SECRET PROJECTS
FLYING WINGS
AND TAILLESS AIRCRAFT

SECRET PROJECTS
FLYING WINGS
AND TAILLESS AIRCRAFT

BILL ROSE

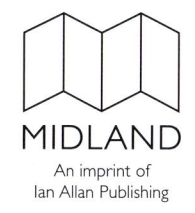

MIDLAND
An imprint of
Ian Allan Publishing

SECRET PROJECTS:
FLYING WINGS AND TAILLESS AIRCRAFT
by Bill Rose

First published 2010

ISBN 978 185780 320 4

All rights reserved. No part of this book may be
reproduced or transmitted in any form or by any means,
electronic or mechanical, including photocopying,
recording, scanning or by any information storage
and retrieval system, on the internet or elsewhere,
without permission from the Publisher in writing.

© Ian Allan Publishing Ltd 2010

Published by Midland Publishing

an imprint of Ian Allan Publishing Ltd, Hersham, Surrey
KT12 4RG.

Printed in England by Ian Allan Printing Ltd,
Hersham, Surrey KT12 4RG.

Mixed Sources
Product group from well-managed
forests and other controlled sources
www.fsc.org Cert no. SGS-COC-005526
© 1996 Forest Stewardship Council

Visit the Ian Allan Publishing website at
www.ianallanpublishing.com

Distributed in the United States of America and Canada
by BookMasters Distribution Services.

Copyright
Illegal copying and selling of publications deprives
authors, publishers and booksellers of income, without
which there would be no investment in new publications.
Unauthorised versions of publications are also likely to be
inferior in quality and contain incorrect information.
You can help by reporting copyright infringements and
acts of piracy to the Publisher or the UK Copyright Service.

Photograph on half-title page:
**The first unmarked XB-35 seen as it is towed
across the runway at Northrop's Hawthorne facility.**
Northrop Grumman

Photograph on title page:
**A B-2A strategic bomber of the 509th Bomb Wing
in flight.** USAF

Contents

	Introduction	6
Chapter One	**British Tailless Aircraft**	10
Chapter Two	**German World War 2 Flying Wing Development**	34
Chapter Three	**US Flying Wings (1935-1950)**	70
Chapter Four	**US Flying Wings (1950-1990)**	95
Chapter Five	**US Manned Tailless Aircraft (1980-2030)**	109
Chapter Six	**Soviet Tailless Designs**	130
	Glossary	143
	Index	144

Introduction

The flying wing is the purest form in aviation. Millions of years before mankind existed it was evolved by nature as a simple and efficient way of transporting seeds over considerable distances. When men first enviously cast their eyes skywards and considered the idea of undertaking flight, birds were the obvious inspiration; however, some pioneers studied the way that certain trees used the wind to carry aerodynamic seeds to new locations. This would encourage experiments with flying wing models and large manned gliders. However, various technical problems and a resistance to new ideas restrained the development of powered designs, with relatively slow progress being made until World War 2 when engine performance improved dramatically. The flying wing was then considered for the role of advanced fighters and intercontinental bombers.

The perfect flying wing is a shape reduced to the bare minimum, with few, if any protuberances, no significant visible fuselage section and the efficient use of internal space. This type of aircraft promises high lift and low drag, although stability and handling were challenges for early designers. Subsequently, many flying wing aircraft were aerodynamic compromises. The early flying wings required vertical stabilisers for effective control, while fuselage sections spread beyond the wing's boundaries, and in some cases, engine pods were added. Because of this, many so-called flying wings were more accurately defined as 'tailless aircraft' and the wing could be swept back, swept forward, swivelling in an oblique manner, straight, of variable geometry, or delta-shaped.

Typically, the flying wing and closely related configurations are unsuitable for development as a supersonic aircraft because of their large wingspans. Nevertheless, there are some interesting exceptions to the rule and scope for supersonic performance with certain highly-swept tailless designs. That aside, the flying wing is potentially a very efficient aerodynamic configuration for carrying substantial payloads at subsonic speeds over long distances.

Some historians will rightly attribute the earliest designs for a manned flying wing to Leonardo da Vinci (1452-1519) who produced a detailed drawing of a man-powered ornithopter (flapping wing device) around 1485. The design was little more than a fanciful idea, but interest in the possibility of manned flight gathered momentum during the following centuries, eventually leading to experiments with balloons and small hand-launched gliding models.

One particularly interesting idea that stemmed from a simple paper dart was a flying wing design produced by James William Butler and Edmund Edwards in 1867. They envisaged a scaled-up man-carrying aircraft, powered by some form of steam propulsion and patented the design, although many aspects of the concept were ahead of its time. This was followed by the first demonstration of sustained flight when Alphonse Pénaud (1850-1880) flew a rubber band-powered model for a distance of 131ft (40m) on 18 August 1871 in Paris. Having shown that powered flight was possible, Pénaud went on to conceive a series of astonishingly advanced flying wing aircraft that were never flown, but set the standard for all future designs. Pénaud was succeeded by the aviation pioneer Louis Pierre Mouillard (1834-1897) who, it is believed, made a short flight of 90ft (27m) at an altitude of 30ft (9m) in his fourth glider near Cairo, Egypt, on 3 January 1878.

While Otto Lilienthal (1848-1896) is often credited with flying the first successful manned glider in 1891, it is widely claimed that Mouillard and Lilienthal were following in the footsteps of English inventor Sir George Cayley (1773-1857). He designed and built several gliders, which were reportedly tested by an unknown 10-year-old boy and Cayley's coachman on several occasions between 1799 and 1853. Whether or not Cayley deserves to be credited with the first manned glider flight remains open to debate. Another early pioneer was Igo Etrich (1879-1967) who built gliders based on the winged liana seed and this work proved to be influential to many future designers. The application of an internal combustion engine to a tailless design was then adopted by pioneers such as French engineer René Arnoux and British designer John William Dunne (1875-1949).

World War 1 saw vast improvements in aviation technology with aircraft becoming a valuable military asset. After hostilities ceased in 1918, German engineer Hugo Junkers turned his attention towards building an efficient aircraft known as the JG-1 that

The German glider pioneer Otto Lilienthal undertaking a short flight at Berlin on an unspecified date in 1896. He experienced many accidents during these trials and died as a result of serious injuries sustained in a crash on 9 August 1896. His last words were 'Sacrifices must be made'. Bill Rose Collection

would seat passengers within the wing. Unfortunately for Junkers, the design was deemed to have contravened conditions of aircraft construction set out by the Allies and the JG-1 was therefore scrapped. Junkers had patented a flying wing aircraft in 1910 and was a strong supporter of this configuration, envisaging future giant transporters capable of carrying 1,000 passengers.

Although such a design never materialised, there would be significant progress made in Germany during the following decades by Alexander Lippisch and the Horten brothers who were responsible for a number of highly significant tailless designs. World War 2 saw major developments of their work with Lippisch and the Hortens designing advanced jet and rocket-powered aircraft that pushed towards the boundaries of supersonic flight. In North America, the main advocate and developer of the flying wing was Jack (John) Northrop, although it should be noted that Vincent Burnelli (1895-1964), who is often overlooked, made great strides with lifting body designs.

At one stage during World War 2, American strategists believed that Britain would fall to Germany and Jack Northrop was given the task of designing a new US Army Air Corps bomber capable of reaching Europe. This project led to construction of the futuristic B-35 flying wing; however, by the time it flew, the propeller-driven warplane was virtually obsolete. The design was re-engineered into the jet-powered B-49, but the new Northrop aircraft was technically flawed and could not compete with the relatively straightforward B-47 produced by Boeing. Subsequently, the B-49 never became operational and interest in flying wings sharply declined.

While designers continued to study the flying wing, no significant aircraft of this type were built for many years, although British post-war interest in tailless aircraft led to the successful delta-wing Avro Vulcan bomber. By the 1970s, advances in computer technology were making the flight control of unusual designs a reality and scientists recognised the potential of the flying wing as an aircraft with an exceptionally low radar cross section.

The Burgess-Dunne Flying Wing Biplane of 1914. Bill Rose Collection

'Le Stablavion' (stable aircraft) was built by French constructor René Arnoux and demonstrated to the public in 1913. Powered by a 55hp (41kW) Chenu piston engine, the performance and handling were said to be disappointing. Bill Rose Collection

Featuring a pusher configuration, René Arnoux's two-seat flying wing monoplane was demonstrated in Paris during 1914. Bill Rose Collection

Secret Projects: Flying Wings and Tailless Aircraft

It had been apparent that flying wings were harder to detect with radar than conventional aircraft and this was believed to be a feature of the Horten jet fighter that first flew at the end of World War 2. It is now suggested that any stealth qualities the Horten jet fighter possessed were more accidental than intentional, even when considering the significant advances in radar countermeasures made by German scientists during the war.

It has been reported on several occasions that post-war aircraft such as the Northrop B-49 and Avro Vulcan proved hard to detect with prevailing ground-based radar systems. An ability to hide aircraft from enemy detection would have many advantages and this resulted in highly classified US research during the 1970s to produce a low-visibility combat aeroplane. This eventually resulted in the Lockheed F-117A that was developed from a diamond shape, and although it was described as a fighter, was designed as a specialised subsonic attack aircraft that was incapable of air-to-air combat. The ability to launch a small-scale surprise attack was obvious, but the F-117A was not expected to fare well in a major confrontation with the Soviet Union, whose air defence capabilities remained significant and were under constant revision. Therefore, the USAF required a next-generation bomber with an intercontinental range, a substantial payload capability and relative invisibility to all existing and anticipated radar systems. This led to proposals for an advanced bomber that resulted in the Northrop-Grumman B-2A Spirit making its first flight in 1986. Developed and built in great secrecy, the B-2A strategic bomber became to be the most expensive combat aircraft in history, with its eventual use in small regional conflicts widely regarded as overkill.

Nevertheless, the B-2A remains a technical masterpiece and is a true flying wing aircraft in every respect, although its shape was selected for reasons of low visibility and the sleek appearance was almost a by-product. The US Navy also sought a new carrier-borne, multi-role combat aircraft with a stealth capability and this led to the A-12A Avenger II, a triangular-shaped flying wing developed by General Dynamics and McDonnell Douglas. In some respects, this aircraft was more advanced than the B-2A. However, spiralling development costs brought the A-12A programme to an abrupt halt.

A new US manned bomber is currently in its initial development phase and is widely visualised as a second-generation B-2. However, the main application for low-observable technology at the present time is for increasingly sophisticated remote-control aircraft that often feature flying wing configurations. Further tailless aircraft seem inevitable as designers look towards aerodynamically efficient blended wing body (BWB) configurations to satisfy demands for new tactical airlifters, tankers and airliners. These aircraft are likely to become a common sight in our skies during the coming decades. BWBs will not be capable of higher speeds than existing aircraft in the same class, but will transport greater payloads over longer ranges at lower cost. On the down side, there may be ground

Engineer, aviation pioneer and founder of the famous aircraft manufacturing concern, Hugo Junkers was an advocate of the flying wing and did much to secure its widespread acceptance.
Bill Rose Collection

Hugo Junker's influential 1910 patent for a new type of aircraft that would contain its most important features inside the wing.
ESP Patent Office

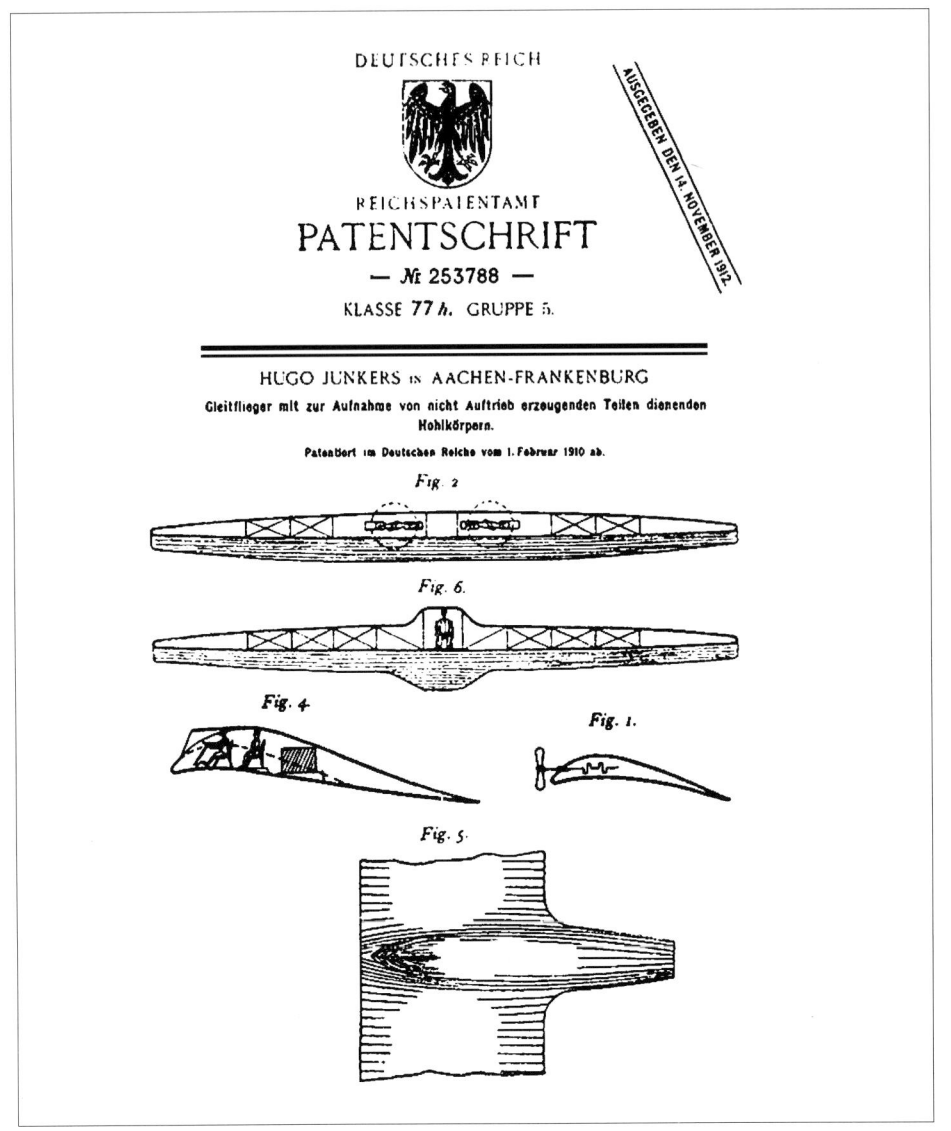

Secret Projects: Flying Wings and Tailless Aircraft

An illustration of the experimental Northrop N-1M flying wing during a test flight. Bill Rose/ Northrop Grumman

The futuristic Vickers Swallow supersonic nuclear strike aircraft was designed in the 1950s and is shown resplendent in RAF markings and anti-flash white finish. The Swallow was too far ahead of its time to be a realistic proposition.
Bill Rose Collection

Northrop Grumman's proposal for the USAF's next generation bomber expected to enter service in 2018. Northrop Grumman/Bill Rose Collection

handling problems for civil versions and few airports could accommodate BWBs at present.

Because there are many grey areas between true flying wings, tailless aircraft, BWB designs and deltas, I have tried to avoid setting definite limits on what kind of aircraft are suitable for inclusion in this book. This has proved to be quite a challenge, as it is often unclear where to draw the line despite considerable consultation with colleagues. As an example, it now appears acceptable to describe an aircraft in technical papers as a 'tailed' flying wing and some authors regard designs such as the Mirage or Concorde as belonging in the flying wing category. Therefore, I have set my own guidelines and have included various interesting tailless aircraft ranging from the British World War 2 experimental GAL gliders and the German Me 163 rocket fighter to the advanced variable geometry of the Vickers Swallow and exotic oblique wing designs.

This book mainly deals with manned aircraft as the detailed additional coverage required for unmanned tailless designs would at least double the space and there are practical limits in producing such a publication. I have not attempted to write an exhaustive technical appraisal of the flying wing or tailless design and this book is not a definitive reference work containing examples of every known design. That said, I have tried to provide background information on many – often lesser-known – military concepts and designs that have (in a few cases) been built as prototypes and occasionally reached production.

Many individuals provided assistance with background material for this book, but I would like to especially thank Chris Gibson and Tony Buttler, Dr Iain Murray, Robert Bradley of the San Diego Air & Space Museum, Martin Müller, Alexi Malinovsky and Tony Chong of Northrop-Grumman.

Bill Rose, Norfolk, England
February 2010

Secret Projects: Flying Wings and Tailless Aircraft

Chapter One

British Tailless Aircraft

In late 1942, the UK Director of Scientific Research decided to form the Tailless Aircraft Advisory Committee (TAAC) to oversee development of new designs. German aircraft designers were known to be interested in developing tailless military aircraft and considerable research was also taking place in America. Northrop was working on a long-range, flying wing bomber and the National Advisory Committee for Aeronautics (NACA – the forerunner of NASA) was undertaking extensive research into laminar flow aerofoils. Therefore, the British hoped to take advantage of US developments for a future jet propelled tailless bomber.

Geoffrey Hill

Tailless aircraft were nothing new in Britain with the early pioneering work of John William Dunne inspiring more advanced designs by Geoffrey Terence Roland Hill (1895-1955). Hill had become preoccupied with the problem of stalling and this led him to design the Pterodactyl Mk1, a flying wing with a 31° leading edge sweep and all-moving wingtips. The aircraft was built during an 18-month period with Air Ministry support and flew as a glider in December 1924. It was then equipped with a 33hp (24.6kW) Bristol Cherub engine and flew towards the end of 1925. In 1926, Hill joined Westland Aircraft, which secured Air Ministry backing for further development of the Pterodactyl design and filed a patent for a wing adjustment design in 1930.

A series of small aircraft followed with Hill designing a two-seat fighter version of the aircraft for Specification F3/32, known as the MkV. Construction began in 1932 with duralumin and steel being used for the majority of the fuselage framework and main wing. From the outset, Hill decided to add short, unswept lower wings for strengthening purposes, making the MkV a sesquiplane. The undercarriage consisted of tandem wheels located beneath the centre of the fuselage and skids below each lower wingtip with small trailing wheels. A very troublesome Rolls-Royce Goshawk 1 engine in a forward mounted position powered the MkV, providing a maximum speed in level flight of around 190mph (306kph) and a service ceiling of 30,000ft (9,144m). When empty, the MkV weighed 3,534lb (1,602kg) and around 5,100lb (2,313kg) when fully loaded. The wingspan was 46ft 8in (14.2m) with a wing area of 396ft² (36.78m²) and the overall length was 20ft 6in (6.24m). As a fighter, the aircraft would be equipped with several machine guns and was capable of carrying a small bomb load. The prototype was ready to fly in 1933. During tests the performance was said to be comparable to a Hawker Demon and longitudinal stability was certainly superior to earlier Pterodactyl designs. Despite its promise, the MkV failed to win support for further development. Although disappointed, Hill continued to work on the Pterodactyl design producing further tailless aircraft concepts, but the project was effectively at an end.

The Pterodactyl Bombers

In 1939, Professor Hill was recruited by the Air Ministry to oversee various specialised military research projects and his first assignment involved a programme to assess various ways of allowing an aircraft to cut enemy barrage balloons' cables without stalling. In addition to a range of consultative work, Hill became the chief scientific liaison officer between the British and Canadian governments in 1942. At the start of this period, he began a private design project for an advanced tailless bomber with initial plans being completed on 22 July 1942.

Hill's first proposal was a boomerang-shaped flying wing with a straight central leading edge and the outer wing sections swept (at the leading edge) by approximately 44°. The wingspan was 140ft (42.6m) with a wing area of 3,350ft² (311m²) and the overall length appears to have been around 50ft (15.24m). The wing would have a central depth of 7ft 6in (2.28m), making a substantial pressurised crew compartment possible. Quoted weight is 85,000lb (38,555kg) and was presumably an all-up estimate.

Hill envisaged six forward-positioned piston engines mounted in side-by-side pairs, driving three rear-mounted pusher configuration contra-rotating propeller assemblies via lengthy drive shafts. The use of turbojets was

Designed by Geoffrey Hill, the MkV Pterodactyl was a military variant of this pre-war series of aircraft developed to meet Specification F.3/32. A sesquiplane in configuration with a small, unswept lower wing, the Pterodactyl MkV was fitted with two forward-firing machine guns and carried a rear gunner who enjoyed an unrestricted view.
Bill Rose Collection

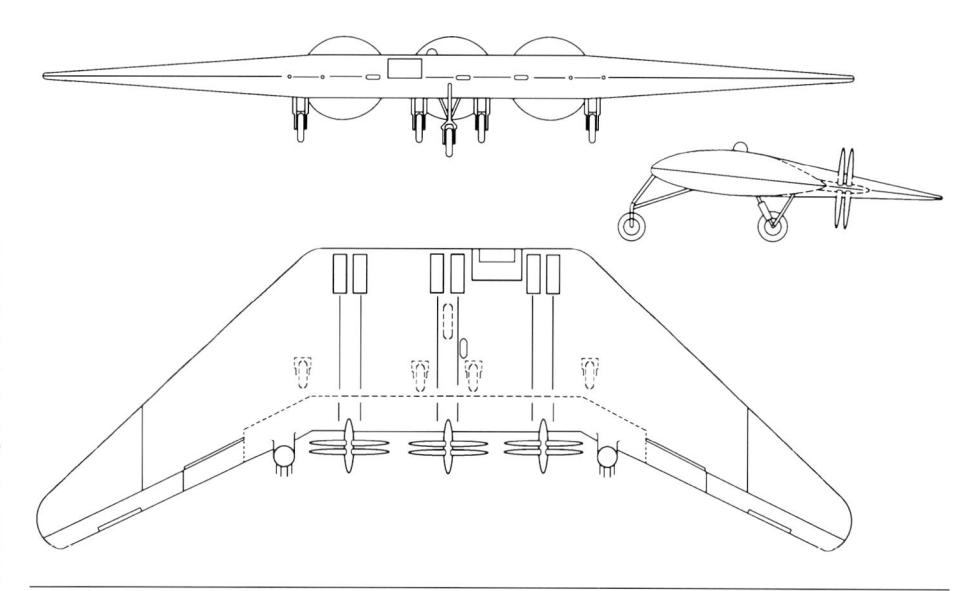

A proposed six-engine, three contra-prop Pterodactyl flying wing bomber, with an estimated weight of 85,000 lb (38,555kg). Bill Rose Collection

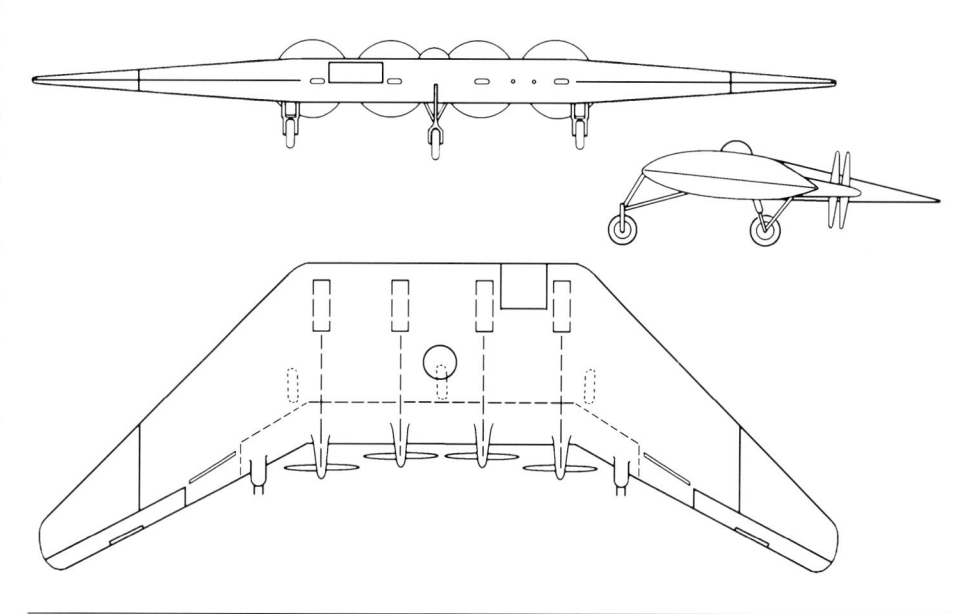

Professor Hill's wartime proposal for a four-engine, propeller-driven flying wing Pterodactyl Bomber. Bill Rose Collection

also considered and Hill believed this design could easily be modified when jet propulsion became available. Estimates of performance are not quoted in any available documentation. The Pterodactyl bomber would be supported on a rather unusual fully retractable undercarriage consisting of four large main wheels, positioned across the underside of the wing at the centre of gravity and a single nose-wheel. During take-offs and landings, the pilot would sit in a capsule located towards the centre of the aircraft. This would be extended below the wing to afford the pilot a better view of the runway and it would be possible to use the front wheel as a positioning aid. For normal flight, the pilot would sit behind a windshield in the leading edge of the wing, positioned slightly starboard of centre. Hill also planned to seat the navigator alongside the pilot at the front of the aircraft, with extra windows allowing downward observation.

The bomber would be equipped with four remote-controlled machine gun turrets, all outboard of the engine bays and propellers. Details of bomb carriage are unknown, although it seems certain that at least two separate bays were envisaged on either side of the cabin area. There were no vertical control surfaces, although in addition to elevons and flaps, Hill proposed movable wingtips. One development of this design was an aircraft carrier, able to transport up to three piston-engine fighters (presumably Spitfires or Hurricanes) on the upper wing. This would make it possible to operate at ranges much greater than might normally be available. Presumably the fighters would return to base under their own power, or the pilots would bail out at a pre-arranged location.

Hill also designed a smaller version of the Pterodactyl bomber with a wingspan of approximately 100ft (30.4m) and a length of about 38ft (11.5m). It would have an anticipated weight of approximately 45,000 lb (20,411kg). This design differed in having four separate unspecified piston engines, each driving a tail-mounted propeller. The fully-retractable undercarriage would be slightly simpler than the larger bomber, using three separate main wheels and a single nose-wheel. It appears that Professor Hill did not consider the retractable pilot's capsule necessary for this aircraft. Rear facing remote-controlled machine gun turrets were mounted outboard of the propellers on each trailing edge and a single forward firing gun turret was positioned on the leading edge, to the port side of centre. The control surfaces appear similar to the larger design.

These designs were undoubtedly submitted for official consideration, but went no further as they were probably considered far too unconventional. Undeterred, Professor Hill continued to work on the concept, which he now envisaged as a large trans-Atlantic airliner suitable for post-war operations. This proposal was known as the Pterodactyl MkVIII and was to be powered by five Rolls-Royce Griffon engines driving pusher propellers. The airliner was to have a cockpit section protruding from the central leading edge. Despite interest from Short Brothers, nothing came of this project.

Baynes Bat

After leaving school, Leslie Everett Baynes (1902-1989) became immediately involved with the aviation industry. He worked for the Aircraft Engineering Company in Hendon, North London, became a designer for Short Brothers at Rochester and then devised the very successful Scud 1 light sailplane. This led him into a manufacturing partnership with F.D. Abbot, forming the company Abbot-Baynes Sailplanes Ltd of Farnham, Surrey. In 1935, a powered version of the Scud was built to meet a request made by Sir John Carden who ran a company developing armoured vehicles. As a consequence of this order, a new partnership was formed, called Carden-Baynes Aircraft, with a factory located at Heston, Middlesex where powered aircraft were manufactured. Baynes and Carden began

British Tailless Aircraft

Three-view drawing of the Baynes BAT. Bill Rose Collection

The Baynes BAT during a test flight. This small glider was designed during World War 2 to test the possibility of building a much larger 'Carrier Wing' capable of transporting a light tank to a combat zone. Bill Rose Collection

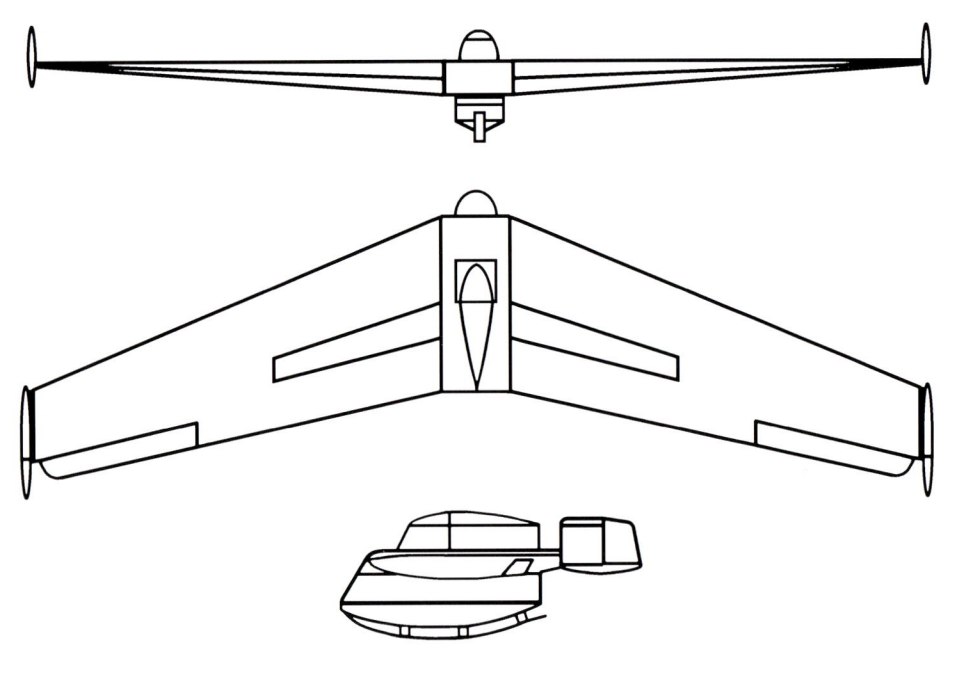

producing a sailplane (which was essentially a Scud 3) equipped with a small retractable 249cc Villiers engine. The unit was mounted above the aircraft in a pusher configuration and a small tank carried enough fuel to run the engine for about 30 minutes.

At the start of World War 2, Baynes had become a scientific advisor to the Alan Muntz Company in Heston and he took responsibility for organising its aircraft division. At this time there were no suitable transport aircraft and the army was looking for ways to airlift military cargo and equipment to operational areas. In 1941, Baynes designed an unpowered 'Carrier Wing' capable of transporting a light tank to a combat zone, which was generally referred to as the Baynes Aerial Tank (BAT).

Taking the form of a towed glider, it would transport a light armoured vehicle, which was expected to be the Armstrong Whitworth MkVII Light Tank developed in 1938 and later known as the Tetrarch. This vehicle had a combat weight of 16,800 lb (7,620kg) and carried a crew of three. The glider's swept wing would have a 100ft (30m) span with vertical stabilisers at the wingtips. It was proposed that just before landing the tank's engine would be started, allowing it to go into action immediately after touchdown.

The Baynes BAT received enthusiastic official support and it was decided to build a one-third-scale, proof-of-concept tailless manned glider, with a wingspan of 33ft 4in (10m) and using a single main spar. A small cockpit accommodated the pilot and the undercarriage was composed of a lower centrally located skid and wingtip skids. A wheeled trolley was used for ground handling and take-offs. A nacelle replaced the area beneath the glider where the tank would be carried. On the full-sized version, the wing would be released at the moment of touchdown and drawn away from the tank. A contract was issued to Slingsby Sailplanes at Kirkbymoorside for the manufacture of a prototype. Built almost entirely from wood, the glider was completed during spring 1943 and issued with the serial RA809. The first test flight took place in the summer of 1943 at Airborne Forces Experimental Establishment (AFEE), Sherburn-in-Elmet, Yorkshire. With Flt Lt Robert Kronfeld at the controls, the Baynes BAT was towed into the air behind an Avro Tutor.

Kronfeld later reported that, 'In spite of its unorthodox design the aircraft handles similarly to other light gliders with very light and responsive controls and is safe to be flown by service pilots in all normal attitudes of flight.' However, the RAE's chief test pilot Capt Eric

Baynes Bat

Crew	1
Wingspan	33ft 4in (10.15m)
Sweep	22° (leading edge)
Wing area	160ft² (14.86m²)
Aspect ratio	7:1
Length	11ft 4in (3.45m)
Empty weight	763 lb (346kg)
Gross weight	963 lb (437kg)
Cruising speed	90mph (145kph)
Maximum speed	120mph (193kph)
Stalling speed	40mph (64kph)

Melrose 'Winkle' Brown was less enthusiastic about the Baynes BAT when he tested it, finding the controls disappointing.

Why this difference of opinion arose is hard to say, but the tests were still judged successful. Unfortunately, there were ongoing problems concerning tank suitability and it had been realised that landing faster than the tank's maximum speed was a serious issue. This led to the idea of fitting an undercarriage to the BAT, but it was considered over-complex and the Baynes BAT was then moved onto the back burner. At the same time, a heavy glider was being developed by General Aircraft called the GAL.49 Hamilcar, which had been designed from the outset to carry a substantial payload that included a Tetrarch or the US-designed M22 Locust light tank.

While the Hamilcar eventually entered service, the Baynes BAT never progressed to a full-sized carrier wing glider. It was then transferred to the Royal Aircraft Establishment at Farnborough, which made good use of it for stability tests that continued after the war. In late 1946, the Baynes BAT was formally disposed of as surplus equipment, being purchased by British Light Aircars of Redhill, Surrey. It seems that the BAT was then moved to Croydon Airport where it was last seen behind a hangar in 1958, apparently in poor condition. Soon after this, the glider was scrapped. Baynes, known to his friends and family as 'Baron', worked on many other interesting wartime projects that included an unusual tilt-rotor aircraft design and he was responsible for design work on converting Lancasters to carry the Barnes Wallis bouncing bomb used to breach several dams in the Ruhr Valley during May 1943.

Handley Page Manx

In the late 1930s, Dr Gustav Victor Lachman (1896-1966), an Austrian scientist who headed the Design Office at Handley Page Aircraft, turned his attention towards the possibility of improving aircraft performance by a significant reduction in drag. He favoured the flying wing design and the company chairman, Frederick Handley Page, fully supported this research and agreed to authorise the construction of a small experimental aircraft. The initial assembly would be contracted out to Dart Aircraft of Dunstable, Bedfordshire, which was a small specialist company building gliders and replica light aircraft. Work seemed to proceed well and the airframe was returned to Handley Page at Radlett, Hertfordshire, during September 1939, for completion. But the aircraft was found to be substantially overweight and there were serious problems with the type of glue used during assembly. As a consequence, the aircraft underwent a programme of modifications and the main spar was largely rebuilt. It is possible that this had some bearing on the fact that Dart Aircraft had ceased trading by the end of 1939.

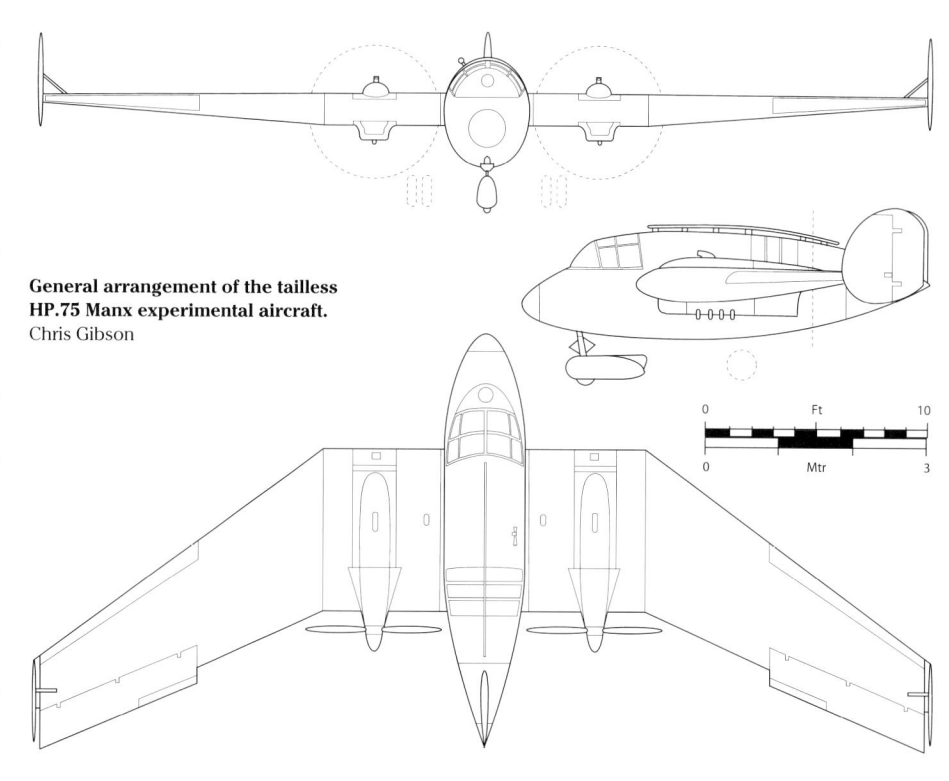

Built mostly from wood, this aircraft received the semi-official name Manx (after the tailless cat). It has been claimed that the company designation HP.75 may not have been applied until 1945, although the official registration H-0222 was issued at an early stage in this project. The Manx was fitted with two rear-mounted de Havilland Gipsy Major II four-cylinder piston engines, each rated at 140hp (104kW) and fitted with two blade propellers acting as pushers. The overall wingspan was 39ft 10in (12.1m), wing area was 245ft^2 (22.76m^2), the length was 18ft 3in (5.5m) and the empty weight was 3,000lb (1,360kg). Maximum take-off weight was estimated at 4,000lb (1,814kg) allowing a maximum speed of approximately 146mph (234kph) and a service ceiling of about 10-12,000ft (3,000-3,650m). The central section of the wing on either side of the cockpit was straight and the outer section was swept back by 35° with elevons and leading edge slots. An upright fin and rudder was attached to each wingtip and an additional fin was located on the upper rear of the fuselage to enhance flight control.

General arrangement of the tailless HP.75 Manx experimental aircraft.
Chris Gibson

The quite distinctive central fuselage section accommodated a two-man crew with the flight observer sitting directly behind the pilot and facing rearward. The Manx was equipped with a tricycle undercarriage with the rear wheels able to retract, but the nose wheel fixed. This was normally fitted with a streamlined fairing to reduce drag. Taxiing trials began at Radlett in late 1940, although tests became long and drawn out, with more pressing wartime work often taking priority.

The company's senior test pilot, James Richard Talbot (1909-1945), was now involved with these trials, along with Edgar Alexander 'Ginger' Wright (1914-1945), a Handley Page test pilot who headed the Observer's Office. On 12 September 1942, during high speed taxiing trials, the Manx became momentarily airborne, achieving a height of about 12ft (3.65m), but after touchdown, it was evident that the nose-wheel had been damaged, so repairs and modifications were made. Further attempts to fly the Manx followed and it finally became airborne on 11 June 1943, with Talbot at the controls. However, the cockpit canopy became detached soon after take-off and the flight was immediately terminated. As trials continued on an intermittent basis, the renowned glider pilot Robert Kronfeld was invited to test fly the Manx. Kronfeld was now an RAF Squadron Leader, assigned to General Aircraft Ltd (GAL) of Feltham, Middlesex, which was working on its own experimental tailless glider project.

British Tailless Aircraft

He made at least two flights in the Manx and reported that the aircraft handled well in comparison to other tailless designs he had flown. By late 1945, the Manx had logged up to 30 test flights lasting for a total of around 17 hours. Talbot and Wright had flown many of the missions, but both were killed on 3 December 1945 when a prototype Hermes 1 airliner they were flying crashed shortly after leaving Radlett Aerodrome. This loss had a direct impact on the Manx programme and the aircraft made one more test flight in April 1946 and was then placed in storage.

The Manx was an interesting design, which was briefly considered for development as a twin-engine transport aircraft, or possibly a light bomber, with a canard configuration. Nothing came of this and the Manx remained in storage until 1952 when it was broken up for scrap.

HP.75 Manx

Crew	2
Wingspan	39ft 10in (12.1m)
Wing area	245ft² (22.76m²)
Length	18ft 3in (5.5m)
Empty weight	3,000 lb (1,360kg)
Gross weight	4,000 lb (1,814kg)
Powerplant	Two de Havilland Gipsy Major II four-cylinder in-line piston engines each rated at 140hp (104kW)
Maximum speed	146mph (234kph)
Ceiling	10-12,000ft (3,000-3,650m)

Above: **Receiving the semi-official name of Manx (after the tailless cat), the experimental HP.75 was mainly built from wood and powered by two rear-mounted de Havilland Gipsy Major II four-cylinder piston engines.** Bill Rose Collection

Below: **The HP.75 Manx in flight.** Bill Rose Collection

GAL Gliders

Soon after it became established at the end of 1942, the Tailless Aircraft Advisory Committee (TAAC) invited a number of aircraft contractors to submit plans for experimental tailless aircraft that could be used for research purposes. Many companies (including de Havilland, Saunders Roe, Hawker and Fairey) declined to take part, leaving Armstrong Whitworth and General Aircraft Ltd (GAL) as the principal participants, followed by Handley Page which had already built the Manx. Designers at GAL had been interested in developing tailless aircraft since the mid-1930s and proposals were submitted to the TAAC, which swiftly approved several swept-wing prototypes that would be used to test low-speed handling characteristics. Initially, it was planned to build six prototypes, but this was reduced to four. Two would be gliders designated GAL.56 and two powered versions referred to as GAL57, using a single Lycoming R-680-13 radial engine in a pusher configuration.

Construction would have to be cost effective, utilising common parts wherever possible. This was necessary to avoid diverting too many resources away from war production. It was decided from an early stage to use a standard centre section with common attachment points for wing anchorage. However, it became apparent that there would be problems interchanging wings with different profiles on a standard body and a decision was taken to abandon the powered versions and build four different gliders, taking the simplest route to keep the project on course. It was also agreed that GAL test pilots and observers would conduct most of the initial test flight. Refinement and construction were then passed to an engineering team at the Hanworth factory, Feltham, Middlesex, which was headed by a Czech engineer called Otto Wels (no connection to the pre-war German politician), who specialised in flight control systems.

Each central section utilised a tubular steel framework covered in plywood and the wings were mainly of wooden construction, supported by a single spar. Off-the-shelf landing gear was used for the GAL56, with the main wheels being Dowty units designed for the Lysander and the tail wheel normally used on a Bisley. The serial numbers TS507, TS510, TS513 and TS515 were issued on 21 October 1944, although it was finally decided not to proceed with construction of TS515. Each GAL56 accommodated a pilot and observer in the centre section, with the main difference between each model being the wing profile. Fins with rudders were fitted to

Secret Projects: Flying Wings and Tailless Aircraft

GAL56 'Medium V'

Crew	2
Wingspan	45ft 4in (13.8m)
Wing sweep	28.4° (leading edge)
Wing area (net)	317ft² (29.45m²)
Wing area (gross)	350ft² (32.5m²)
Aspect ratio	5.8
Length	19ft (5.79m)
Height	8ft 9in (2.66m)
Aerofoil section	RAF 34 Modified
Chord-root	11ft 4in (3.45m)
Chord-tip	43½in (1.1m)
Dihedral-normal	0.5°
Flying weight (crew + max ballast)	4,400 lb (1,996kg)
Stalling speed	58mph. E.A.S. (93.3kph)
Max towing speed	150mph. E.A.S. (241kph)

GAL61

Crew	2
	Pilot and space for prone observer
Wingspan	51ft 11in (15.8m)
Wing sweep	36.4° (leading edge)
Length	24ft 8in (7.5m)
Flying weight	5,174 lb (2,348kg)

the wingtips and it was decided to add anti-spin parachutes in wingtip containers for emergency use.

No overall name was assigned to the glider, but the models were referred to by their wing configuration. The first to be completed during autumn 1944 was the GAL56/01 (TS507) 'Medium V' which identified its 28.4° leading edge sweep. An RAF-34 aerofoil section was used and it had a modified contour to enhance the elevon performance. The wingspan was 45ft 4in (13.8m), length was 19ft (5.79m) and it was 8ft 9in (2.66m) high. The aircraft undertook taxiing trials at Aldermaston during November 1944 and made its first flight on 17 January 1945 at RAF Dunholm Lodge in Lincolnshire. This location had been assigned to GAL as a facility to store Hamilcar heavy gliders and it was chosen for testing because the GAL56 was a secret project and there was less chance of the trials being observed by anyone.

For the flight at Dunholm Lodge, an Armstrong Whitley V bomber was used to tow the glider into the air and test pilot Robert Kronfeld was at the GAL56's controls. He reported that the aircraft handled fairly well except in extreme conditions and after making 48 flights at Dunholme Lodge, TS507 was transferred to RAE Farnborough in June 1945. However, when RAE test pilot Capt Eric Brown flew the GAL56, he was far from impressed with it, describing it as very difficult to control and noting that he 'could not relax for a second, beginning right away with takeoff'.

The second aircraft known as GAL56/04 (TS510) was designated 'Medium U'. It differed from the first aircraft in having a parallel chord centre section and swept outer leading edge of 28.4°. The wingspan was 51ft (15.54m, height 21ft (6.4) and length 10ft

Top: **The third GAL56 glider 'Maximum V' (TS513), which made its maiden flight on 30 May 1947 at Lasham.** Bill Rose Collection

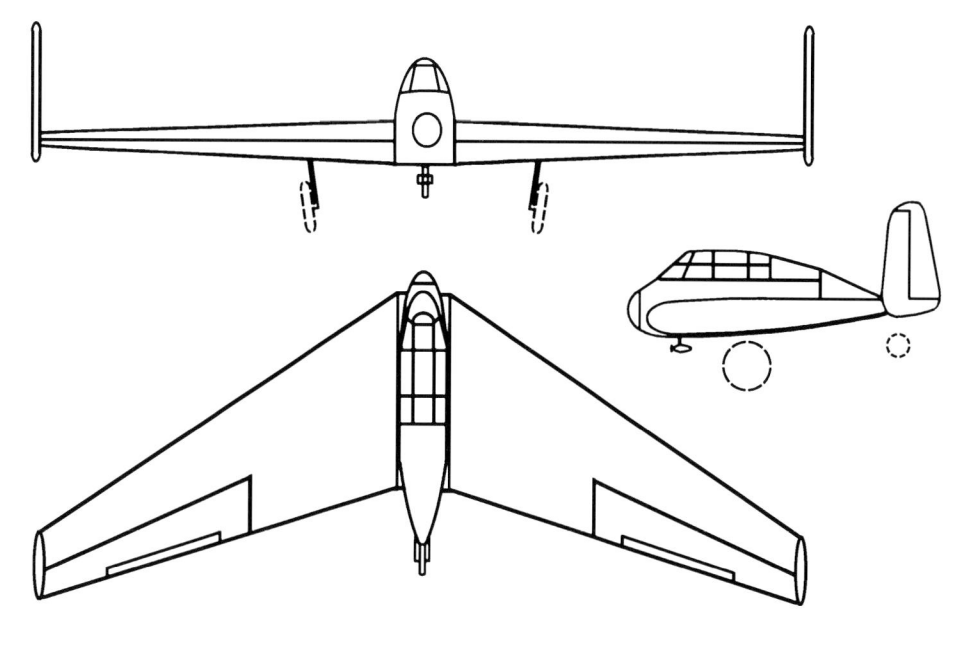

Above: **Three-view drawing of the GAL56 'Medium V'.** Bill Rose Collection

Below: **The GAL56 'Medium U' glider (TS510) piloted by Flt Lt Robert Kronfeld, after release from a Halifax tow aircraft.** Bill Rose Collection

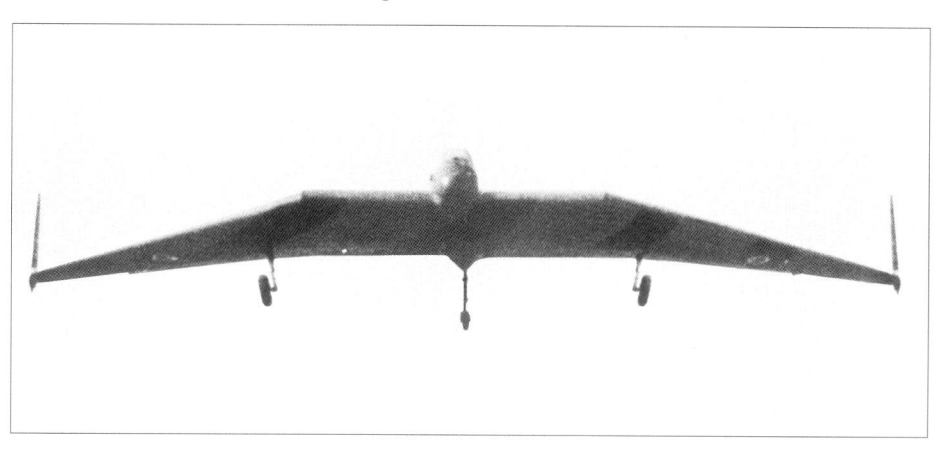

British Tailless Aircraft

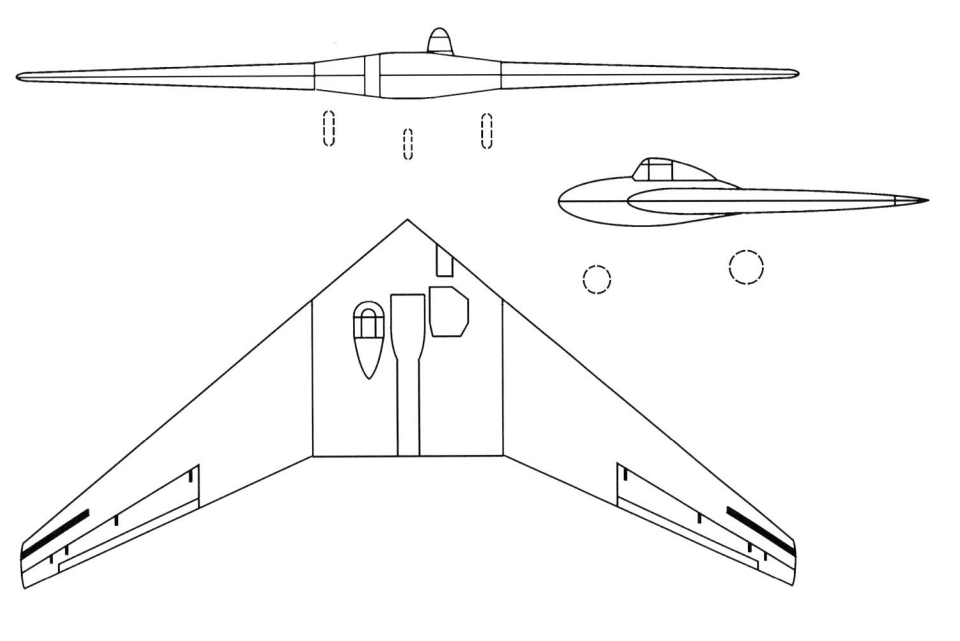

The final and most advanced glider in the GAL experimental series was the GAL61 (TS515). It was completed in 1948 and shown at the SBAC Air Show at Radlett during the same year. It was then prepared for testing at Lasham, but never flew. Bill Rose Collection

the glider entered a steep dive and became inverted. Kronfeld told McGowan that he had lost control of the glider and his observer immediately bailed out. The altitude was approximately 1,000ft (300m) and his parachute opened at about 100ft (30m) making it a close call. Regrettably, Kronfeld stayed in the aircraft until it hit the ground.

A significantly more advanced GAL experimental glider was nearing completion at this time, called the GAL61. It had been reassigned the original designation TS515 that was intended for use with a fourth GAL56 prototype. GAL61 featured a raised cockpit in the centre of the aircraft, with a prone position for an observer within the wing. This design had the same 36.4° leading edge sweep as the GAL56 Maximum V and in overall appearance, it loosely resembled the powered Northrop N-1M flying wing. GAL61 had a wingspan of 51ft 11in (15.8m), an overall length of 24ft 8in (7.5m) and a gross weight of approximately 5,174lb (2,346kg). A fully retractable undercarriage was fitted as standard equipment and the GAL.61 was a true flying wing in all respects. There were no vertical stabilisers and the aircraft used elevons and wingtip drag rudders for control. GAL61 was completed by mid-1948 and displayed statically at the 1948 SBAC Air Show at Radlett. It was then returned to Lasham for testing, but approval to begin test flights was never granted and the project was finally cancelled in mid-1949. Although it was the most interesting of the four gliders, GAL61 never flew and is thought to have been broken up for scrap in 1950.

(3m). Medium U was assigned the reference TS510D and it flew for the first time on 27 February 1946 at Aldermaston and was then moved to Lasham. It was damaged in an accident during 1949 and subsequently scrapped. The third GAL56/03 (TS513) was called 'Maximum V' and featured a 36.4° sweep. It flew for the first time on 30 May 1947 at Lasham. This version of the glider featured nose flaps and was designed to allow adjustment of the wing dihedral on the ground. It was equipped with two sets of split flaps. The first hinged at the 50 per cent chord line, with the second rear set hinged at 70 per cent. Used one set at a time, this was selected on the ground. The wingspan of 'Maximum V' was 45ft 4in (13.8m), with a length 23ft 6in (7.16m) and a height of 9ft (2.74m).

All three gliders were exhibited at the September 1947 SBAC show held at Radlett Aerodrome and the second GAL56 'Medium U' was demonstrated by Robert Kronfeld after a Halifax towed it into the air. But the programme was dealt a severe blow on 12 February 1948 when Kronfeld was killed while testing GAL56/01 (TS507). He had left Lashman Airfield with his observer Barry McGowan and they were towed behind a Halifax until reaching 16,000ft (4,876m) where separation took place. The purpose of the flight was to carry out stall tests, but having made a normal recovery from his first stall

Armstrong Whitworth Flying Wings

In 1942, the Directorate of Scientific Research approached Armstrong Whitworth Aircraft (AWA) to develop an aerofoil section for wind tunnel laminar flow experiments. As a result of this, the company's chief designer John 'Jimmy' Lloyd (1888-1978) began work on proposals for a military flying wing aircraft. Lloyd produced an initial design study of an advanced flying wing jet bomber for the RAF, which carried the company reference AW.50 and he was authorised to continue with this

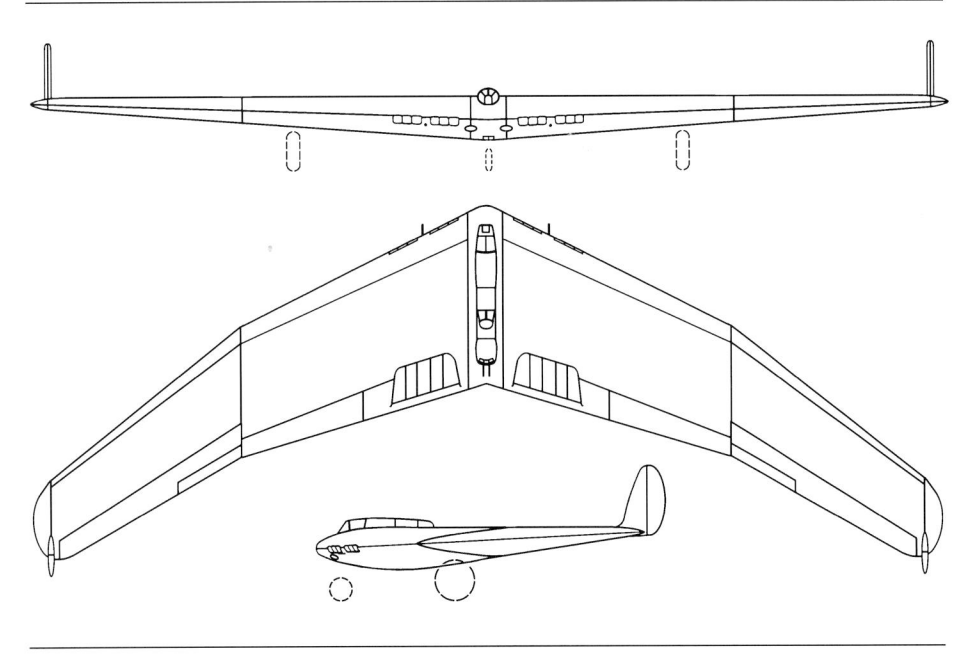

An initial Armstrong Whitworth design study for an advanced RAF flying wing jet bomber with the company reference AW.50. Bill Rose Collection

Secret Projects: Flying Wings and Tailless Aircraft

Right: **One of John Lloyd's early design for an experimental twin-jet aircraft, which appeared in a UK Patent (2,474,685) filed during 1944 and released in 1949. This would eventually lead to the AW.52.** Bill Rose Collection/UK Patent Office

Bottom: **AW.52G is towed into the air during a test flight.** Bill Rose Collection

work, which was supported by the Ministry of Aircraft Production (MAP). Lloyd envisaged the use of a smooth surface for the aircraft's skin, fabricated from a fairly thick alloy, strengthened by rolled corrugations of lighter gauge metal to maintain adequate rigidity. At the centre of the aircraft was a cockpit affording good visibility, with a slightly raised crew section and a tail-mounted, rear-facing, remotely controlled turret containing two 20mm cannons. In addition, it was also proposed to equip the aircraft with two forward-facing 20mm cannons located in the wings between each engine.

Propulsion would be provided by four advanced Metropolitan-Vickers (Metrovick) F.2/4 Beryl axial flow turbojet engines. This design was producing 3,500 lb (15.5kN) of static thrust by 1944, but the F.2/4 remained too unreliable for use in any production aircraft. Lloyd hoped that the ongoing problems with the F.2/4 would be largely resolved by the time the AW.50 was ready for production and improved thrust might be available. The engines would be located within the wings on each side of the cockpit drawing air from four separate intakes along the leading edge of the wing.

Split-flaps would be used, plus wingtip fins equipped with rudders. The AW.50 was to be equipped with a fully retractable tricycle undercarriage. Lloyd's initial plans were for an aircraft with a wingspan of 120ft (36.6m), a wing area of 2,000ft² (185.8m²) and an overall length of 45ft (13/7m). The estimated maximum speed was 470mph (756kph) at sea level and 480mph (772kph) at 30,000ft (9,144m), with a rate of climb slightly better than 3,000ft/per min (914m/per min). The anticipated service ceiling is unknown, but range was expected to be 1,500 miles (2,424km). Gross weight was 49,765 lb (22,573kg) with the bomb load accounting for 12,000 lb (5,443kg) of this figure. However, within months, the design underwent a significant revision, with the wingspan being reduced to 112ft 6in (34.3m) and the wing becoming thinner. As a consequence, the centre section became recognisable as a fuselage and the rear gun turret was removed, leading to nominal changes in weight and performance. A smaller twin-engine experimental version of this aircraft was considered at some point during the early design phase, but engine problems appear to have ruled this out.

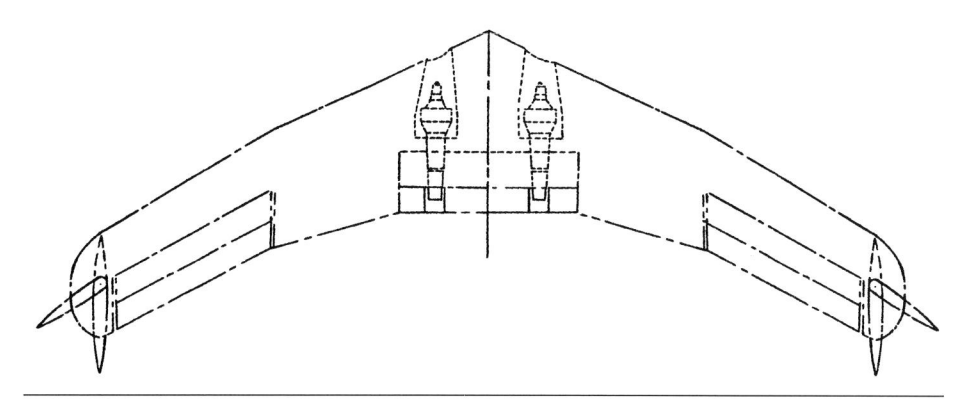

However, it was decided that a one-third-scale size glider should be built to test the aerodynamics, as there was little data to draw on regarding the behaviour of flying wing aircraft at low speeds or in unusual attitudes. Initially assigned the company reference AW.51, design work started in May 1943, with the project altering to AW.52, which finally became AW.52G, with the last letter referring to its status as a glider.

Assembly started at the beginning of March 1944, although proceedings were relatively slow as priority was being given to more pressing war production work. Wind tunnel testing continued and AW.52G was finally completed in early 1945. It was then assigned the official registration RG324, but by this time, the original flying wing bomber had been cancelled. Nevertheless, AW.52G was seen as a useful research tool and on 2 March 1945 was towed into the air behind a Whitley bomber. This first flight was undertaken by the company's test pilot Charles K. Turner-Hughes, who reported no unexpected handling difficulties.

Spruce and plywood (used for the single box spar and ribs) were utilised in much of the construction, with the outer skin fabricated from Plymax (a thin sheet of duralumin bonded to a thicker sheet of plywood). This allowed a very smooth finish that met the requirements for effective laminar flow. The central cockpit area accommodated a pilot

Armstrong Whitworth AW.50

Crew	6
Wingspan	120ft (36.6m), later reduced to 112ft 6in (34.3m)
Wing area	2,000.04ft² (185.8m²)
Length	45ft (13.7m)
Gross weight	49,765 lb (22,573kg)
Maximum speed	
at sea level	470mph (756kph)
at 30,000ft (9,144m)	480mph (772kph)
Rate of climb	3,000ft/per min (914m/per min)
Ceiling	Unknown
Range	1,500 miles (2,414km)
Powerplant	4 x Metropolitan-Vickers (Metrovick) F.2/4 Beryl axial-flow turbojet engines, initially producing 3,500 lb (15.5kN) static thrust
Armament	Provisionally, 2 x 20mm forward firing cannons and one rear firing remote controlled turret with 2 x 20mm cannons.
Bomb load	12,000 lb (5,443kg)

British Tailless Aircraft

The AW.52G on the ground. Bill Rose Collection

A staged company photograph of the AW.52G with crew and observers. The unusual attachment to the trailing edge of the port wing is a frame for the pitot comb used to measure airflow. Bill Rose Collection

The first of two AW.52 experimental jet aircraft (TG363) which were based on designs for the larger AW.50 bomber. Two Rolls-Royce Nene turbojets provided propulsion, each rated at 5,000 lb (22.24kN) static thrust. Bill Rose Collection

and rear seated observer, with conventional flight controls, aside from a large handbrake style lever used to actuate additional hydraulically-operated, horizontal control surfaces called 'correctors'. In addition to the other control surfaces, a substantial hydraulically operated one-piece slotted flap with a length of 15ft 4in (4.67m) is positioned along the entire trailing edge of the central wing section. As a precaution during testing, anti-spin parachutes were housed in canisters on each wingtip.

AW.52G utilised a fixed tricycle undercarriage with brakes and a non-steering nosewheel. The wingspan was 53ft 10in (16.41m), with a wing area of 443.04ft² (41.16m²). Overall length was 19ft 4in (5.89m), the height was 8ft 4in (2.54m). The gross weight of the aircraft was approximately 6,000lb (2,724kg). The

Armstrong Whitworth AW.52G

Crew	2
Wingspan	53ft 10in (16.41m)
Wing area	443.04ft² (41.16m²)
Length	19ft 4in (5.89m)
Height	8ft 4in (2.54m)
Gross weight	6,000lb (2,724kg) approx
Powerplant	None
Glide speed	100-120 mpg (160-190kph) approx
Max permitted speed	250mph (400kph)

Armstrong Whitworth AW.52 Jet (TG363)

Crew	2
Sweep	Initial 17.5°, followed by 34° to the wingtips (leading edge)
Wingspan	90ft (27.4m)
Wing area	1,314ft² (122m²)
Length	37ft 4in (11.4m)
Height	14ft 4in (4.4m)
Empty weight	19,662 lb (8,919kg)
Gross weight	34,154 lb (15,492kg)
Powerplant	2 x Rolls-Royce Nene 2 turbojets, each rated at 5,000 lb (22.2kN) static thrust
Maximum speed	500mph (800kph) approx
Ceiling	35-40,000ft (10-12,000m) approx
Range	1,000 miles (1,600km) approx

AW.52G would normally glide at around 100-120mph (160-190kph), with a maximum permitted speed of 250mph (400kph) and stall occurring at about 60-65mph (96-104kph).

Because there was so much interest in boundary layer control, an experimental system was devised to draw in air through a slot forward of the elevons. The idea was to reduce the possibility of wingtip stall at lower speeds and to achieve the suction, small wind-powered pumps were fitted to each of the main wheel struts. Trials continued throughout 1945, with the aircraft usually being flown by company test pilots Charles Turner-Hughes or Eric George Franklin. Some refinements were made to the glider as the project progressed and it was then decided to build two somewhat larger experimental jet-powered flying wings. The project would receive the company reference AW.52 and approval under the original MAP specification E.9/44 by the Ministry of Supply.

The new aircraft would be approximately three quarters the size of Lloyd's initial design for the AW.50. Its gross weight would be about 34,000lb (15,422kg) and two Rolls-Royce turbojets would provide propulsion. In overall appearance the larger jet-powered AW.52 was similar to the glider, although the centre of the wing now contained a recognisable fuselage section that protruded forward. The two turbojet engines were buried in the wing on each side of the cockpit section and the aircraft's internal structure was somewhat different to the AW.52G, with metal being used throughout. The first AW.52 (TS363) was completed in Armstrong Whitworth's assembly shop at Whitley, Coventry, by early 1947. It had already been revealed to the public as a mail-carrying aircraft, although this appears to have been largely public relations spin.

Like the glider, this aircraft had an initial sweep of 17.5°, followed by 34° to the wingtip, which provided the distinctive boomerang shape. The AW.52 had a wingspan of 90ft (27.4m), a length of 37ft 4in (11.4m) and a height of 14ft 4in (4.4m). Empty, the aircraft weighed 19,662lb (8,919kg), with a gross weight of 34,154lb (15,492kg) and the aircraft carried a crew of two. The engines chosen for the first aircraft were Rolls-Royce Nene 2 turbojets, each rated at 5,000lb (22.2kN) of static thrust. The estimated maximum speed of the AW.52 was about 500mph (800kph), with a ceiling of about 35-40,000ft (10-12,000m) and a range of approximately 1,000 miles (1,600km). The aircraft featured a pressurised cockpit and the pilot was equipped with a Martin Baker Mk1 ejector seat, although not the passenger. The AW.52 was fitted with a thermal de-icing system using exhaust from the engines and there was a boundary layer control system connected to the engine air intakes and pressure balanced control surfaces. The aircraft also utilised a fully retractable tricycle undercarriage with a steerable nose-wheel.

Like the AW.52G, the AW.52 was equipped with vertical wingtip fins and rudders and canisters were attached that contained anti-spin parachutes for emergency use. The trailing edge of the flying wing was occupied by a substantial Fowler flap, which was contoured to allow for each jet exhaust pipe. After a period of tests and minor modifications, the aircraft was partly dismantled and transported by road to the RAF Experimental Establishment at Boscombe Down. Having been reassembled, AW.52 spent the next couple of months undertaking ground tests and taxiing trials until a break in the weather allowed the first flight to be made on 13 November 1947.

The trial was undertaken by Armstrong Whitworth test pilot Eric Franklin who reported that the aircraft handled as anticipated. Following this success the AW.52 was returned to Bitteswell Airfield (no longer in existence) for further testing. The second AW.52 (TS368) was completed in the Whitley workshops during the summer of 1948 and differed slightly by having two less powerful Rolls-Royce Derwent 5 engines, each producing 3,500lb (15,56kN) of static thrust. Rolls-Royce engines appear to have been chosen for reasons of reliability, although it remains unclear why Derwent turbojets were fitted to the second aircraft in preference to the similar Nene units. TS368 first flew on 1 September 1948 and flight-testing with both aircraft continued until 30 May 1949.

On this date, John Lancaster was undertaking a series of trials in the vicinity of the Bitteswell Aerodrome with TS363. After entering a dive at about 320mph (510kph), Lancaster encountered severe pitch oscillation and realising that the aircraft was about to break up, he ejected, becoming the first British pilot to use this system in an emergency. The second AW.52 was transferred to the RAE Farnborough in October 1950 where testing continued until September 1953 when Armstrong Whitworth left the programme. As a consequence, the RAE decided to conclude operations.

Exactly how useful the Armstrong Whitworth flying wing programme proved to be remains debatable. Lloyd hoped that this work would lead to a large flying wing airliner powered by six turbojets, but there were too many technical obstacles. Laminar flow proved to be largely unworkable, control of the AW.52 prototypes was often difficult and take-off and landing distances were unsatisfactory. In May 1954, the second AW.52 was broken up for scrap and it is thought that the glider met the same fate.

AW.56

In late 1946, the UK Air Staff requested proposals for an advanced medium range jet bomber. Known as Operational Requirement (OR) 229, this set out the RAF's future needs for a fast, high-altitude aircraft, capable of delivering a 10,000lb (4,535kg) bomb to a release point 1,500nm (1726 miles or 2,776km) distant. Although the primary objective was the carriage and delivery of a single atomic bomb, no British nuclear weapon had been produced at this time and a second requirement designated OR.1001 (later given the codename 'Blue Danube') was issued by the Air Staff to develop a plutonium bomb. Both the aircraft and the bomb represented a significant technical challenge. The RAF was seeking a bomber that was capable of sustaining a speed of 500kts (926kph) at an altitude of 50,000ft (15,240m) with a gross weight of 100,000lb (45,359kg). Bearing in mind the state of aerodynamic knowledge and gas turbine technology at the time, this was a very tall order.

Armstrong Whitworth AW.56 Flying Wing Medium Bomber Project (OR.229)

Crew	5
Wingspan	120ft (36.58m)
(revised)	102ft (31m)
Wing area	2,611ft² (242.56m²)
(revised)	2,250ft² (209m²)
Length	80ft (24.38m)
(revised)	75ft (22.8m)
Height	32ft (9.75m) unconfirmed
Gross weight	113,000lb (51,256kg)
(revised)	101,150lb (45,881kg)
Powerplant	5 x Rolls-Royce AJ65 Avon turbojets, each rated at 6,500lb (28.9kN) static thrust
(revised)	4 x AJ65 engines, or possibly RR RB77 at 7,500lb static thrust
Maximum speed	640mph 1,030Kph
(revised)	575mph (925kph)
Service ceiling	50,000ft (15,240m)
Range	Carrying a 10,000lb (4,535kg) bomb load, initially expected to be 1,724 miles (2,776km)
Armament	Maximum 20,000lb (9,071kg) bomb load. Either, one nuclear weapon, two ground penetrating bombs, 3 x 6,000lb (2,721kg) bombs, or various smaller free fall bombs

Armstrong Whitworth responded to OR.229 with an initial submission and not surprisingly the designers drew heavily on their flying wing and laminar flow research. After the Ministry of Supply issued the more specific Specification B.35/46 in early 1947, Armstrong Whitworth submitted detailed plans for a swept-wing tailless jet bomber, incorporating a host of advanced features with the company reference AW.56.

From the outset, Armstrong Whitworth believed that a tailless configuration would generate fewer aerodynamic problems at transonic speeds. They also proposed a series of wing slots that would allow boundary layer control at all speeds, leading to theoretically effective laminar flow. At this time, experiments to determine the viability of laminar flow had been sponsored by Armstrong Whitworth and were being conducted at RAE Farnborough with a modified Hurricane fighter (Z3687). Initial results had been disappointing, but research continued, with a modified Gloster Meteor MkIII jet fighter and AWA's flying wing programme. The Armstrong Whitworth laminar flow wing for the AW.56 was to have a span of 120ft (36.58m) and an area of 2,611ft² (242.56m²). The overall length of the aircraft was initially 80ft (24.38m) with an unconfirmed height of 32ft (9.75m) and a gross weight of 113,000lb (51,256kg). To meet the performance requirement of B.35/46, five Rolls-Royce AJ65 Avon turbojets would be used for propulsion, each rated at 6,500lb (28.9kN) static thrust. Four engines would be installed in the wing roots with air intakes on each side of the cockpit and another engine would be located in the tail, with its own dorsal air inlet located mid-way along the fuselage. The gross weight was calculated at 113,000lb (51,256kg), which suggested that the aircraft would have a maximum speed of 640mph (1,030kph) and a ceiling in excess of 50,000ft (15,240m).

The AW.56's fuselage section would be built using fairly conventional materials and construction methods, although the two-spar wing would be covered with an unusual multi-layer skin similar to that developed for the experimental AW.52 flying wing.

A fully retractable tricycle undercarriage was planned for the bomber and a flight control system developed for the AW.52 would be used, comprising of two tandem control surfaces called a 'corrector' and a 'controller'. The 'corrector' acted as a longitudinal trim control and the 'controller' was similar in function to an elevon. A crew of five would man the aircraft, housed in a pressurised nose section, with access to the bomb bay to allow in-flight arming of the nuclear weapon. No ejector seats would be installed, but it was proposed that the entire nose section would be jettisoned in an emergency and could be lowered to the ground by four substantial parachutes. As an alternative to a nuclear weapon, the AW.56 could carry a variety of conventional stores with a maximum weight of 20,000lb (9,071kg). Another interesting design feature was the bomb bay doors which opened transversely with sections sliding fore and aft. This was considered an effective way of minimising impact on the aircraft's speed and trim.

A long-range mission would involve the aircraft ascending to an altitude of 40,000ft

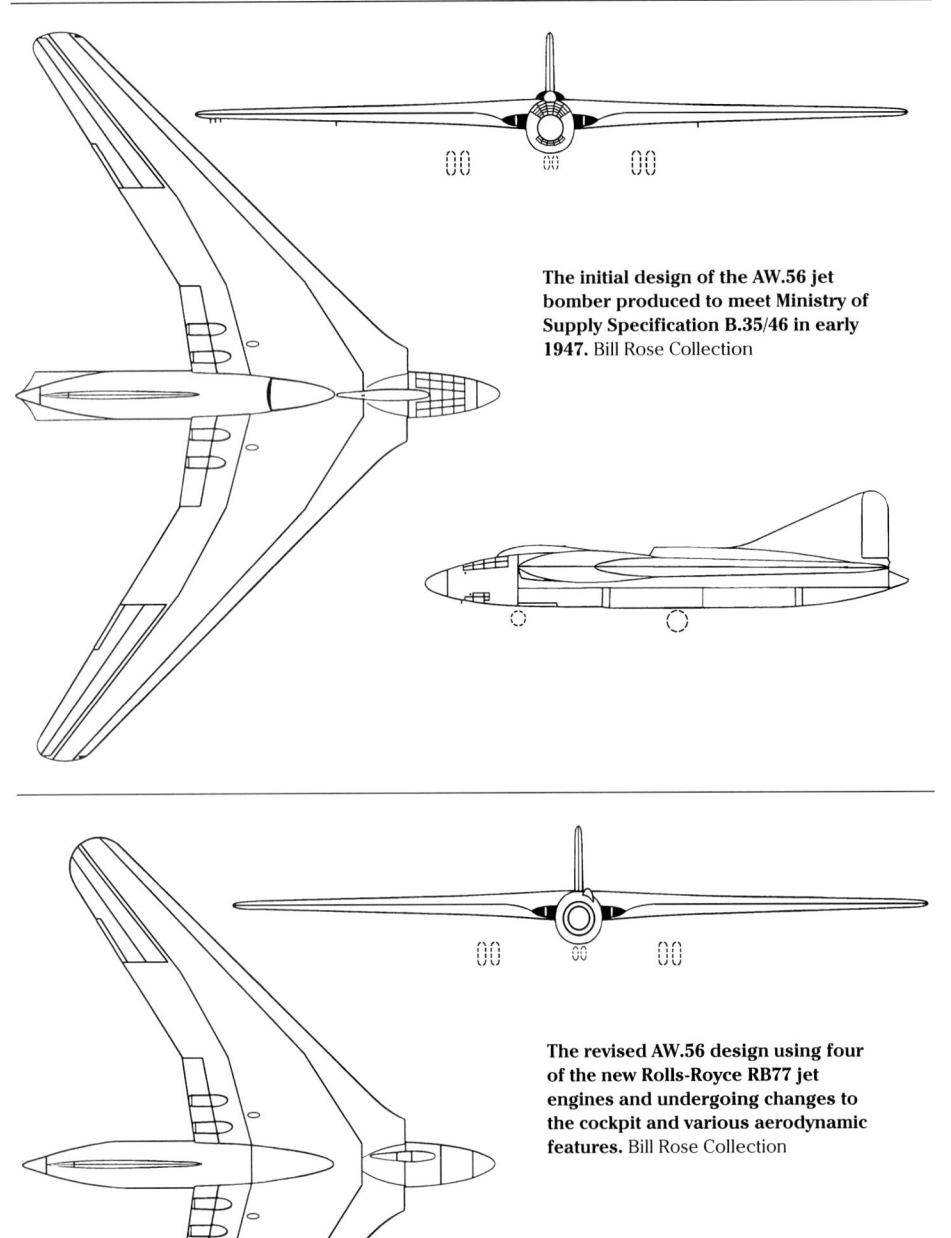

The initial design of the AW.56 jet bomber produced to meet Ministry of Supply Specification B.35/46 in early 1947. Bill Rose Collection

The revised AW.56 design using four of the new Rolls-Royce RB77 jet engines and undergoing changes to the cockpit and various aerodynamic features. Bill Rose Collection

Secret Projects: Flying Wings and Tailless Aircraft

(12,192m) and progressively climbing to 50,000ft (15,240m), which would be attained after approximately 2 hours and 30 minutes. It was suggested that the Avon engines might be replaced by MetroVick F.9s, which would offer improved thrust, lower fuel consumption and the ability to climb directly to 50,000ft (15,240m). However, the requirements for a new bomber were lowered after the Tender Design Conference took place and this led to a significant revision of the AW.56 proposal, resulting in a slightly smaller aircraft. The redesigned AW.56 would be fitted with the new Rolls-Royce RB.77 engines, allowing the use of four rather than five units. This meant that the tail engine was removed, leading to better streamlining and a noticeable weight reduction. This improvement would provide the AW.56 with performance similar to the proposed F.9 powered version.

Another alteration to the revised aircraft was the use of a raised cockpit canopy for the pilot. Offset to the port side, this would have improved visibility considerably. AWA anticipated full completion of this second design within two years and testing of the first prototype about five months later. But the design was finally rejected by the MoS in favour of the Avro 698 and Handley Page H.P.80 which became the Vulcan and Victor.

AW.171

The AW.171 is often listed as a supersonic flying wing by aviation sources and therefore deserves to be briefly mentioned. Armstrong Whitworth produced several designs during the mid-1950s to meet a MoS specification for a one-man supersonic research aircraft with a vertical take-off and landing (VTOL) capability. The first was the highly swept AW.171 which would be powered by two Bristol Orpheus turbojets for horizontal flight and 10 centrally located Rolls-Royce RB.108 engines mounted in an upright position for lift. This was followed by the AW.172 which utilised a slightly different wing profile and propulsion system. It appears that Rolls-Royce's leading engine designer, Alan Arnold Griffith, was involved with this project and he produced a number of broadly similar designs which also utilised centrally located lift engines. Although the supersonic VTOL demonstrator was cancelled at an early stage, there was some lingering interest in the idea of a larger VTOL bomber or transport aircraft based on the AW.171, which continued until 1957 when a wide number of advanced research projects were officially cancelled.

Underside view of DH.108 TG283 in flight.
Bill Rose Collection

Armstrong Whitworth AW.171

Crew	1
Wingspan	17ft 6in (5.36m)
Sweep	83°
Length	70ft 7in (21.59m)
Gross weight	16,309 lb (7,398kg)
Powerplant	
(horizontal flight)	2 x Bristol Orpheus turbojets, each rated at 4,859 lb (21.6kN) static thrust.
(VTOL operations)	10 x Rolls-Royce RB108 turbojets, each rated at 2,101 lb (9.34kN) static thrust
Maximum speed	1,483mph (2,387kph)
Endurance	unknown
Range	unknown

DH.108 Swallow

In 1943, the Brabazon Committee was formed to consider requirements for civil air transportation once the war had ended. This resulted in approaches being made to a number of aircraft contractors for submissions and one company who responded was de Havilland, which had studied the Committee's Type 1V requirement for a jet-powered 100-seat airliner. This resulted in proposals for a scaled up Vampire fighter, a tailless flying wing using four Ghost turbojets and a more conventional concept that would eventually become the DH.106 Comet. However, such a project would take the designers and engineers into uncharted territory and it was recognised that a small demonstrator was required to establish the viability of various swept wing configurations.

During October 1945, the company's Chief Designer Ronald Bishop finally selected a small experimental tailless proposal known as DH.108, which was based on a Vampire with a single swept tail fin. Propulsion was to be provided by a single de Havilland Goblin 2 turbojet and because this prototype drew heavily on a proven design, the development time and cost could be minimised. In early 1946, the Air Ministry approved full development of what would be Britain's first swept wing aircraft. Two similar, but slightly different prototypes would be built to provide data for the proposed jet airliner, plus future jet fighters like the DH.110 Sea Vixen. One of the experimental aircraft would be used to evaluate the performance of the swept wing at relatively low speeds while the other would have a transonic capability. These aircraft were now assigned the official (Experimental) references E.1/45 and E.11/45.

Much of the DH.108's design can be credited to John Carver Meadows Frost (1915-1979) who is now remembered for his work on the Avrocar project in Canada. Both of the DH.108 aircraft started life as fuselages for Vampire F.1 jet fighters that were taken directly from the production line. As originally planned, the first aircraft was fitted with a Goblin 2 turbojet engine, producing 3,000 lb (13.4kN) static thrust. A new wing with a 43° sweep and fixed leading edge slats were fit-

British Tailless Aircraft

The clean, compact de Havilland DH.108 tailless experimental aircraft, which was based on the Vampire jet fighter and drew heavily on wartime German aeronautical research. This photograph shows the second prototype, TG306.
Bill Rose Collection

ted. Utilising quite a lot of wood in its construction, the new wing had a span of 39ft (11.88m) and an area of 328ft² (30.4m²), which was 15% greater than the Vampire. Control of roll and pitch was undertaken by elevons located outboard of the trailing edge split flaps and containers were fitted to the wingtips that carried small anti-spin parachutes for emergency use.

A single vertical fin now replaced the twin tail boom fitted to the Vampire and this resulted in a sleeker more elegant looking aircraft which was given the name Swallow, although it was never formally adopted. As a result, this elegant-looking aircraft appeared to be something of a Vampire crossed with a wartime Messerschmitt Me 163B rocket interceptor, perhaps reflecting the fact that German aeronautical development had influenced this design. Having been completed in what would now be regarded as an astonishingly short period of time, the aircraft was assigned the official serial number TG283 and the DH.108 made its first flight on 15 May 1946, with test pilot Geoffrey Roald de Havilland Jr OBE (1910-1946) at the controls. (Son of the original Geoffrey de Havilland.) The test flight was relatively uneventful and de Havilland reported the DH.108 handled well, despite being restricted to a maximum speed of 280mph (450kph).

While the DH.108 was not a classified project, some of the aircraft's technology was considered sensitive and details of flight trials were treated with secrecy. There were runway repair problems at Hatfield, so it was an easy decision to continue with trials at RAF Woodbridge in Suffolk. At that time, Woodbridge was being used for classified RAF experimental work and its lengthy, well-maintained runway made this an especially suitable location. Somewhat surprisingly, the base was closed in March 1948 and passed to the USAF several years later.

The secrecy surrounding the DH.108 continued until the beginning of June 1946 when Parliamentary Secretary of the Ministry of Supply Arthur Woodburn visited de Havilland at Hatfield and disclosed the aircraft's existence (which had now returned to the facility). While minor modifications were being made to the aircraft, it was already apparent that a tailless design based on prevailing technology was less than ideal for an airliner. Meanwhile, work continued on construction of the second prototype designed for high-speed flight, which was fitted with a slightly more powerful Goblin 3 engine rated at 3,350 lb (14.9kN) static thrust. The aircraft was marginally shorter than the first DH.108 with an overall length of 25ft 10in (7.874m) as opposed to 24ft 6in (7.467m) and featured a 45° leading edge wing sweep. Automatic leading edge slots were fitted that could be locked by the pilot, a more streamlined cockpit canopy was used and there were improvements to the flight controls.

This aircraft received the serial number TG306 and was built to explore flight at much higher speeds and perhaps supersede the existing air speed record of 616mph (991kph).

TG306 first flew during June 1946 and appeared at the Society of British Aircraft Constructors (SBAC) September 1946 show at Radlett (which moved to Farnborough in 1948). As well as being a static exhibit, it was flown by Geoffrey de Havilland during the show's final event and clearly impressed the visitors. A couple of weeks later, on 27 September 1946, Geoffrey de Havilland took off from Hatfield in the second DH.108. He had now logged 13 hours in the aircraft and intended to push it towards its limits during preparations for an attempt on the air speed record, which had now been unofficially broken in this aircraft. The emergency anti-spin parachute containers had been removed and the aircraft's metallic surface had been polished to a bright finish. However, things went disastrously wrong above the Thames Estuary when de Havilland encountered pitch oscillations at Mach 0.9.

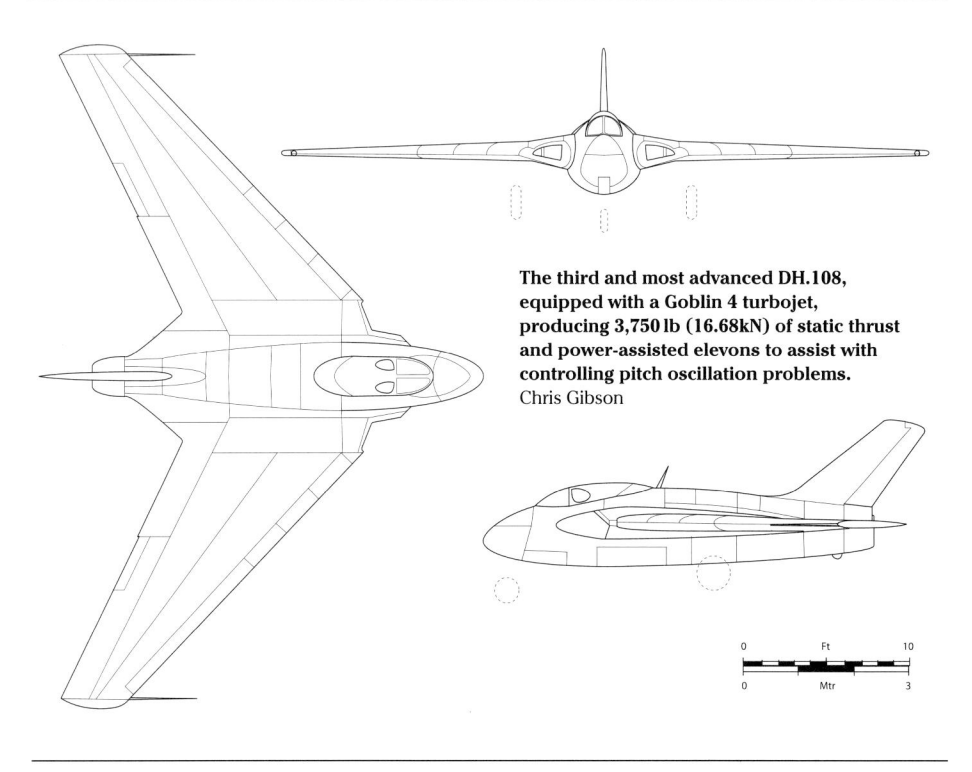

The third and most advanced DH.108, equipped with a Goblin 4 turbojet, producing 3,750 lb (16.68kN) of static thrust and power-assisted elevons to assist with controlling pitch oscillation problems.
Chris Gibson

Secret Projects: Flying Wings and Tailless Aircraft

De Havilland's third DH.108, based on a production Vampire F.5 fighter and configured for high-speed flight, was given the official reference VW120. Piloted by John Derry, it set a world air speed record of 605.23mph (974kph) on a 62-mile (100km) closed circuit during April 1948.
Bill Rose Collection

As a consequence, the main spar fractured, the wings sheared off and the fuselage came apart. Wreckage showered down into the muddy waters of Egypt Bay near Gravesend, Kent, and de Havilland was killed. Recovery of debris proved especially difficult and Geoffrey de Havilland's body could not be located, although it finally washed ashore at Whitstable on 7 October 1946. This tragic accident would hold up high-speed flight testing for another year, during which time it was decided that the problems that had caused the accident could be effectively dealt with. In July 1947, a decision was taken to replace the second DH.108 with a similar aircraft, albeit with a number of modifications and improvements.

The third DH.108 was based on a production Vampire F.5 fighter and it received the official serial number VW120. It was slightly more streamlined than TG306 with a pointed nose, giving it an overall length of 26ft 9½in (8.165m). A sleeker, more aerodynamic cockpit canopy was fitted, the pilot's ejector seat was lowered, which reduced visibility and the cockpit remained unpressurised. With engine performance steadily (although slowly) improving, this aircraft was fitted with the latest Goblin 4 turbojet, producing 3,750 lb (16.68kN) of static thrust. As a final major upgrade, the third Swallow was fitted with power-assisted elevons to address the problem of pitch oscillations.

Replacing Geoffrey de Havilland as the company's chief test pilot was wartime night-fighter ace John Cunningham (1917-2002) who made his first flight in the new Swallow on 24 July 1947. The following year on 12 April 1948, this aircraft piloted by de Havilland test pilot John Derry (1921-1952), set a new world air speed record of 605.23mph (974kph) on a 62 mile (100km) closed circuit, later earning him the prestigious Segrave Memorial Trophy. Flying this aircraft, Derry would also become the first British pilot to exceed the speed of sound, which took place on the morning of 6 September 1948 above Windsor.

For some weeks the Swallow had been tested at gradually increasing speed and on this occasion Derry decided that conditions were good enough to push the aircraft a little further. Rapidly descending from about 40,000ft (12,000m), the aircraft nudged past Mach 1 just before Derry pulled out of the descent at 30,000ft (9,000m). Although there was no serious instability, Derry later reported that the controls became heavy and unresponsive, despite the power boost system. But once he dropped down below Mach 0.96, everything returned to normal and Derry resumed his flight to the de Havilland facility at Hatfield.

Trials with the third DH.108 continued into the following year, when the aircraft appeared at the Farnborough Air Show and took third place in the SBAC's Challenge Trophy Air Race. It was then officially passed to the Ministry of Supply which continued with testing at RAE Farnborough. Unfortunately, the third DH.108 was lost on 15 February 1950 with its pilot Squadron Leader Stuart Muller-Rowland being killed. He had been undertaking dives at high transonic speeds above Buckinghamshire when the aircraft broke up. Wreckage came down in the Little Brickhill area, with a number of parts found near Bow Brickhill Church and some components as far removed as Husborne Crawley. The local fire service was mobilised, along with the police, who were instructed to cordon off the area as some aspects of the aircraft remained classified. Witnesses reported hearing an explosion, although this may have been a sonic boom. The cause of the accident was later determined to have been an oxygen system failure, resulting in the pilot losing consciousness.

The first DH.108 was still flying, but on 1 May 1950, it crashed at Hartley Wintney, Hants, during stalling trials killing the pilot Squadron Leader George Genders. The three DH.108 Swallow aircraft completed a total of 480 flights, which provided invaluable data, despite all being lost in fatal accidents. Many observers have claimed the aircraft were jinxed, cursed or the design was fatally flawed, but others believe these are not entirely fair comments. At that time, the DH.108 represented the cutting edge of aeronautical research and these aircraft were regularly flown at their performance limits. Much of the research undertaken in the immediate post-war era meant actually going out and trying an idea to see if it worked. Both the US and Russians lost experimental aircraft during this period, simply as a result of pushing the envelope that little bit further.

As a footnote, the DH.108 trials would inspire the British film director David Lean to make a fictional movie called *The Sound Barrier*, which was released in 1952. Starring Ralph Richardson and Ann Todd, it was very successful at the time, but is now largely forgotten. The film featured a 'new' jet fighter called the Prometheus that was used in an attempt to break the sound barrier. Prometheus was actually a Nene-powered Supermarine Swift Type 535 prototype (VV119).

De Havilland DH.108 (TG283)

Crew	1
Wingspan	39ft (11.88m)
Length	25ft 10in (7.9m)
Gross weight	8,800 lb (3,991kg)
Powerplant	1 x de Havilland Goblin II turbojet rated at 3,100 lb (13.8kN) static thrust
Maximum speed	280mph (450kph)
Ceiling	N/A
Range	730 miles (1,174km)

De Havilland DH.108 (VW120)

Crew	1
Wingspan	39ft (11.89m)
Wing area	327.86ft² (30.47m²)
Wing loading	133kg/m² (27 lb/ft²)
Length	26ft 10in (8.17m)
Height	14ft (4.27m)
Gross weight	8,940 lb (4,064kg)
Powerplant	1 x de Havilland Goblin 4 turbojet rated at 3,738 lb (16.67kN) static thrust
Thrust/weight	0.42
Maximum speed	677mph (1,090kph)
Ceiling	40,000ft (12,192m)

Westland PJD.144

In the immediate post-war years, the Royal Navy began to consider its future needs for a more advanced carrier-borne twin jet fighter with the ability to operate at night. It would need to be capable of achieving a maximum speed of 500kts (927kph), have a gross weight of no more than 30,000lb (13,608kg). A maximum wingspan of 55ft (16.8m) was recommended and folded, the span could be no greater than 18ft (5.5m). The maximum permissible length was 43ft (13.1m). Assisted take-off was anticipated and the armament would comprise two or ideally four 30mm cannons. This Operational Requirement (OR.246) led to Specification N.40/46 being issued to a number of aircraft contractors and one of the companies that responded was Westland. It undertook a detailed study, which resulted in an initial proposal designated PJD.129, followed by three differing variations. These were PJD.142, PJD.143 and PJD.144, with the designs completed in late 1947.

The version preferred by Westland was the PJD.144, which was similar in overall appearance to the initial PJD.129 proposal. It was a completely tailless design with vertical wingtip fins and rudders and this proposal utilised two turbojets in a stacked configuration along similar lines to the later English Electric Lightning. Air intakes for the engines were positioned on each side of cockpit with a split central duct feeding both engines. The PJD.129/144 concept has been compared with the Junkers EF.128 which was a German proposal produced for the 1945 Emergency Fighter Competition. To what extent the designers at Westland were influenced by captured research material is hard to say as much of the documentation for the EF.128 project fell into Soviet hands. But it appears that the Westland fuselage had more in common with aircraft like the de Havilland Vampire and the similarities to the German design are rather superficial.

The main differences between the PJD.129 and the PJD.144 were alterations to the wings and fins. The leading edge wing sweep was reduced from 45° to 38°, made possible by changes to the wing's outer chord and the fin size was slightly increased. PJD.142 was broadly similar to this aircraft, but lacked the vertical wingtip fins and utilised a single upright tailfin. PJD.143 was the most conventional of these studies with an upright fin and horizontal tail surfaces. It was also decided to alter the engine layout and have the turbojets side-by-side. Initially, Westland designed these concepts around two unspecified turbojet engines in the Rolls-Royce Nene class with a static thrust of about 5,000lb (22.24kN), although the RAE decided that the newly prototyped and more advanced Rolls-Royce axial-flow Avon (then known as the Axial Jet – AJ.65) was the preferred choice. Estimated maximum speed at altitude was about 630mph (1,013kph) and general dimensions and weights complied with the N.40/46 specification. Armament appears to have been the same type for all variants and in this case, three 30mm cannons were proposed.

A fully retractable tricycle undercarriage was proposed for all models and the aircraft would have been equipped with arrestor landing gear. A radar dish for airborne interception was housed in the aircraft's nose and this system would have been operated by a second crew member who was seated directly behind the pilot and facing rearward. On 15 December 1947, a Design Study Conference was chaired by the Director-General of Technical Development (Air) for the MoS, Stewart Scott-Hall, to assess all the submissions for N.40/46. The Westland proposals were an early casualty and it was decided that performance projections for this aircraft were unsatisfactory and there were general concerns about the tailless design. Delegates felt that in addition to lacking adequate performance, the Westland proposal might suffer from tip stalling and the anticipated approach speed was too high. The Conference also decided that Westland had not fully

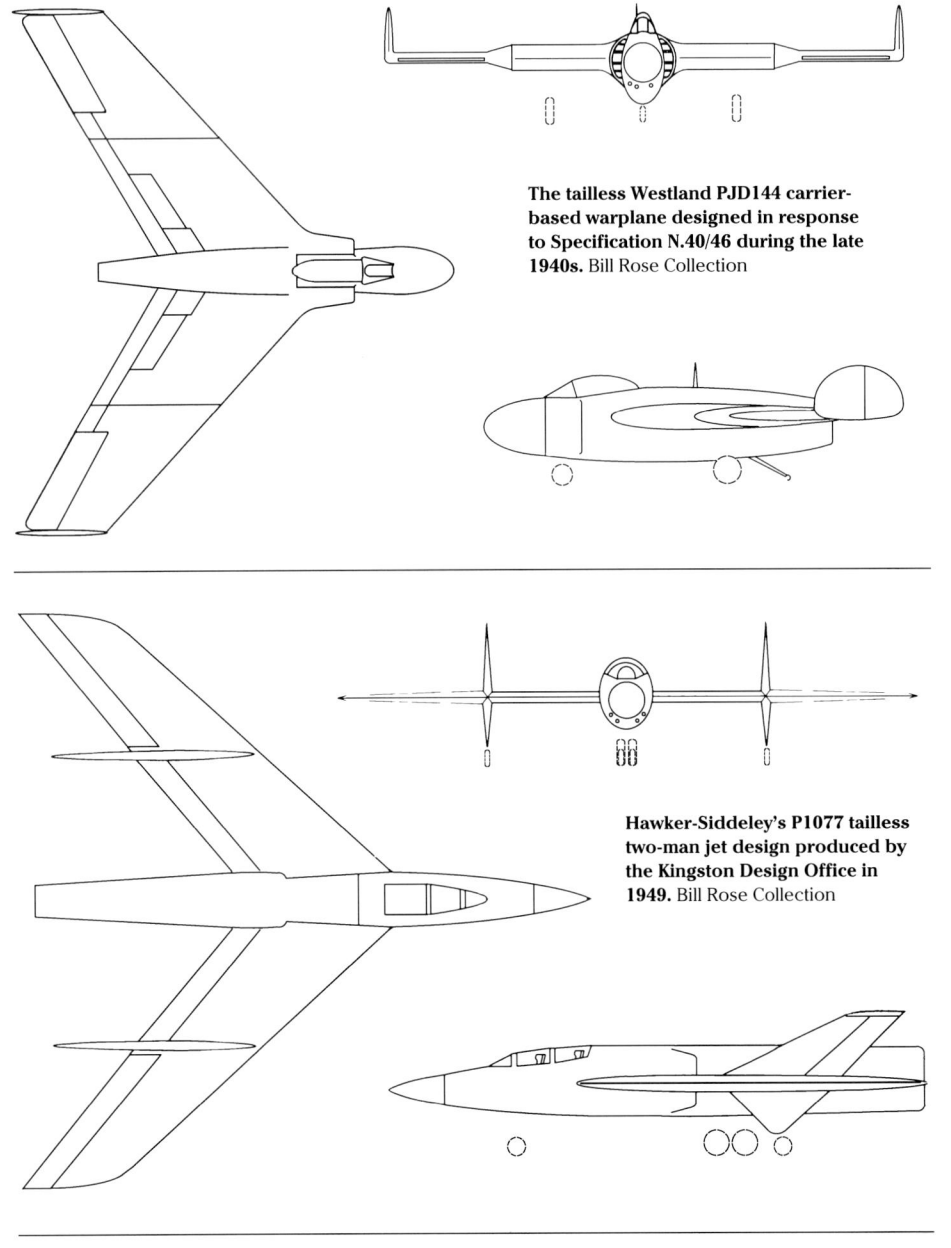

The tailless Westland PJD144 carrier-based warplane designed in response to Specification N.40/46 during the late 1940s. Bill Rose Collection

Hawker-Siddeley's P1077 tailless two-man jet design produced by the Kingston Design Office in 1949. Bill Rose Collection

Westland PJD.144

Crew	1
Wingspan	55ft (16.8m)
Wing area	745ft² (69.2m²)
Length	43ft 6in (13.3m)
Gross weight	27,260 lb (12,365kg)
Powerplant	2 x Rolls-Royce AJ65 Avon turbojets, each providing 6,500 lb (28.9kN) static thrust
Maximum speed	632mph (1,017kph) at sea level
Ceiling	50,000ft+ (15,240m+) estimate
Armament	3 x 30mm Aden cannons

considered their options for an aircraft with a tail and fitting one would negate any drag reduction advantages of the tailless design. The selection process continued during the following year with the de Havilland DH.110 finally being chosen as the best available design. This led to a contract being issued in October 1948 for the construction of a DH.110 prototype to meet Specification N.40/46 and for evaluation as a new RAF night fighter under Specification F.4/48.

Hawker Siddeley PJD.144

One of the more unusual fighter designs to emerge from Hawker Siddeley's design office at Kingston during 1949 was the tailless two-man P.1077 jet fighter, possibly intended to meet Specification F.4/48. It is almost as if the designers had taken a look at the Westland PJD.144 proposal and then set about upgrading it. The wingspan was 58ft (17.67m), the length was 55ft (16.76m) and was to be powered by two stacked Rolls-Royce Avon turbojets equipped with afterburners. Air intakes for the engines would be positioned around the fuselage about mid-wing and the P.1077 would carry 1,000 Imp gallons (4,546 litres) of fuel. Specific performance figures are unknown, but this design was probably intended to be capable of high transonic speed at altitude with a ceiling in the region of 50,000ft (15,240m). The aircraft carried a crew of two and would be equipped with air intercept radar. The undercarriage consisted of a bicycle configuration with fully retractable twin nose wheels and four larger main wheels. It seems almost certain that outrigger stabilising wheels would have been necessary. A radar dish would be fitted within the nose of the aircraft and two large vertical fins and rudders were positioned in the centre of each wing. Proposed armament were four 30mm cannons in a ventral pack. Needless to say, this interesting design never progressed beyond the drawing board.

Hawker P.1077

Crew	2
Wingspan	58ft (17.6m)
Wing area	750ft² (69.67m²)
Length	55ft (16.7m)
Powerplant	2 x Rolls-Royce AJ65 Avon turbojets, each provided 6,500 lb (28.9kN) static thrust. Specific afterburner performance unknown.
Maximum speed	650-700mph (1,000-1,100kph) estimate
Ceiling	50,000ft+ (15,240m+) estimate
Armament	4 x 30mm Aden cannons

Rolls-Royce VTOL Flying Wing

In 1956, Geoffrey Light Wilde was appointed as the Head of the Advanced Projects Design Office at Rolls-Royce in Derby. An outstanding engineer, Wilde is now best remembered for his initial work on the RB211 engine, but back in 1956, his newly formed department began detailed studies of many different ideas for civil and military engine applications, including a number of VTOL aircraft designs. Wilde was particularly interested in developing a fixed wing VTOL aircraft and specifically, a flying wing, which would use a cluster of small engines for lift with separate propulsion for horizontal flight. He began to develop this particular idea in association with one of his designers called John Coplin and it seems very likely that A.A. Griffith, who was the company's leading VTOL proponent, also took part in this study.

They settled on a basic layout that would utilise a large number of vertically positioned turbojets in the centre of the aircraft to provide lift. An illustration shows the use of 30 jet engines, but the complexity of such a system would probably have made this design unattractive for a production aircraft. Louvred inlet and exhaust shutters would be used to cover the engines in level flight and four jet engines in ducts mounted on the trailing edge of the aircraft would be used in forward flight. Wilde also envisaged a boundary layer, drag reduction system with air being drawn through conduits from the wing and fed to the intakes of the rear-mounted engines.

Proposed dimensions of this VTOL design are unknown, although the cluster of engines at the centre of gravity would result in a substantial wing thickness/chord ratio of as much as 20 per cent. Combined with a relatively low structural weight, this would allow a considerable payload capacity for cargo or passengers within the forward wing on either side of the central cockpit area. As a light military transport, it might have been especially useful for inserting and extracting Special Forces during unusual operations.

General performance figures are unknown, but it seems likely that speed, range and payload capacity would have been superior to the present day Bell-Boeing V-22 Osprey. Nothing came of this paperwork study, although Rolls-Royce applied for a patent in 1959, naming Wilde and Coplin as the inventors. This was published in 1963 and it received the reference GB920875. There was no further notable interest in flying wings at Rolls-Royce.

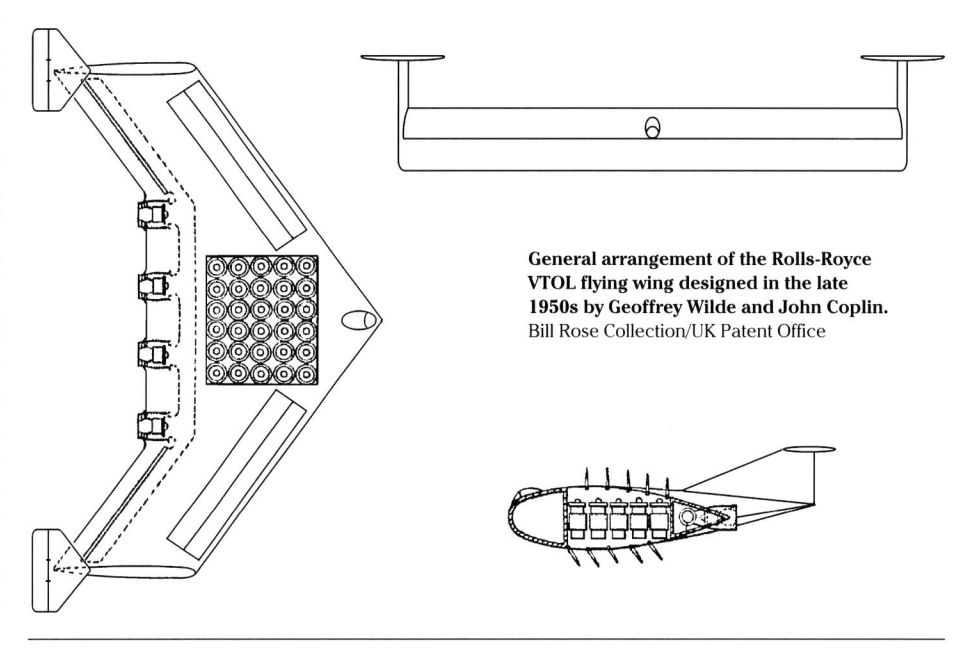

General arrangement of the Rolls-Royce VTOL flying wing designed in the late 1950s by Geoffrey Wilde and John Coplin.
Bill Rose Collection/UK Patent Office

British Tailless Aircraft

Early Avro Vulcan Studies

In 1944, the Air Ministry produced a paper with the title 'Future Bomber Requirements'. This outlined ideas for aircraft to follow the most successful types in service such as the Avro Lancaster. With the war over, there were new adversaries in the East and the RAF began to seriously consider ideas for an advanced, five-man strategic bomber powered by jet propulsion. This led to an Air Staff Operational Requirement (OR) 229 being issued in late 1946 for a fast, high-altitude aircraft, capable of delivering an atomic bomb with an estimated weight of 10,000 lb (4,535kg), to a target 1,500nm (1726 miles or 2,776km) distant. A more detailed official requirement was issued on 7 January 1947 known as Specification B.35/46. The companies responding to this request were quickly narrowed down to Avro, which developed a proposal called the Type 698, Handley Page with its HP.80 design and Armstrong Whitworth which suggested a tailless aircraft called the AW.56 (see earlier description). The AW.56 was rejected, while a preliminary study undertaken by Avro's Project Office at Chadderton, Manchester, received enthusiastic support in official circles and was given the go-ahead.

Handley Page was also contracted to develop the HP.80, which was seen as a fallback against failure of the Avro design. The advanced Handley Page proposal used an unusual crescent-shaped wing with decreasing sweep and decreasing chord, which was intended to provide a constant limiting Mach number across the entire wing at a high cruise speed. Based on early research by Dr Gustav Victor Lachmann (1896-1966), it would become the Handley Page Victor. In addition to the chosen bomber designs, Vickers-Armstrong had been working on ideas for jet bombers since 1944 and submitted a proposal for OR.229. Their design was considered too conservative and met with rejection, but the company's chief designer George Edwards managed to maintain interest in his concept and the Air Ministry finally decided to allow further development on the promise of a prototype by 1951. Subsequently, Specification B.9/48 was issued and the Vickers bomber received the company designation Type 660. Considered as further insurance against development problems with the more advanced Vulcan and Victor, this aircraft would become the Valiant.

However, prior to reaching the completion date for OR.229, the design team at Avro considered several ideas that differed considerably from the later Vulcan delta wing bomber. Heading the design office was Avro's Technical Director Roy Chadwick (1893-1947) who created the Avro Lancaster and is now generally regarded as one of Britain's greatest aircraft designers.

Initially, Chadwick envisaged a fairly conventional jet-powered bomber that was not totally dissimilar to the Vickers-Armstrong proposal. It would have a streamlined fuselage, four jet engines buried in the wing roots and a conventional tailplane. Unfortunately, Chadwick contracted shingles in January 1947 and had to leave the bomber project to his design team who included Bob Lindley, Stuart Davies and Donald Wood.

Influenced by the work that had been undertaken in Germany by Alexander Lippisch on delta configurations, Chadwick's deputy Bob Lindley moved away from the early outlines and began to draw up proposals for a bomber which was for all intents and purposes a flying wing with no vertical stabilisers. It would use a boundary layer control system with power provided by five centrally located Avon or Sapphire turbojets. The intake for the jet engines would be a large forward letterbox-shaped duct at the front of the aircraft. One of the most interesting features of this particular design was the directional engine exhaust system using large upper and lower flaps.

The aircraft would be fitted with two separate cockpits and the forward section was capable of tilting to provide better visibility under certain circumstances. Lindley also

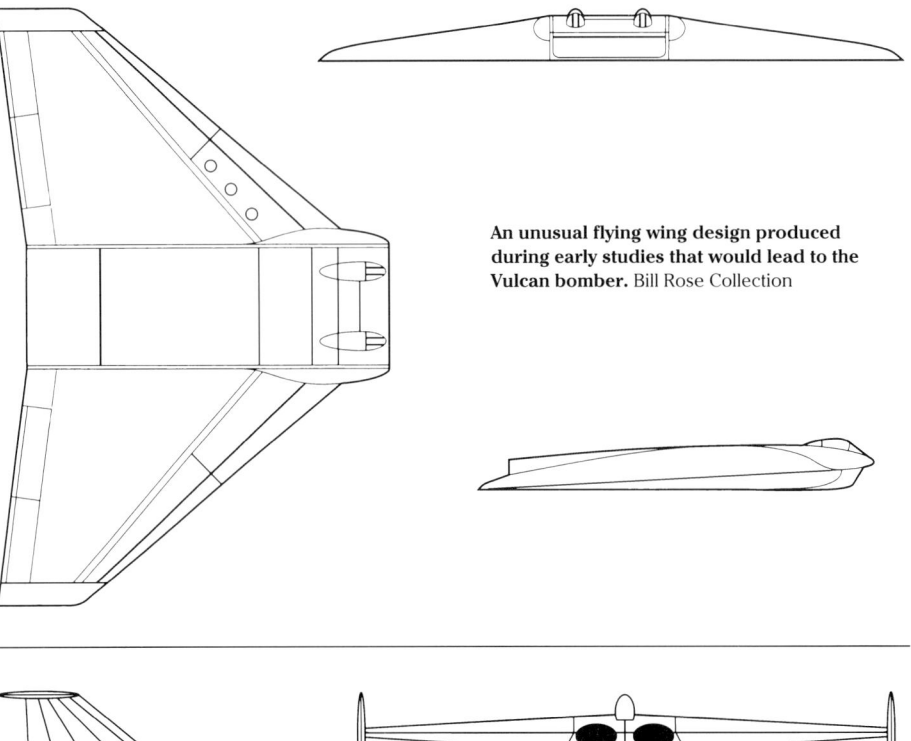

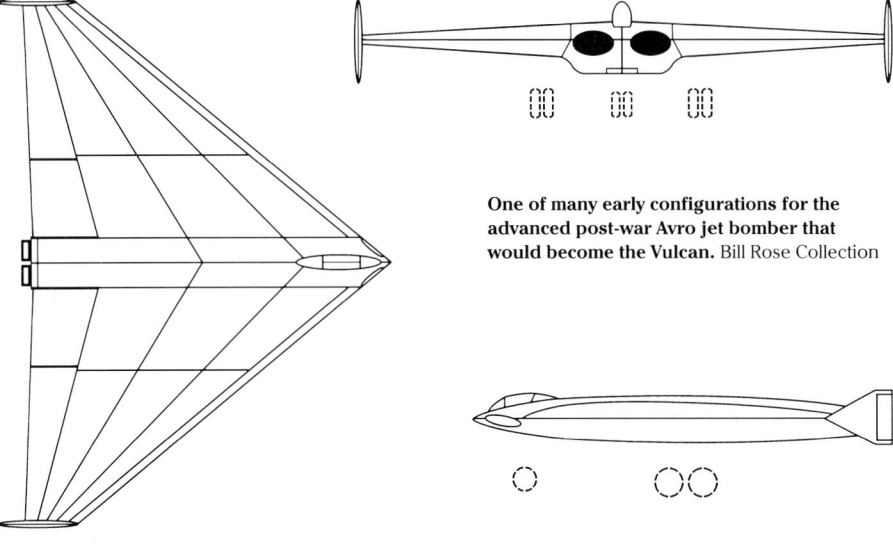

An unusual flying wing design produced during early studies that would lead to the Vulcan bomber. Bill Rose Collection

One of many early configurations for the advanced post-war Avro jet bomber that would become the Vulcan. Bill Rose Collection

proposed an additional crew area within the leading edge of the port wing. There would be two separate bomb bays at each side of the engine compartment, each having enough space to contain a single large bomb. The fully retractable undercarriage layout is a little less clear from the one available drawing of this early design, but it appears to comprise two rear-mounted main wheels and two separate nose wheels. The whole package was something of a design tour-de-force, combining many new ideas in a largely unproven aerodynamic shape.

When Roy Chadwick finally returned to the office he was not entirely pleased with the direction the project had taken and it seems there were disagreements about what he perceived to have become a science fiction concept. However, Roy Chadwick finally came around to the idea of flying wing design and soon began to suggest modifications and improvements. The appearance of the new Type 698 began to evolve towards a triangular delta-winged shape, although some of the existing features were retained. The forward engine inlet was replaced with two intakes at the leading edge and the rather strange dual cockpit layout was replaced with a single enclosure. Chadwick kept the two bomb bays, but now decided that wingtip stabilisers were necessary. The undercarriage underwent considerable revision with the favoured choice being a bicycle arrangement supplemented by outrigger wheels.

There were also attempts to design various crew capsule escape systems, but this was considered too complicated and the idea was finally abandoned. With concerns about weight, Chadwick hoped to reduce the number of turbojets to two, assuming it became possible to build an engine with 20,000 lb (89kN) static thrust. This twin-engine delta wing bomber continued to evolve and a fuselage began to form in the centre of the wing and protrude forward beyond the leading edge, making it easier to produce a pressurised crew compartment and allow extra space for essential equipment. But it was clear that two engines remained an unrealistic option and the Avro team eventually accepted that four turbojets were necessary.

Modifications continued and the Type 698 now featured upright wingtip fins with rudders and four Bristol BE.10 (later Olympus) turbojets arranged with two, staggered above the others. Air intakes for upper and lower engines on each side of the aircraft were located on each side of the forward fuselage section. On 23 August 1947, Roy Chadwick was being carried as an observer on the test flight of an Avro Tudor II. Incorrect servicing of the ailerons resulted in the aircraft crashing into the ground moments after it left the runway. Both test pilots and Chadwick were killed. This represented a significant setback to the programme and almost led to cancellation of the contract. Within a matter of weeks, (Sir) William Farren had been appointed as the new Technical Director and soon managed to calm official worries. This ensured continuation of the project, with Ministry confirmation being received on 27 November 1947.

Longitudinal stability remained a problem and the idea of utilising a horizontal tailfin similar to the Gloster Javelin was briefly considered. This was eventually dropped, but a single upright tailfin was retained. There were also issues with the staggered engine layout and this was finally dropped in favour of a less complicated side-by-side arrangement. Work on the jet bomber continued and Avro was awarded a contract to proceed to the hardware stage on 1 January 1948. The company would now build a full-sized mock-up of the bomber, two scale-sized proof-of-concept demonstrators and two full sized prototypes.

The demonstrators initially comprised a half-sized aircraft called the Avro 710, which would be powered by two Rolls-Royce Avon turbojets, and a one-third sized single Rolls-Royce Derwent-engine version with the reference Avro 707. Work began on the prototypes in 1948, but it was realised that building the Avro 710 would be as complex and expensive as a full sized aircraft, so construction of this aircraft was stopped. However, it was decided that the number of Avro 707s should be increased and five would eventually be built.

The first Avro 707 (VX784) flew on 4 September 1949, but crashed on 30 September 1949, killing the pilot Flt Lt Eric Esler after entering a low-speed stall which is believed to have been caused by faulty air brakes.

At this time, the design that would be used for the first two full-sized prototypes (VX770 and VX777) was essentially complete, although the RAE had insisted on some significant changes to the wing structure in late 1948, which would delay the start of construction at Chadderton and Woodford until early 1951. Roly Falk undertook the maiden flight of the first Type 698 prototype (VX770) on 30 August 1952. The test went well, aside from problems with trailing undercarriage doors which required careful inspection by a Vampire chase plane and a company 707. It was finally determined that this didn't interfere with the aircraft's ability to land and Falk put VX770 down on the runway with no problems.

Production aircraft were to be powered with Bristol Olympus engines, but these were not available at that time, so VX770 was fitted with four lower-powered Rolls-Royce RA.3 Avons. In October 1952, it was decided that the new bomber should be given a proper name and a Commonwealth capital city was favoured. Ottawa was the preferred choice, but this idea was soon dropped and Vulcan was selected.

Vickers Swallow

Sir Barnes Wallis Kt, CBE, FRS, RDI, FRAeS (1887-1979) is best remembered as the scientist who devised the bouncing bomb that was used by the RAF in May 1943 to attack the Möhne, Sorpe and Eder dams in the Ruhr. This mission was called Operation 'Chastise' (more widely known as the Dambusters Raid) and it eventually earned Barnes Wallis international fame, making him one of the relatively few British aircraft designers to be portrayed in a feature film (*The Dambusters*, 1954). The bouncing bomb project was essentially a one-off undertaking and when it

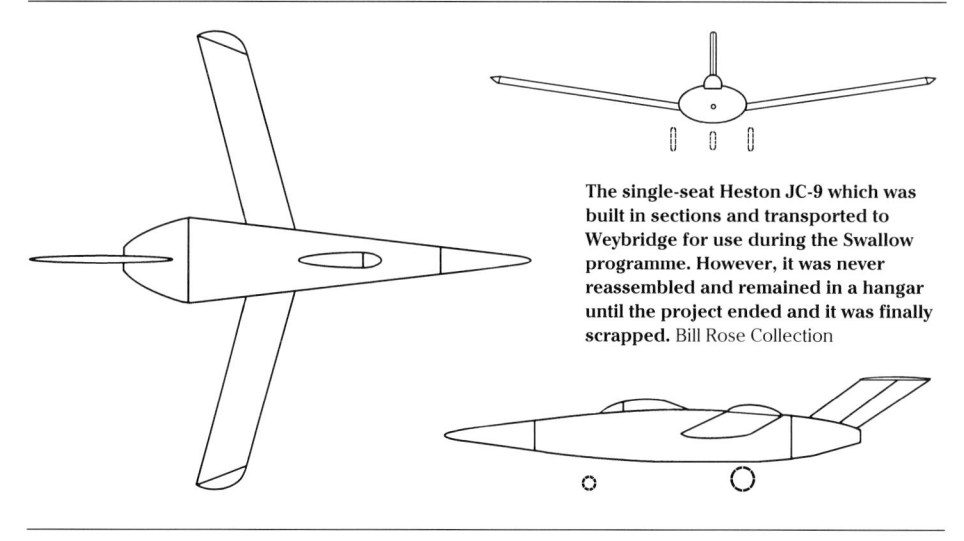

The single-seat Heston JC-9 which was built in sections and transported to Weybridge for use during the Swallow programme. However, it was never reassembled and remained in a hangar until the project ended and it was finally scrapped. Bill Rose Collection

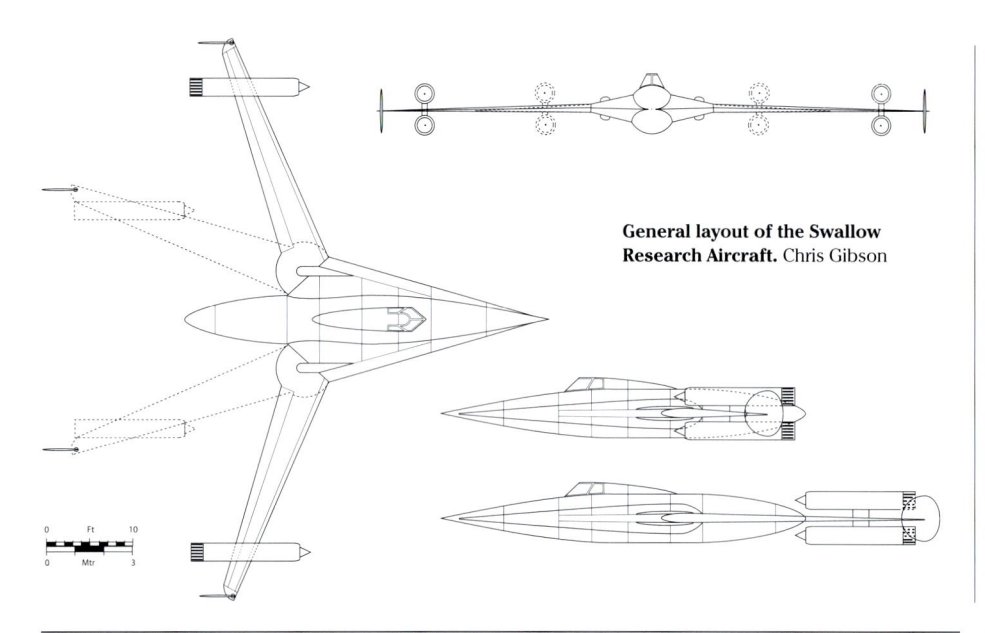

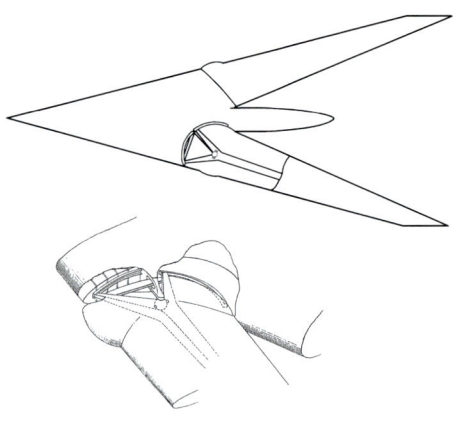

General layout of the Swallow Research Aircraft. Chris Gibson

This drawing from a 1964 UK Patent (GB950400) shows the internal system of rotary adjustment for the Swallow's wings. UK Patents Office

was completed, Wallis returned to designing massive ground-penetrating bombs such as the Tallboy (12,000 lb – 5.44 metric tons) and the even bigger Grand Slam (22,000 lb – 9.9 metric tons) which were used with considerable success against special targets such as rocket launching facilities, the German battleship *Tirpitz* and massively hardened U-Boat pens.

Towards the end of World War 2, Barnes Wallis began to take an interest in the possibility of supersonic flight and considered the idea of a tailless aircraft with movable wings. In 1946, he wrote a technical paper entitled 'The Application of the Aerodynamic Properties of Three Dimensional Bodies to the Stabilisation and Control of Aerodynes'. This was followed by work on the design of a flying model that would provide useful data on the use of laminar flow techniques. Starting with small hand-launched models, Wallis progressed to larger versions, propelled from a trolley on rails at 100mph (160kph). These models comprised slender, smooth ovoid bodies with aft mounted variable sweep wings and a highly swept tail fin.

Vickers had been awarded a half million pound contract for supersonic tests as part of the abandoned M.52 project and the money was now reallocated for Wallis' project that had been called Wild Goose. It would utilise models for wind tunnel and flight-testing. In addition to the wind tunnel models, 12 larger Wild Goose test vehicles were built and issued with serials XA197-202 and XA947-952. The models were slender with the wings mounted towards the rear and the vehicle was equipped with a single upright tailfin. There was also provision to fit a small rocket motor as the trials progressed.

In late 1949, flight tests began at Predannack Aerodrome near the Lizard in Cornwall and considerable secrecy surrounded the project which was regarded as pure military research. The Wild Goose models would be flown initially as gliders and controlled using rather basic radio equipment. This presented many challenges to Wallis' team as separate operators were required for pitch and roll. The models remained fairly stable in flight with the team graduating to powered tests using rocket propulsion. The National Physical Laboratory at Teddington, Middlesex, was also conducting wind tunnel tests on Wild Goose models and there was official interest in using this research to develop a new surface-to-air missile. The first really successful flight of a Wild Goose test vehicle took place in April 1952, although the model was written-off in crash soon afterwards. The Wild Goose trials continued until late 1954 when it was realised that laminar flow was unattainable.

However, much of this research was being supported by a classified weapons system called Green Lizard which would comprise a compact missile fired from a launch tube. Early designs began soon after the end of World War 2, with several patent applications being made in 1949 and held unpublished until 1956. The design was considered as a surface-to-surface and surface-to-air missile, eventually becoming a turbojet-powered AA missile that was equipped with flip-out swept wings. It would be based around the British Isles to protect against Soviet bombers and, when used, it would dispense 100 sub-munitions in the path of attacking bombers. Work on this project was abandoned in the early 1950s, but some design features can be seen on current air-launched weapons.

The proposed Vickers Swallow supersonic nuclear strike aircraft in RAF markings and anti-flash white finish. Bill Rose Collection

By 1951, Wallis was considering ideas for a manned variable geometry aircraft that would perform well across wide a range of different speeds and the next stage in his programme would be the construction of a small demonstrator. George Cornwall was the chief designer for Heston Aircraft and his company was heavily involved in the Wild Goose project as the main sub-contractor. Wallis had drawn up proposals for a small manned variable geometry aircraft and Cornwall was asked to finalise the design. A contract was then issued to Heston Aircraft leading to the construction of a prototype which received the designation JC.9.

The single-seat JC.9 was 46ft 6in (14.1m) in length with a maximum wingspan of 38ft (11.58m) and a height of 8ft 4in (2.5m). It was fitted with a retractable tricycle undercarriage and appears to have been intended for use as a glider with the possibility of installing a turbojet later. In appearance, the JC.9 was quite unusual having a bulbous rear fuselage which tapered towards the nose and a single swept, vertical tailfin. It was built in sections and transported to Weybridge for final assembly where it remained uncompleted in a hangar for some time until the JC.9 was finally scrapped. Exactly why this happened remains unknown, although there is some conjecture that Barnes Wallis was 'encouraged' to have this aircraft built despite his strong opposition to the manned tests of new prototypes. Could it be that he delayed the aircraft's construction until it was no longer required?

Before the Wild Goose trials ended in 1954, Wallis had started to work on the design of a high-performance variable-geometry tailless aircraft that might be developed to fly intercontinental distances. At the same time, the RAF was beginning to consider ideas for a future high flying supersonic reconnaissance bomber and OR.330 was issued. Vickers was not approached to submit a design for this aircraft, but Wallis obtained a copy of OR.330 and adapted his variable geometry concept to meet this need. He envisaged a sleek arrow shaped tailless aircraft with a flattened profile and variable geometry wings pivoted towards the rear of the fuselage, using a form of knuckle joint. Engines in pods would be mounted towards the wingtips which would swivel and also be adjustable in pitch. This would allow the propulsive system to take over from conventional control surfaces. Position of the engines was also important for minimising centre of gravity problems as the wing angle altered.

Small models of Wallis' new design called Swallow were initially tested in the Vickers Armstrong wind tunnel. Then trials began with 10 models, each having full wingspans of 30ft (9.1m) and wingtip fins and elevons. The models were built and issued with the serials XK831-835 and XK850-854, with tests beginning at Predannack Aerodrome in 1955 and continued until the late 1950s. On one occasion, a model powered by two rocket motors reached a speed of Mach 2.5, while fully developed models with dummy engine pods underwent supersonic tests in the wind tunnel at RAE Bedford. Although the Swallow was not chosen for OR.330, official interest in Wallis' project was considerable. Vickers continued to receive financial support for the Swallow trials and serious discussions about building two different manned research aircraft took place in 1957.

The initial proposal was for a small one-man demonstrator with an approximate weight of 10,000 lb (4,535kg), which gave way to a similar but larger aircraft with a gross weight of 25,000 lb (11,339kg). This aircraft would have a similar airframe to later production versions with a conventional forward cockpit that accommodated a pilot and could be adapted for a second crew member.

The Research Swallow had a proposed length of 68ft 9in (20.95m) with the wings fully swept, a wingspan of 75ft (22.86m) with the wings fully forward and a wingspan of 30ft 9in (9.37m) fully swept. One noticeable difference between the manned aircraft and earlier models was the extension of the fuselage rearwards to house additional equipment, fuel or, in later versions, a military payload. Height of the aircraft is unclear, although it is known that a substantial ground clearance was considered necessary for take-offs and landings. The undercarriage was to be a multi-wheel tricycle design with take-off speed calculated at 155mph (250kph) and landings made at 130mph (209kph). At low speed the Research Swallow would have an

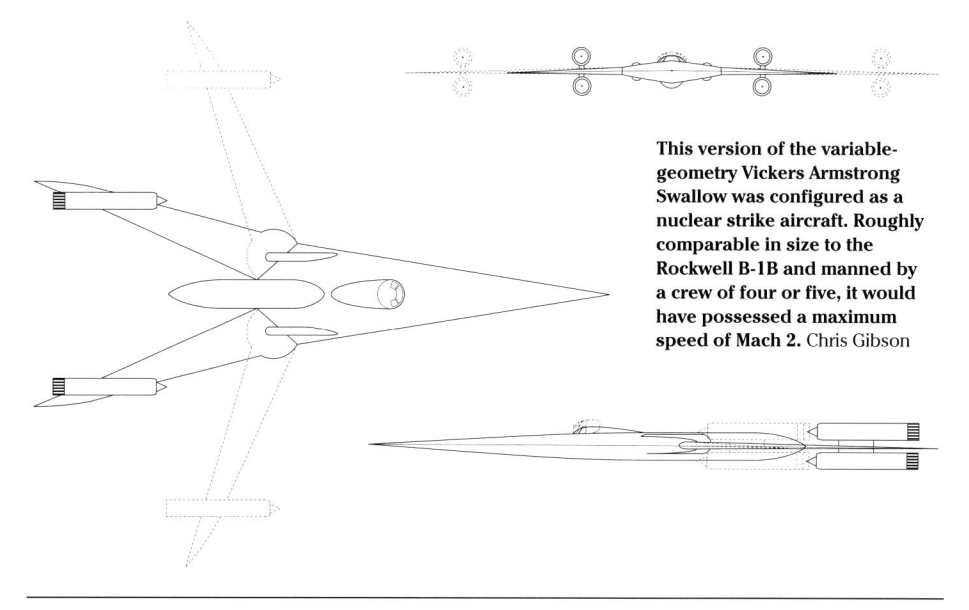

Heston JC.9

Crew	1
Wingspan	38ft (11.58m)
Length	46ft 6in (14.17m)
Height	8ft 4in (2.5m)
Powerplant	Unknown
Performance	Unknown

Vickers Research Swallow 1958

Crew	1 (possibly 2)
Wingspan	
(fully forward)	75ft (22.86m)
(fully swept)	30ft 9in (9.37m)
Aspect ratio	
(low speed)	10.7 (16.7 wing only)
(swept)	1.88
Length	68ft 9in (20.95m)
Height	Unknown
Empty weight	14,500 lb (6,577kg)
Gross weight	25,000 lb (11,339kg)
Fuel weight	9,000 lb (4,082kg).
Payload capacity	1,500 lb (680kg)
Powerplant	4 x Bristol afterburning turbojets
Engine pod dimensions	34in x 24ft (0.86m x 7.3m)
Maximum speed	Mach 1.6
Take-off speed	155mph (250kph)
Landing speed	130mph (209kph)
Cruise altitude	35-40,000ft (10,668-12,192m)
Ceiling	50,000ft (15,240m).
Range	Unknown
Armament	None

This version of the variable-geometry Vickers Armstrong Swallow was configured as a nuclear strike aircraft. Roughly comparable in size to the Rockwell B-1B and manned by a crew of four or five, it would have possessed a maximum speed of Mach 2. Chris Gibson

British Tailless Aircraft

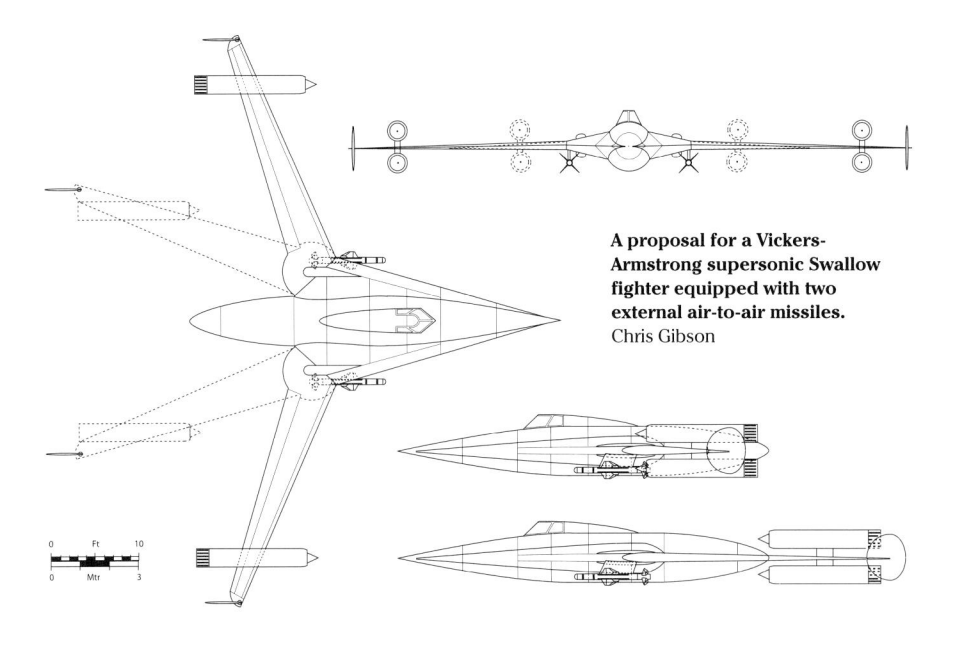

A proposal for a Vickers-Armstrong supersonic Swallow fighter equipped with two external air-to-air missiles. Chris Gibson

aspect ratio of 10.7 and this would alter to 1.88 fully swept. Wingtip stabilising fins were also proposed. Empty, the aircraft would weigh 14,500 lb (6,577kg) and the additional fuel weight would be 9,000 lb (4,082kg).

Four Bristol turbojet engines with afterburners would be housed in wing pods measuring 34in (863mm) in diameter and 24ft (7.3m) in length. Suggested maximum speed was Mach 1.6 with a cruise altitude of 35-40,000ft (10,668-12,192m) and a ceiling of about 50,000ft (15,240m). Developed into a military aircraft, the Swallow would have the same overall dimensions as the Research prototype. Two different variants were proposed for the RAF and the Royal Navy. The first was a high/low level bomber or naval strike aircraft and the second was a high performance fighter.

As a bomber, the Swallow would have a maximum performance of Mach 2 at a typical altitude of 36,000ft (10,972m). In the low level role, it would have a maximum speed of Mach 0.95 at an altitude of 500ft (152m). The service ceiling would be 80,000ft (24,382m). Gross weight was estimated at 30,000 lb (13,607kg) and a payload was probably a single rearward-ejected free-fall nuclear bomb in the Red Beard (15 kiloton yield) class. It is hard to see this aircraft being considered for the delivery of conventional ordnance. Range for the bomber is thought to have been about 5,000 miles (8,000km). This variant would be capable of operating from an improvised tactical airstrip such as a good stretch of straight adequately wide roadway, or the deck of an aircraft carrier, although it would require some structural strengthening and modifications for the latter. The most likely choice of propulsion for the Strike-Swallow was four afterburning Bristol Siddeley BE.38 turbojet engines. The BE.38 was a proposed high-performance variant of the Orpheus engine, but it was never completed.

The fighter version of the Swallow was similar in many respects, although the maximum speed quoted was Mach 2.5 and a realistic range might have been approximately 1,500 miles (2,414km), although some documentation suggests substantially more allowing for economic cruise. Armament is unknown, but it seems probable that two or four air-to-air missiles would be carried externally.

Several larger variable geometry versions of the Swallow were proposed that included a bomber with an overall length (at full 80° wing sweep) of approximately 130ft (39.6m) and a wingspan (with the wings fully extended) of about 130ft (39.6m), making it quite close in size to the Rockwell B-1B variable geometry bomber. This version of the Swallow would probably have carried a crew of 4-5 and posses a maximum speed of about Mach 2. The payload would have been a single nuclear weapon ejected rearward from the extended tail section.

As a supersonic military transport aircraft, Wallis proposed a version of the Swallow with an overall length (with full wing sweep) of 160ft (48.76m), a fully extended wingspan of 174ft (53m) and a fully swept wingspan of 71ft 6in (21.8m). It would have exactly the same aspect ratios as the smaller designs. The aircraft would utilise a multi-wheeled tricycle undercarriage layout with a substantial ground clearance of about 20ft (6m), considered necessary during take-off and landing. Its gross weight was set at 150,000 lb (68,038kg) with a maximum speed of Mach 2.5 and a cruise altitude of 67,000ft (20,421m). Operation range would be 4,600 miles (7,400km) and the payload capability would be 25,000 lb (11,339kg). Powered by four engines in wing-mounted nacelles, the size of each unit would suggest that Wallis was considering a choice of several different afterburning turbojets.

While this aircraft was envisaged for military use, Wallis also considered the idea of a slightly smaller commercial supercruise airliner, capable of carrying 60 passengers to Australia without any refuelling stops.

A further variant of the airliner would use eight turbojets mounted in individual wing pods. Various ideas were studied for cockpit layouts that included a rising capsule that would allow improved visibility at low speeds. Nevertheless, it was now recognised

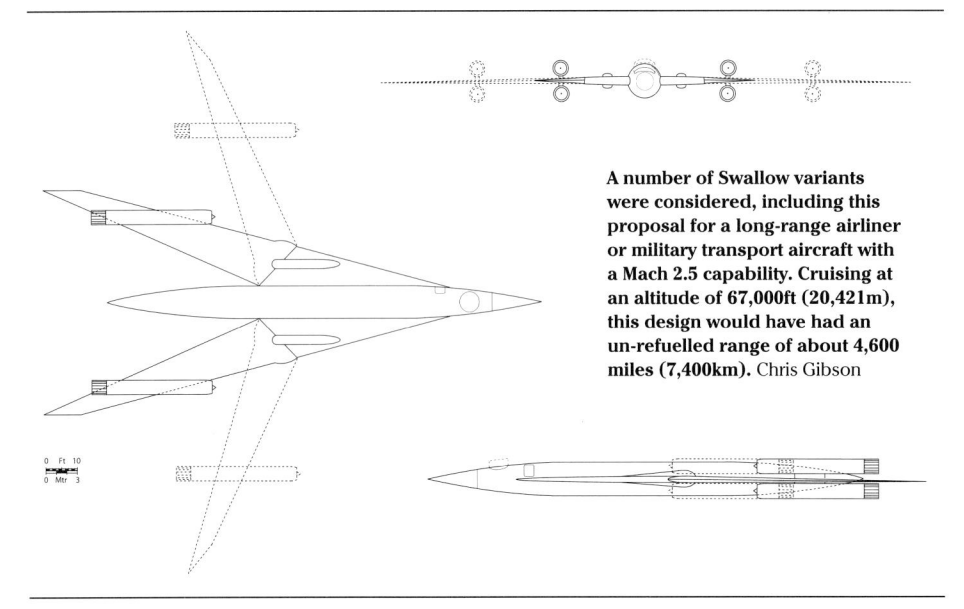

A number of Swallow variants were considered, including this proposal for a long-range airliner or military transport aircraft with a Mach 2.5 capability. Cruising at an altitude of 67,000ft (20,421m), this design would have had an un-refuelled range of about 4,600 miles (7,400km). Chris Gibson

Secret Projects: Flying Wings and Tailless Aircraft

Vickers High/Low Level Bomber/ Naval Strike Swallow

Crew	1-2
Wingspan	
(fully forward)	75ft (22.86m)
(fully swept)	30ft 9in (9.37m)
Aspect ratio	
(low speed)	10.7 (16.7 wing only)
(swept)	1.88
Overall length	68ft 9in (20.95m)
Height	Unknown
Empty weight	16,100 lb (7,302kg)
Gross weight	30,000 lb (13,607kg)
Fuel weight	12,250 lb (5,556kg)
Powerplant	4 x Bristol afterburning turbojets
Engine pod dimensions	34in x 24ft (0.86m x 7.3m)
Maximum speed	
(high Level)	Mach 2
(low Level)	Mach 0.95
Take-off speed	172mph (276kph)
Landing speed	130mph (209kph)
Cruise altitude	36,000ft (10,972m)
Ceiling	80,000ft (24,382m)
Range	Unknown
Payload capacity	1,500-2,000 lb (680-907kg)
Armament	Single tactical nuclear weapon

Vickers Swallow Fighter

Crew	1
Wingspan	
(fully forward)	75ft (22.86m)
(fully swept)	30ft 9in (9.37m)
Aspect ratio	
(low speed)	10.7 (16.7 wing only)
(swept)	1.88
Height	Unknown
Overall length	68ft 9in (20.95m)
Empty weight	15,250 lb (6,917kg)
Gross weight	30,000 lb (13,607kg)
Fuel weight	13,220 lb (5,996kg)
Payload capacity	1,530 lb (680kg)
Powerplant	4 x Bristol afterburning Orpheus turbojets
Maximum speed	Mach 2.5
Take-off speed	172mph (276kph)
Landing speed	130mph (209kph)
Cruise altitude	40,000ft (12,192m)
Ceiling	80,000ft (24.384m)
Improvised tactical airstrip	
take-off distance	3,000ft (914m) loaded
Range	1,500 miles (2,414km) estimated
Armament	AAMs

Vickers Military Transport Swallow/ Long Range Bomber

Crew	4-5?
Wingspan	
(open)	174ft (53m)
(folded)	71ft 6in (21.79m)
Aspect ratio	
(low speed)	10.7 (16.7 wing only)
(swept)	1.88
Overall length (swept)	160ft (48.76m)
Height	Unknown
Gross weight	150,000 lb (68,038kg)
Landing weight	95,750 lb (43,431kg)
Fuel weight	58,750 lb (26,648kg)
Powerplant	4 x afterburning turbojets, each producing 12,850 lb (57kN) static thrust
Engine pod dimensions	40in x 30ft (1m x 9m)
Payload capacity	25,000 lb (11,339kg)
Maximum speed	Mach 2.5
Take-off speed	164mph (263kph)
Landing speed	131mph (210kph)
Cruise altitude	67,000ft (20,421m)
Range	4,600 miles (7,400km)
Armament	One, possibly two free fall nuclear weapons

that development of the Swallow would take at least 10 years to complete. Unfortunately, 1957 was the year of the infamous Duncan Sandys' White Paper that suggested that the era of manned military aircraft was drawing to a close. As a direct consequence, many advanced programmes were terminated. Further official funding for the Swallow was cut and Wallis was allowed to approach the American Mutual Weapons Development Programme (MWDP) Office in Paris for help. This led to a US team visiting Weybridge and a small delegation led by Wallis visiting NASA at Langley.

All the Swallow research data was then passed to the US and although a six-month joint US-UK development programme was discussed with MWDP staff, much of the research was undertaken at Langley.

By June 1959, NASA was reporting lift/drag ratio and pitch-up problems with the Swallow design and it was angling to use the variable geometry design for an entirely different tailed design. Wallis' concept was effectively dead, although a good deal of the research undertaken during the Swallow programme would find its way into the future F-111 swing-wing bomber. The Swallow was a superb looking proposal and still seems futuristic today. It is interesting to speculate on whether this very complex design could have been developed into an operational military aircraft had sufficient funding been available.

HP.117 Flying Wing Studies

The flying wing project described in this section was another attempt to exploit boundary layer reduction which is theoretically well suited to this type of aircraft. The designers hoped to develop an advanced transport aircraft that was primarily aimed at the commercial sector with secondary military aircraft.

Boundary Layer Theory (BLT) can be traced back to the beginning of the 20th century and it is generally attributed to the German scientist Ludwig Prandtl. Many sources also acknowledge concurrent research undertaken in England by Frederick William Lanchester and it is quite common to find references to Lanchester-Prandtl Theory. However, it was some years before anyone was in a position to experiment with boundary layer control (BLC) and the first practical tests were undertaken in 1936 by the Swiss aerodynamicist Dr Werner Pfenninger, working at the Institute for Aerodynamics in Zurich.

In 1939, NACA Langley conducted some elementary BLC experiments using suction slots, but the programme ended after the US joined the war, with the focus of attention switching to the perfection of laminar flow aerofoils. At about the same time, Miles Aircraft in Britain carried out similar trials and scientists in Germany experimented with BLC, using a modified Me 109. Aerodynamicists recognised that an aircraft flying at subsonic speed wasted about half the fuel required to maintain level flight through drag at the boundary layer. But an effective and reliable system of control remained elusive. In the post-war years, the US Navy tested various boundary layer control methods with a modified Cessna 170 and a Grumman Panther jet fighter, while the USAF sponsored tests conducted at Edwards AFB, using an adapted F-84 fighter.

The RAE at Farnborough was using the AW.52 flying wing for BLC trials, although results proved disappointing and the project was abandoned in 1953. Nevertheless, some research continued at Handley Page's Radlett facility under the direction of the company's chief aerodynamicist Dr Gustav Lachmann and his deputy Godfrey H. Lee. Mainly funded by the Ministry of Supply, this took the form of wind tunnel testing and airborne trials using the prototype DH.113 Vampire fighter.

Certain aspects of this research had military implications and were classified, but many details found their way into the public domain with Dr Lachmann outlining his project to the Royal Aeronautical Society on 11 November 1954. By 1956, Lachmann was hoping to utilise BLC methods with a fairly conventional aircraft design, which initially looked like a de Havilland Comet and steadily evolved into an airliner resembling the Boeing 707.

Lachmann and Lee then concluded that an entirely new kind of aircraft was required for

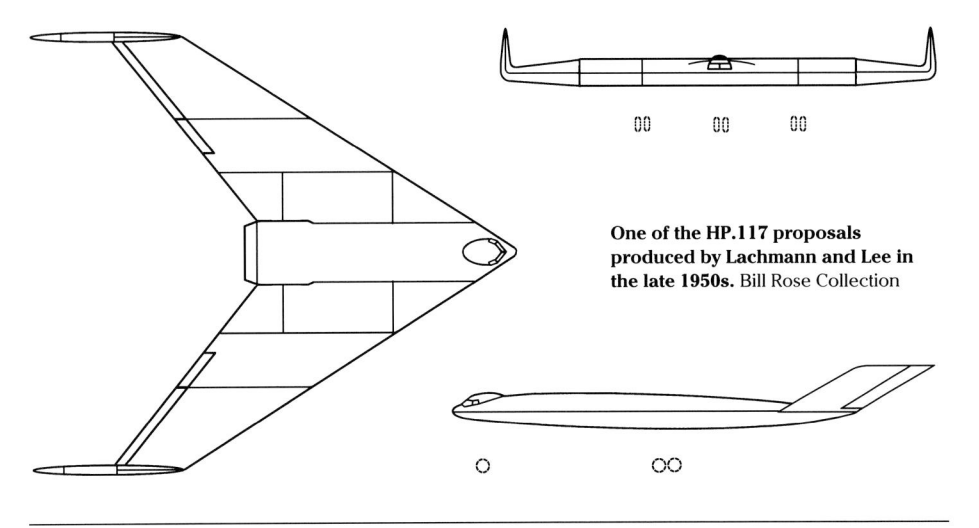

One of the HP.117 proposals produced by Lachmann and Lee in the late 1950s. Bill Rose Collection

this project and a flying wing was the optimal shape for a long-range transport aircraft making full use of boundary layer reduction methods. By 1958, both the RAE and NACA had generally lost interest in BLC, although work continued at Northrop under the direction of Dr Werner Pfenninger who had been recruited by Jack Northrop in the late 1940s.

This ongoing research was enough to keep the Handley Page programme alive, especially with Northrop preparing to construct three X-21A research aircraft which had started life as Douglas WB-66Ds. Subsequently, Lachmann managed to maintain

HP.117

Crew	4-6 (plus 200 passengers)
Wingspan	125ft (38m)
Sweep	44° at mid chord
Wing area	5,820ft² (540m²)
Length	101ft (30.78m)
Height	42ft (12.8m)
Cruise speed	527mph (848kph)
Ceiling	55,000ft (16,764m)
Range	5,000 miles (8,046km)
Gross weight	330,000lb (149,685kg) later revised to 305,000lb (138,345kg)
Powerplant	3 or 4 Rolls-Royce RB.163 turbofans

HP.119

Crew	2
Wingspan	44ft 8in (13.6m)
Sweep	50°
Gross weight	30,000lb (13,607kg)
Powerplant	3 Bristol Siddeley Viper BSV.20 turbojets, each rated at 3,000lb (13.3kN) static thrust. Two engines for propulsion, the third to draw off air from the boundary layer.
Range	6,700 miles (10,000km) at 527mph (848kph) at 40,000ft (12,192m)

official support for his research, which would result in the development and testing of a highly modified Folland Midge wing with a 45° sweep. This was mounted in an upright position on the dorsal section of an Avro Lancaster (PA474) which belonged to the College of Aeronautics at Cranfield. The first test was considerably delayed and did not take place until 2 October 1962.

The new aircraft proposed by Lachmann and Lee was assigned the company reference HP.117 and the first rather loose set of designs was completed by April 1959. Their concept took the form of a swept flying wing with wingtip stabilising fins, although various options were reviewed for different performance and payload requirements. Three to six turbofan engines would power the HP.117 and a pusher turboprop arrangement was considered at one stage, but found unsatisfactory. The HP.117 would accommodate 200 to 300 passengers and it was finally decided that the ideal wingspan was 125ft (38m) with a sweep of 44° at mid-chord.

A scale model of HP.117 was exhibited at Le Bourget in 1961 with claims to the media that this design could reduce transatlantic fares by as much as 30 per cent and make long distance travel a reality for many ordinary people. Progress with the project remained sluggish and although Lachmann met with representatives of the Ministry of Aviation during 1961, he failed to secure any financial support for the construction of prototypes once the wing trials at Cranfield had been completed.

Lachmann wanted to start with the conversion of a Victor bomber for use as a test bed and if this aircraft performed well with the boundary layer reduction system installed, it would be followed by the construction of two scale size demonstrators based on the HP.117, which would be designated HP.119. Although the response from the ministry was less than encouraging, Lachmann and Lee continued to evolve their design for the HP.117 as a 300-seat airliner. It would now have a wingspan of 148ft (45m) and be powered by four or six Rolls-Royce turbofans with the gross weight reaching 330,000lb (149,685kg) and an estimated range of 5,000 miles (8,000km).

Although there was a reluctance to continue spending government money on this Handley Page programme, the Ministry of Aviation agreed in 1963 to follow the research taking place at Cranfield with trials of a test wing fitted to a Hawker Siddeley HS.125 transport jet. Continuing development of the HP.117 led to a somewhat different design for a very substantial military transport designated HP.135, which was displayed in model form, but failed to attract the kind of interest required for further development. In 1965, Lachmann retired and one year later was sadly dead. So was the HP.117 project. Work on boundary layer control was now at a standstill in Britain and the X-21A trials concluded in the US at about the same time. Northrop showed that boundary layer reduction could be made to work, but many of the previously identified problems remained unresolved. In the 1980s, there was a revival of US interest with trials involving an F-111 and F-14 flown from Dryden, later followed by supersonic experiments with the F-16XL. However, at the present time, an application of this technology remains elusive.

Davidson's Aerobus

1952 saw the beginning of a project at Britain's National Gas Turbine Establishment (NGTE) to utilise a system of directing a jet flow through a wing's trailing edge to improve low-speed performance. The idea was not entirely new and the German aerodynamicists H. Hagedorn and P. Ruden had noted interesting trailing edge effects during boundary layer control research in 1938.

After examining the data from these wind tunnel tests, scientists at NGTE undertook some very elementary experiments with small desktop-sized models. This indicated that increased lift and thrust might be achieved by ducting a certain amount of jet engine exhaust to the wing's trailing edge. A thin jet sheet produced behind an aircraft could be used in much the same manner as a hinged wing flap, leading to the term 'jet flap'. There were various ways the jet flow might be directed that included long slots, nozzles and flaps positioned in the jet flow.

Heading the NGTE jet flap project was Ivor Davidson who soon began to consider practical uses for this technology, although he recognised that a wing capable of vectoring a jet flow along most of its trailing edge would present various engineering problems. There was also the matter of how to maintain control in the event of an engine failure. At cruising speed, an aircraft using jet flaps would behave like a conventional fixed wing design, but at lower speeds the jet flow would be directed downwards, generating considerable lift and providing outstanding STOL performance.

The research programme continued with Ivor Davidson presenting an outline of jet flap development to the Royal Aeronautical Society in October 1955. But it was now becoming clear that this technology would be difficult to use with the majority of existing fixed wing designs and he realised that a new type of aircraft was needed.

By the end of the 1950s, Davidson had outlined a compact transport aircraft called Aerobus that would take advantage of laminar flow aerodynamics and use the jet flap system. This all-wing design would have a wingspan of 50ft (15.24m), a wing area of 1,240ft² (115m²) and a length of 57ft (17.37m). The aircraft would be supported on the ground by a retractable tricycle undercarriage and the gross weight (as an airliner) was estimated at 64,000 lb (29,030kg) with the anticipated payload being 100 passengers and their luggage. Propulsion would be provided by a total of four turbojets in wingtip nacelles connected to 16 trailing edge outlets via ducting. This short-haul aircraft would cruise at approximately 444mph (716kph) with an operating altitude of 20,000ft (6,096m). The Aerobus project continued into the early 1960s with the operating cost initially estimated at 1.2 pence (old) per passenger mile.

Despite limited commercial and military interest in Aerobus, the State-funded NGTE continued to develop jet flap technology, having already requested the construction of a proof-of-concept aircraft during the late 1950s.

This received Ministry of Aviation approval and Hunting Aircraft of Luton, Bedfordshire, was issued with a contract in June 1959 to build two small demonstrators. The first prototype known as H.126 (serial XN714) undertook its maiden flight at RAE Bedford on 26 March 1963 with Hunting's Chief Test Pilot Stanley Oliver at the controls. By this time, the second prototype was considered unnecessary and had been cancelled.

The jet flap system used on the H.126 consisted of 16 nozzles located along the wing's trailing edge, releasing approximately half of the jet engine's exhaust gas. A small amount of gas was also ducted to the wingtips for low speed control and the remainder was exhausted on each side of the lower fuselage.

The H.126 was a compact, single-seat aircraft, built around its turbojet engine. The cockpit was located in a forward position, offering good visibility and the tricycle undercarriage was of a simple, fixed position design. Trials were mainly undertaken at RAE Bedford between 1963 and 1967 with no serious problems occurring and the aircraft was then loaned to NASA who conducted wind tunnel tests at the Ames Flight Research Center during 1969. H.126 was returned the following year and is now on display at the RAF Cosford Museum.

The jet flap experiments showed that the idea could be made to work, but it also became apparent that the nozzle system was too complex to be practical and the power requirements were much greater than originally anticipated.

A related, although much simpler system using air ducted from the compressor stage, was utilised by several 1960s combat aircraft to improve low speed performance. This 'blown flap' can be found on several current military transport aircraft.

Hunting Aircraft H.126

Crew	1
Wingspan	45ft 4in (13.8m)
Wing area	221ft² (20.58m²)
Length	50ft 2in (15.2m)
Height	15ft 6in (4.72m)
Gross weight	10,740 lb (4,871kg)
Powerplant	1 x Bristol-Siddeley Orpheus BOr.3 Mk.805 turbojet, producing 4,000 lb (17.79kN) static thrust
Maximum speed	Unknown, although the H.126 was designed to explore low speed and could fly at 32mph (51.5kph)
Ceiling	Unknown

Aerobus (1962 proposal)

Crew	3 flight 2 cabin
Wingspan	50ft (15.24m)
Wing area	1,240ft² (115m²)
Length	57ft (17.37m)
Height	15ft (4.57m)
Gross weight	64,000 lb (29,030kg)
Cruise speed	444mph (716kph)
Powerplant	4 x turbofan engines
Payload	100 passengers (as an airliner)

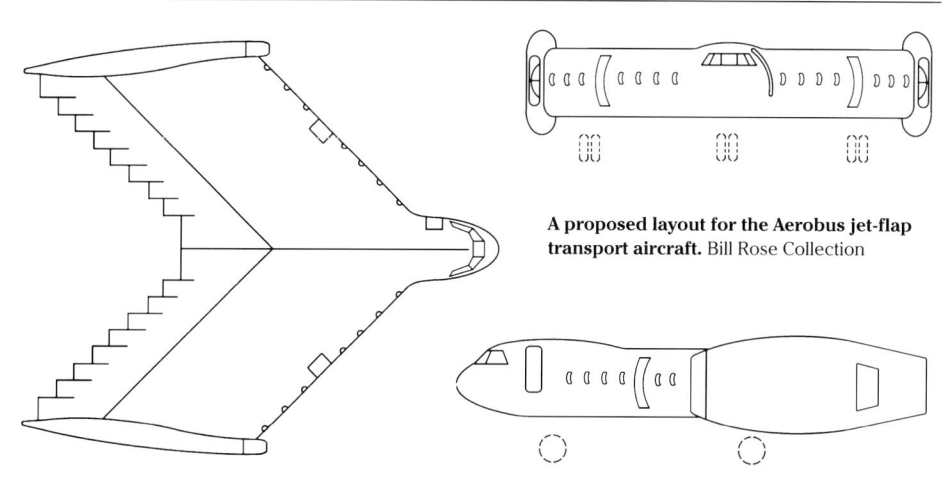

A proposed layout for the Aerobus jet-flap transport aircraft. Bill Rose Collection

The Hunting H.126 prototype. BAE Systems

British Tailless Aircraft

Chapter Two

German World War 2 Flying Wing Development

German interest in flying wings and tailless aircraft pre-dates powered flight, although the most important early designer to set out specific rules for this type of aircraft was Hugo Junkers (1859-1935) who had spent the first half of his life working as a very successful heating appliance design engineer. During his spare time, Junkers developed advanced aircraft concepts and in February 1910, he filed a Patent (253788) for a powered flying wing aircraft that represented a significant advance in aviation design. Known as a Nurflugel (wing only) aircraft, Junkers recognised the advantages of housing crew, engines and payload within the wing. Once the design had been registered, Junkers established an aircraft design bureau at his water heater factory in Dessau and this led to small-scale manufacturing.

Although the Nurflugel was too far ahead of its time to be built, Junkers began to produce technical innovations that found their way into conventional aircraft, such as all-metal construction. World War 1 gave the company a significant boost with Junkers building hundreds of warplanes in association with Fokker and becoming established as a major manufacturer. In 1924, Junkers produced plans for a giant airliner capable of carrying 100 passengers over long distances, but it was too advanced for practical development. But some elements of this concept were used in the Junkers G.38 transport aircraft which flew in 1929 and became the world's largest land based aircraft. At the beginning of the 1930s, Reimar Horten (1915-1994) and his older brother Walter (1903-1998) started work on their first tailless glider called the Ho1. Apparently, this project received their parents' full support and some of the construction took place in their dining room.

The Ho1 was followed by the Ho2 in 1934 and during the following year was upgraded by the addition of an 80hp (59kW) Hirth HM60R engine connected to a rear mounted pusher propeller with a drive shaft. This aircraft was flown by the well-known test pilot Hanna Reitsch (1912-1979) on 17 November 1938, who was quite critical of the design. Nevertheless, her involvement with the project was sufficient to encourage the construction of a larger design called the Ho3 and it would eventually secure official government interest that would lead to the most sophisticated experimental aircraft produced during World War 2.

Another early aviation pioneer was Alexander Martin Lippisch (1894-1976) who witnessed a demonstration flight by Orville Wright at Berlin in September 1909. This experience made a lasting impression on the 14-year-old Lippisch and, having served in the Luftstreitkräfte (Imperial German Army Air Service) during World War 1 (as an aerial photographer), he then secured a job with Zeppelin and later Dornier as an aeronautical designer. During his spare time, Lippisch produced plans for gliders and the well-known glider pilot Gottlob Espenlaub built a full-sized aircraft from one of his designs in 1921. This would be followed by dozens of different tailless designs and by 1925, Alexander Lippisch had become Director of the Technical Department at the Rhön-Rossitten Gesellschaft (RRG), which later became the German Research Institute for Soaring Flight (Deutsche Forschungsanstalt fur Segelflug – DFS).

Lippisch now began work on his first powered aircraft called 'Storch' (Stork) and undertook development of the delta wing. He is credited with coining the term 'delta' for this type of aircraft, having taken it from the three-sided Greek letter and not surprisingly,

A classic Horten design, the Ho 111e Motorglider was powered by a Volkswagen engine and was flown during 1944. Peter Nash Collection

Dr Alexander Lippisch, one of the most influential aircraft designers of the 20th century, photographed after World War 2. Bill Rose Collection

Secret Projects: Flying Wings and Tailless Aircraft

his first full-sized delta wing design was called Delta 1. A series of aircraft developed from the Storch and Delta followed, with Lippisch eventually vacating his position with the DFS to join Messerschmitt in 1939 where he worked on a rocket powered tailless aircraft.

As World War 2 progressed, German aircraft designers became increasingly convinced that jet and rocket powered tailless designs represented the next generation of high-performance warplanes. Most of the major aircraft manufacturers produced tailless proposals, with many being tested as wind tunnel models. Only a few reached the early stages of construction. Had the war taken a different course and lasted longer, it is a certainty that some of these impressive designs would have entered operational service. Indeed, once hostilities ceased, the Allies wasted no time securing German aircraft research documentation and equipment while making every effort to track down those scientists and engineers who had worked on the most advanced projects.

Arado Flying Wing Projects

Towards the end of 1943, the design office of Arado Flugzeugwerke GmbH at Landeshut in Silesia (now Kamienna Góra in Poland) began work on a highly advanced flying wing jet-powered bomber, intended to meet future requirements of the Reichsluftfahrtsministerium (RLM – German Air Ministry). The objective was to develop an aircraft capable of delivering a payload of at least 8,818 lb (4,000kg) over a range of at least 3,100 miles (5,000km). Although the request for a new long-range bomber had yet to be officially issued, Arado was already at the forefront of jet bomber development and had received advanced warning of what was likely to be required in the coming months. They now hoped to utilise a flying wing design with a laminar high-speed profile to provide the expected level of performance.

Under the leadership of Arado's Dr W. Laute, 15 different concepts were developed from research undertaken by Dipl. Ing. Kosin and Lehmann who had produced a study called 'Flying Wing Aircraft for Long-Ranges and High Speeds'. Laute's new study was designated E.555 (the E prefix signifies Entwurf – Draft Project) and the variations became E.555-1 to E.555-15. In most cases, the main difference between each design was the number of engines, their locations and minor variations in wingspan or length, but the possibility of extending the fuselage rearwards or utilising tail booms was also considered. All available jet engines were reviewed during the study and included the BMW109 003, Junkers Jumo 004 and Heinkel Hirth He S 011, which would be housed in external nacelles.

The initial studies were completed in early 1944 and a meeting between Arado representatives and the RLM took place on 20 April 1944. Details of the new flying wing bomber were then informally finalised. Within a matter of weeks, a decision had been taken to proceed with further refinement of the Arado E.555-1, which was intended for use against targets on America's Eastern Seaboard and deep within Russia.

Built almost entirely from steel and duralumin, E.555-1 would be powered by six BMW 003A turbojets, each providing a maximum static thrust of 1,760 lb (7.8kN). The aircraft would have a wingspan of 69ft 6½in (21.2m) with a wing area of 1,345.5ft² (125m²). The overall length was approximately 60ft (18m) and the height was calculated at 16ft 4in (5m). Two substantial vertical stabilising fins with rudders would be fitted and the anticipated gross take-off weight was 52,911 lb (24,000kg) with a payload of 8,818 lb (4,000kg) payload. Maximum speed at altitude was expected to be 534mph (860kph) with an economic cruise speed of 444mph (714kph) and a ceiling of almost 50,000ft (15,240m). A crew of three would be accommodated in a fully pressurised cockpit and the aircraft would be supported on the ground by a tricycle undercarriage. It was also suggested that a 'jettisonable' take-off trolley might be used (possibly with rocket assistance) to improve range when carrying a full payload and E.555-1 could be equipped with extra internal fuel tanks. Defensive armament would comprise two fixed forward-firing 30mm Mk103 cannons, plus a remotely-controlled tail turret with two 20mm MG151/20 cannon and a remotely controlled dorsal turret also fitted with two 20mm MG151/20 cannons. The turrets would be controlled from a pressurised cabin behind the main crew compartment with the operator using a periscope system.

The operational range of this aircraft remained a major issue and attacking distant targets meant that there would be little or no loiter time available in the bombing area, so

Arado Ar E.555-1

Crew	3
Wingspan	69ft 6½in (21.2m)
Length	60ft (18m)
Height	16ft 4in (5m)
Wing area	1,345.5ft² (125m²)
Maximum speed	534mph (860km/h)
Ceiling	50,000ft (15,240m)
Maximum range*	2,982 miles+ (4,800km+)
Take-off weight	52,911 lb (24,000kg)
Powerplant	Six BMW003A turbojets, each providing a maximum static thrust of 1,760 lb (7.8kN)
Armament	Two fixed forward mounted Mk103 30mm cannons, two MG151/20 20mm in tail turret and two MG151/20 20mm cannons in dorsal turret
Bomb load	8,818 lb (4,000kg)

* With supplementary fuel tanks and full bomb load

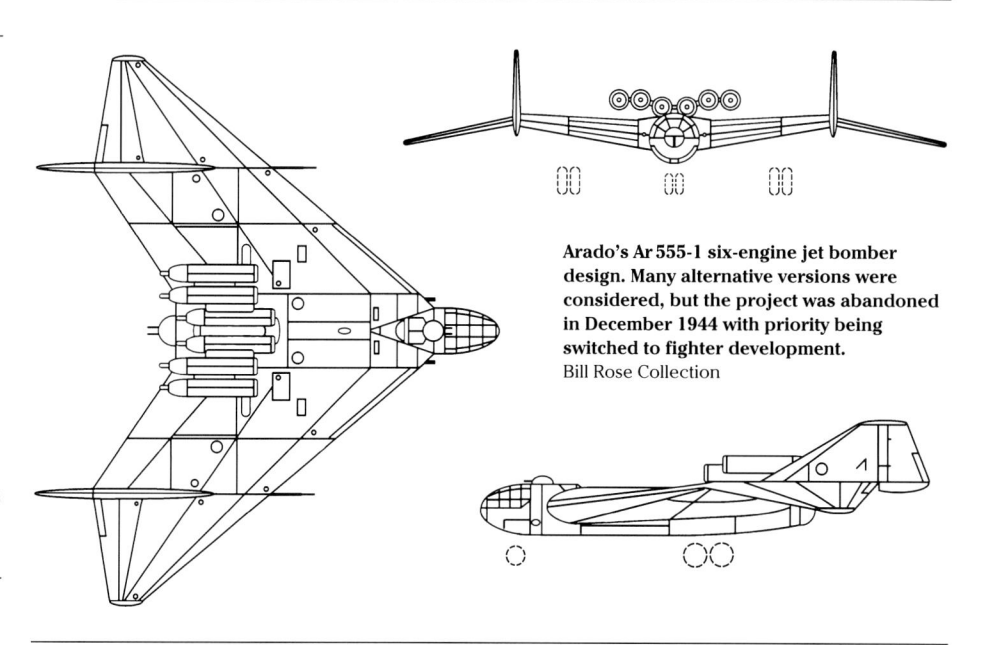

Arado's Ar 555-1 six-engine jet bomber design. Many alternative versions were considered, but the project was abandoned in December 1944 with priority being switched to fighter development.
Bill Rose Collection

German World War 2 Flying Wing Development

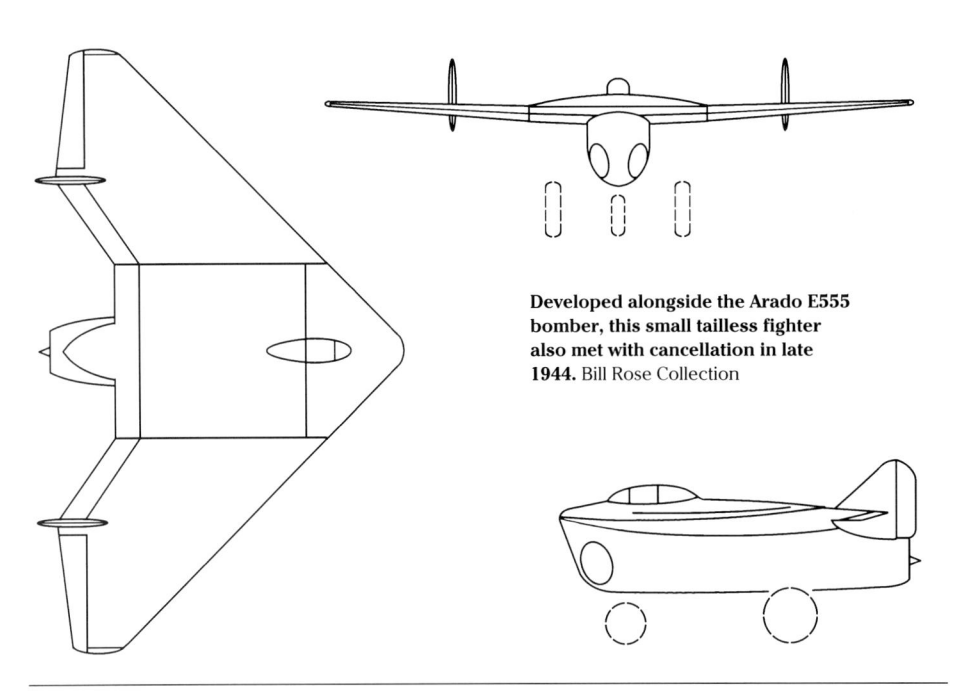

Developed alongside the Arado E555 bomber, this small tailless fighter also met with cancellation in late 1944. Bill Rose Collection

methods of improving the aircraft's performance remained under study. Dr Laute hoped that the performance of jet engines would continue to improve and progressively reduce this shortcoming. It is believed that models were wind tunnel tested and although E.555-1 was a very advanced concept with considerable promise, it was also showing signs of becoming a very expensive project that would become a drain on essential war resources. As a consequence, the Entwicklungs-HauptKomission (EHK) ordered the project's immediate cancellation on 28 December 1944.

Arado's Flying Wing Fighter

Running alongside the Arado E.555 project was a study for a high-speed single seat fighter that would utilise some of the same aerodynamic properties. The name of this project was Arado E.581 and there are known to have been at least five separate proposals. Details of E.581-1 to E.581-3 remain obscure, although they are thought to have been extremely compact configurations. The slightly larger Arado E.581-4 and very similar E.581-5 were built around a single Heinkel HeS 011 turbojet housed in the fuselage below the wing with the air intake below the nose.

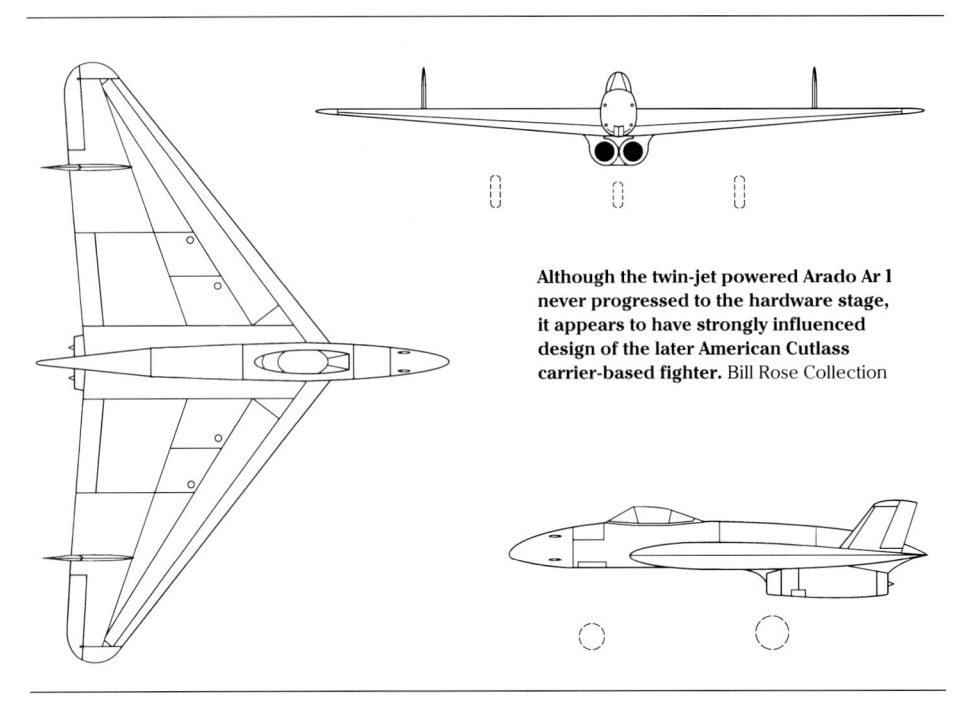

The design was virtually a delta shape in appearance, using two vertical stabilisers with rudders and it would have been equipped with a retractable tricycle undercarriage. The E.581-4/5 was fairly ugly when seen side on with the fuselage looking rather like a bathtub. However, there is no reason to suspect that it wouldn't have performed reasonably well and the estimated maximum speed was 530mph (854kph). Endurance would have been fairly limited and its primary role would have been as an interceptor. Nevertheless, this project did not progress very far and was scrapped at the same time as the E.555-1.

Arado Ar 1

Although the E.555 and E.581 both met with cancellation at the end of 1944, the aerodynamic research had already been made available to the company's design group headed by Professor Walter Blume (1896-1964) who was working on ideas for an all-weather/night interceptor and a ground attack light bomber. His team produced two distinctly different concepts for this project. The first was an advanced tailless jet-powered design designated Ar 1 and the second was a conventional tailed alternative with an engine beneath each wing known as Ar 2. This second proposal utilised experience gained from development of the Arado Ar 234 Blitz jet bomber and was probably regarded as something of a fallback option. The normal 'E' code does not appear to have been assigned to this study.

The tailless Ar 1 combat aircraft utilised what was effectively a delta wing with a 35° sweep and two vertical stabilisers with rudders. The fuselage extended ahead of the wing to allow the carriage of weapons and a forward installed centimetric radar system. There would also be a pressurised cockpit able to accommodate two crew members. Power for the Ar 1 would be provided by two Heinkel He S 011 turbojets or two BMW003A turbojets located on the underside of the wing. The aircraft would be supported on the ground with a tricycle undercarriage. At a review of the Ar 1 project in March 1945, concerns were expressed about problems of drag induced by the wing's surface area and the engine installation.

A decision was then taken to make immediate corrections to the design, most noticeably by an alteration to the profile of the wing's trailing edge. This revised version of the Ar 1 also included changes to the fuselage and a rearrangement of the cockpit layout to allow the carriage of a third crew member. It is hard to know if the project progressed very far beyond these proposals as the war in

Although the twin-jet powered Arado Ar 1 never progressed to the hardware stage, it appears to have strongly influenced design of the later American Cutlass carrier-based fighter. Bill Rose Collection

Arado E.581-4

Crew	1
Wingspan	29ft 2½in (8.95m)
Sweep	45° (leading edge)
Wing area	263ft² (24.5m²)
Length	18ft 6in (5.65m)
Height	8ft 6in (2.6m)
Gross weight	8,231 lb (3,734kg)
Empty weight	5,410 lb (2,454kg)
Maximum speed	530mph (854kph)
Engine	1x Heinkel He S 011A turbojet rated at 2,865 lb (12.75kN) static thrust
Armament	2 x 30mm Mk108 cannon

Arado Ar 1 (E.583)

Crew	2 or 3
Wingspan	60ft 4in 18.40m
Wing area	807ft² (75.0m²)
Sweep	35° (leading edge)
Aspect ratio	4.5 : 1
Length	42ft 6in 12.95m
Height	12ft 6in (3.80m)
Empty weight	20,502 lb (9,300kg)
Gross weight	34,612 lb (15,700kg)
Powerplant	2 x Heinkel He S 011A turbojets, each rated at 2,865 lb (12.75kN) static thrust, or 2 x BMW003A turbojets, each rated at 1,760 lb (7.8kN) static thrust
Maximum speed	503mph (810kph)
Endurance	2h 36m at economic cruise
Ceiling	42,000ft (12,800m)
Armament	2 or 4 x 30mm Mk213 cannon, forward firing; 2 x 30mm Mk213 cannon, rearward firing; 2 x 30mm Mk213 cannon firing upwards from the centre of the aircraft In the ground attack role: 2 x 1,102 lb (500kg) bombs

Note: Some figures for the Arado designs detailed on these pages are the best available estimates and should not be regarded as definitive.

Europe was almost over. The Ar 1 may have been tested as a wind tunnel model, but never got much further than the early design phase.

Details of the Ar 1 and other Arado flying wing projects were secured by US Intelligence and the documentation appears to have been passed to the US aircraft company Vought, which used them to develop the F7U-1 Cutlass jet fighter.

Blohm und Voss Flying Wing Projects

The Blohm und Voss Shipbuilding Company was established in 1877 at Hamburg, Germany, and it produced many famous vessels including the battleship *Bismarck*. In 1933, the company turned its attention to aircraft, becoming well known as a constructor of flying boats. Accompanying this move into the realm of aviation was the recruitment of Dr Richard Vogt (1894-1979) who was appointed as the company's chief designer and is now remembered for some of his highly unorthodox concepts that reached the prototype stage in a few instances.

In late 1943, Vogt began work on a series of ideas for a new lightweight interceptor, initially using a rear-mounted Argus, Junkers or Daimler Benz piston engine driving a pusher propeller. As the study evolved, Vogt developed this design into a turbojet-powered interceptor to meet the Luftwaffe's future needs. Despite heading the design office, Vogt undertook much of the work himself, with assistance from Hans Amtmann and the company's aerodynamicists, George Haag and Richard Schubert. The initial proposals began to emerge in autumn 1944 with the reference P.208, which was generally known within the company as the 'Arrow Wing'.

As a starting point, Vogt had taken some features from his earlier P.207 design for a straight-winged fighter with a rear-mounted three-blade propeller. Keeping most of the fuselage section, he then dispensed with the straight wing and tail control surfaces, fitting a new 30° swept wing with a constant cross section and tip-mounted down-turned control fins. There were several objectives for this design and Vogt saw potential for improving maximum speed by minimising surface area and reducing weight. The simple all-metal construction would also help to bring down the cost of manufacturing the aircraft.

The P.208 project had started out with the intention of evolving quite quickly towards turbojet propulsion, but there were endless delays with the jet engines, so priority was given to refining the aerodynamics. The first three studies for the P.208 only differed in engine installation, utilising the Jumo 222E, Argus AS413 or Daimler Benz DB603L. The P.208-3 was then selected, which used the liquid-cooled Daimler Benz 12-cylinder DB603L engine, equipped with a two-stage supercharger and methanol-water injection. This prototype engine was expected to provide a maximum (sea level) power output of 2,761hp (2,059kW) at 3,000rpm. The engine's air intake and radiator was positioned on the underside of the fuselage, directly below the cockpit.

While wind tunnel models of the P.208 were being tested, a twin-boom, single seat Skoda-Kauba SK V-6 (itself a prototype aircraft designed by Austrian engineer Otto Kauba) was requisitioned and extensively modified to validate the Arrow Wing concept. The pusher propeller design made the SK V-6 particularly suitable for these experiments and the extensively modified aircraft, now minus its original tail unit, was redesignated as the SK SL6. Very little information is available for this test programme, which may have been undertaken at Prague. On 30 April 1945, almost all documentation relating to Skoda-Kauba Flugzeugbau projects was burnt and Otto Kauba made a swift exit from the city. It is not thought that any of the Skoda-Kauba prototypes survived the war.

However, it is understood that test flights had started in late 1944 and may have continued into early 1945, demonstrating the viability of the unusual Blohm und Voss concept. Vogt now began working on the P.209, a more sophisticated Arrow Wing fighter design with a fuselage built around a Heinkel He S 011 turbojet engine drawing air from a forward nose intake. The aircraft would be equipped with a tricycle undercarriage and armed with two 30mm Mk108 cannon in the lower forward fuselage. Using a similar design of wing and control surfaces, the P.209 was slightly more compact than the P.208 with a wingspan of 35ft (10.66m) and an increased sweep of 35°. Maximum speed was estimated at 559mph (900km).

The next design in this series was the P.210-01, which Vogt entered for the 1944 Volksjäger (People's fighter) competition. This was the RLM's attempt to obtain a lightweight, relatively inexpensive jet fighter that could be produced by a semi-skilled workforce at dispersed sites. The single-seat P.210-01 was very similar to the P.209 in overall design, utilising a central tubular spar that formed the

BV P.208-3

Crew	1
Wingspan	31ft 2in (9.5m)
Sweep	30°
Length	30ft 2in (9.2m)
Height	11ft 4in (3.45m)
Empty weight	9,138 lb (4,144kg)
Gross weight	11,033 lb (5,004kg)
Powerplant	1 x liquid cooled Daimler Benz 12-cylinder DB603L engine, utilising a two-stage supercharger and methanol-water injection
Maximum speed	490mph (788kph)
Range	760 miles (1,223km)
Armament	3 x 30mm Mk108 cannons

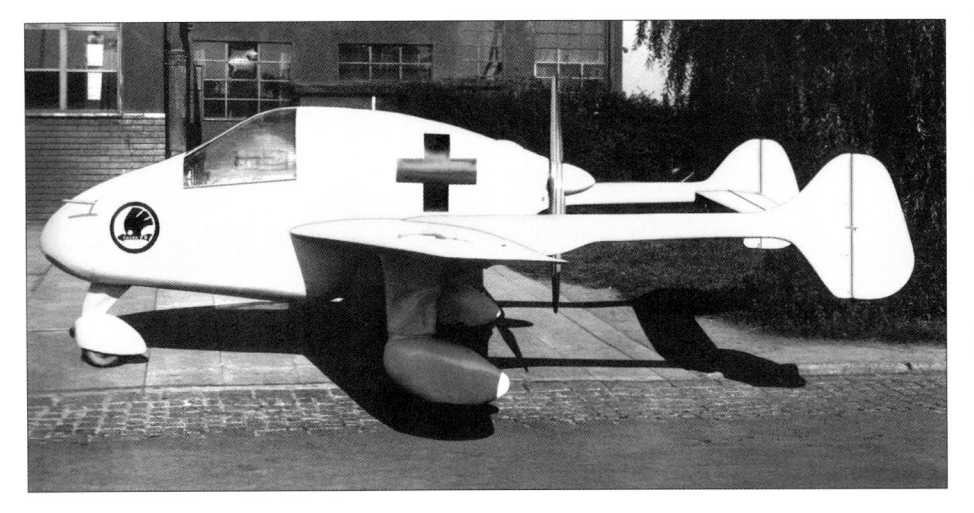

The Skoda-Kauba V-6 Experimental aircraft is seen in its completed form before undergoing modification that allowed testing of wing designs for Blohm & Voss' advanced jet fighters. The fate of this aircraft is unknown. Bill Rose Collection

engine duct and supported the wings. For propulsion, a BMW003A turbojet would be used, providing 1,760 lb (7.8kN) static thrust. It is difficult to verify the exact wingspan of this design, but the best sources suggest an overall figure of 37ft 10in (11.52m). Sweep also appears reduced to 30°. The overall length was about 24ft (7.32m) and take-off weight would have been approximately 7,500 lb (3,402kg). There are no details available of estimated performance, but it seems likely that a maximum speed in excess of 500mph (805kph) was anticipated, with a ceiling of at least 35,000ft (10,000m). The armament was to be two forward firing 30mm Mk108 cannons fitted on each side of the cockpit.

While this project was underway, Vogt and Amtmann started working on a more conventional alternative. There is some confusion about the designation of this design, which appears to have started out as P.210-02 and then became P.211-02. The proposal was for a rather crude-looking straight-winged aircraft with a tail, powered by a BMW turbojet within the fuselage. But the B&V designers also produced an altogether superior concept called the P.211-01. This had a similar wing shape and sweep to the P.210-01, but without the booms and wingtip fins. In overall appearance, the P.211-01 was somewhat similar to the advanced Messerschmitt P.1101 jet fighter, which had almost been completed at the end of the war and was secured by US forces.

Although the tailless B&V design was considered to be the best submission for the RLM's Volksjäger contest, the Heinkel He 162A was finally selected for full development. This lightweight fighter not only flew before the end of the year but also saw operational service when fuel supplies permitted. Despite losing out, Vogt was encouraged to continue with development of the tailless series of jet fighters and his next proposal was the P.212. It had been under development since autumn 1944, with initial plans to begin the construction of three prototypes in February 1945, with test flight commencing in August 1945. The Blohm und Voss P.212-03 would be powered by a Heinkel He S 011 turbojet and came to be regarded as the most refined version of this tailless series with an estimated maximum speed of almost 600mph (965kph) at 20,000ft (6,000m), a service ceiling of 40,000ft (12,192m) and unspecified but apparently good endurance. The forward positioned fully pressurised cockpit would have provided good visibility and the aircraft was to be supported on the ground by a tricycle undercarriage. A wide range of armament options were studied for this design which included various numbers of forward firing cannons, R4M rockets or bombs for limited ground attack missions.

The overall wingspan was to be 31ft 2in (9.5m) although this was shortened slightly during a review. It was also decided that the 45° sweep would be reduced to 40° and the chord would be altered to allow larger fuel tanks and improved structural provision for external stores. Although Vogt favoured an all-steel construction, allowances were made for the P.212-03 to utilise wood and alu-

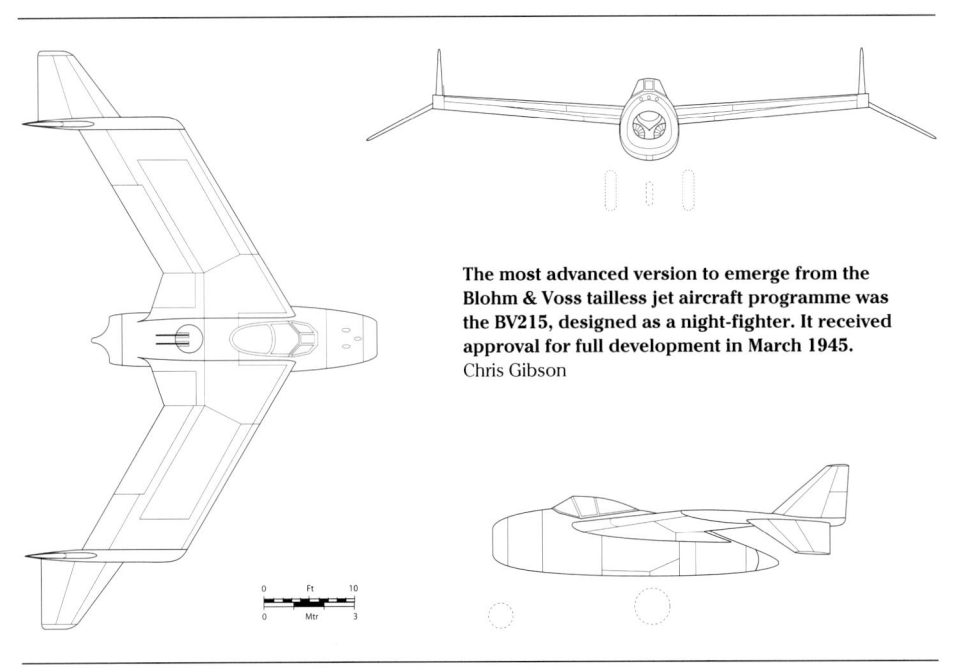

The most advanced version to emerge from the Blohm & Voss tailless jet aircraft programme was the BV215, designed as a night-fighter. It received approval for full development in March 1945.
Chris Gibson

BV P.209-01

Crew	1
Wingspan	35ft (10.66m)
Sweep	35°
Length	24ft (7.3m)
Powerplant	1 x Heinkel He S 011A turbojet rated at 2,865 lb (12.75kN) static thrust
Maximum speed	559mph (900kph)
Armament	2 x 30mm Mk108 cannons

BV P.210-01

Crew	1
Wingspan	37ft 10in (11.52m)
Sweep	30°
Length	24ft (7.32m)
Empty weight	5.467 lb
Gross weight	7,500 lb
Powerplant	1 x BMW003A turbojet rated at 1,760 lb (7.8kN) static thrust
Maximum speed	+500mph (+805kph) approx
Ceiling	35-40,000ft (10-12,000m) approx
Armament	2 x 30mm Mk108 cannons

Secret Projects: Flying Wings and Tailless Aircraft

minium in non-load-bearing areas of the wings. With wind tunnel testing underway, the P.212-03 was entered for the Luftwaffe's Emergency Fighter Competition, which had been organised by the Oberkommando der Luftwaffe (OKL – Luftwaffe High Command). Other designs were submitted by Heinkel, Junkers, Messerschmitt and Focke-Wulf, with Focke-Wulf's Ta-183 being selected for development and production.

However, the P.212-3 was considered sufficiently interesting to remain under consideration as a future Luftwaffe combat aircraft. Meanwhile, another tailless Vogt design that carried the reference P.215-02 was under review for the role of night fighter to meet a 1944 specification issued by the Technische Luftrüstung (Technical Air Armaments Office). They required a new combat aircraft with a maximum speed of 559mph (900kph), a minimum endurance of four hours, the ability to carry FuG240 or FuG244 radar and an armament of four 30mm cannons. Vogt responded with a broadly similar design to the tailless P.212, but somewhat larger in size to accommodate two side-by-side Heinkel He S 011A turbojets, air intercept radar equipment and a pressurised cockpit capable of accommodating three crew members.

Construction-wise, the Blohm und Voss P.215-02 was built using all the same techniques developed for earlier designs, with the majority of components made from steel, although some non-load bearing parts would be aluminium and control surfaces would be fabricated from wood. It was also planned to make the nose section from shaped wooden panels, as this component covered the radar unit and needed to be non-metallic. Aside from a short section of inner trailing edges, the wing's chord was constant along its length like all earlier proposals in this series. The sweep was reduced to 30° and the wingtip fin arrangement was almost identical to the P.212. The overall wingspan including the dihedral winglets was 61ft 8in (18.8m), reducing to 47ft 3in (14.40m) for the main wing. The main supporting feature of the wing was a centrally-located steel-welded box and it was planned to divert warm air from the engine compartment into the wings for de-icing. A tricycle undercarriage supported the aircraft on the ground, comprising of a rearward-retracting nose-wheel that was normally used on the Heinkel He 219 and two forward-retracting main wheels.

Several different cockpit layouts were considered, that included a side-by-side arrangement for two crew members a two seat tandem arrangement and provision for a rearward facing radar operator. All options considered included ejection seats. By most standards, the P.215-02 would have been heavily armed with five forward-facing 30mm cannons, one or two rear-facing 30mm cannons in a remotely controlled backward-facing turret and the option of two 'Schräge Musik' (Jazz/Slanted Music) upward firing cannons to be used while passing beneath an enemy bomber. The aircraft could also be used as a light bomber with provision to carry two 1,102 lb (500kg) bombs beneath the fuselage.

Like the other Blohm und Voss tailless fighter proposals, the P.215-02 could be easily transported by road once the wings were removed, allowing for use at improvised dispersed sites such as suitable stretches of autobahn.

The Technische Luftrüstung modified its requirements for a future jet-powered night fighter in late February 1945 which was too demanding for the P.215-02 and its fellow competitors. Subsequently, it was decided to go ahead with development and testing which received official approval in March 1945. But with only weeks remaining before the war ended, no further progress was made with this interesting series of tailless aircraft. Although these B&V jet fighters had rather an unorthodox appearance, wind tunnel tests indicated that the P.212 and P.215 would have performed well. This appears to have been confirmed in recent times by model aircraft constructors who have built and flown scale sized jet-powered replicas.

There was one other advanced Blohm und Voss fighter project under development during the final months of World War 2 with the reference Ae 607 or P.217. This design differed considerably from all those previously discussed. It was a small, single-seat lightweight highly-swept flying wing fighter, powered by a Heinkel He S 011A turbojet. Because of the very compact nature of this aircraft, it was necessary to offset the cockpit, placing it alongside the engine in a central position. Another unusual feature was the small canard control surfaces that were added to improve low-speed stability. Few details of this study are available, but it is understood that the Ae 607 was shelved in favour of the P.212-03.

After hostilities ceased, Dr Richard Vogt was recruited by the Americans under Operation 'Paperclip' and taken to the United States. He worked for the USAF until 1954, later becoming head of the design office at the Astrophysics Development Corporation. In 1960, Dr Vogt joined Boeing where he worked on VTOL systems and hydrofoils. His final work with the company involved post-launch evaluation of the Boeing 747.

Dr Richard Vogt was one of the great aeronautical designers of the 20th century. He died at Santa Barbara, California, in 1979, aged 84.

BV P.212-03

Wingspan	31ft 2in (9.5m)
Sweep	40°
Length	24ft 10in (7.55m)
Empty weight	5,974 lb (2,710kg)
Gross weight	9,215 lb (4,180kg)
Powerplant	1 x Heinkel He S 011A turbojet rated at 2,865 lb (12.75kN) static thrust
Maximum speed	600mph (965kph) at 20,000ft (6,000m)
Ceiling	40,000ft (12,192m)
Armament	Different configurations including 2-7 forward firing 30mm Mk108 cannons, R4M rockets or bombs

BV P.215.02

Crew	2 or 3
Wingspan (overall)	61ft 8in (18.8m)
(main)	47ft 3in (14.4m)
Sweep	30°
Length	38ft 1in (11.6m)
Height	16ft 5in (5.0m)
Wing area	678.13ft^2 (63m^2)
Empty weight	16,314 lb (7,400kg)
Gross weight	32,363 lb (14,679kg)
Powerplant	2 x Heinkel He S 011A turbojets, each rated at 2,865 lb (12.75kN) static thrust
Maximum speed	560mph (900kph)
Ceiling	48,500ft (14,783m)
Range	1,400 miles (2,253km)
Endurance	5 hours
Armament	5 x 30mm Mk108 cannons

mounted in the nose, although various alternative layouts were considered. It was also planned to fit two Mk108 cannons in a remote-controlled rear-facing turret and the idea of having two upward-facing cannons was considered. Other options were R4M unguided rockets and the possibility of carrying bombs for use in the ground strike role.

BV Ae 607 P.217

Crew	1
Wingspan	26ft 3in (8m)
Sweep	45° at 0.5 chord
Length	23ft 4in (7.41m)
Gross weight	9,260 lb (4,200kg) (estimated)
Powerplant	1 x Heinkel He S 011A turbojet rated at 2,865 lb (12.75kN) static thrust
Maximum speed	500mph (800kph) at altitude (estimated)
Armament	3 x 30mm Mk108 cannons in the nose

German World War 2 Flying Wing Development

BMW Strahlbomber II

BMW is not usually associated with the design of combat aircraft, but during World War 2, the company developed two proposals for a Strahlbomber (jet bomber). The first design produced in 1944 was to be powered by six BMW003A engines, with four of the engines buried in the wings and two located in a fairing beneath the cockpit at the front of the fuselage. The aircraft would be a swept wing design with no tailplane, flown by a two-man crew. BMW's initial concept soon gave way to a more sophisticated, twin-engine flying wing bomber, powered by two side-by-side BMW109-018 turbojets. This advanced axial flow gas turbine was expected to deliver 7,496 lb (33.3kN) of static thrust and it remained in development until the end of the war. BMW engineers placed these jet engines at the second Strahlbomber's centre of gravity to ensure stability and continued flight should one engine fail. There were no vertical control surfaces and by using the higher performance 109-018 engines this aircraft was expected to provide a significantly better maximum speed and range than the first design.

The engines carried by the swept-wing Strahlbomber II would be fed from an intake at the nose, with the airflow ducted around the cockpit. A crew of three would man this aircraft, with the bomb aimer accommodated in a ventral bay, and each pressurised crew compartment would be separate. The Strahlbomber II would be equipped with a remotely controlled gun turret in the tail fitted with two 20mm MG151/20 cannons and the aircraft would be capable of carrying an 11,020 lb (5,000kg) bomb load. The aircraft would be supported on the ground by a substantial tricycle undercarriage and the design suggests that BMW may have been aiming for good high-altitude performance. Relatively little is known about these studies, but like many other advanced German wartime projects, this particular design never left the drawing board.

BMW Strahlbomber II

Crew	3
Wingspan	113ft 3in (34.5m) estimated (all sources vary slightly)
Length	60ft (18.28m)
Height	14ft 9in (4.5m)
Gross weight	69,400 lb (31,480kg)
Powerplant	2 x BMW109-018 turbojets, each rated at 7,496 lb (33.3kN) static thrust
Maximum speed	600mph (965kph) estimated (sources vary)
Ceiling	Unknown
Range	2,485 miles (4,000km)
Armament	2 x 20mm cannons in remote-controlled tail turret and 11,020 lb (5,000kg) bomb load

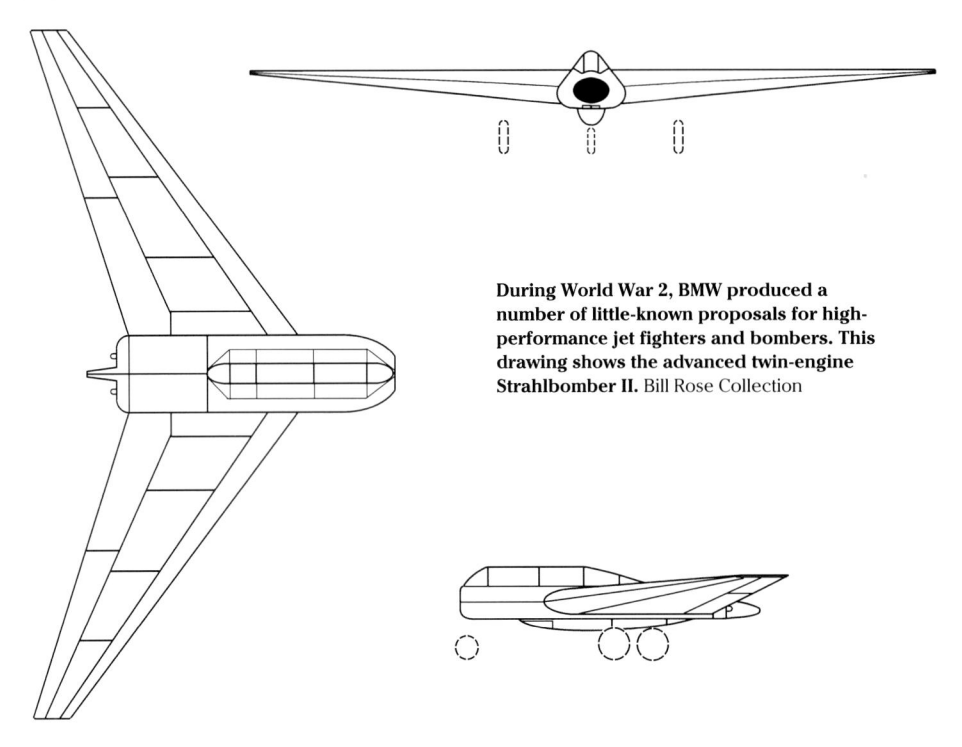

During World War 2, BMW produced a number of little-known proposals for high-performance jet fighters and bombers. This drawing shows the advanced twin-engine Strahlbomber II. Bill Rose Collection

Focke-Wulf Fw 1000 x 1000 x 1000 Bomber Project B

In 1944, Focke-Wulf began a series of studies to fulfil the RLM's requirement for a jet bomber capable of reaching a maximum speed of 1,000kph (621mph) and carrying a 1,000kg (2,204 lb) bomb load over a distance of 1,000km (621miles). This specification then became the name of the project: 1000 x 1000 x 1000. Focke-Wulf is known to have worked on three different proposals. All were to be powered by two Heinkel Hirth 109-11A turbojets and the first two studies were conventional in appearance, rather like the post-war Yakovlev Yak-25 (which might have utilised some of this design work), while the third was a tailless flying wing.

There is confusion about whether these studies were simply called Project A, B and C, or Project A-1, A-11 and B. In addition, there is one source that claims this study was designated 031 0239/10, which may have been the correct company project number. On the strength of what details are available, it is best to simply refer to the Focke-Wulf flying wing proposal under discussion as Project B. The designer primarily responsible for this work was Dr Heinz von Halem, who is now remembered for his very exotic Triebflügel (thrust wing) fighter concept produced in late 1944. While developing Project B, he was assisted by the brilliant aerodynamicist Dr Dietrich Küchemann, who later became a senior official at RAE Farnborough, worked on Concorde and was honoured with a CBE.

The aircraft that emerged from this collaboration was the delta-shaped flying wing, with its two engines located in a central position and fed from leading edge air intakes at the wing roots. It is also possible that deflector plates were proposed as a means of vectoring jet exhaust flow and providing

Focke-Wulf FW 1000x1000x1000 Project B

Crew	1 or possibly 2
Wingspan	46ft (14m)
Sweep	45° (leading edge)
Wing area	592ft² (55m²)
Length	19ft (5.8m)
Height	9ft (2.74m)
Gross weight	17,857 lb (8,100kg)
Powerplant	2 x Heinkel He S 011A turbojets, each rated at 2,865 lb (12.75kN) static thrust
Maximum speed	659mph (10,60kph)
Ceiling	46,000ft (14,000m)
Range	1,305 miles (2,100km)
Armament	Over 2,204 lb (1,000kg) bomb load. Initially, no defensive weapons.

additional flight control. Down-turned stabilising fins and rudders were positioned at the wingtips and the wing's sweep was to be 45° (some sources claim slightly less). The aircraft was supported on the ground by a fully retracting tricycle undercarriage and the cockpit was fully pressurised with the potential for expansion to accommodate a second crew member. Although this Focke-Wulf project progressed little further than the early design stage, some aspects of the study appear to have proved influential with US and British designers during the post-war years.

Heinkel Tailless Projects

Heading Heinkel's design office was Siegfried Günter (1899-1969) who was unquestionably one of the company's greatest assets. He had worked alongside his twin brother Walter on a number of important Heinkel aircraft that included the He 51, He 70 and He 111. Walter was killed in a car accident in 1937, but Siegfried continued as a designer with the company. Having been involved with the early development of jet aircraft, Siegfried Günter and his chief engineer Karl Schwaerzler took direct control of Heinkel's entry for the Volksjäger Competition, which led to the successful He 162A Salamander. The aircraft was built, undertook its first test flight on 6 December 1944, underwent various revisions to correct serious problems (thanks to the assistance of Dr Alexander Lippisch) and entered production almost immediately, with a small number of He 162A fighters becoming operational by March 1945.

With the He 162A in production, work at Heinkel's design office in Vienna was focussed on the development of more advanced versions of this warplane and a suitable proposal for the OKL's Emergency Fighter Competition. This quickly led to three very unusual concepts. Designated P.1078, the first study in this series (P.1078A) was the most conventional looking and took the form of a single-seat jet fighter with nose intake, forward cockpit and straightforward tail unit. In many respects, the fuselage was similar to that of the Messerschmitt P.1101 jet fighter, but was fitted with rather unusual gull wings with a 40° leading edge sweep.

The second design (P.1078B) was for a compact single-seat flying wing fighter, powered by a single Heinkel He S 011 turbojet. However, this proposal had a very usual layout with two forward fuselage nacelles. One would accommodate the cockpit and the other would house two 30mm Mk108 cannons and the forward undercarriage wheel.

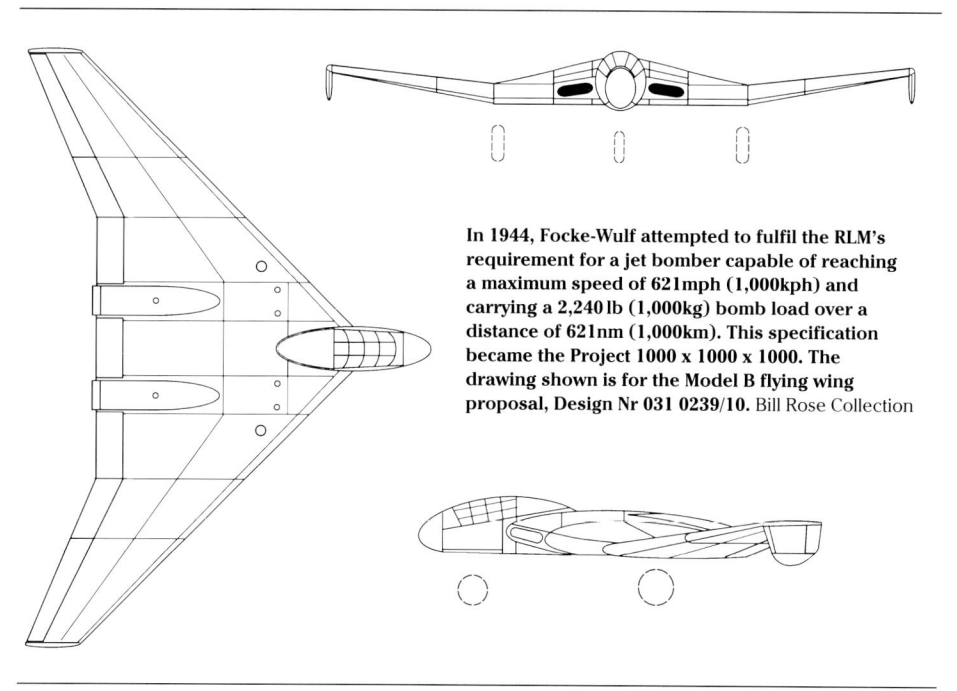

In 1944, Focke-Wulf attempted to fulfil the RLM's requirement for a jet bomber capable of reaching a maximum speed of 621mph (1,000kph) and carrying a 2,240 lb (1,000kg) bomb load over a distance of 621nm (1,000km). This specification became the Project 1000 x 1000 x 1000. The drawing shown is for the Model B flying wing proposal, Design Nr 031 0239/10. Bill Rose Collection

The engine's air-inlet was positioned between both nacelles, there were no upright control surfaces and the gull-wing profile was virtually identical to that of the P.1078A. The third design for the emergency fighter competition known as the P.1078C also retained this 40° sweep gull wing, but used a short fuselage section without any upright control surfaces. With an appearance more like the Blohm und Voss P.212-03, this single-seat design was chosen as Heinkel's preferred entry for the competition. Powered by a single Heinkel He S 011 turbojet fed from a nose intake, the fuselage was constructed mainly from steel with the wings built from wood. This was also where the aircraft's entire fuel supply was accommodated. A fully retracting tricycle undercarriage was chosen with wheels turning through 90° to lie flat along the fuselage and the proposed armament was two 30mm Mk108 cannons installed below the cockpit, each with 100 rounds of ammunition.

The Luftwaffe expressed concerns about many of the aircraft's features such as the unprotected fuel tanks in the wings and the aerodynamic shape of the fuselage. It concluded that this proposal was less satisfactory than the other leading entries and as a consequence Heinkel abandoned further development work in late February 1945. Günter's department was now concentrating on designs for a larger twin-engine night fighter called the P.1079 which began with a reasonably conventional design using engines in the wing roots, a modest 35° wing leading edge sweep and V-tail. This was soon replaced by a tailless twin-engine concept (P.1079B-1) that used the same gull-wing wing profile as the P.1078 designs. For stability, this aircraft would use a single upright tailfin. Günter chose the same complicated folding tricycle

Heinkel P.1078B

Crew	1
Wingspan	31ft (9.44m)
Sweep	40° (leading edge)
Length	19ft 10in (6.04m)
Gross weight	8,576 lb (3,890kg)
Maximum speed	636mph (1,023kph)
Ceiling	45,000ft (13,716m)
Powerplant	1 x Heinkel He S 011A turbojets, rated at 2,865 lb (12.75kN) static thrust
Armament	2 x 30mm Mk108 cannons

Heinkel P.1078C

Crew	1
Wingspan	29ft 6in (9m)
Sweep	40° (leading edge)
Wing area	191.6ft² (17.8m²)
Length	20ft (6.1m)
Height	7ft 8in (2.33m)
Empty weight	5,410
Gross weight	8,643 lb
Maximum speed	637mph (1,027kph) at sea level
Ceiling	40,000ft+ (12,192m+) (estimated)
Powerplant	1 x Heinkel He S 011A turbojets, rated at 2,865 lb (12.75kN) static thrust
Armament	2 x 30mm Mk108 cannons

German World War 2 Flying Wing Development

The second completely tailless version of the Heinkel He1079 jet fighter designed by Siegfried Günter. Chris Gibson

Heinkel He P.1080

Crew	1
Wingspan	29ft 3in (8.9m)
Wing area	215ft² (19.97m²)
Length	26ft 9in (8.15m)
Maximum speed	621mph (1,000kph)
Powerplant	2 x 900mm diameter Lorin-Rohr ramjets, each providing an estimated 3,440 lb (15.3kN) of thrust at altitude, plus four solid fuel booster rockets used for take-off, each providing 2,204 lb (9.8kN) thrust
Armament	2 x 30mm Mk108 cannons

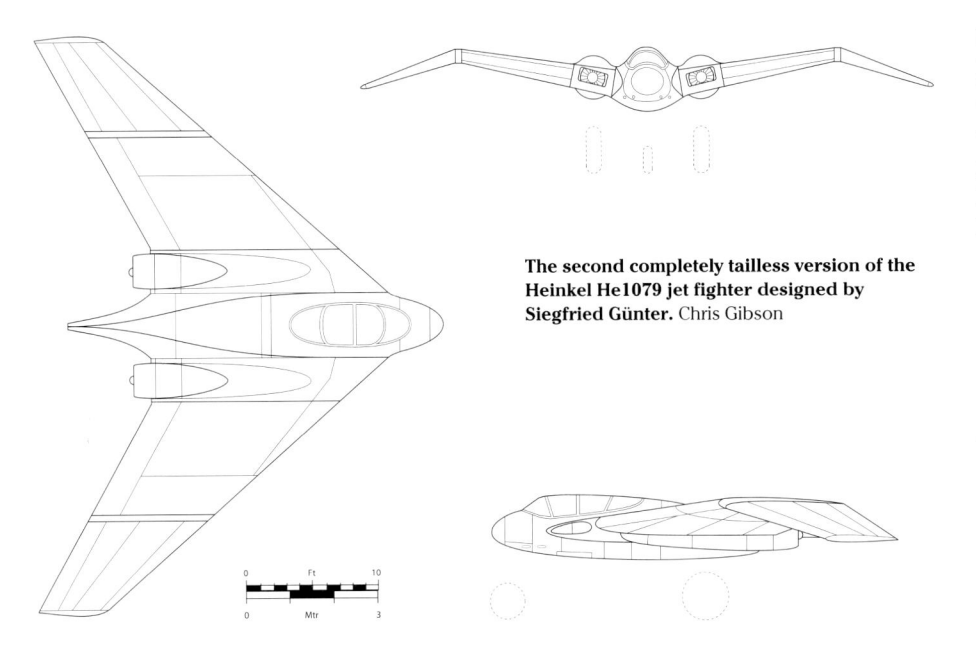

undercarriage arrangement which minimised the amount of internal space required when retracted. Armament was to be four 30mm cannons in the nose and the aircraft would be equipped with centimetric radar.

Heinkel He P.1079B-1

Crew	2
Wingspan	43ft (13.1m)
Sweep	45° (leading edge)
Length	31ft (9.44m)
Maximum speed	630mph 1,013kph (630mph)
Ceiling	+40,000ft (+12,192m) (estimated)
Range	1,678 miles (2,700km)
Powerplant	2 x Heinkel He S 011A turbojets, each rated at 2,865 lb (12.75kN) static thrust, or 2 x Junkers Jumo 004B turbojets (providing reduced performance)
Armament	4 x 30mm Mk108 cannons (3 x Mk108 cannons in the Jumo-powered version)

Heinkel He P.1079B-2

Crew	2
Wingspan	43ft (13.1m)
Sweep	45° (leading edge)
Length	31ft (9.44m)
Maximum speed	630mph (1,013kph)
Ceiling	+40,000ft (+12,192m) (estimated)
Powerplant	2 x Heinkel He S 011A turbojets, each rated at 2,865 lb (12.75kN) static thrust
Range	1,678 miles (2,700km)
Armament	4 x 30mm Mk108 cannons

Although Heinkel He S 011 turbojets were the preferred choice for propulsion, the option to install Junkers Jumo 004B engines was also considered, although this would have reduced internal space and led to a reduction in offensive armament, resulting in three 30mm cannons as opposed to four. A further development of this design was the P.1079B-2 which was broadly similar, but dispensed with the tail fin. Various cockpit arrangements were considered with the preferred option to have the second crew member facing rearward.

One of the last projects undertaken by Heinkel's Vienna design bureau was the P.1080 ramjet fighter which utilised a number of features borrowed from earlier tailless concepts. The P.1080 was to be equipped with two large ramjet engines on each side of the fuselage, drawing fuel from tanks carried between both units. To achieve the speed required for these engines to become operational, four solid-fuel boosters would launch the aircraft. Presumably, this would have been undertaken with a trolley on a hard runway. The P.1080 was not equipped with a retractable undercarriage and would utilise a single extendable landing skid. Armament comprised two 30mm cannons.

Work on these advanced designs continued until the end of March when Heinkel hastily vacated its facilities in Vienna in response to approaching Soviet forces. Much documentation was destroyed and Günter's team moved to a safer location. However, they were eventually detained by the US and according to one report US Intelligence encouraged them to continue working on Günter's most advanced Heinkel projects until autumn 1945. There are two conflicting stories about what happened to Siegfried Günter after this period. He is known to have briefly worked for a Berlin car repair shop owned by his father-in-law and was allegedly kidnapped by the KGB and taken to Russia where he was forced to undertake design work on advanced military aircraft. Alternatively, Günter is said to have sought a job in the US aviation industry. He was turned down and subsequently approached the Russians who made him an immediate offer. According to one unconfirmed source, the German designer then travelled to Russia and undertook much of the initial development for the MiG-15 and MiG-17 jet fighters. It should be mentioned that the early design history of the MiG-15 remains somewhat obscure, although the use of German research has always been acknowledged. Having spent several years in the Soviet Union, Günter finally returned to West Germany where he joined the reformed Heinkel Company and worked on supersonic VTOL projects. He died in Berlin in June 1969.

Henschel P.135

Henschel came into existence during the mid-19th Century as a constructor of locomotives and by the mid-1930s, had become a major manufacturer or armoured fighting vehicles. The company produced huge numbers of Panther and Tiger tanks during World War 2, made possible by the extensive use of slave labour.

Henschel also operated an aircraft division that developed a small number of combat aircraft and several advanced guided missiles. One particularly interesting Henschel Flugzeugwerke AG proposal for the OKL Emergency Fighter Competition of late 1944 was a small tailless single engine design created by Chief Engineer Friedrich Nicolaus and known as the P.135.

Powered by a Heinkel He S 011 turbojet, the aircraft consisted of a compact fuselage with a nose inlet for the jet engine and a centrally located cockpit. The aircraft would be supported on the ground with a tricycle undercarriage and the P.135 used a sophisticated compound swept wing with straight edge wingtip sections. This was intended to counteract turbulence at high speed by spreading the effect of compression along the length of the wing. This was an interesting design, but it could not compete against the Focke-Wulf Ta 183 and the project was shelved.

The compact Henschel P.135 designed for the Emergency Fighter Requirement of 1944.
Bill Rose Collection

Henschel P.135

Crew	1
Wingspan	30ft 2in (9.2m)
Length	25ft 6in (7.77m)
Maximum speed	612mph (985kph)
Ceiling	46,000ft (14,020m)
Gross weight	9,038 lb (5,000kg)
Powerplant	1 x Heinkel He S 011A turbojet rated at 2,865 lb (12.75kN) static thrust
Armament	4 x 30mm Mk108 cannons

Advanced Horten Projects

Having established themselves as constructors of elegant and advanced gliders during the 1930s, the Horten Brothers (Reimar and Walter) joined the Luftwaffe in 1936 as pilots. However, they were encouraged to continue designing and building aircraft, leading to the extraordinary Parabola that was damaged during storage in 1938 and subsequently destroyed having never flown.

In 1939, Reimar and Walter were offered jobs with Heinkel and Messerschmitt, but disagreements over the ownership of future patents prevented the brothers from accepting. Nevertheless, Walter had many high-level connections within the Luftwaffe and Reimar was married to Air Minister Ernst Udet's secretary which allowed them almost unprecedented scope to continue working on their own aviation projects. It's also worth mentioning that there was a third Horten brother, Wolfram Horten, who played some part in the development of their early designs. He was killed when his Heinkel He 111 was shot down over Dunkirk.

Walter Horten (left) and Reimar Horten (right) who produced designs for some of Germany's most advanced combat aircraft during the World War 2. Courtesy David Myhra

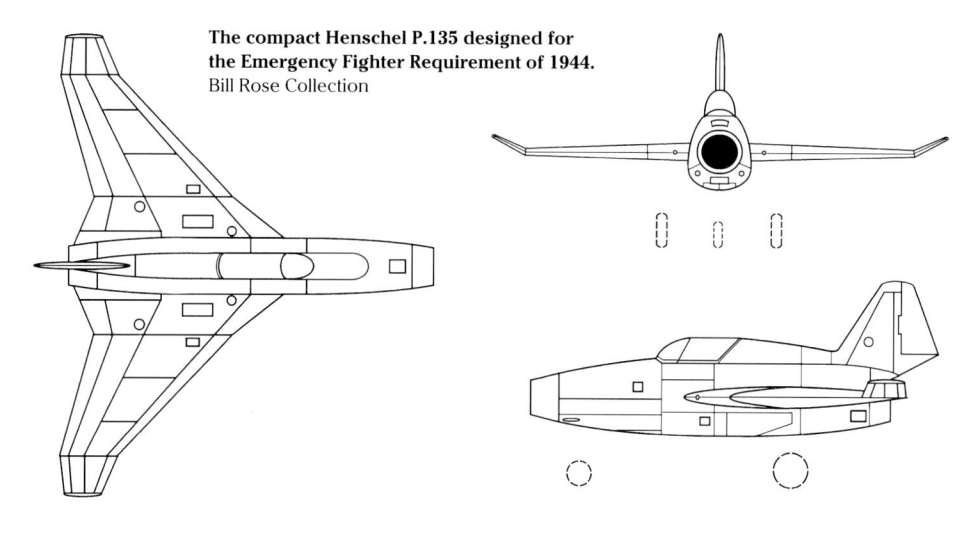

With a full-scale war taking place and awareness that Northrop was working on flying wing aircraft in the United States, senior RLM officials agreed that the Horten's projects were of special importance. Subsequently, an entire facility known as Sonderkommando (Special Detachment) 9 based at Göttingen Airfield was made available to them for the design and construction of new military aircraft. In 1942, Major Walter Horten took command of the installation and Reimar soon joined him. In addition to Sonderkommando 9, the Peschke furniture factory at Minden was placed at their disposal for skilled fabrication work.

The brothers began by designing a propeller driven two-seat tandem trainer called the Horten Ho VII. Peschke was requested to begin construction of a small batch of Ho VII aircraft, but after the first aircraft was completed and test flown at Minden in 1943, the RLM cancelled the contract. They now instructed the Hortens to proceed with development of their proposed jet powered flying wing fighter-bomber that would become the Horten Ho IX. At this point, all the initial studies for this aircraft had been completed and construction work was starting on the first prototype Ho IX V1 (Versuchs 1 – Experimental or Version One), which would be an unpowered glider. The Hortens planned to undertake extensive testing with this first aircraft and once the bugs had been ironed out they would move to construction of the Ho IX V2, which would be powered by two BMW003 turbojets.

Work on this project progressed at a fairly pedestrian rate until it was brought to the attention of Reichsmarschall Hermann Göring who took a personal interest in the

German World War 2 Flying Wing Development

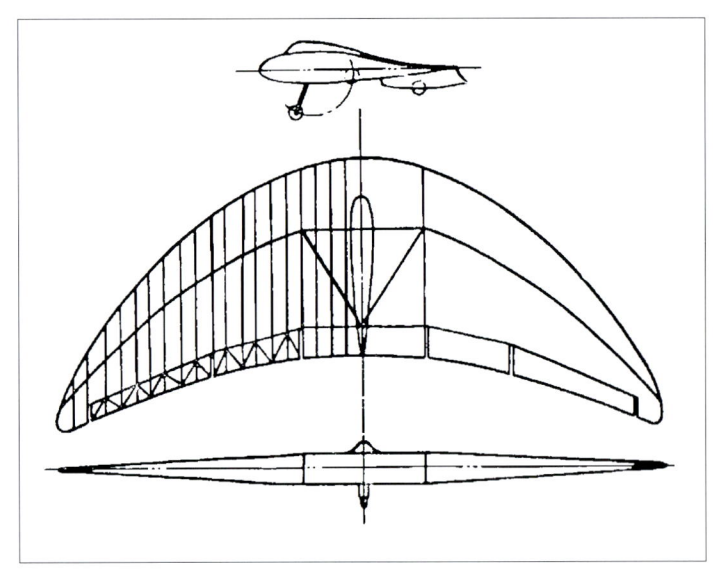

44   *Secret Projects: Flying Wings and Tailless Aircraft*

project and provided them with his full support. It was obviously encouraging to have backing from the head of the Luftwaffe when trying to obtain prioritised components like jet engines, but it also put the Hortens under considerable pressure with Göring setting schedules for the rapid introduction of this new fighter aircraft.

The Ho IX V1 was a flying wing in every respect with no vertical stabilisers or control surfaces, although it is said that Walter Horten was strongly in favour of including a single upright fin on the aircraft. Various materials were used in the Ho IX's construction, but the main parts of the airframe were a central welded tubular steel framework with the wings being mostly fabricated from wood. The one-man cockpit was located just behind the central leading edge and the glider utilised a tricycle undercarriage. The retractable nose-wheel was salvaged from a crashed Heinkel He 177 bomber, the two main wheels were fixed in position and the struts were enclosed in fairings. This was apparently considered necessary to assist with stability because there was no propulsion. Unusual for this time was a braking parachute fitted in the tail that would be deployed on landing to slow the aircraft.

The Ho IX V1 was first flown by test pilot Heinz Scheidhauer at Göttingen Airfield on 1 March 1944. Following several successful flights, V1 was transferred to Oranienburg Airfield near Berlin for testing by members of the Luftwaffe. When these trials concluded, V1 was transported to Brandis. It remained there until 1945 when members of the American 9th Armored Division discovered the glider and eventually destroyed it.

Meanwhile, the second prototype had been assembled in a large garage at Göttingen Airfield, although the planned use of BMW turbojets was in doubt due to ongoing engine reliability issues and uncertain delivery dates. The only option was to modify the fuselage to take a pair of slightly larger Junkers Jumo 004 jet engines. With changes made to the engine bays, steel protector plates were fitted to shield the central trailing edge from hot exhaust from the engines.

By the time both 1,980 lb (8.8kN) static thrust jet engines were installed in the Ho IX V2, it was late 1944 and the project was behind schedule. This second prototype was closer to a production aircraft, although it carried no armament. V2 was fitted with a fully-retractable undercarriage comprising of a nose-wheel salvaged from a Heinkel He 177 and main wheels from a Messerschmitt Bf 109.

The first test flight was undertaken on 2 February 1945 at Oranienburg by Leutnant Erwin Ziller, an experienced test pilot who had already gained some useful experience flying an Me 262 jet fighter at the Rechlin test centre. The initial flight of the new Horten aircraft was considered successful, but at the end of the second trial on the following day, Ziller ran into problems deploying the parachute too early and it resulted in damage to the undercarriage. This was repaired, but it meant that testing was delayed until 18 February 1945. Unfortunately, things went disastrously wrong on this occasion. Ziller suffered a turbojet failure and attempted to land on one engine. He lost control of the aircraft and was killed in the crash. The exact cause of the accident was never discovered and the investigation that followed could not rule out sabotage.

Nevertheless, these brief trials were judged so successful that Reichsmarschall Hermann Göring ordered the aircraft into immediate

Opposite page:

Top left: **The constructional detail of the Horten Parabola's airframe during assembly in 1938.** Bill Rose Collection

Top right: **Drawing of the Horten Parabola that was built as a glider but never flown.** US Army

Centre left: **The Horten Parabola was found to have suffered damage following storage and apparently repair was not an option. After the war, knowledge of this glider led US Intelligence to suggest that the Hortens had been secretly involved in the development of flying disc-shaped aircraft, although there was no truth to the idea.** Courtesy David Myhra

Centre right: **The Horten Parabola glider was deliberately set on fire after it was determined that the aircraft had been damaged beyond practical repair.** Courtesy David Myhra

Bottom left: **The prototype Ho IX V1 flying wing glider being moved by a ground crew in preparation for a test flight at Oranienburg Airfield during mid-1944.** Courtesy David Myhra

Bottom right: **The sleek Horten Ho IX V1 at Oranienburg Airfield.** Courtesy David Myhra

This page:

Horten Ho IX V1 being towed by a small truck across a snow-covered airfield during 1944. Courtesy David Myhra

The badly damaged centre section of the Ho IX V1, prior to being scrapped. US Army

German World War 2 Flying Wing Development

production as a new fighter-bomber. Plans had already been drawn up for Gotha Waggonfabrik A.G to begin assembly of several experimental prototypes and a further batch of 20 pre-production aircraft at the Friedrichsroda factory. This aircraft would be called the Gotha Go 229A and the company's engineers were officially requested to make a number of general upgrades to the design and minor modifications that would assist with manufacture. These included cockpit changes and the installation of a rudimentary ejector seat, alterations to the undercarriage, some aerodynamic modifications to the engine intakes and structural improvements within the engine bays. It was decided to install four 30mm Mk108 cannons just outboard of the engines and provide hardpoints beneath the fuselage for either two bombs or two drop tanks.

By spring 1945, production was underway at Friedrichsroda with the first prototype Go 229A V3 (sometimes also called the Ho IX V3) at an advanced stage of assembly. Several variants of the Go 229 were also being assembled and these were the V4, V5, V6 and V7. In addition, components were being readied for production of the first 20 Go 229A fighter-bombers. The Go 229A V3 was almost ready to begin flight-testing when US forces secured the Friedrichsroda plant in April 1945. The two-seat V6 was about half finished and work was underway on the other pre-production aircraft. V3 was then shipped to the RAE at Farnborough, England, for initial evaluation and from there taken to the United States where there were plans to make it airworthy. But this never happened and the aircraft was finally passed from the USAF to the National Air and Space Museum which intended to fully restore it.

Unfortunately at the time of writing this interesting aircraft remains in rather a poor state and it may be some time before this happens.

After the Americans removed V3 from Gotha Waggonfabrik A.G, it is understood that a team of engineers were instructed to destroy the remaining uncompleted prototypes before Soviet forces arrived.

Controversy surrounds the supposed stealth capabilities of the Go 229A flying wing and whether it was intended to have a low radar signature from the outset. The smooth boomerang shape and predominantly wooden construction were a good combination for this. It is also worth noting that 17mm thick sheets of plywood used for the skin contained a middle layer of resin-bonded sawdust and charcoal which worked quite well as a radar absorbing material (RAM).

The Germans had certainly made progress with radar countermeasures during World War 2 and managed to effectively mask U-Boat periscopes with the use of a RAM coating. It is also claimed that during a conversation in 1950, Reimar Horten remarked that the largely wooden construction of the Go 229A would have made the aircraft hard to detect by radar. While it remains conceivable that this aircraft was intended to have a stealth capability, it seems more likely that this feature arose accidentally from the use of low-cost materials. No documentation that refers to the development or testing of RAM for this aircraft has been located. Nevertheless, the possibility can't be entirely ruled out and evidence could surface in the future.

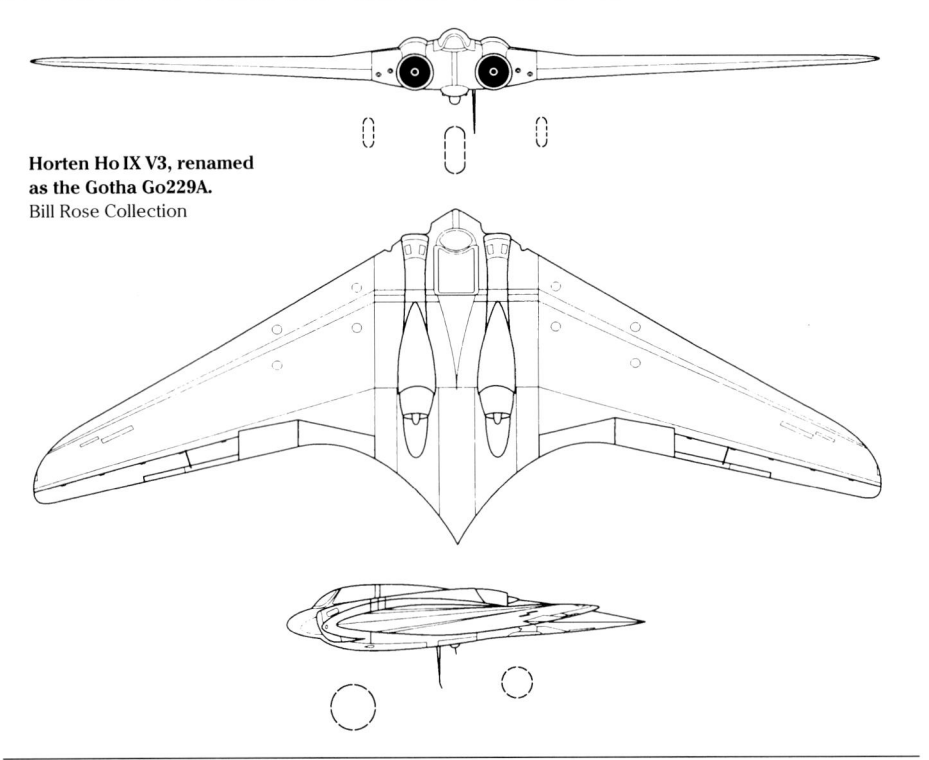

Horten Ho IX V3, renamed as the Gotha Go229A.
Bill Rose Collection

Horten Ho IX V3/Gotha Go 229A

Crew	1
Wingspan	55ft (16.78m)
Sweep	28° (leading edge)
Wing area	576.9ft² (53.59m²)
Length	24ft 6in (7.47m)
Height	9ft 2in (2.81m)
Wing area	576.9ft²
Empty weight	11,175 lb (5,067kg)
Gross weight	18,740 lb (8,500kg)
Powerplant	2 x Junkers Jumo 004B turbojets, each rated at 1,980 lb (8.8kN) static thrust
Maximum speed	590mph (946kph) at sea level and 607mph (976kph) at high altitude
Initial climb rate	4,330ft/min (1,319m/min)
Ceiling	52,500ft (16,000m)
Range	932 miles (1,500km). This could be doubled with two 275 Imp gal (1,350 litre) external drop tanks
Armament	2 or 4 x 30mm Mk108 cannons and provision for 2 x 2,204 lb (1,000kg) SC1000 bombs

Secret Projects: Flying Wings and Tailless Aircraft

Opposite, top: **The Horten Ho IX V2 jet-powered prototype under construction at Gottingen Airfield.** Bill Rose Collection/David Myhra Collection

Right: **The largely completed centre section of the Horten Ho IX V3.** US Army

Below left: **Nearly fully-assembled, the Horten Ho IX V3, soon after discovery by members of the US 3rd Army VII Corps on 14 April 1945.** US Army

Below right: **The Horten Ho IX V6 was also discovered by members of the US 3rd Army VII Corps on 14 April 1945 at the Gotha works, Friedrichsroda.** US Army

Bottom left: **The engines already installed into the Ho IX V6 airframe which was at an advanced stage of assembly at the Gotha works by the end of World War 2.** US Army

Bottom right: **The Horten Ho IX V3 at the Smithsonian Institution's Garber Restoration Facility in 2000.** Courtesy Michael Katzmann

German World War 2 Flying Wing Development

Gotha Projects

Once Gotha Waggonfabrik A.G had been selected to manufacture the Horten-designed fighter-bomber, a team of company engineers headed by Dr Hünerjäger set about undertaking various improvements to the aircraft that would make it more suitable for Luftwaffe service and as easy and cost effective to produce as possible. Their initial assessment of the Horten design led Gotha's team to begin work on an alternative concept for a flying wing aircraft that utilised many of the same constructional features, but was generally more advanced than the Go 229A and could be upgraded with less difficulty. Major differences included the use of externally mounted engines in nacelles and an entirely different cockpit layout. The initial proposal for this design was submitted to the RLM in early 1945, which were sufficiently impressed to commission further research.

This project now received the reference Gotha P.60A. It would be built from a combination of steel and wood with propulsion provided by a pair of turbojets mounted above and below the centre of the wing. The initial choice was BMW003A turbojets, although these could easily be replaced with more advanced versions, or engines manufactured by Junkers or Heinkel. Because the turbojets were carried outside the aircraft's body, maintenance or replacement of these units would have been much simpler than found with the Horten fighter. A further development of the P.60A was to install an additional Walter HWK509B rocket engine and increase the aircraft's ceiling and climb rate. This proposal was referred to as the Höhenjäger (High Altitude Fighter) and assigned the project designation P.60A/R. The pressurised cockpit was flush with the aircraft's wing and took the form of a glazed forward section with accommodation for two crew members, although they would be lying side-by-side in prone positions.

While this would allow the crew to stand higher g forces, it also raised serious questions about their ability to escape from the aircraft in an emergency. To address this question, the idea of mounting both engines below the wing was studied, but found to reduce the roll rate. The problem of abandoning the P.60A in an emergency was never resolved, although there were suggestions to develop some kind of crew ejection mechanism. The P.60A would be supported on a tricycle undercarriage with a lengthy strut for the nose-wheel which turned through 90° during retraction to minimise the use of internal space when stowed. Control surfaces on the trailing edge of the wing were supplemented by drag rudders at the wingtips. To counteract stall during landings, the wing's leading edge was fitted with hydraulically controlled split flaps.

Probable armament for the P.60A would have been four 30mm Mk108 cannons. This aircraft could have been fitted with a camera pack for high altitude reconnaissance missions. A further development was the slightly bigger P.60B that would benefit from a simplified internal structure, a modest re-arrangement of the cockpit and an engine upgrade to Heinkel He S 011 turbojets. Assembly of the first prototype P.60B was underway during February 1945, although a change of requirements within the RLM led to its cancellation and a switch to development of a third version intended for use as a night fighter called the P.60C.

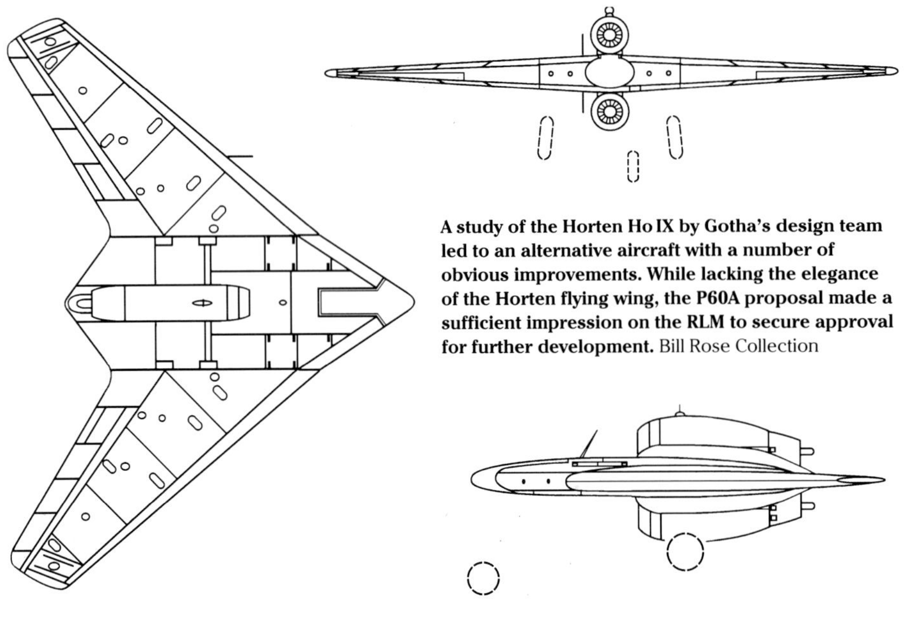

Gotha Go P.60A

Crew	2
Wingspan	40ft 1in (12.2m)
Sweep	45° (leading edge)
Wing area	504ft² (46.8m²)
Length	28ft 11in (8.82m)
Height	11ft 6in (3.5m)
Gross weight	16,424 lb (7,450kg)
Maximum speed	569mph (915kph)
Ceiling	41,000ft (12,500m)
Range	994 miles (1,600km)
Powerplant	2 x BMW003A turbojets, each rated at 1,760 lb (7.8kN) static thrust
Armament	4 x 30mm MK108 cannon
Reconnaissance role	2 x Rb50/18 cameras

Gotha Go P.60B

Crew	2
Wingspan	44ft 4in (13.5m)
Sweep	45° (leading edge)
Wing area	588.78ft² (54.7m²)
Length	32ft 6in (9.9m)
Height	11ft 6in (3.5m)
Gross weight	21,943 lb (9,953kg)
Maximum speed	604mph (973kph)
Ceiling	40,500ft (12,400m)
Range	1,740 miles (2,800km)
Powerplant	2x Heinkel He S 011 each rated at 2,865 lb (12.74kN) static thrust
Armament	4 x 30mm MK108 cannons
Reconnaissance role	1 x Rb50/18 camera and 1 x Rb30/18 camera

Gotha Go P.60C

Crew	2, later 3
Wingspan	44ft 4in (13.5m)
Sweep	45° (leading edge)
Wing area	588.78ft² (54.7m²)
Length	35ft 9in (11.5m)
Height	11ft 6in (3.5m)
Gross weight	23,082 miles (10,470kg)
Maximum speed	596mph (959kph)
Ceiling	43,600ft (13,300m)
Range	1,367 miles (2,200km)
Endurance	3.55 hrs
Powerplant	2x Heinkel He S 011 each rated at 2,865 lb (12.74kN) static thrust
Armament	2 x Mk108 30mm cannons firing forward, plus 2 x 30mm Mk108 cannons in centre section firing upwards at an oblique angle. Extensive radar and electronic equipment for the night fighter role.

A study of the Horten Ho IX by Gotha's design team led to an alternative aircraft with a number of obvious improvements. While lacking the elegance of the Horten flying wing, the P60A proposal made a sufficient impression on the RLM to secure approval for further development. Bill Rose Collection

This aircraft was largely based on the P.60B, but featured a tandem cockpit with conventional upright seating and an extended nose section containing air intercept radar equipment and a 'Morgenstern' (Morningstar) antenna. A variant of this design was considered which would accommodate three crew members and another change was the provision of vertical stabilisers and rudders. It is believed that construction of a prototype P.60C continued until quite late in the war, but the aircraft was finally destroyed. Apparently, very little documentation for this project survived.

The Hortens earned a reputation for being difficult to get along with and it appears they were not entirely happy about anyone else trying to improve on their work. However, the RLM recognised the superior features of the P.60 series and so did the American scientists who studied the project after the war. They concluded that although the P.60 showed greater induced drag resulting in a slight loss of climbing rate and ceiling when compared to the Go 229, the P.60 was a more stable design with better directional control. Although the RLM had been impressed with the P.60, further developments of the Gotha Go 299 were planned which included a radar-equipped night-fighter known as the Go 229B.

Following completion of the Go 229 prototypes at Friedrichsroda, a brief period of flight-testing was anticipated before the first batch of production aircraft were transported to Brandis for operational deployment as replacements for the Messerschmitt Me 163B rocket interceptors.

The limited trials that had taken place with the powered and unpowered Horten Ho IX aircraft indicated that it was faster than the Me 262 jet fighter, but less manoeuvrable than the Me 163B rocket-powered interceptor. Nevertheless, it was still more than capable of attacking the anticipated high-altitude USAAF B-29 bombers.

Horten People's Fighter

Before manufacture of the Go 229 commenced, the Hortens were already working on an improved successor to this aircraft designated as the Ho X which was expected to enter service in 1946 as the new Volksjäger (People's fighter). There is some confusion about this design because the designation Ho X appears to have been applied to several different projects. This was apparently done for security and disinformation purposes. However, the intended successor to the Go 229 was a compact one-man flying wing aircraft with a central fuselage section and a completely faired-in cockpit accommodating the pilot in a seated position. The design had two intakes for the turbojet just behind the cockpit on each side of the fuselage. It utilised a tricycle undercarriage and a production fighter would have been armed with three forward firing cannons.

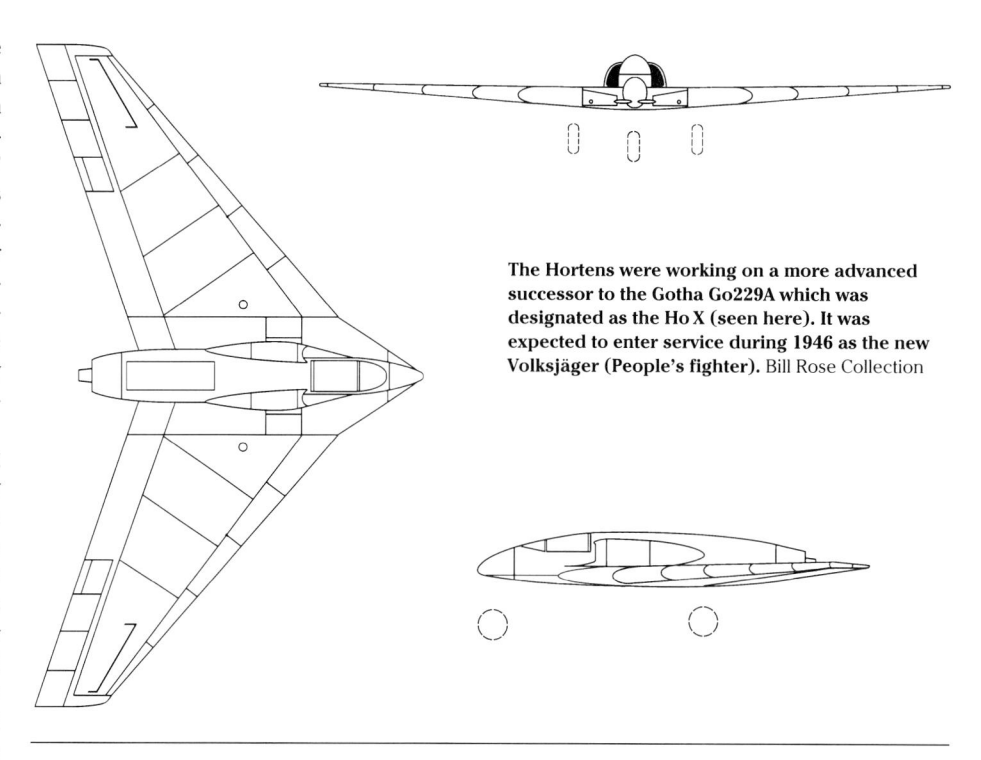

A second, more advanced design with an arrowhead appearance was also called the Ho X. It had a 60° leading edge sweep and was powered by a single turbojet in the rear of the body with the inlet just above and behind the cockpit canopy. Some illustrations indicate an engine nacelle beneath the wing. No vertical control surfaces appear to have been envisaged and the aircraft would be supported on the ground by a tricycle undercarriage. The pilot would fly this aircraft in a prone position. Almost nothing is known about this design and may have been more closely related to the Ho XIII which is discussed shortly. During autumn 1944, several small models of Ho X designs were built and test flown. These are said to have had wingspans of about 9ft 10in (3m). Nothing is currently known about these trials, but the construction of a full sized prototype followed at Göttingen Airfield. The Ho X aircraft was assembled using the same materials and methods as the Ho IX with a welded tubular steel central framework and wings made from wooden components covered with plywood panels. The aircraft may have been either of previously mentioned designs and was intended to be flown as a glider first then fitted with a 240hp (179kW) Argus As10C inverted V8 piston engine and a pusher propeller for powered trials. This would be followed by a more refined second version, probably equipped with a BMW003A turbojet.

It is not clear what stage of development this project reached by the end of the war, but Luftwaffe personnel destroyed the Ho X before Allied forces arrived. Nearly all documentation for the Ho X was burnt or simply disappeared and the Horten Brothers remained less than forthcoming about this project after hostilities ceased.

The Hortens were working on a more advanced successor to the Gotha Go229A which was designated as the Ho X (seen here). It was expected to enter service during 1946 as the new Volksjäger (People's fighter). Bill Rose Collection

Horten Ho X Volksjäger

Crew	1
Wingspan	45ft 11in (14m)
Sweep	Initially 60° at the nose and 43° to the wingtips. (Leading edge)
Wing area	376.7ft² (35m²)
Wing loading	35.5 lb/ft² (173.3kg/m²)
Length	23ft 8in (7.21m)
Height	7ft 6in (2.28m)
Gross weight	13,393 lb (6,075kg)
Powerplant	1 x BMW003A turbojet rated at 1,760 lb (7.8kN) static thrust, or preferably 1 x Heinkel HeS 011A turbojet, rated at 2,865 lb (12.74kN) static thrust. (Early prototype: 1 x 240hp (179kW) Argus As10C V 8 piston engine in pusher configuration)
Maximum speed	684mph (1,100kph) – He S 011A
Ceiling	50,000ft (15,250m) – He S 011A
Range	1,243 miles (2,000km) – He S 011A
Armament	1 x 30mm Mk108 cannon and 2 x 20mm MG151 cannons

German World War 2 Flying Wing Development

Left: **Developed from small models, the Horten Ho XIIIa was a single-seat glider built with a sweep of 60° to test various ideas about future supersonic flight. Trials began in 1944 and the next (eventual) step would have been construction of a Ho XIIIb prototype with supersonic performance.**
Bill Rose Collection

Bottom: **The Ho XIIIb supersonic fighter was the Horten brothers' most advanced concept that would have used a mixture of rocket and jet propulsion. This is believed to be the general appearance of the design.** Bill Rose Collection

Horten Supersonic Fighter

By 1943, the Hortens were discussing the possibility of supersonic flight. While this remained uncharted territory, they decided to experiment with a highly swept glider that would provide an understanding of slow speed handling with a highly swept configuration that might by capable of reaching or exceeding Mach 1.

The glider was designated Ho XIIIa and construction is believed to have begun in early 1944. The aircraft used wings from the Ho III attached to a new central section which provided a span of 39ft 4in (12m) and a sweep of 60°. The design was very clean with few protrusions apart from a dorsal spoiler and there were no vertical control surfaces. The pilot was housed in a gondola arrangement, mounted below the centre section, with access via a tail cone cover. In an emergency, the pilot would jettison this cover and slide out the back of the unit. The first test flight took place at Göttingen Airfield on 27 November 1944 and a further 19 flights were conducted at Hornberg by Hermann Strebel who reported that the glider handled well although he complained about poor roll control, limited forward visibility and landing problems caused by the extended skid.

Nevertheless, the Hortens were contemplating the construction of a more advanced prototype that would be powered by an Argus As10 piston engine in a pusher configuration. But this never came about and at the end of the war a group of Russian soldiers who had just been liberated from a prison camp discovered Ho XIIIa and destroyed it. Furthermore, all the plans and research material for this project vanished without a trace. It now appears that the Ho XIIIb was the anticipated final development of this programme and it was expected to have supersonic performance under certain conditions. Looking very much like an advance Lippisch design, this fighter would have been about the same size as the Ho XIIIa with the same 60° wing sweep. But unlike the glider, there would have been a substantial upright fin containing the cockpit in very similar fashion to the proposed supersonic Lippisch P.13.

This similarity has often been remarked on although Reimar Horten denied any knowledge of Lippisch's work during his time in post-war London. However, this seems highly unlikely and there was almost certainly wartime contact between the Hortens and

Horten Ho XIIIa Glider

Crew	1
Wingspan	39ft 4in (12m)
Wing area	387.5ft² (36m²)
Sweep	60° (leading edge)
Length	32ft 9in (10m)
Height	Unknown
Aspect ratio	4.0
Empty weight	550 lb (250kg)
Take-off weight	727 lb (330kg) approx
Powerplant	None
Maximum speed	111mph (180kph)
Stall speed	27mph (44kph)
Landing speed	27mph (44kph)
Ceiling	Unknown
Range	N/A
Ballast	Water
Armament	None

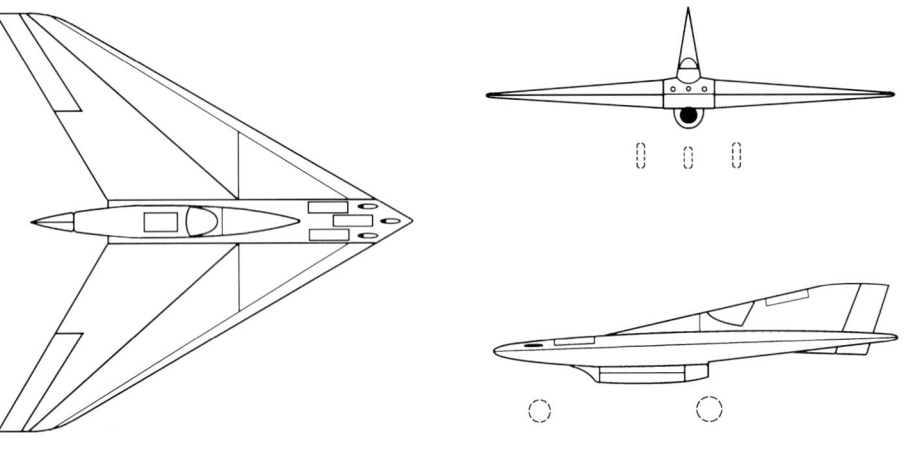

Horten XIIIb (Ho X) Supersonic Fighter

Crew	1
Wingspan	39ft 4in (12m)
Sweep	60° (leading edge)
Length	39ft 4in (12m)
Height	Unknown
Powerplant	1 x BMW003R combined turbojet, producing 2,205 lb (9.8kN) static thrust and a BMW109-718 liquid fuel rocket engine providing 882 lb (3.92kN) thrust
Maximum speed	1,118mph (1,800kph)
Ceiling	50,000ft (15,240m) approx
Range	Unknown
Armament	2 x 30mm MG213 cannons

Secret Projects: Flying Wings and Tailless Aircraft

Original artwork for the Horten Ho XVIII strategic jet bomber, looking decidedly advanced for its time. Bill Rose Collection

Lippisch. The supersonic Ho XIIIb would have been powered by a mixed propulsion system. This could have been either a BMW003R combined turbojet linked to a BMW109-718 rocket engine or a Heinkel He S 011 turbojet and a supplementary Walter rocket engine. The fighter was expected to have a high rate of climb and be capable of maintaining supersonic level flight during a combat mission. The Hortens believed that a maximum speed of Mach 1.4 was realistic, although this may have been rather optimistic. Supported on the ground by a retractable tricycle undercarriage, the Ho XIIIb would have been armed with two 30mm MG 213 cannons. The Ho XIIIb represented the cutting edge of aircraft design in 1945. Proposals to have this aircraft in service by 1946 seem like wishful thinking, but the Ho XIII project shows how much progress had been made in a few short years and explains why the Allies were so eager to secure details of these programmes.

Horten Amerika Bomber

Another major design project to be undertaken by the Horten brothers was a long-range flying wing bomber. In 1944, the RLM issued a requirement to the leading German aircraft contractors for a long-range bomber that was capable of undertaking attacks on America's eastern seaboard. The Luftwaffe wanted a high altitude aircraft capable of delivering four tons of bombs (or possibly one special weapon) to a chosen target and completing the round trip of about 7,000 miles (11,265km) without refuelling.

Five submissions were received by the RLM, although every company expressed concerns that the requirement was too demanding with prevailing technology. As a consequence, these designs were rejected and the RLM requested fresh proposals. The Hortens had not been approached to participate in the first competition but were aware that it had not been a success, so they decided to start design work on a flying wing aircraft which they called the Ho XVIII Amerika Bomber. By 1 January 1945, the brothers had produced about 10 initial concepts, mainly differing in the number of engines used and their positioning.

The design preferred by the Hortens was a large, smoothly-contoured flying wing with four or six buried engines. This resembled a cross between the Ho IX fighter and the modern B-2A bomber in appearance. Advanced Heinkel He S 011 turbojets were the preferred method of propulsion, although it was accepted that Jumo 004B turbojets might be adequate. The possibility of using turboprops in a similar configuration to the Northrop B-35 was also briefly considered and rejected. Engine intakes were located in the inner leading edge and the idea of using a rocket assisted launch trolley and landing skids was discussed as a weight saving measure. One further idea considered by the Hortens was in-flight refuelling, although it remained relatively new and unexplored technology and met with final rejection. On 25 February 1945, the Hortens were invited to present the details of their Amerika Bomber proposals at an RLM review in Berlin that was attended by representatives of the five other aircraft companies who were participants in the contest.

No decisions were made at that time, although several days later the Hortens were invited to Reichsmarshall Göring's office and advised by him that their design had been selected. They were told that Junkers would be responsible for building the new Amerika Bomber with assistance from Messerschmitt. A meeting between the Hortens and engineers from Junkers and Messerschmitt was arranged and when it took place there was considerable disagreement about the design with Junkers engineers recommending a major revision of the Horten's Ho XVIIIa proposal. Junkers wanted to add a large central fin and rudder to the bomber and the Hortens reluctantly agreed to this, plus the use of six Jumo 004B turbojets located beneath the wing in two nacelles and a fully retractable tricycle undercarriage.

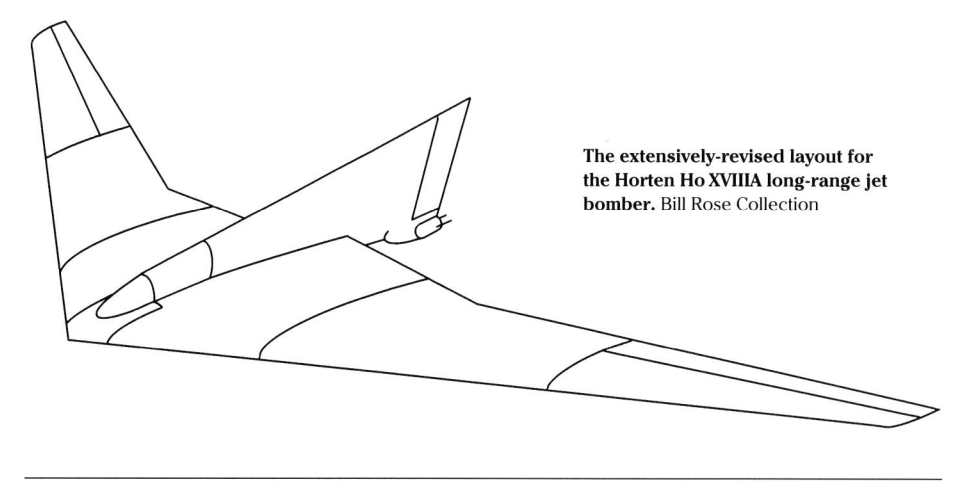

The extensively-revised layout for the Horten Ho XVIIIA long-range jet bomber. Bill Rose Collection

German World War 2 Flying Wing Development

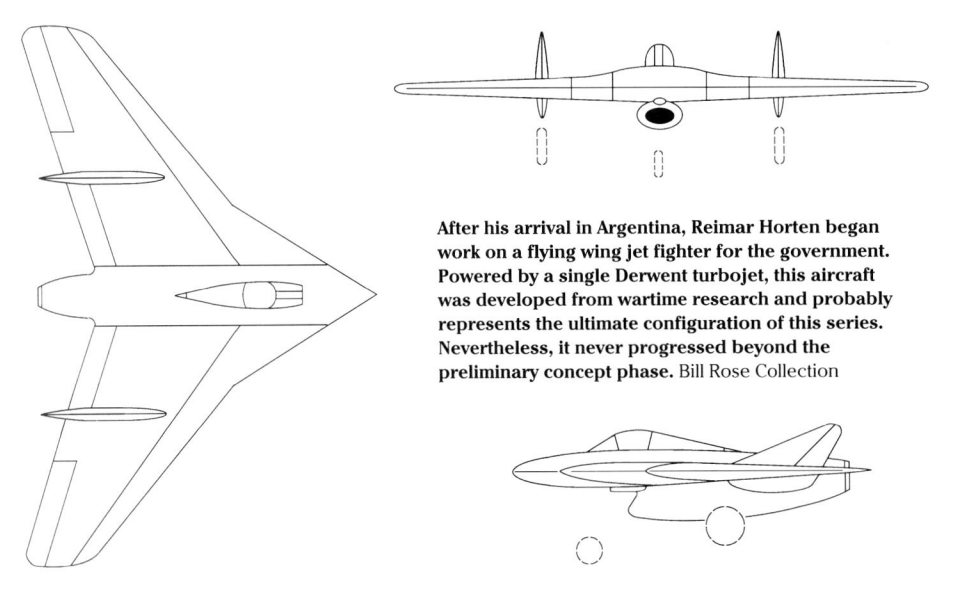

After his arrival in Argentina, Reimar Horten began work on a flying wing jet fighter for the government. Powered by a single Derwent turbojet, this aircraft was developed from wartime research and probably represents the ultimate configuration of this series. Nevertheless, it never progressed beyond the preliminary concept phase. Bill Rose Collection

Horten Ho XVIIIa Early Specification

Crew	4
Wingspan	98ft 6in (30m)
Wing area	1,780ft² (165.3m²)
Sweep	Unknown
Length	Unknown
Gross weight	73,000lb (33,112kg)
Fuel capacity (max)	6,000 US gal
Powerplant	6 x Junkers Jumo 004B turbojets, each rated at 1,980lb (8.8kN) static thrust
Maximum speed	560mph (900kph)
Ceiling	52,500ft (16,000m)
Range	5,593 miles (9,000km)
Armament	Forward and rearward firing defensive 30mm Mk108 cannons.
Bomb load	8,820lb (4,000kg)

Horten XVIIIb Bomber

Crew	3
Wingspan	137ft 9in (42m)
Length	62ft 4in (19m)
Sweep	35° (leading edge)
Gross weight	97,000lb (44,000kg)
Powerplant	4 x Heinkel He S 011 each rated at 2,865lb (12.74kN) of static thrust
Maximum speed	530mph (852kph)
Ceiling	Unknown
Range	6,835 miles (11,000km)
Endurance	27 hours
Armament	Forward and rearward firing defensive 30mm Mk108 cannons.
Bomb load	8,820lb (4,000kg)

Although initially agreeing to these proposals, Reimar Horten remained unhappy about the modifications and set about making further alterations that resulted in a new aircraft called the Ho XVIIIb.

His revisions were accepted and it was now agreed that four Heinkel He S 011 turbojets would power the aircraft and these would be located in underwing pods attached to struts containing the landing gear. It is clear that there was considerable pressure being exerted on everyone involved with this project. The RLM wanted the long-range bomber in service at the earliest possible date and Junkers was instructed to start production as soon as was practical. Subsequently, two huge bomb-proof underground hangars near Kahla were prepared for manufacture and assembly, while suitable runways were built at the site to facilitate testing. It is possible that some rudimentary construction of the first Ho XVIIIb was underway when the war ended and the RLM expected this prototype to be completed during autumn 1945, which seems to have been very wishful thinking! Exactly how the aircraft would have performed is debatable, especially as gas turbine technology was still at an early stage. Engine reliability was poor and turbojets like the Junkers Jumo 004 were worn out after 25 hours of use. Even if the war had lasted long enough for the Luftwaffe to field a few intercontinental jet bombers capable of reaching America or Soviet industrial areas beyond the Urals, it would have made little difference to the outcome of events.

Following the defeat of Nazi Germany, Reimar and Walter Horten briefly worked for the British. Reimar then travelled to Argentina where he undertook a number of officially sponsored aviation projects, while Walter remained in West Germany. Having assembled a small team of engineers at the Instituto Aerotécnico at Córdoba (later the Fábrica Militar de Aviones – FMA), Reimar Horten produced an initial design for a single-seat jet fighter, which was classified as top-secret.

These studies began with a flying wing concept, heavily based on the Horten Ho IX and Horten Ho X. Powered by a single Rolls-Royce Derwent turbojet with a dorsal intake, the aircraft utilised mid-wing stabilising fins with rudders and a fully retractable undercarriage. The armament would probably have been two or four cannons and although performance estimates are unknown, it would have been in the class of other contemporary single-engine jet fighters. Although this concept was never built, Reimar Horten worked on many other aircraft designs.

One project that began in 1951 and finally flew in 1960 was the IAe.38 cargo aircraft. This was a four-engine flying wing design with a span of 105ft (32m) that flew on four occasions. It was an interesting aircraft that reflected wartime developments, but finally met with cancellation in 1962.

The partly completed IA38 transport aircraft, designed by Reimar Horten in Argentina during the 1950s. The slow pace of construction meant that it was outclassed by the time it finally flew and met with cancellation in 1962. Peter Nash

Secret Projects: Flying Wings and Tailless Aircraft

Junkers Flying Wing Projects

In 1943, a team of designers working under Dr Heinrich Hertel (1902-1982) began to consider possible ways of meeting future RLM requirements for a new long-range high performance bomber. Their favoured choice was a flying wing aircraft. The project was designated EF.130 and as the concept steadily evolved, a decision was made to power the aircraft with four BMW003 or preferable Heinkel He S 011 turbojets which would be mounted side-by-side towards the centre-rear of the flying wing's upper side.

Junkers Ju EF128

Crew	1 (2 seats for a proposed all-weather variant)
Wingspan	29ft 2in (8.9m)
Sweep	45° (leading edge)
Wing area	189.4ft² (17.6m²)
Length	23ft (7.05m)
Height	8ft 8in (2.65m)
Fuselage width	4ft 2in (1.27m)
Fuselage area	231.42ft² (21.5m²)
Empty weight	5,747 lb (2,607kg)
Gross weight	8,988 lb (4,077kg)
Max wing loading	47 lb/ft² (231kg/m²)
Fuel weight	2,755 lb (1,250kg)
Powerplant	1 x Heinkel He S 011A turbojet rated at 2,865 lb (12.74kN) static thrust
Maximum speed	562mph (905kph) at sea level, 615mph (990kph) at altitude
Ceiling	45,000ft (13,716m)
Armament	2 x 30mm Mk108 cannons

Junkers EF.130

Crew	3
Wingspan	78ft 9in (24m)
Sweep	Unknown
Wing area	1,291ft² (120m²)
Length	36ft (11m)
Height	Unknown
Gross weight	83,790 lb (38,000kg)
Maximum speed	615mph (990kph)
Ceiling	40,000ft (12,192m)
Range	4,350 miles (7,000km)
Powerplant	4 x BMW003A turbojets, each rated at 1,760 lb (7.8kN) static thrust or 4 x Heinkel He S 011A turbojets, each rated at 2,865 lb (12.74kN) static thrust
Armament	8,820 lb (4,000kg) bomb load, defensive rearward firing 30mm cannons possibly two forward 30mm cannons

Much of the initial aerodynamic work for this project was undertaken by DFS which resulted in the aircraft sometimes being referred to as the DFS 130.

Construction-wise, the EF.130 would be fabricated from low-cost materials with steel components in critical or load bearing areas and wooden sections wherever possible. A crew of three would be housed in a pressurised glazed cockpit that protruded forward from the leading edge and the aircraft would be supported by a tricycle undercarriage. Two vertical stabilisers with rudders were envisaged. The design was in the same general class as Arado's Ar E.555 and the tailless Messerschmitt P.1108. Wind tunnel models were constructed and tested, but the aircraft failed to win acceptance with the RLM.

At the same time, Dr Hertel's office was undertaking a parallel study for a smaller flying wing fighter which received the reference EF.128. The design was for a compact single-seat, single-engine jet fighter armed with two 30mm Mk108 cannons, each carrying 100 rounds and there was the option of fitting two additional cannons. The fuselage would be constructed from welded steel and many parts of the wings would be made from wood.

Each wing carried a vertical stabiliser with a rudder and the aircraft would be supported on the ground by a retractable tricycle undercarriage. Junkers engineers hoped to use a Heinkel He S 011A turbojet rated at 2,865 lb (12.74kN) static thrust for propulsion, although it is likely that the option of fitting a Jumo 004 engine was considered. Air intakes for the turbojet were located on each side of the fuselage beneath the wings. Each wing carried a 118 Imp Gallon (540 litre) fuel tank and the main 225 Imp Gallon (1,025 litre) fuel tank was positioned at the centre of the aircraft between the cockpit and engine. The pressurised cockpit was extensively armoured and an ejector seat was fitted.

In February 1945, proposals for the EF.128 were submitted to the Emergency Fighter Competition. The outcome is not entirely clear as Junkers continued to work on this design, producing an engineering mock-up complete with a Heinkel He S 011 engine and undertaking wind tunnel testing with scale models. Plans were also drawn up for a stretched version of the fighter able to carry a second crew member with a radar system and greater fuel load. It is unclear how far this project had progressed by the end of the war, but relatively little hardware or documentation survived.

Another very interesting Hertel flying wing project came about during the final months of the war while he was heavily involved in development of the Horten Amerika bomber. Carrying double the Horten aircraft's bomb load, this larger aircraft was designed to have true intercontinental range, allowing strikes deep into America and Russia. The design reference is uncertain, but Hertel later called this study the Very Long Range Bomber (VLRB) project and he anticipated a crew of eight to ten. Hertel also believed that this large flying wing would make a good peacetime transport and passenger aircraft.

The fuselage was fully integrated with the wing and there was a rather ugly nose intake for the engines positioned directly below the cockpit. Hertel planned to use eight Heinkel He S 109 011 or eight Jumo 109 012 engines turbojets buried in the fuselage. The aircraft

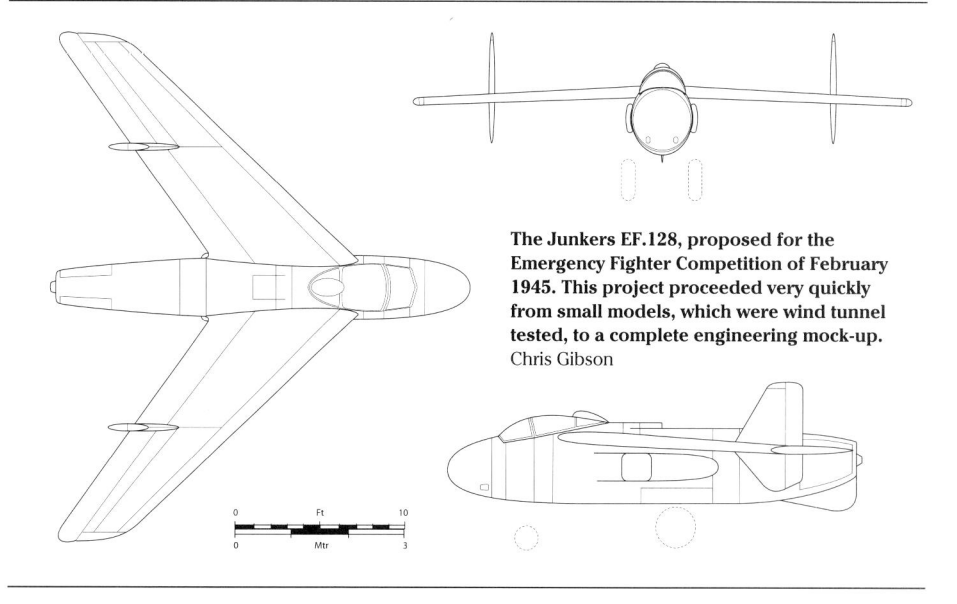

The Junkers EF.128, proposed for the Emergency Fighter Competition of February 1945. This project proceeded very quickly from small models, which were wind tunnel tested, to a complete engineering mock-up.
Chris Gibson

German World War 2 Flying Wing Development

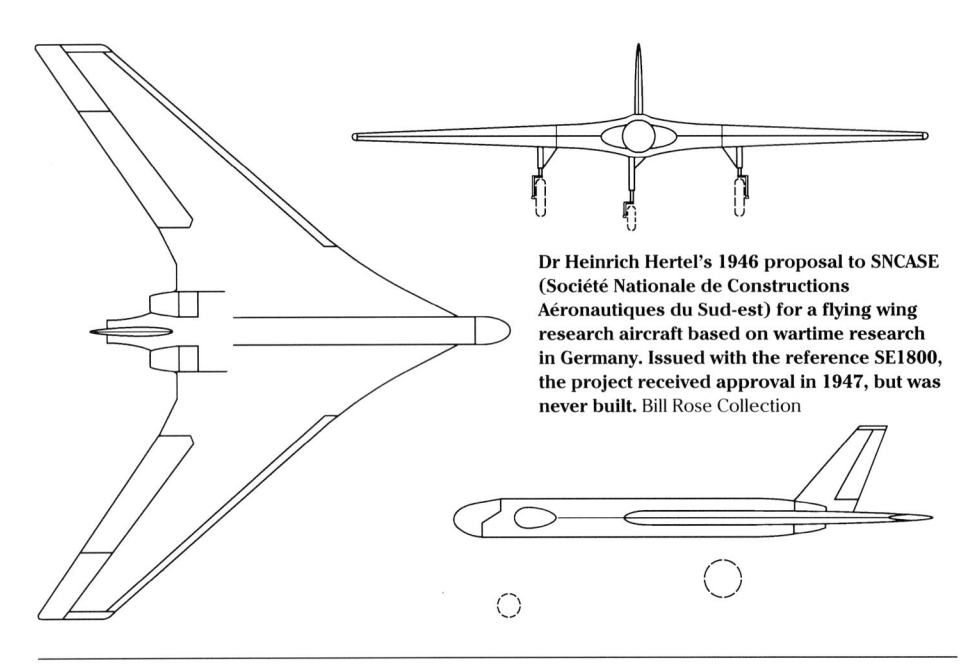

Dr Heinrich Hertel's 1946 proposal to SNCASE (Société Nationale de Constructions Aéronautiques du Sud-est) for a flying wing research aircraft based on wartime research in Germany. Issued with the reference SE1800, the project received approval in 1947, but was never built. Bill Rose Collection

Junkers Very Long Range Bomber (VLRB)

Crew	8-10
Wingspan	168ft 3in (51.2m)
Sweep	45° (leading edge)
Wing area	11,840ft² (1,100m²)
Length	101ft 8in (31m)
Gross weight	198,360lb (88,974kg)
Max wing loading	47 lb/ft² (231kg/m²)
Powerplant	8 x Heinkel He S 011A turbojet rated at 2,865 lb (12.74kN) static thrust or 8 x Junkers Jumo 109 012 turbojets
Maximum speed	640mph (1,030kph)
Ceiling	Unknown
Range	10,557 miles (17,000km)
Armament	Defensive cannons in upper and lower remote controlled turrets. 17,636 lb (8,000kg) bomb load

Project SE.1800

Crew	1 (possibly 2)
Wingspan	55ft 9in (17m)
Wing area	785ft² (73m²)
Sweep	45° (leading edge)
Length	39ft 6in (12m)
Empty weight	20,086 lb (9,111kg)
Gross weight	33,069 lb (15,000kg)
Maximum speed	621mph (1,000kph)
Endurance	2 hours
Powerplant	2 x Rolls-Royce Nene turbojets rated at 5,000 lb (22.2kN) static thrust, or 2 x SNECMA Atar 101 turbojets, initially rated at 3,700 lb (16.45kN) static thrust
Armament	None

would be fitted with a single upright stabilising fin and rudder with support on the ground provided by a robust tricycle undercarriage and two-wheel nose unit and four wheels on each main strut. It was also suggested that small outrigger wheels might have been required during landings.

Assistance with the aerodynamics for this design was provided by DFS and an initial proposal was submitted to the RLM in the last month of the European war although nothing came of this very ambitious project. However, the story did not end there and when hostilities ceased Dr Hertel was recruited by the French to work on new aircraft projects.

In 1946, the Marignane design office of Société Nationale de Constructions Aéronautiques du Sud-est (SNCASE) began to consider various ideas for a flying wing research aircraft and Dr Hertel took the opportunity to propose a design that drew heavily on his VLRB study. SNCASE was impressed with Hertel's ideas and assigned the project reference SE.1800. Official approval was granted on 30 April 1947 (Document No 07776) with the aim of drawing up plans for a tailless subsonic flying wing aircraft.

This was almost a twin-engine, one-third-size demonstrator version of the large flying wing bomber that Hertel designed in 1945.

It was hoped this study would lead to several military options, which included a high performance transport aircraft with a gross weight of 250 metric tons and a heavy fighter with a cruise speed of 600mph (970kph) and a range of 2,050 miles (3,300km). In appearance, SE.1800 was more elegant than the VLRB. It had a contoured cockpit and engine intakes in the wing root leading edges. A tri-

cycle undercarriage was planned and the wing profile remained very similar to the wartime bomber design. But the French authorities finally concluded that the project was too ambitious and cancelled it on 1 December 1948.

At this time, Hertel was working with the German scientist Dr Helmut Zborowski who was in the process of setting up an aviation design consultancy at Brunoy called Bureau Technique Zborowski (BTZ). But Hertel decided not to remain in France and he returned to West Germany during 1950, accepting an academic post at the Berlin Technical University. In 1959, he joined Focke-Wulf in Bremen where he worked as a design consultant until his retirement.

Messerschmitt Me 163

In the late 1930s, Heinkel at Rostock-Marienehe secretly built a small experimental rocket-powered aircraft called the He 176. The He 176 flew and was not a great success, but it indirectly led to a separate RLM sponsored rocketplane programme called Projekt X that was undertaken by Dr Alexander Lippisch and his team at DFS. Lippisch had produced an advanced tailless glider known as the DFS 40 and his new rocket-propelled design was partly based on this aircraft. In 1938, an area of the DFS facility was prepared for assembly of the mainly wooden prototype that had been given the reference DFS 194. But working space was extremely limited and it was agreed that only the wings would be built at DFS and Heinkel would assist with construction of the fuselage.

Because the project was classified as top secret, there were security restrictions that began to cause problems, so the RLM decided that Lippisch and his team of 12 engineers would move to Messerschmitt at Augsburg. This took place on 2 January 1939 and Projekt X was able to continue in an enclosed environment with less outside meddling. Lippisch's group was assigned a new design office called Department L and the relocation seemed to work well, although Willy Messerschmitt considered this an unwelcome imposition from the outset.

The DFS 194 had been largely completed at Darmstadt by the time Lippisch and his staff moved to Messerschmitt, so the airframe was transported to Augsburg where it was finished by skilled assembly workers borrowed from the Bf 110 production line.

Lippisch had originally intended to test the DFS 194 with a piston engine driving a pusher propeller, but this idea was dropped and the

DFS 194 was adapted to accept a Walter RI-203 rocket engine, modified to provide a reduced maximum thrust of 660 lb (2.93kN) for the purpose of improving endurance. When the work was completed in early 1940, the DFS 194 was transported to Peenemünde-Karlshagen where the engine was installed.

Heinrich 'Heini' Dittmar was the test pilot assigned to this project. He began with gliding trials which graduated to powered flights (after being towed into the air), followed by sharp starts (on the ground) using the rocket engine. Initially, the speed was limited to about 190mph (300kph), but Dittmar had soon pushed this to 342mph (550kph). The construction of two Me 163A prototypes was now underway at Augsburg and although Projekt X was highly classified, the programme did not receive priority, so assembly of these aircraft was slow with much of the work only taking place when skilled personnel could be spared from the Messerschmitt production lines. Because the rocket-powered Heinkel He 176 had proved disappointing, there was half-hearted official interest in Projekt X. But once reports of the DFS 194 trials at Peenemünde-Karlshagen reached the RLM, there was an abrupt change of attitude. Lippisch was now receiving the kind of support he needed with the RLM deciding that Department L would receive more staff and the number of prototypes should be increased to six.

Lippisch had initially considered a military adaptation of the DFS 194 which progressed to a more refined proposal known as P.01-111 that was completed in September 1939. His designers then began to consider an armed version of the more sophisticated Me 163A prototype. This resulted in a series of proposals and minor variants that are too numerous to list, but all adhered to the same basic design philosophy.

Development of the interceptor continued for some time after the Me 163A had been selected for prototyping. Two variants considered by Lippisch in 1941 utilised the same overall dimensions as the Me 163, but differed in the cockpit arrangement. The P.01-117 was conceived with a flush, pressurised cockpit, accommodating the pilot in a prone position and P.01-118 was to have a complicated internal arrangement that allowed the pilot to swivel for the optimal position. Both these designs received serious consideration, but neither was accepted for further development.

Lippisch also examined the possibility of producing a turbojet version of the Me 163 after early details of production jet engines had been reviewed. This resulted in several proposals and the most notable was the P.01-115 conceived in mid-1941 that would be powered by a BMW003 engine. This aircraft was similar to the Me 163, but the fuselage was broader along its entire length and there was an engine intake above and behind the cockpit canopy. A supplementary rocket engine was also considered as an option. Nothing came of these studies, but the idea would resurface in the future.

With construction of the first Me 163A prototypes at an advanced stage, work began on formalising the rocket-propelled interceptor that received the reference Me 163B. This design resembled the Me 163A, but it would steadily evolve into a new aircraft during the months that followed. Me 163A V1 was completed in early 1941 and transported to Lechfeld for unpowered glide tests. Dittmar flew the aircraft which was towed into the air by a Messerschmitt Bf 110 twin-engine fighter. The Me 163A performed well, although there were landing problems due to its very flat gliding angle. With a sinking speed of about 5ft (1.52m) per second at 137mph (220kph) and lack of flaps, precise touchdowns were very difficult and this led to a couple of potentially dangerous incidents.

By mid-1941, the first two Me 163A prototypes (V1 and V4) had undergone minor modifications and were taken to Peenemünde-Karlshagen for installation of their Walter HWK RII-203b rocket engines and further testing. The fuel used by the RII-203b was

DFS 194

Crew	1
Wingspan	30ft 6in (9.29m)
Wing area	188.84ft^2 (17.54m^2)
Length	17ft 8in (5.38m)
Weight	4,620 lb (2,095kg)
Maximum speed	342mph (550kph)
Powerplant	1 x Walter HWK R.1-203 liquid fuel rocket engine providing a max thrust of 661 lb (2.94kN)

Below left: **Alexander Lippisch's Delta IVc, which received the official designation DFS39. The Delta IVc was the final incarnation of this small flying wing. The aircraft handled well and was considered extremely stable, providing invaluable aerodynamic data for the Projekt X programme, which eventually resulted in the Messerschmitt Me 163 rocket-powered interceptor.** Bill Rose Collection

Below: **One of the Projekt X wind-tunnel test models built during the late 1930s. It bears a close resemblance to the final design and is seen suspended upside down, which was standard practice during these trials.** Bill Rose Collection

German World War 2 Flying Wing Development

Me 163B-1A

Crew	1
Wingspan	30ft 7in (9.32m)
Wing area	199.13ft² (18.49m²)
Sweep	23.3° (quarter-chord)
Length	18ft 8in (5.73m)
Height (on dolly)	9ft (2.76m)
Empty weight	4,200lb (1,905kg)
Gross weight	9,500lb (4,309kg)
Maximum speed	596mph (959kph) at altitude
Rate of climb	11,500ft/min (3,505m/min)
Ceiling	39,000ft (11,887m)
Powered endurance	7min 30sec
Range	50 miles (80km)
Powerplant	1 x Walter HWK 509A-2 liquid fuel rocket engine providing a max thrust of 3,750lb (16.68kN)
Armament	2 x 20mm MG151 cannons with 100rpg or 2 x 30mm Mk108 cannons with 60rpg

The first prototype Me 163A (Werk Nr 1630000001) assigned the reference V4, which made its initial test flight at Lechfeld in spring 1941. Deutsches Bundesarchiv

Accidents, sometimes with fatal consequences were continual throughout Germany's rocket interceptor programme, primarily due to the extremely dangerous fuels used to power the rocket engine. This photograph is believed to show Me 163A (GG-EA) V5 after an incident at Peenemünde. Bill Rose Collection

Me 163A V4 making a rocket-powered take-off. Bill Rose Collection

a mixture of highly corrosive concentrated hydrogen peroxide (T-Stoff) and a calcium permanganate liquid catalyst (Z-Stoff), which converted the hydrogen peroxide to a hot steam. This was a truly dangerous blend that could easily explode, even when carefully handled by highly trained operatives. Such were the hazards posed by the use of Z-Stoff and its tendency to clog jets that a replacement was urgently sought. Nevertheless, thrust produced by these early engines was considerable and the Walter RII-203 provided a controlled output that could be varied from about 330lb (1.46kN) to 1,650lb (7.33kN).

Powered flights began during September 1941 and on 2 October 1941 the fully-fuelled Me 163A V4 piloted by Dittmar was towed into the air behind a Bf 110C and released at an altitude of 13,124ft (4,000m). Dittmar then ignited the Walter rocket engine and accelerated to a speed of 624mph (1,004kph) where he ran into severe stability problems and had to throttle back. He had broken all existing air speed records by a significant margin, but the achievement remained secret. Meanwhile, the RLM was so impressed by the flight they ordered the newly designed Me 163B into immediate production.

Having analysed the problems encountered by Dittmar, Lippisch's team decided that the wing profile of the forthcoming Me 163B required alteration to protect against wingtip stall. This resulted in special fixed slots being fitted to the outer wing section just ahead of the elevons. Although production of the Me 163B began on 1 December 1941, there were continuing problems with development of the higher performance 'Hot' Walter HWK109-509A rocket engine. The tricky Z Stoff catalyst had now been replaced with a mixture of methyl alcohol, hydrazine hydrate and water called C-Stoff, but Walter's scientists at Kiel had run into major difficulties with the new engine. This meant that when the first Me 163B rolled off the production line in April 1942, there was no propulsion system for it. It would be another year before these problems were resolved and late July 1943 before the new engines were delivered.

The Me 163B differed considerably from the Me 163A and it was designed to carry more fuel which improved the maximum speed, ceiling and range. It was initially intended to arm the aircraft with two 20mm MG151 cannons, but these were later replaced by more effective 30mm Mk108 cannons. The cockpit was unpressurised and pressurisation was considered unnecessary for a relatively short duration mission with the pilot using a face mask. It was also decided to install a substantial amount of forward and rearward armour. However, the unsatisfactory two-wheel dolly that dropped away after take-off was retained and the aircraft would land on a deployable skid and tail wheel.

Difficulties with development of the more advanced rocket engine encouraged Lippisch to design an alternative 'contingency' propeller-driven version of the Me 163B which was assigned the reference Me 334. This aircraft would utilise some of the existing Me 163B components and could be assembled on existing production lines. A forward located 1,475hp (1,100kW) 12-cylinder piston engine would drive a rear-mounted three bladed pusher propeller. The Me 334 would be equipped with a fully retractable tricycle undercarriage and a tailfin and rudder were positioned beneath the rear of the fuselage, offering some protection to the propeller blades during take-offs and landings.

Lippisch also designed a jet-powered Me 163B, which undoubtedly drew on earlier studies. This proposal was called the P.20 and it would be propelled by a single Jumo 004B turbojet, rated at 1,980lb (8.8kN) static thrust. With an engine intake in the lower nose, the fuselage dimensions remained similar to the Me 163B, but there was just enough space to accommodate the Junkers turbojet which had a length of 12ft 8in (3,85m) plus the forward cockpit and fuel tanks. Like the Me 334, this design would also use a fully retractable tricycle undercarriage. Performance estimates were very good for this proposal with a maximum speed of 568mph (914kph), a ceiling of 40,000ft (12,192m) and a range in excess of 500 miles (800km). Armed with two 20mm and two 30mm cannons, the P.20 might have been a very effective low-cost jet interceptor that would have been superior to the later He 162 and perhaps safer to fly. However, a company review compared the P.20 to the rival twin-jet Me 262 and Lippisch's proposal was dropped.

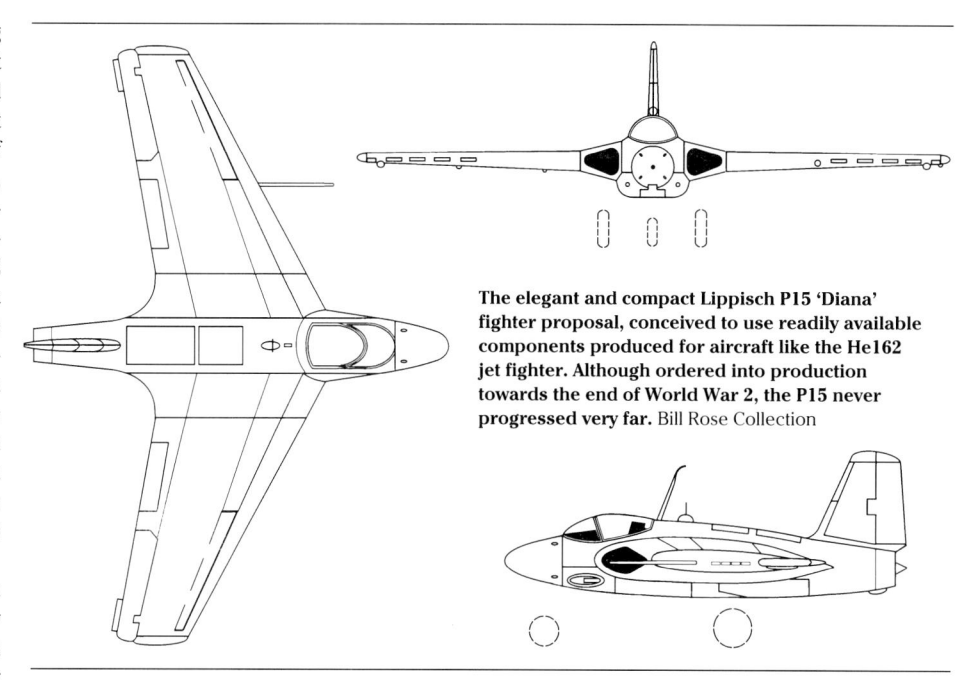

Soon after this, on 1 May 1943, Lippisch left Messerschmitt to become Director of the Vienna Aviation Research Institute and most of his staff went with him. It was undoubtedly for the best as Lippisch was no longer on speaking terms with Willy Messerschmitt.

Dr Lippisch designed one further very promising warplane that was related to the Me 163. In early 1945, he was officially requested to develop an inexpensive alternative to the Heinkel He 162 jet fighter that could be easily assembled from readily available components. He responded by proposing a more streamlined version of the P.20, which evolved into a fighter called the P.15 based around a new fuselage containing a Heinkel He S 011A turbojet, mated to the forward section of a Heinkel He 162. A tricycle undercarriage would be used, employing the main wheels from a Messerschmitt Bf 109 and the wings and tailfin would be very similar to those built for the Me 163C. Intakes for the jet engine would be in the wing roots and the fighter would be armed with two or four can-

The elegant and compact Lippisch P15 'Diana' fighter proposal, conceived to use readily available components produced for aircraft like the He 162 jet fighter. Although ordered into production towards the end of World War 2, the P15 never progressed very far. Bill Rose Collection

Messerschmitt (Lippisch) P.20

Crew	1
Wingspan	30ft 6in (9.3m)
Wing area	186ft² (17.27m²)
Sweep	22° (leading edge)
Aspect ratio	5.0:1
Length	18ft 10in (5.7m)
Height	9ft 10in (3m)
Empty weight	5,707 lb (2,588kg)
Gross weight	7,996 lb (3,628kg)
Maximum speed	560mph (900kph) at altitude
Rate of climb	60ft/sec (18m/sec)
Ceiling	38,000ft (11,582m)
Range	584 miles (940km)
Powerplant	1 x Junkers Jumo 004B turbojet rated at 1,980 lb (8.8kN) static thrust
Armament	2 x 20mm Mk103 cannons and 2 x 30mm Mk108 cannons

Lippisch P.15

Crew	1
Wingspan	33ft 1in (10.08m)
Wing area	215ft² (19.97m²)
Sweep	23° (leading edge)
Length	21ft (6.4m)
Gross weight	7,936 lb (3,600kg)
Powerplant	One Heinkel He S 011A turbojet rated at 2,865 lb (12.74kN) static thrust
Maximum speed	621mph (1,000kph) approx
Armament	2 x 30mm Mk108 cannons in the fuselage and 2 x 20mm MG151 cannons in the wings

German World War 2 Flying Wing Development

Unquestionably the most famous German pilot of the Nazi era, Hanna Reitsch was involved with the testing of several advanced military aircraft and suffered serious injuries in 1942 after crash-landing a defective Me 163B. Bill Rose Collection

nons. Bearing some resemblance to the Me 163 series of designs, this hybrid tailless aircraft offered a good combination of features and it received the name Diana. Production was assigned to Wiener Neustadt Aviation, but the P.15 Diana progressed no further than a scale model by the end of the war.

Development of the Me 163B had been complex and troublesome, but the first production aircraft was test flown as a glider on 26 June 1942 at Lechfeld, having been towed into the air by a Bf 110. By the start of the following year, an evaluation unit known as Erprobungskommando 16 (EK16) had been assembled at Peenemünde-Karlshagen under the leadership of Hauptmann Wolfgang Späte who would go on to become one of Germany's most highly decorated pilots. Soon after their formation, EK16 was relocated to the Bad Zwischenahn Airfield northwest of Oldenberg.

Hanna Reitsch was also involved with early testing of the Me 163 and had been assigned the task of conducting acceptance flights for each Me 163B that left the Regensburg production line. On 30 October 1942, she made a glide test with the fifth aircraft, but the undercarriage dolly failed to separate. Reitsch was forced to make a crash landing and it put her in hospital for many months.

Accidents with these aircraft were common and test pilot Heini Dittmar was badly injured during an uncontrolled Me 163 crash landing on a section of concrete apron. The sudden 20G deceleration caused him serious spinal injuries which confined him to hospital for the next two years. His deputy Rudolph Opitz also experienced a very hard landing in a defective Me 163, and although not so severe, it kept him in hospital for several months. The accidents were investigated by Dr Justus Schneider, who was a consultant working for the Luftwaffe, and he made a number of recommendations. As a consequence, there were attempts to improve the landing skid and make it more capable of absorbing severe impacts, but this turned out to be more difficult than envisaged. Attention then switched to redesigning the pilot's seat to make it torsion-sprung and this became a standard feature for all Me 163 aircraft.

Walter rocket engines were now installed in the Me 163B aircraft and tested, although frequent problems arose with their operation such as the engines cutting out due to turbulence in the fuel outlet. Luftwaffe pilots assigned to EK16 were being trained to fly the Me 163A gliders and by autumn 1943, a significant number of production Me 163B aircraft had been completed at Regensburg. However, a B-17 bombing raid on 17 August 1943 resulted in most of the remaining airframes being destroyed and production was passed to Klemm Technik GmbH which would coordinate dispersed production of components in much smaller facilities. The Me 163B had now received the name Komet (Comet), although pilots often referred to the aircraft within the EK16 as 'The Powered Egg' or 'The Devil's Sledge'.

The best way to deploy the new interceptor remained under consideration and Hauptmann Späte proposed a chain of bases for the aircraft, each separated by a distance of about 90 miles (150km). The rocket fighters would attack the increasing waves of Allied bombers during the inbound and outbound stages of their missions.

The Luftwaffe accepted aspects of the proposal with new bases being selected at Wittmundhafen, Udetfeld, Stargard, Deelen, Husum and Venlo. The first functional rocket fighter staffel (squadron) known as I/JG400 was created during May 1944 and based at Wittmundhafen with most of the personnel being drawn from EK16. But the combat ready aircraft did not arrive until July 1944 and then a decision was taken to relocate operations to Brandis Airfield near Leipzig because

Me 163C

Crew	1
Wingspan	32ft 2in (9.8m)
Wing area	219.583ft² (20.39m²)
Length	23ft 1in (7m)
Height (on dolly)	10ft (3m)
Empty weight	4,850 lb (2,199kg)
Gross weight	11,684 lb (5,299kg)
Max speed at altitude	569mph (915kph)
Service ceiling	40,000ft (12,192m)
Powered endurance	12 minutes
Range	78 miles (125km)
Powerplant	1 x Walter HWK 509C-1 liquid fuel rocket engine providing a max thrust of 4,410 lb (19.61kN)
Armament	2 x 20mm MG151 cannons with 100rpg or 2 x 30mm Mk108 cannons with 60rpg

A Me 163B interceptor during take-off. Like the earlier Me 163A, it had a two-wheel dolly that was dropped after leaving the ground and the aircraft would make a glide landing, touching down on a deployable skid and tail wheel. This saved weight avoided the need for a complicated undercarriage. Bill Rose Collection

Secret Projects: Flying Wings and Tailless Aircraft

A Me 163B caught by the gun camera of a USAAF P-51 Mustang fighter just before it was shot down. USAAF

protection of the local Leuna synthetic fuel plant had been given high priority. Brandis was relatively small and a second-rate airfield – workshops were inadequate, general facilities were poor and there was nowhere safe to store the dangerous fuels used by the Komets which had to be shipped to the airfield by rail. Furthermore, the Leuna facility was close to the limits of the Komet's range. It was a very unsatisfactory situation, but Brandis still became the centre of Komet operations during the remainder of World War 2.

There had been one or two fleeting encounters with Allied aircraft, but the first operational mission took place at the end of July and several kills had been recorded by the beginning of August 1944. By now, the shortcomings of the Me 163B were becoming apparent and the high approach speed during an attack made it difficult for pilots to hit their targets. Additionally, the Mk108 cannons would often jam.

Attacking the bomber formations at high speed with cannon fire presented various problems and consideration had been given to the use of air-to-air R4M rockets. EK16 undertook trials with an adapted Me 163A that was fitted with underwing racks carrying R4Ms, but this did not work out and the idea seems to have been abandoned.

A somewhat different and rather unorthodox idea was then adopted which involved the use of 10 upward-firing 50mm projectiles configured to be recoilless by simultaneously discharging a downward counterweight. A Komet equipped with this system would pass beneath the enemy bomber at high speed and a photoelectric cell would automatically trigger the release of the projectiles at exactly the right moment. Known as the SG-500 Jagdfaust (Fighter Fist), this weapon had been fitted to 12 Me 163Bs by the end of the war and was used operationally with Lt Fritz Kelbs shooting down a B-17G during an interception.

Aside from that, the Me 163B's combat record was poor. It is hard to determine the exact number of kills that can be credited to this aircraft, but it is certainly no more than 15 and the majority were USAAF B-17s.

Although the Me 163 enjoyed an astonishing rate of climb and maximum speed, the fuel burnt at a phenomenal rate of 18.3 lb (8,3kg) per second, leading to rapid depletion. Then the aircraft became very vulnerable and Allied fighter pilots identified this weakness, realising that the best time to attack one of the rocket fighters was during its glide back to base.

Work continued to improve the rocket fighter and two Me 163Bs (V6 and V18) underwent modifications to accept the more powerful two-chamber Walter HWK 109-509 C rocket engine. This was intended for use in the enhanced Messerschmitt Me 163C that entered development after Lippisch and his team left Messerschmitt. Three Me 163C prototypes were completed by Messerschmitt and had been test flown by 1945. This aircraft was a considerable improvement on the Me 163B with a lengthened fuselage and pres-

A Me 163B glides back to base after an operational flight. Bill Rose Collection

German World War 2 Flying Wing Development

Me 263A-1/Junkers Ju 248 V1

Crew	1
Wingspan	31ft 2in (9.5m)
Wing area	191.6ft² (17.8m²)
Aspect ratio	5.07
Length	25ft 10in (7.88m)
Height	10ft 5in (3.17m)
Empty weight	4,640lb (2,105kg)
Gross weight	11,354lb (5,150kg)
Maximum speed	621mph (1,000kph) (HWK509C-4)
Rate of climb	16,400ft/min (HWK509C-4)
Ceiling	45,000ft (13,716m)
Powered endurance	13min
Range	90 miles (144km)
Powerplant	1 x Walther HWK509C-4 liquid fuel rocket engine producing a max thrust of 4,410lb (19.61kN), or 1 x BMW708 rocket engine producing an estimated 5,500lb (24.46kN) thrust
Armament	2 x 30mm Mk108 cannons with 60rpg

surised cockpit. A landing skid was still used, although the tail wheel retracted. Armament was similar but it was planned to fit the Me 163C with the SG-500 Jagdfaust system. The Me 163C addressed some of the earlier criticisms and in overall terms the aircraft was an improvement over the Me 163B, but the Luftwaffe was unimpressed, mainly because the aircraft retained the landing skid system. This saved weight and avoided the need for a complicated undercarriage, but it was possible for a dolly to bounce up from the ground after release and hit the aircraft, or fail to detach, which could be almost as bad.

Using a landing skid also created ground-handling problems and could leave the aircraft vulnerable to attack prior to retrieval. Messerschmitt responded to these concerns at the end of 1943 with proposals for a more advanced aircraft that would be built alongside the Me 163C. Designated as the Me 163D, this new design was wind tunnel tested in model form and then a wooden mock-up was built and shown to RLM officials. Immediate approval was given to proceed with the construction of a prototype and this aircraft was completed by spring 1944 with gliding tests following within a matter of weeks. The Me 163D V1 was essentially a stretched version of the Me 163B with a similar cockpit arrangement, a fully retractable tricycle undercarriage, the improved two chamber Walter rocket engine and larger fuel tanks.

But the RLM were not entirely satisfied with the Me 163D V1 and voiced concerns that Messerschmitt resources had become too stretched to continue with the project. It was then decided that further development of the Me 163D V1 should be passed to Heinrich Hertel's design office at Junkers. The project was now renamed Ju 248 and Hertel's engineers made a series of immediate improvements. These included lowering of the fuselage dorsal section and revising the cockpit which they heavily armoured, pressurised and covered with a blister canopy. Production aircraft would be built in three sections with a removable tail unit to facilitate easy engine maintenance. The wings were similar to those found on the Me 163B, but now used automatic slots and had larger flaps. The aircraft was designed around the Walter HWK109-509C rocket engine, but allowances were made for upgrading to the more advanced BMW708 rocket engine which promised significantly better performance and ran on S Stoff (mostly nitric acid) and R Stoff (crude oxide monoxylidene and triethylamine).

By August 1944, the Ju 248 V1 had been completed at Dessau, and soon after this, glide trials commenced using a Ju 188 bomber as a tow aircraft. For each of these flights the undercarriage was fixed in an extended position and the Ju 248 V1 proved to handle more safely than the Me 163 at low speeds. According to most reliable references, powered flights followed during September or October with speeds in excess of 590mph (950kph) being attained. But there were problems encountered as the centre of pressure moved rearward beyond Mach 0.8 and this was an issue that needed to be addressed. Then a rather petty disagreement arose about the aircraft's designation and Willy Messerschmitt complained to the RLM which instructed Junkers to start using the original reference Me 263.

At an RLM meeting in Berlin during December 1944, it was decided to press ahead with production of the new aircraft, although development slowed with other work taking priority and serious fuel shortages limited further testing. When hostilities ended, the Me 263 V1 was the only example to be completed, but airframes for the V2 and V3 had reached an advanced stage of construction. When Soviet forces secured the Junkers plant, V1 was shipped back to Russia, along with most of the documentation and manufacturing equipment. While the Komet was impressive for its time, this programme can only be regarded as a failure, having diverted valuable manpower and resources from more worthwhile aircraft such as the Me 262 jet fighter. When the final Me 163B rolled off the production line in February 1945, about 365 of these aircraft had been produced.

Japan

During the Me 163's development, Japanese officials were invited to observe test flights under a joint technical exchange agreement. The Japanese were impressed with the aircraft and knew about America's forthcoming Boeing B-29 bomber which would present interception problems for existing fighters. Following a visit to Bad Zwischenahn airfield in 1943 by the Japanese military attachés, a contract was signed for licensed production of the Me 163B and its rocket engine. The Germans would provide blueprints, technical material, fuel formulations and allow inspection of the manufacturing facilities. In addition they would provide several fully functional Walter rocket engines and one airframe with the deal being completed by 1 March 1944.

The Japanese 3,600 ton diesel-electric submarine I-29 *Matsu* (Pine Tree) was used for several highly classified missions during World War 2 and during December 1943, I-29 was sent to German-occupied France with a special delivery of rare metals and various high-priority materials such as morphine. The submarine arrived at Lorient on 11 March 1944 and before returning to Japan, the boat was loaded with a secret cargo that included blueprints and technical documentation for the Me 163, plus several examples of the Walter HWK 509A rocket engine and possibly a Me 163B airframe. On 16 April 1944, 18 passengers boarded the boat and she slipped out of the port. I-29 arrived at Singapore on 14 July and disembarked its passengers. Amongst these was the Berlin naval attaché Eiichi Iwaya, who had been involved in securing the Me 163 deal. He then flew on to Japan and the special cargo remained onboard I-29 for return directly to Kure, Japan. On 26 July 1944, I-29 was detected in the Balintang Channel by Wilkin's USN Submarine Taskforce and attacked by the submarine USS *Sawfish* which fired four torpedoes at her. Three hit I-29 and she sank immediately.

Mitsubishi already had enough technical documentation to begin producing copies of the Walter rocket engine (some sources indicate that an engine was already in its possession), but it had no aircraft capable of using it. With the disappearance and presumed loss of I-29, its only reference material was a Me 163B handbook that had been provided to Eiichi Iwaya. The accuracy of this claim remains open to question with one unconfirmed report suggesting that some of the Me 163B documentation plus a Walter rocket engine (and a Junkers Jumo 004 turbojet) were unloaded at Singapore and transported directly to Japan.

A Japanese MXY8 Akigusa (Autumn Grass) training glider built by the Naval Arsenal in Yokosuka.
Bill Rose Collection

B-29 raids were now underway and there was an urgent need to produce an interceptor capable of engaging these fast, high-flying bombers. Something had to be done and there was general agreement that waiting for the next submarine to arrive was not an option. After some discussion, it was decided to build a reasonably authentic copy of the Me 163B based on available information. It was felt that there should be no significant differences with the specification as the Messerschmitt aircraft was a proven design.

Mitsubishi was immediately assigned the task of developing the aircraft and the project was co-ordinated by Kiro Takahashi and Tetsuro Hikida. This design was given the designation J8M1 and would receive the name Shusui (roughly translated as Sharp Sword). By September 1944, a mock-up had been completed and by October 1944, several modifications had been made (mainly to simplify production) with approval to commence immediate production. Alongside this project, a glider for training flights was being assembled at the Naval Arsenal in Yokosuka under the direction of Hidemasa Kimura. This received the designation MXY8 and was called Akigusa (Autumn Grass). MXY8 was completed by the end of the year and test flown at the Hyakurigahara Airfield by Lt Cdr Toyohiko Inuzuka. He reported that the glider handled very well and as a consequence two further MXY8 gliders were built and supplied to the Army and Navy for further evaluation. At the same time, a manufacturing contract was issued to Yokoi Koku KK to begin manufacture of a production glider called Ku 13.

Work was now proceeding at Mitsubishi on the construction of 12 J8M1 (Ki-202) prototypes which externally resembled the original Komet, but differed in certain detail such as the lack of a small nose airscrew to drive a generator. Two slightly different versions of the aircraft would be manufactured for the Army and Navy. Aside from minor differences in the type of equipment carried, the weapons varied. The Navy's J8M1 would be equipped with two 30mm Type 5 cannons and the Army's version designated Ki-200 would carry two 30mm Ho105 cannons, although it appears that neither of these weapons compared to the German Mk108 design.

During trials, the Mitsubishi KR10 (Tokuro-2) rocket engine based on the Walter design delivered slightly less thrust than anticipated, but it was considered adequate for test flights while development continued. Fuel for the rocket engine was identical to the German C Stoff and T Stoff, referred to in Japan as Ko and Otsu. The Imperial Japanese Navy received priority and the first pre-production J8M1 came off the Mitsubishi production line at Nagoya in June 1945. It was then transported to Yokosuka where a rocket engine was fitted. With half full fuel tanks, the first Shusui flight took place on 7 July 1945. The project's senior test pilot Toyohiko Inuzuka made a sharp start and left the ground, successfully jettisoning the undercarriage and pulling up into a steep 45° climb. But seconds later, the rocket engine cut out and the aircraft stalled.

In the first account of this accident, the aircraft went into a steep vertical dive, hit the ground and Inuzuka was killed instantly. Alternatively, it has been suggested that he managed to glide back to the airfield, but struck the roof of a small building on the perimeter and crash-landed. The prototype caught fire and Inuzuka was rescued but died the following day. Whatever the exact course of events may have been, this accident was a setback to the programme. Engineers finally concluded that there were problems with the engine's automatic cut-out system, probably caused by an air lock in the fuel supply, resulting from the tanks only being partially filled. Urgent modifications were made to the design of the engine, although this does not appear to have held up aircraft production at Mitsubishi.

It was planned to have the first Shusui interceptor unit operational by the beginning of 1946, but Japan had surrendered before the next test flight could take place. By the end of the war, approximately 50 gliders had been completed and seven or eight Shusui aircraft built. A development of the glider called MXY9 Shuka (Autumn Fire) received some consideration by the Navy. This version would utilise a Kugisho Hatsukaze 11 (Tsu-11) ducted fan jet engine, although it never progressed beyond the concept stage. The Navy was also planning to build a derivative of the Shusui called the J8M2 which would only be fitted with one cannon to allow the carriage of a greater fuel load.

Yokosuka MXY8 Akigusa (Autumn Grass) Training Glider

Crew	1
Wingspan	31ft 2in (9.50m)
Wing area	190ft² (17.7 m²)
Length	19ft 10in (6.05m)
Height	8ft 10in (2.70m)

Mitsubishi J8M Shusui (Sharp Sword)

Crew	1
Wingspan	31ft 2in (9.5m)
Wing area	191ft² (17.7 m²)
Length	19ft 10in (6.05m)
Height	8ft 10in (2.70m)
Empty weight	3,318 lb (1,505kg)
Loaded weight	8,565 lb (3,885kg)
Maximum speed	559mph (900kph) at 30,000ft (9,144m)
Rate of climb	9,113ft/min (2,777m/min)
Ceiling	39,000ft (11,887m)
Powered endurance	5min 30sec
Powerplant	1 x Mitsubishi KR10 (Tokuro-2 or Ro.2) liquid fuel rocket engine producing 3,300 lb (14.7kN) of thrust
Armament	(J8M1) 2 x 30mm Type 5 cannon (J8M2) 1 x 30mm Type 5 cannon (Ki-200) 2 x 30mm Ho-105 cannon

German World War 2 Flying Wing Development

Post-War British Komet Trials

When the war in Europe ended, British forces retrieved a great deal of German aeronautical hardware for evaluation. The quality of the equipment varied from brand-new condition to badly damaged, but almost anything of interest was transported to the Royal Aircraft Establishment (RAE) at Farnborough where it was examined and tested by the secretive Experimental Flying Department.

In May 1945, the RAE took delivery of an intact Me 163B, although the early history of this Komet remains unknown. It was assigned the official UK serial VF241, partly repainted to show RAF colours and the engine was removed. This space would be filled with test equipment and ballast. Wg Cdr Roly Falk undertook the first glide flights in July 1945, but there were problems with the aircraft's hydraulic system which held up testing for the remainder of the year. It was also decided by the Ministry of Supply that there should be no powered flights made in this aircraft as it was too dangerous. Whether or not this was ever a serious consideration remains unknown.

Glide trials with VF241 resumed during February 1946 using a Spitfire IX as the towing aircraft. The flights were undertaken from Wisley Airfield in Surrey which was owned by Vickers-Armstrong, but is now derelict. Later flights were made at RAF Wittering, although it's not entirely clear why this more distant location was chosen. However, both sites were able to provide a grass landing area which was essential for the Komet. Many of the flights were undertaken by senior RAE test pilot Capt Eric Brown, who is now credited with having flown more different types of aircraft than anyone else in history.

One of the purposes of these trials was to gain experience with skid landing techniques as the RAE was developing proposals for an experimental swept-wing supersonic aircraft designed by the German engineers Hans Multhropp and Martin Winter. It was hoped that the Multhropp-Winter aircraft would reach at least Mach 1.26 and climb to an altitude of 60,000ft (18,288m). This alternative to the supersonic Miles M.52 that was under development carried the pilot in a prone position and utilised a landing skid system to minimise weight.

But on 15 November 1947, VF241's hydraulic landing skid failed as Brown touched down and the Komet was badly damaged. Brown was slightly injured, but the aircraft was a write-off. The supersonic project was cancelled at around the same time and this would be one of the last captured German aircraft to be test flown by RAE personnel. Nevertheless, the small rocketplane had quite an impact on British designers and it is clear that the experimental DH.108 programme (described in the previous chapter) was strongly influenced by the Me 163. The idea of a rocket-powered interceptor also persisted for several years with the Me 163 making a lasting impression on Britain's senior air staff who were increasingly concerned about the threat from future high-flying Soviet bombers.

The jet engine was still relatively crude, unreliable and incapable of delivering the kind of performance needed by an interceptor. This led to a requirement for an advanced pure rocket-powered interceptor issued as Specification F.124. Several military aircraft contractors made submissions and the winner was an advanced delta-winged design from Shorts known as PD.7. However, it was soon replaced by a proposal from Saunders Roe for a high-performance mixed propulsion interceptor called the SR.53 which was finally accepted for development under a revised Specification F.138. Two examples were built and there were plans to progress to the Saunders Roe SR.177 which would enter service with the RAF, Royal Navy and Luftwaffe. The programme continued until the late 1950s when it met with sudden cancellation during major defence cuts. Since the SR.53's inception, gas turbine technology had made considerable strides and as a consequence, combat aircraft using rocket propulsion were effectively dead.

US Komets

At the end of World War 2, five Messerschmitt Me 163B Komets were shipped to the US for evaluation by the USAAF. Each Me 163 received a Foreign Equipment serial number: FE-495, FE-500, FE-501, FE-502 and FE-503. Of these aircraft, FE-500 (also marked T-2-500) was the example used for testing. This Me 163B-1a (Werke Nr 191301) arrived at Freeman Field, Indiana, on 10 August 1945 and it was displayed at the Wright Field Air Fair during October 1945. Following this, the aircraft was restored to fully operational condition using components salvaged from other Komets and work was completed by March 1946. FE-500 was then shipped to Muroc Field (now Edwards AFB), California, on 12 April 1946. It was planned to test the Me 163B as a glider and then switch to rocket-powered trials, so a request was made to the US Navy for a supply of Hydrazine hydrate. Dr Lippisch had been detained in Austria by the USAAF's Air Technical Intelligence branch and was taken to Paris and London for debriefings. He was then offered the opportunity to work in the United States along with senior members of his staff that included Ernst Sielaff and Friedrich Ringleb under a scheme called Operation 'Paperclip'.

Lippisch arrived in the US during January 1946 and was then transferred to Wright Field (now Wright-Patterson AFB), Dayton, Ohio. One of the first programmes he was asked to participate in was a USAAF evaluation of the Me 163B and on 30 April 1946, Dr Lippisch and former test pilot Ludwig Vogel were flown to Muroc Field. The next day Lippisch and Vogel examined FE-500 and pointed out various faults with the landing gear, control system and wing delamination. This resulted in immediate work on the aircraft, with the wings being replaced by those belonging to FE-495. The Komet was finally judged airworthy on 3 May 1946 and preparations were made to undertake the first glide flight. Major Gustav E. 'Gus' Lundquist had also been flown in from Wright Field where he headed the Fighter Test Section and was assigned to make the initial glide flights in FE-500.

Several Me 163B Komets were secured by the British during 1945 and the best example was provided to the RAE for testing and evaluation, having been given the reference VF241. The engine was replaced with ballast and VF241 was partly repainted with RAF markings. Bill Rose Collection

At the end of hostilities in Europe, the US Army shipped vast quantities of advanced German military hardware back to America for evaluation. This included complete examples of aircraft such as the Messerschmitt Me 163. Five of these aircraft are known to have been shipped to the US and this photograph shows one of these examples being loaded into a Douglas C-54 transport aircraft. USAF

Restored to fully operational condition in the USA, this Me 163B was assigned the reference FE500 and delivered to Muroc Field (now Edwards AFB), California, on 12 April 1946. It was flown as a glider and there were plans to test the aircraft under rocket power, but the idea was finally abandoned on the grounds of safety. USAF

The first attempt to fly the aircraft took place on 3 May 1946 at Rogers Dry Lake using a B-29 bomber as the tow aircraft. But there were problems with the tow cable being inadvertently released and the trials were delayed. When flight tests finally got under way, Lundquist experienced very serious wake turbulence problems caused by the B-29, but he was lifted to an altitude of about 32,000ft (9,753m) before gliding back to land on the lake bed.

Further flights were made and it was planned that Robert Hoover would fly FE-500 under full rocket power, although it was finally decided not to proceed for safety reasons. With the trials concluded, FE-500 was moved to Norton AFB where it was stored until 1954 and then handed over to the Smithsonian Institution (now the National Air and Space Museum). It remained on display until 1996 when it was loaned to the Mighty Eighth Air Force Museum in Georgia which undertook a full restoration. At the time of writing it is in the process of being returned to the National Air and Space Museum's Silver Hill facility.

Details of this aircraft's earlier history in Germany remain unknown. As far as is known, the other Komets taken to Freeman Field had all been scrapped by the late 1940s with some of the parts being retained as spares for FE-500.

In addition to FE-500, two Japanese J8M1 Shusui aircraft were shipped to the United States onboard the USS *Barnes* in November 1945. The first example received the serial FE-300 (or T2-300), but the reference for the second is unknown at present. This was briefly displayed at Naval Air Station Glenview, Illinois, and then scrapped. FE-300 was evaluated by the Navy and then passed to the Planes of Fame Museum, California, where it currently resides.

In 1960, a J8M1 was discovered hidden in a cave at the Yokosuka region south of Tokyo. Although in very poor condition, the aircraft was displayed outdoors at a Japanese Air Force base near Gifu for many years. In 1999, Mitsubishi purchased this example and undertook a full restoration which was virtually a complete replication. The aircraft is now kept at the company's Komari Plant Museum.

Postwar Russian Komet Research

In early 1944, Mikoyan-Gurevich (MiG) and at least one other Opytnoe Konstruktorskoe Byuro (OKB or Experimental Design Bureau) were requested to start work on developing a Russian version of the rocket-powered Me 163B interceptor. Proposals were drawn up, but further development had not been approved by the end of the war in Europe. It remains unclear how similar this proposal was to the German aircraft. After hostilities ceased, the Russians secured several examples of the Me 163B, an example of the Me 163S (two-seat trainer) and the very advanced Junkers 248/Me 263V1 prototype. In addition to the aircraft, there were huge quantities of documents, factory equipment and engineers who had worked on these programmes.

Many captured German aircraft of interest, including the German rocket fighters, were transported to the Gromov Flight Research Institute which had been established in 1941 south-east of Moscow. But when it came to testing the rocket aircraft there was no fuel for the Walter rocket engines and there were insufficient means within the Soviet Union or captured territories to produce the quantities of hydrogen peroxide required.

Nevertheless, glide flights began in 1945 using a Tupolev Tu-2 bomber to tow a Me 163B into the air with M.L. Gallay becoming the first Soviet test pilot to fly the Komet. Further flights, with and without water ballast, were undertaken by institute pilots. It was soon determined that the Me 163B could dive at higher speeds than any other unpowered design and it possessed good longitudinal and roll stability. The institute's chief test pilot, Lt Col V. Ye. Golofastov, remarked that the Komet behaved like a conventional fighter in unpowered flight and had good aerobatic qualities. However, it is clear that the Me 163B was not a popular aircraft with the Russians who nicknamed it Karas (Carp) and none of them liked the landing skid system which was blamed for several minor accidents.

German World War 2 Flying Wing Development

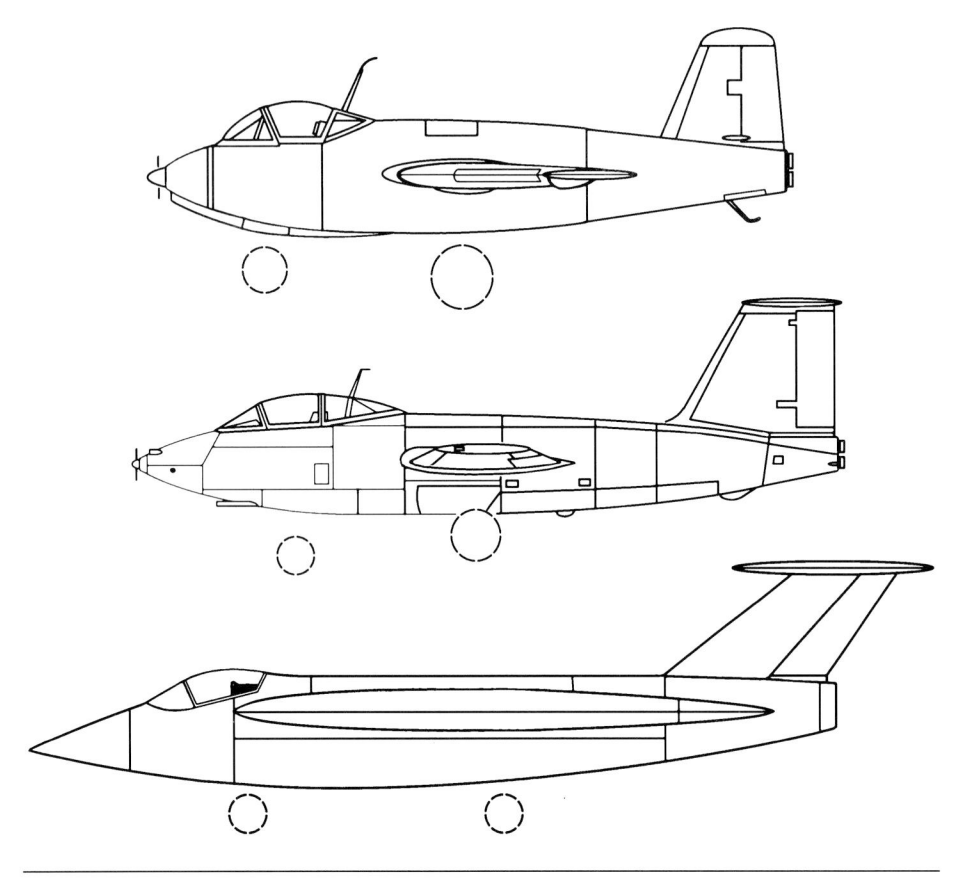

Mikoyan-Gurevich I-270

Crew	1
Wingspan	25ft 5in (7.75m)
Wing area	129ft² (12m²)
Length	29ft 2in (8.91m)
Height	10ft 1in (3.08m)
Empty weight	3,408lb (1,546kg)
Gross weight	9,150lb (4,150kg)
Powerplant	1 x Dushkin-Glushko RD-2M-3V liquid fuel rocket engine producing 3,190lb (14.2kN) thrust
Maximum speed	621mph (1,000kph)
Landing speed	104mph (168kph)
Ceiling	55,775ft (17,000m)
Rate of climb	13,800ft/min (4,220m/min)
Endurance	9min
Armament (proposed)	2 x 23mm Nudelman NS-23 cannons with 40rpg and 8 x RS-82 rockets

Lippisch DM-1

Crew	1
Wingspan	19ft 5in (5.9m)
Length	21ft 7in (6.6m)
Height	10ft 5in (3.17m)
Weight	655lb (297kg)

At the end of World War 2, Soviet forces captured a Me 263 prototype, research documentation and a number of German technicians. This led to a project at the Mikoyan-Gurevich OKB to improve on the rocket fighter's design and build two prototypes assigned the reference MiG I-270. Bill Rose Collection

It is not clear if this is the first or second MiG I-270 rocket-powered prototype interceptor, but it appears to differ in minor detail from photographs of the MiG I-270 seen on the snow field. Bill Rose Collection

The Messerschmitt Me 263 (top) was Germany's most advanced wartime rocket-powered interceptor. It was built in prototype form and underwent limited trials towards the end of hostilities. This aircraft and much of the research material that fell into Soviet hands formed the basis of the MiG I-270 (centre). Although the MiG was a considerable improvement over the original design, it was eventually abandoned. Germany's advanced wartime rocket fighter programme also made a deep impression on British officials who commissioned a series of studies for purely rocket-powered interceptors. The ultimate design to emerge was the high-performance Short PD7 (bottom). However, it was soon realised that despite possessing phenomenal performance when compared to prevailing turbojet-powered fighters, this type of aircraft was essentially impractical due to its substantial fuel consumption. The Short PD7 represents the most advanced and final pure rocket fighter concept of any note. However, the British persevered with mixed propulsion until the late 1950s before finally giving up on the idea. Bill Rose Collection

Secret Projects: Flying Wings and Tailless Aircraft

Built by students from the Darmstadt and Munich Universities, the Lippisch-designed DM-1 was expected to lead to several supersonic combat aircraft and become a successor to the Me 163B.
Bill Rose Collection

In a parallel programme, work was underway at the Mikoyan-Gurevich OKB to develop the captured Me 263 into a point defence rocket interceptor. This lead to an improved version of the aircraft called the MiG I-270 (Zh). It differed in a number of respects from its German predecessor, having straight thin wings and a 30° swept tailplane. It was structurally superior to the Junkers prototype with a larger pressurised cockpit and the I-270 was the first Soviet aircraft to be fitted with an ejector seat. Had this design entered production it would have been armed with two 23mm cannons and eight air-to-air rockets.

Two prototypes were built during 1946 with the assistance of German engineers, although the first aircraft had no engine and was only intended for glide trials so water was carried as ballast. Test pilot Victor Yuganov flew the first MiG I-270 during December 1946 with a Tupolev Tu-2 used as the tow aircraft. The second I-270 was completed at the beginning of 1947 and was fitted with a two-chamber GRD-2M-3V rocket engine designed by Leonid Dushkin and Valentin Glushko. This engine was developed from an advanced design for the experimental pre-war Soviet BI rocket plane, but probably utilised some later German engineering techniques. The GRD-2M-3V was fuelled with nitric acid and kerosene, providing a maximum thrust of about 3,190 lb (14.2kN). Powered flights began in early 1947, but the second prototype was badly damaged after Yuganov made a hard landing. Soon after this, the first prototype was seriously damaged in another landing incident. It was then decided to abandon the project with rapid advances being made in the field of turbojet propulsion and the promise of effective surface-to-air missiles.

Lippisch DM-1

Although it barely qualifies for inclusion in this book, Lippisch designed a very advanced pure delta shaped glider called the DM-1 after leaving Messerschmitt. The name of this aircraft reflected the fact that a group of talented students from Darmstadt and Munich Universities were recruited to work on the project under his direction. The DM-1 was seen as a stepping-stone to more advanced experimental aircraft powered by turbojet, rocket and ramjet engines. Wind tunnel tests showed that this unusual design remained stable at speeds up to Mach 2.6 and Lippisch believed that much higher Mach numbers would be possible with the right type of propulsion. One anticipated relatively short-term development of the DM-1 was a supersonic ramjet-powered interceptor that was given the provisional reference P.13A.

When Germany surrendered, the DM-1 glider had almost been completed at Prien am Chiemsee in southern Germany. It was then secured by the US Army, which allowed completion of the project before shipping it back to America and ultimately NACA Langley. Lippisch's research data from this project would prove extremely influential with all postwar American and British designers.

Lippisch Heavy Fighters and Fast Bombers

During his time at Messerschmitt in the early 1940s, Lippisch studied a number of designs for heavy fighters and light bombers with Dr Rudolf Rentel. The first series of proposals were for the Lippisch Li P.04-106A to P.04-114A flying wings (most appear to differ only in minor detail) which were an attempt to produce a more effective competitor to the Messerschmitt Bf 110 Zerstörer (Heavy Fighter). The P.04-106A's wing had an initial sweep of 13°, becoming 30° from just outside the engine nacelles. The aircraft was to be powered by two Daimler Benz 601E engines each rated at 1,200hp (895kW) driving pusher propellers. Stabilising fins and rudders were positioned on the wings and the aircraft was equipped with a fully retracting undercarriage that included an extending tailwheel. The pilot was positioned right at the front of the cockpit, affording him good unobstructed visibility and the radio operator/rear gunner faced rearward. Armament would consist of four fixed forward firing cannons and two rearward firing machine guns. This design would have provided some advantages over the Bf 110, but it was not accepted for further development by the RLM.

In late 1941, Lippisch was advised about jet engine developments at Junkers and he produced preliminary designs for a twin-engine fighter called P.09 which utilised the Me 163's aerodynamics. Messerschmitt rejected the P.09 as it clashed with development of the Me 262, but Lippisch evolved the proposal into a slightly larger two-man fast jet bomber called the Li P.10. By the end of 1941, the tailless P.10 had been given a wingspan of 43ft 11in (13.4m) with a 33° sweep and the aircraft's overall length was 26ft 9in (7.5m). Gross weight was 24,250 lb (11,000kg) and two of the still experimental Junkers Jumo turbojets would be used for propulsion, also enclosed within the wing roots. It was planned to equip the aircraft with a fully retractable undercarriage with the rear end rested on a tail wheel and the crew of two would sit side-by-side in a flush cockpit. P.10 would be armed with forward and rearward firing cannons and capable of carrying a 2,205 lb (1,000kg) bomb load internally.

Dr Hermann Wurster produced a closely related design with a different propulsion system and, rather confusingly, this received the same Lippisch P.10 reference (but probably had a different unknown suffix). This version of the P.10 was to be powered by a centrally positioned Daimler Benz 606 piston engine rated at 2,700hp (2,014kW) which connected to a tail-mounted pusher propeller via a shaft. This P.10 utilised a similar undercarriage, had the same wingspan and a similar gross weight to the jet powered P.10. It appears that cockpit was only intended to accommodate a pilot. Both the jet and piston engine versions of the P.10 design were conceived as potential successors to the unsatisfactory Messerschmitt Me 210 heavy fighter and a third contender known as the Me 329 (described in a later section) was produced by Messerschmitt's Dr Hermann Wurster.

With design work continuing on a new fast bomber that was adaptable to the heavy fighter role, Lippisch proposed the P.11 in

German World War 2 Flying Wing Development

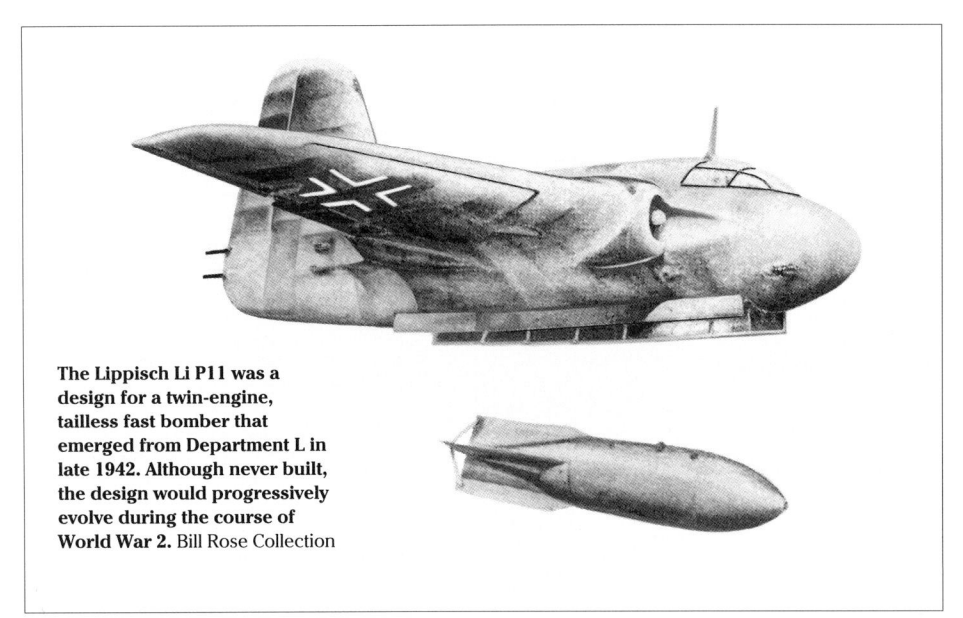

The Lippisch Li P11 was a design for a twin-engine, tailless fast bomber that emerged from Department L in late 1942. Although never built, the design would progressively evolve during the course of World War 2. Bill Rose Collection

Lippisch Li P.04-106 Heavy fighter

Crew	2
Wingspan	52ft 6in (16m)
Length	19ft 1in (5.8m)
Height	10ft 4in (3.15m)
Maximum speed	424mph (682kph)
Ceiling	39,000ft (11,887m)
Range	1,500 miles (2,414km)
Maximum speed	316mph (510kph)
Powerplant	2 x Daimler Benz 601E piston engines each rated at 1,200hp (895kW)
Armament	4 x forward firing MG151 guns located on the fuselage sides and in the wing roots. 2 x remote-controlled MG131 guns firing rearward

Lippisch Li P.10 Jet Powered Fast Bomber (November 1941)

Crew	2
Wingspan	44ft (13.4m)
Sweep	33° (leading edge)
Length	26ft 9in (8.15m)
Height	9ft 10in (2.99m)
Wing area	570.5ft² (53m²)
Gross weight	Unspecified
Maximum speed	Unknown
Powerplant	2 x Junkers turbojets (based on prototype engines)
Armament	2 x 20mm MG151/20 cannon in the nose, and 2 x 20mm MG151/20 cannon in the tail.
Internal bomb load	2,205 lb (1,000kg)

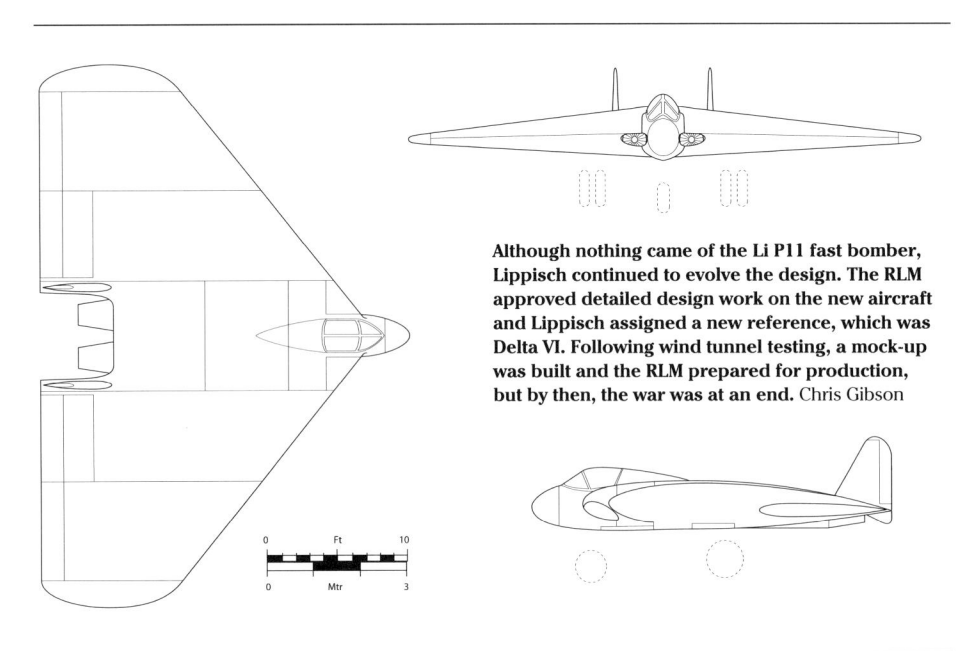

Although nothing came of the Li P11 fast bomber, Lippisch continued to evolve the design. The RLM approved detailed design work on the new aircraft and Lippisch assigned a new reference, which was Delta VI. Following wind tunnel testing, a mock-up was built and the RLM prepared for production, but by then, the war was at an end. Chris Gibson

autumn 1942. This might be regarded as a further refinement of the tailless, jet engine powered P.10 with some aerodynamic improvements and a fully retractable tricycle undercarriage. Powered by two Junkers Jumo 004B turbojets, the P.11 was to be a two-man aircraft with a tandem cockpit, forward firing 20mm cannons and the same payload capability as the P.10. Refinement of the design continued into 1943 with significant changes to the wing profile, engine intakes and cockpit design, which was now reduced to just a pilot. One unusual feature was the hinged stabilisers attached to the tailplane that could be brought into a horizontal position.

Nothing came of this fast bomber project which remained on the drawing board up until the time when Lippisch and his team parted company with Messerschmitt and relocated to Vienna. P.11 seemed to have been passed over for a bomb-carrying Horten Ho IX, but Lippisch was then approached by the RLM to continue work on P.11 and produce a new high-speed version of his aircraft. As the P.11 continued to evolve towards a delta shape, Lippisch assigned it a new reference – Delta VI. The initial prototype (V1) would be a glider and there would be the option of configuring the aircraft as a heavy fighter or fighter-bomber. Following wind tunnel testing of models, a mock-up was completed at the LFA (Aviation Research Institute) in early 1944.

Delta VI was an impressive semi-delta wing design with a forward positioned cockpit, two upright stabilisers and rudders and power provided by two centrally positioned Jumo 004B turbojets. Rocket assisted take off was also considered as an option for short runways and/or heavy loads. The aircraft was supported on the ground by a robust retractable tricycle undercarriage and was capable of carrying the same payload as the earlier aircraft in this series. One interesting suggestion was to equip the heavy-fighter version with a 75mm BK 7.5 cannon in an external pack for an anti-armour role. It is probable that 12 rounds would have been carried in the pack and this cannon was able to penetrate 5in (130mm) of armour at a range of 3,280ft (1,000m).

The aircraft appears to have been a promising design with available literature suggesting that it would have been fast and manoeuvrable with a good range and the ability to be configured for a number of different roles. Naturally, low cost materials would have been used wherever possible in its construction. The RLM approved the Delta VI and commissioned the V1 prototype and three pre-production aircraft for evaluation and development. Henschel was chosen to

Secret Projects: Flying Wings and Tailless Aircraft

Lippisch Li P.10 Piston Engine Powered Fast Bomber (May 1942)

Crew	1
Wingspan	52ft 6in 16m
Length	32ft 4in (9.85m)
Wing area	570.5ft² (53m²)
Gross weight	24,250lb (11,000kg)
Maximum speed	424mph (682kph)
Ceiling	39,000ft (11,887m)
Range	1,500 miles (2,421km)
Powerplant	1 x centrally located Daimler Benz DB606 piston engine (two connected DB601 engines) producing 2,700hp (2,013kW)
Armament	2 x forward firing 20mm MG151 cannons. 2 x 20mm MG151 rearward firing cannons in tail.
Bomb load	2,205lb (1,000kg)

Lippisch Li P.11 (December 1942)

Crew	1
Wingspan	41ft 6in (12.65m)
Wing area	401.5ft² (37.3m²)
Length	26ft 9in (8.15m)
Height	13ft 2in (4.0m)
Empty weight	8,830lb (4,005kg)
Gross weight	16,535lb (7,500kg)
Maximum speed	550mph (885kph) approx
Powerplant	2 x Junkers Jumo 004B turbojets, each rated at 1,980lb (8.8kN) static thrust
Armament	2 x 20mm MG151/20 cannon in the wing roots

Lippisch Delta VI

Crew	1
Wingspan	35ft 5in
Wing area	538ft² (50m²)
Aspect ratio	2.33:1
Sweep	37° (leading edge)
Length	24ft 6in (7.49m)
Height	9ft (2.76m)
Gross weight	17,636lb (8,000kg)
Maximum speed	646mph (1,040kph)
Ceiling	40,000ft (12,192m) estimated
Range	1,864 miles (3,000km) approx
Powerplant	2 x Junkers Jumo 004B turbojets, each rated at 1,980lb (8.8kN) static thrust
Armament	2 x 30mm Mk103 cannons, plus option for two additional 30mm Mk103 cannons or one 75mm BK 7.5 cannon in an external pack
Bomb load capability	2,205lb (1,000kg)

The Me329, designed by Dr Hermann Wurster, was built as a wooden mock-up, but a prototype may also have been constructed and flown at the Rechlin Test Centre in early 1945. Chris Gibson

manufacture the Delta VI prototypes and undertake production at their Berlin plant.

Lippisch had initially planned to have the jet powered Delta VI-V2 ready for testing within six months, but there were major disagreements with Henschel and as a consequence the programme slowed with Lippisch's engineers at Salzburg beginning work on construction of the V1 prototype. By the end of the war in Europe, wind tunnel tests had been completed and the mainly wood/plywood fuselage of Delta VI-V1 was largely finished. It was secured by American forces and may have been shipped to the US for evaluation.

Messerschmitt Tailless Designs

Serious problems with the Messerschmitt Me 210 fighter-bomber led Dr Alexander Lippisch's Department L and Dr Hermann Wurster's design office to initiate design projects that would produce a superior replacement. Lippisch started work on his P.10 series of proposals at the end of 1941, while Wurster contributed with a single engine, tailless concept and separately developed a twin (piston) engine flying wing which was given the company reference Me 329. An additional project was already underway to re-engine and improve the Me 210, leading to the Me 410 Hornisse (Hornet).

Wurster's tailless Me 329 heavy/long-range multi-role combat aircraft would be mainly built from readily available wood/plywood and utilise as many off-the-shelf Me 210/410 components as possible to limit production requirements. The pilot and navigator were accommodated in a spacious cockpit with staggered side-by-side positions offering good visibility. The Me 329's wingspan was slightly greater than the earlier Lippisch Li P.04 proposals or the later piston engine P.10 and propulsion would be provided by two Daimler Benz 601 or Jumo 213 piston engines mounted within the wings and each driving a three-bladed pusher propeller with an 11ft 2in (3.4m) diameter. As a consequence of this layout, the undercarriage was a fully retracting tricycle design, although the amount of ground clearance below the propellers would suggest there was potential for serious problems in certain situations. The Me 329 was fitted with a single swept tailfin and rudder and the aircraft's centrally located bomb bay could accommodate a 2,205lb (1,000kg) payload. Additional bombs, rockets or fuel tanks could be carried externally. Armament comprised of four MG151/20 20mm cannons in the nose, possibly two Mk103 30mm cannons in the wing roots and a remote controlled MG151/20 20mm cannon in the tail. This would be controlled by the navigator using a periscope aiming system.

A full-sized mock-up of the Me 329 was built at Augsburg and comparative estimates suggested that the aircraft would have provided slightly better performance than the piston engine Lippisch (Wurster) P.10 and was a significant improvement over the Me 410. Nevertheless, Willy Messerschmitt turned down both designs, deciding to continue with development of the Me 410. Little is known about the history of the Me 329, but it appears that development of this interesting aircraft continued after Lippisch left Messerschmitt in 1943

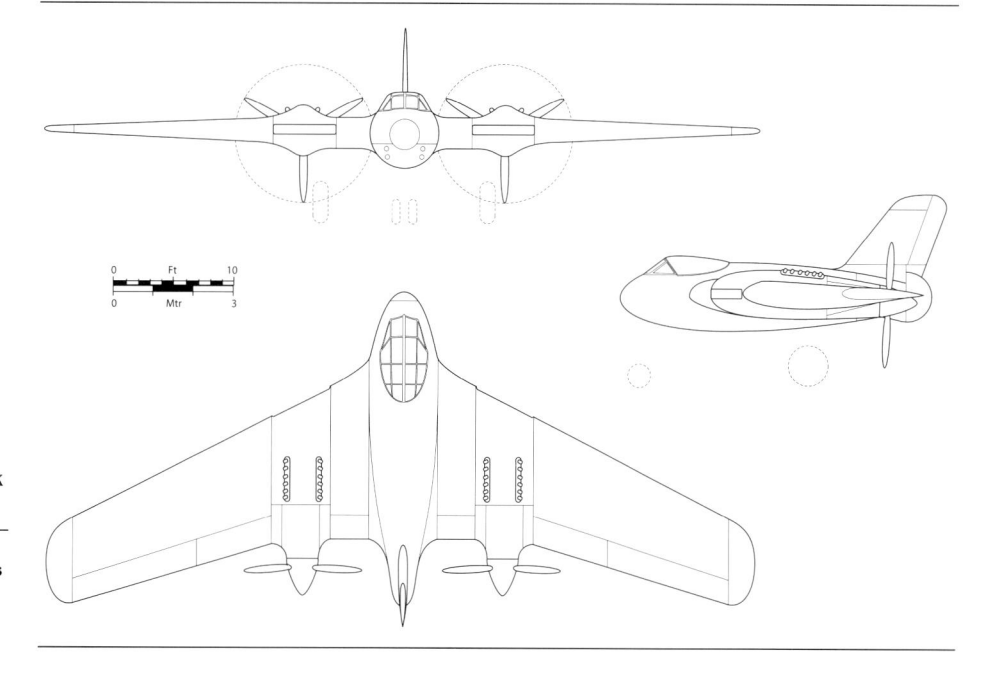

German World War 2 Flying Wing Development

Messerschmitt Me 329

Crew	2
Wingspan	57ft 6in (17.5m)
Sweep	26° (leading edge)
Wing area	592ft² (55m²)
Length	25ft (7.62m)
Height	15ft 6in (4.73m)
Empty weight	15,322 lb (6,950kg)
Gross weight	26,786 lb (12,150kg)
Range	1,566 miles (2,520kph)
Maximum speed	426mph (685kph)
Ceiling	41,000ft (12,496m)
Powerplant	2 x 12-cylinder DB603, each rated at 1,725hp (1,287kW) or 2 x Junkers Jumo 213 12-cylinder piston engines, each rated at 2,020hp (1,508kW), during take-off, using MW50 injection.
Armament	4 x 20mm MG151/20 cannon mounted in the nose, plus 2 x 30mm Mk103 cannon in the wing roots. A remote controlled 20mm MG151/20 cannon in a tail barbette. An internal bomb load of 2,205 lb (1,000kg) and a similar weight in external underwing stores.

and according to one report, a prototype was completed by early 1945 and test flown at the Rechlin Test Centre before hostilities ceased.

Flying Wing Bombers

Messerschmitt undertook a number of studies for long range and heavy bombers during World War 2 and several of these were flying wing designs that are often credited to Lippisch's Department L. Unfortunately, relatively little documentation has survived, although in the case of the P.08.01 study, this can be dated to September 1941 and was produced by Dr Hermann Wurster, apparently with some assistance from Dr Lippisch.

The P.08.01 was a large flying wing powered by four Daimler Benz DB615 piston engines driving pusher propellers. It had almost the same wingspan as a modern Northrop B-2A stealth bomber and Wurster envisaged the P.08.01 being used in a wide range of different roles. As a long-range bomber, the P.08.01 would be capable of crossing the Atlantic and as a shorter-range tactical bomber it would carry a very substantial bomb load. It would be adaptable to the reconnaissance role, a transport aircraft capable of carrying a small tank and a rather unusual airborne anti-aircraft platform equipped with four 88mm anti-aircraft guns. P.08.01 would have also been capable of undertaking maritime, glider towing duties and perhaps launching air-to-surface missiles.

Built almost entirely from metal, the wing featured two different sweep angles and it has been suggested that the P.08.01 might have been capable of surviving encounters with barrage balloon cables. Intakes for each engine radiator would be located in the inner wing section's leading edge and most of the aircraft's fuel was carried in this location, with tanks and engines being heavily armoured. P.08.01 was fitted with a single tailfin and utilised split flaps. The pressurised cockpit protruded slightly ahead of the wing and would have provided good forward visibility. A substantial, fully retractable tricycle undercarriage supported the aircraft on the ground and there was a large centrally positioned bomb/cargo bay. It was also suggested that additional stores could be carried underwing and the aircraft's configuration meant that a certain amount of nose-down attitude was required for bomb release.

Although the P.08.01 was an interesting design, it was over-ambitious and appears to have progressed little further than the initial design phase. A later series of Messerschmitt studies for an advanced high-speed jet powered bomber was undertaken towards the end of the war in an attempt to meet evolving RLM needs. This project generated a number of widely differing concepts that included several tailless designs.

The tailless proposals are said to have been influenced by earlier Lippisch designs, although Lippisch and most of his colleagues had departed from Messerschmitt some time before this project started. Messerschmitt designers, Siefert and Konrad, are credited for these designs. Initially assigned the reference P.1107, the study followed two different lines of development. The first was a fairly conventional four-engine tailed aircraft and the second was a semi-delta shaped tailless design. Unfortunately, there is very little documentation available for the P.1107 project and the available details are often very confusing.

The RLM required an aircraft capable of carrying an 8,818 lb (4,000kg) payload with a maximum speed of about 600mph (965kph) and a range of approximately 4,350 miles (7,000km). It would be powered by Heinkel

Messerschmitt MeP.08.01 Heavy Bomber

Crew	6-10 (depending on the mission)
Wingspan	166ft (50.6m)
Wing area	3,229ft² (300m²)
Length	50ft 4in (15.35m)
Height	28ft 3in (8.6m)
Gross weight	198,414 lb (90,000kg)
Maximum speed	400mph (643kph)
Maximum range	9,320 miles (15,000km) (as a long range bomber)
Powerplant	4 x Daimler Benz DB615 liquid-cooled piston engines, each producing 4,000hp (2,983kW). The DB615 was built from two DB614 engines and development was abandoned in June 1942.
Armament	Unspecified remote controlled cannons in nose and tail units
Free fall bombs	Tactical mission (1,550 miles/ 2,495km), 110,230 lb (50,000kg). Long-range mission (9,315 miles/ 14,991km), 44,095 lb (20,000kg).
Maritime role	Torpedoes, mines or anti-shipping guided weapons
Airborne defence role	4 x 88mm flak cannons

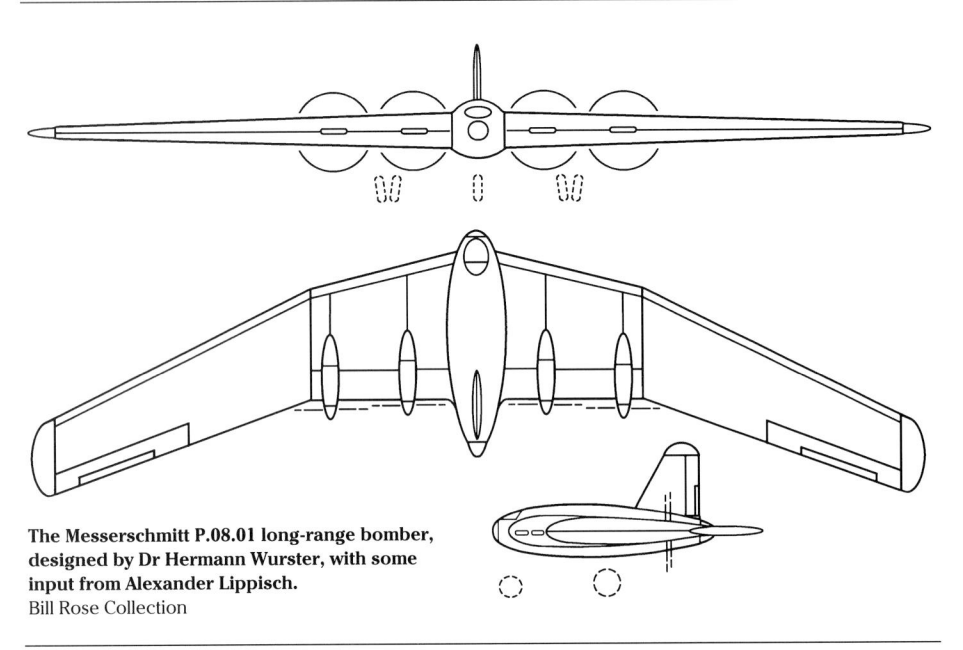

The Messerschmitt P.08.01 long-range bomber, designed by Dr Hermann Wurster, with some input from Alexander Lippisch.
Bill Rose Collection

Messerschmitt P.1107

Crew	4
Wingspan	65ft 7in (20m)
Sweep	45° (leading edge)
Wing area	1,292ft² (120m²)
Length	54ft 5in (16.6m)
Height	19ft 8in (6m)
Powerplant	4 x Heinkel He S 011A turbojets, each rated at 2,865 lb (12.74kN) static thrust
Maximum speed	600mph (965kph)
Ceiling	45,000ft (13,716m) estimated
Range	4,349 miles (7,000km)
Armament	Unspecified forward and rearward defensive cannons. A maximum bomb load of 8,818 lb (4,000kg). Free fall bombs, 2 x torpedoes or guided weapons

turbojets and manned by a crew of four in a pressurised cockpit. The aircraft would be supported on the ground by a retracting tricycle undercarriage and the bomb bay would be adaptable for a range of different ordnance. The materials used for construction would be steel and duralumin around the central area and mainly wood for the wings. The tailless design for the P.1107 study shown in drawing IX-122 (see *Luftwaffe Secret Projects: Strategic Bombers 1939-1945* by Dieter Herwig and Heinz Rode: Midland Counties Publishing) appears to have had a 45° sweep and a wingspan of 65ft 7in (20m). The overall length was approximately 54ft 5in (16.6m) and it was equipped with a single tailfin and rudder, producing an overall height of about 19ft 8in (6m). Four Heinkel He S 011 turbojets located in the wing roots provided propulsion with engine air intakes positioned at the inner leading edge. In addition to meeting requirements for a fast bomber, the P.1107 was to function in maritime and reconnaissance roles.

Project P.1107 had soon given way to a new series of closely related designs called P.1108 that included flying wing proposals which primarily differed in engine layout. Although similar in appearance to the original P.1107 tailless design, the definitive P.1108.11 underwent a major engine bay revision with the air intakes relocated beneath the wing. In addition, the crew requirement was reduced to three. A final proposal in this series was an arrowhead near-delta design with no upright control surfaces and each of the four engines slightly angled inwards to reduce problems with thrust equalisation. P.1108 progressed no further than drawings and discussion and there was no expectation of production before 1948.

Developed in parallel to the P.1108 designs were a series of proposals for an advanced tailless single engine jet fighter with the reference P.1111. A single Heinkel He S 011 turbojet with air intakes positioned in the leading edge wing roots powered this compact design. A relatively low-profile canopy covered the pressurised cockpit and an ejector seat was to be fitted. P.1111 was fitted with a tricycle undercarriage and armament comprised of two 30mm cannons in the nose and two 30mm cannons positioned just outboard of the air intakes. The overall design was very clean with a single swept tailfin and it is believed that aspects of this project influenced development of the de Havilland DH.108.

P.1111 returned good results as a wind tunnel model, but the RLM expressed serious concerns about the unprotected fuel tanks located in the wings considering this to be a serious weakness. Subsequently, the design underwent a significant revision and was allocated the designation P.1112. Main differences with this aircraft were a redesigned wing with slightly less sweep and a reduced span, plus a number of alterations to the cockpit, moving it further forward. Performance was expected to be nominally better. By the end of the war, work was well advanced on construction of a mock-up at Messerschmitt's Oberammergau workshops and Dr Waldemar Voigt who headed this project had anticipated the first test flight by mid-1946. Completed sections of the mock-up and all documentation was captured by US forces and shipped back to America for evaluation. The advanced P.1108 bomber and P.1112 fighter studies were the last projects of any significance undertaken by Messerschmitt before the war ended.

Messerschmitt P.1108.11

Crew	3
Wingspan	65ft 7in (20m)
Sweep	45° (leading edge)
Wing area	1,292ft² (120m²)
Length	54ft 5in (16.6m)
Height	14ft 9in (4.5m)
Gross weight	77,161 lb (35,000kg)
Powerplant	4 x Heinkel He S 011A turbojets, each rated at 2,865 lb (12.74kN) static thrust
Maximum speed	600mph (965kph)
Ceiling	45,000ft (13,716m) estimated
Range	4,349 miles (7,000km)
Armament	Unspecified forward and rearward defensive cannons. A maximum bomb load of 8,818 lb (4,000kg). Free fall bombs, 2 x torpedoes or guided weapons

Messerschmitt P.1111

Crew	1
Wingspan	30ft (9.14m)
Sweep	45° (at 0.41 chord)
Wing area	301ft² (28m²)
Length	29ft 3in (8.91m)
Height	10ft (3.05m)
Empty weight	6,040 lb (2,740kg)
Gross weight	9,437 lb (4,280kg)
Powerplant	1 x Heinkel He S 011A turbojet, rated at 2,865 lb (12.74kN) static thrust
Maximum speed	618mph (995kph)
Ceiling	46,000ft (14,020m)
Armament	4 x 30mm Mk108 cannons

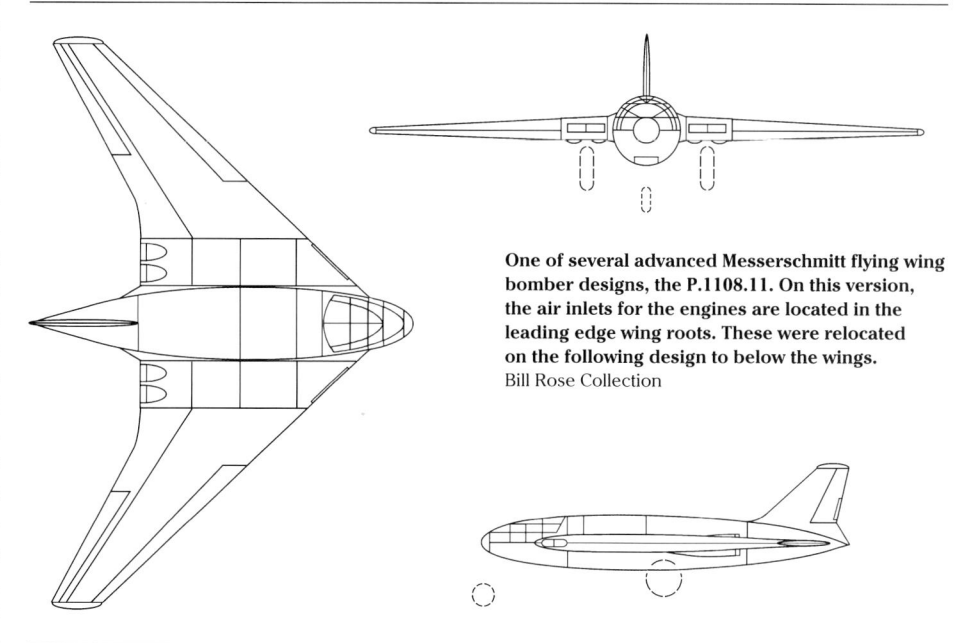

One of several advanced Messerschmitt flying wing bomber designs, the P.1108.11. On this version, the air inlets for the engines are located in the leading edge wing roots. These were relocated on the following design to below the wings.
Bill Rose Collection

German World War 2 Flying Wing Development

Chapter Three

US Flying Wings (1935-1950)

Boeing Studies

A research programme undertaken by the US Army Air Corps Material Division at Wright Field, during 1933 determined that a new fast bomber with a maximum speed of 200mph (320kph), a range of 5,000 miles (8,000km) and the ability to carry a 2,500 lb (1,133kg) bomb load was technically feasible. Both Boeing and Martin expressed an interest in this project and design work commenced in early 1934. This led to contracts being issued for the construction of one prototype by each contractor which became known as the Boeing XB-15 and the Martin XB-16.

The XB-15 was an advanced conventional four-engine all-metal monoplane. It was built as a single prototype which would eventually lead to the B-17 and the B-29. The four engine (later six) Martin XB-16 was a slightly less orthodox design featuring twin tail booms. While the XB-15 was test flown, the XB-16 never reached completion due to the cancellation of this particular bomber programme. Both the XB-15 and XB-16 were judged to have insufficient performance and by this time, the smaller four-engine Boeing B-17 Flying Fortress had been selected for production.

Meanwhile, Boeing was engaged in a secret, almost unknown parallel project to develop a flying wing aircraft which utilised some of the XB-15's features. The company is not generally associated with the early development of flying wing aircraft and their engineers claimed to have no interest in tailless designs as they were considered less stable and harder to control than conventional aircraft. Nevertheless, a series of flying wings were designed during 1935, perhaps in the hope of achieving certain aerodynamic advantages. As work progressed, a total of five different concepts emerged for various roles.

None of these Boeing flying wing studies progressed much further than the drawing board and they remained unknown until relatively recently. Aside from a long-range bomber, there was a flying boat, an airliner and two variations of a compact one-man fighter with all receiving the in-house umbrella designation Model 306. The long-range bomber was completely tailless with swept wings and an unusual system of external elevons supported behind the trailing edge by long struts. Engineers believed this unusual system would be more efficient than normal control surfaces as it avoided any interference with the wing's aerofoil profile. It almost goes without saying that the idea was wind tunnel tested.

The Model 306 flying wing bomber was to be manned by a crew of 10. The wingspan was provisionally set at 140ft (42.6m) and the aircraft's length was 60ft (18.2m). Propulsion took the form of four forward-mounted propellers, each driven by an Allison V-1710 12-cylinder liquid-cooled engine, producing 850hp (633kW). A fully retractable undercarriage was envisaged with the aircraft's rear section resting on a tail wheel. The bomber would have a range of 5,000 miles (8,000km) and carry a 2,500 lb (1,133kg) bomb load with defensive armament consisting of two .50 cal (12.7mm) and two .30 cal (7.62mm) machine guns. Had this aircraft progressed towards production, it seems certain that more guns would have been added. Weights, maximum speed and ceiling are unknown, but slightly better performance than the XB-15 was undoubtedly anticipated.

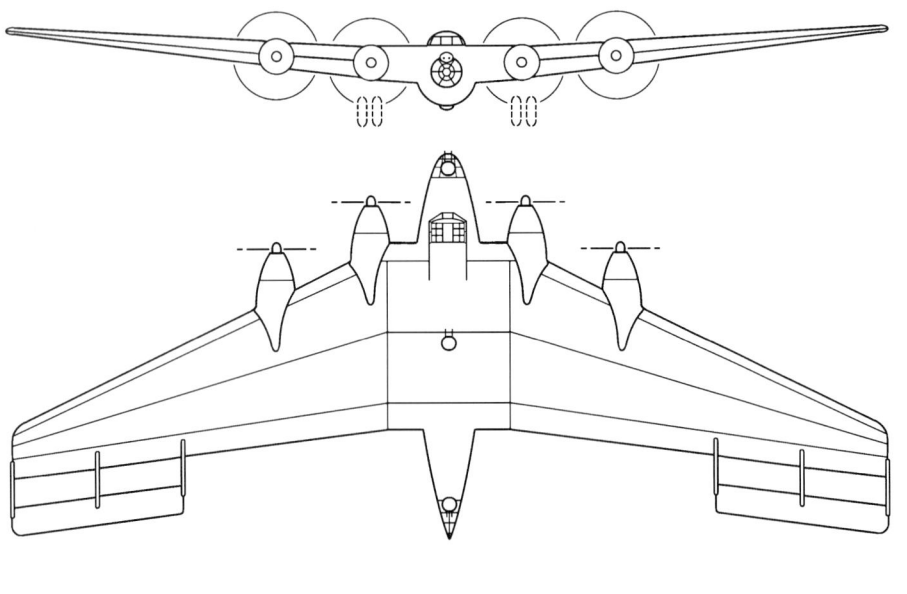

Boeing's 1935 Model 306 long-range, 10-man flying wing bomber proposal, featuring an unusual system of external control surfaces.
Bill Rose Collection

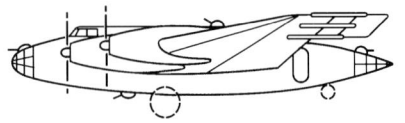

Boeing Model 306 Bomber

Crew	10
Wingspan	140ft (42.6m)
Length	60ft (18.2m)
Height	Unknown
Powerplant	4 x Allison V-1710 12-cylinder liquid-cooled piston engine, each producing 850hp (633kW)
Gross weight	Unknown
Range	5,000 miles (8,000km)
Maximum speed	Unknown
Ceiling	Unknown
Armament	2,500 lb (1,133kg) bomb load.
Defensive armament	2 x .50 cal (12.7mm) machine guns, 2 x .30 cal (7.62mm) machine guns

Boeing Model 306B/C Fighter

Crew	1
Wingspan	306B: 40ft (12m)
	306C: 38ft (11.5m)
Length	306B: 23ft (7m)
	306C: 22ft 2in (6.75m)
Height	Unknown
Gross weight	Unknown
Powerplant	306B: 1 x Allison V-1710 V-12 piston engine rated at 850hp (633kW)
	306C: 2 x Ranger V-770SG V-12 engines, each rated at 420hp (313kW)
Maximum speed	Unknown
Ceiling	306B: 15,000ft+ (4,572m+)
Range	Unknown
Endurance	306B: 3 hours
Armament	One or two .50 cal (12.7mm) machine guns mounted in the nose and possibly one larger calibre cannon

A 1935 Boeing tailless fighter concept produced during the Model 306 study and identified as Model 306B. Powered by a single Allison V-1710 V-12 piston engine, this aircraft used Boeing's externally positioned control surfaces. Bill Rose Collection

A twin-engine version of Boeing's Model 306 fighter study from 1935. The Model 306C design was to be powered by two Ranger V-770SG V-12 engines, each rated at 420hp (313kW). Bill Rose Collection

The second design was for an airliner/transporter with a capacity to carry 28 passengers. Assigned the study reference Model 306A, the airliner had a shorter wingspan of 106ft (32.3m) and was to be powered by four Pratt & Whitney S1EG Hornet radial engines, each rated at 750hp (559kW) and mounted in an unusual push-pull configuration. Initial estimates suggested that the aircraft would be able to cruise at 200mph (321kph) with a range of 1,200 miles (1,931km). Looking quite advanced for its time, the airliner featured a fixed tricycle undercarriage and a flush cockpit in the nose, providing excellent visibility for the pilot. The engine layout was an interesting idea, but calculations showed that the front propeller would disturb its rear counterpart, leading to a 10 per cent loss of power, so the study ended at this point.

The third Model 306 design was for a flying boat based on the Model 306 flying wing bomber with a similar wing profile and engine layout. Details of this design remain sketchy and obviously unfinished with drawings showing no stabilising floats which would have been essential.

The two remaining Model 306 concepts were for much smaller one-man fighter aircraft. The Model 306B was a tailless fighter driven by a single three-bladed propeller in a pusher configuration and powered by a single Allison V-1710 V-12 piston engine. Performance figures for the Model 306B are somewhat vague with an endurance of 3 hours and a ceiling of 15,000ft (4,572m). Maximum speed is unknown, but will not have made this aircraft a class leader. The Model 306B had a project wingspan of 40ft (12m) and a length of 23ft (7m). Armament comprised of two .50 cal (12.7mm) machine guns mounted in the nose and possibly one larger cannon. A fully retractable undercarriage was planned and the position of the cockpit would have provided good visibility. Flight control took the form of Boeing's displaced elevon system and wingtip stabilising fins were planned, probably equipped with rudders.

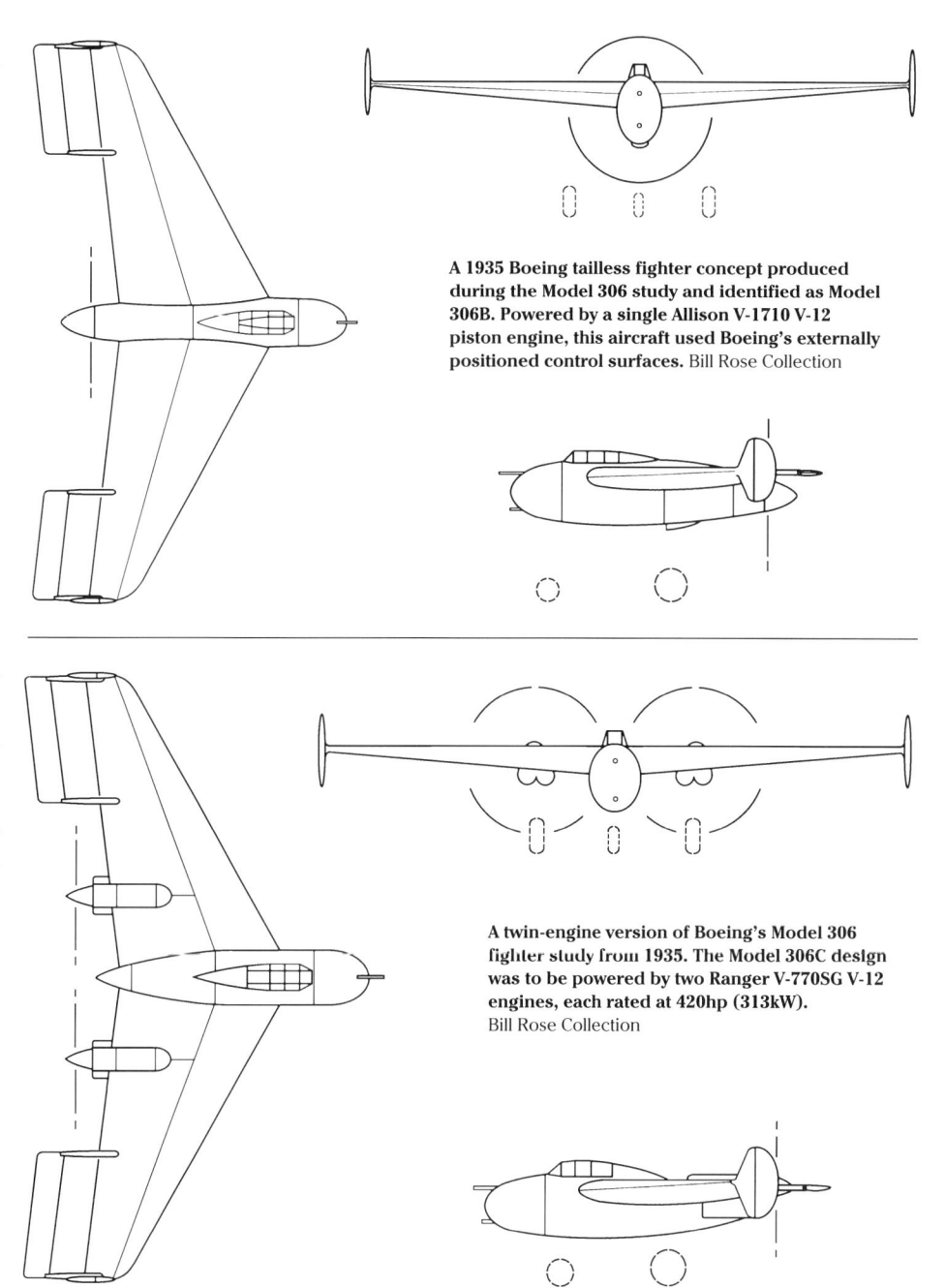

Whether the idea of a contra-rotating propeller unit was considered is unknown, although this might have proved desirable if the design had been taken any further. The Boeing Model 306C was a twin-engine version of the aircraft powered by two Ranger V-770SG V-12 engines, each rated at 420hp (313kW), located at the trailing edge and driving three-blade propellers. The wingspan of the Model 306C was reduced to 38ft (11.5m) and the overall length was 22ft 2in (6.75m). Other details such as armament, cockpit position and control surfaces were virtually the same as found on the single engine design. Needless to say, the Model 306 series of designs progressed no further and remained almost unknown until relatively recently.

US Flying Wings (1935-1950)

Jack Northrop

One man totally dominated US military flying wing development during much of the 20th century and he was John 'Jack' Knudsen Northrop (1895-1981). The Northrop family moved from Newark, New Jersey, to Santa Barbara, California, in 1914 and Jack Northrop joined the Loughead Brothers aviation business (later becoming Lockheed). After several years with the company, Northrop became its chief engineer and much of his time was devoted to working on Curtiss flying boats. Soon after World War 1 ended, the aviation business slumped and Loughead had closed for business by 1921. Jack Northrop worked as a garage mechanic until 1923 when he finally managed to secure a job with the newly established Douglas Aircraft Company at Santa Monica, California. In 1927, he left Douglas to briefly work with his former colleagues at Lockheed and most of this period was spent designing the Vega. Then in 1928, Jack Northrop formed the Avion Company with Kenneth Jay and finally set up Northrop Aviation with help from Donald Douglas of Douglas Aircraft.

Jack Northrop had been interested in the idea of building flying wing aircraft since his earliest days in the aviation business. He had designed many tailless aircraft concepts and built small models made from balsa wood in his spare time. Northrop was convinced that the next major advance in aircraft design was a sleek elegant one-piece wing that did not require a tail. By 1937, he was testing wind tunnel models of tailless aircraft and when he set up a new company in 1939, there was the finance, staff and facilities required to pursue flying wing development.

During the summer of 1939, work began on the construction of a small propeller driven flying wing called the N-1M (NX-28311) which had a wingspan of 38ft (11.58m), a length of 17ft (5.18m) and an empty weight of 4,000lb (1,814kg). Jack Northrop envisaged the N-1M as a one-third sized proof-of-concept demonstrator for a larger commercial or military aircraft. The distinctive yellow coloured N-1M was mainly constructed from wood, with metal only being used when necessary. It was initially powered by two 65hp (48.7kW) Lycoming 0-145 four-cylinder piston engines driving two blade pusher propellers. Because of this propulsive system, a fully retractable tricycle undercarriage was necessary and a small tailwheel in a fairing was added as a safety measure to ensure that any accidental rollback on the ground was limited.

The method of flight control was similar to that employed by the Horten Brothers for their aircraft with the elevons being adjusted together for pitch and differentially for roll. Rudder control was undertaken using split flaps at the wingtips and could be used to induce yaw or reduce speed. The aircraft was also built to allow modest pre-flight changes to the wing profile during testing. Completed by mid-1940, the Northrop N-1M was given the nickname 'Jeep' and trials began at Baker's Dry Lake in California. The test pilot was Vance Breeze and according to reports, the first test flight occurred accidentally during a high-speed taxi run. However, during the tests that followed, the aircraft failed to climb more than a few feet above the ground and two problems were soon recognised. Firstly the aircraft was underpowered and it was decided to replace the Lycoming engines with two 117hp (87.24kW) Franklin six-cylinder, air-cooled units driving three blade propellers.

There was also an aerodynamic problem which was quickly identified by the leading aerodynamicist Dr Theodore von Kármán. He pinpointed an airflow separation problem caused by the N-1M's wing and suggested extending the length of the elevons. Both

Above: **John 'Jack' Knudsen Northrop.** Northrop Grumman

Above right: **The Northrop N-1M proof-of-concept demonstrator with its dihedral wingtips in raised position.** Northrop Grumman

Right: **Jack Northrop (left) talks to the pilot of the experimental N-1M flying wing prototype during tests at Baker's Dry Lake, California, in 1940.** Northrop Grumman

these measures proved totally effective, although the replacement engines were continually operating at their design limits, leading to serious overheating problems. By the summer of 1941, Jack Northrop was considering another engine change to new Lycoming six-cylinder units each providing 150hp (112kW), but this never happened as there were now plans to move forward with a more advanced design.

Towards a Flying Wing Bomber

During April 1941, the US Army Air Corps issued a confidential request to various aircraft contractors for an intercontinental bomber with a range of 10,000 miles (16,000km). It had to be capable of cruising at 300mph (482kph), achieving a maximum altitude of 40,000ft (12,192m) and carrying a 10,000lb (4,535kg) bomb load. There was a widespread expectation in Washington that Britain would surrender to the Nazis and the US required the ability to undertake trans-Atlantic bombing missions. A number of proposals were submitted by Boeing, Consolidated, North American, Canadian Car & Foundry (CC&F) and Northrop.

Northrop's proposal would be a much larger development of the N-1M and during September 1941, it was officially acknowledged that despite some propulsive difficulties, the Northrop N-1M had performed well and showed considerable promise. Subsequently, the Secretary of War approved further development of the company's flying wing bomber.

The other aircraft to receive approval for development was Consolidated's Model 36 (which became the B-36) and a contract to build two Model 36 prototypes was issued during November 1941. The designers at Consolidated also produced an alternative six-engine flying wing bomber which promised superior aerodynamics and better use of internal space. This aircraft would have been substantial in size and manned by a crew of 12. The wingspan was 288ft (87.7m), with a 12° leading edge sweep and an overall length of 78ft (23.7m). Propulsion was broadly similar to the system chosen for the Model 36, comprising of six Pratt & Whitney, 3,000hp (2,237kW) X-Wasp radial piston engines, each driving a 19ft (5.79m) diameter Curtiss three-blade pusher propeller.

A maximum bomb load of 72,000lb (32,658kg) was viable for a limited range mission and the planned defensive armament was substantial with two forward and one rear (remote controlled) turret equipped with 37mm cannons and two aft turrets using .50 cal (12.7mm) machine guns. The flying wing's gross weight was estimated at 237,800lb (107,864kg) with a maximum speed at 30,000ft (9,144m) of 394mph (634kph) and a service ceiling of 42,000ft (12,800m). But it is uncertain if the original target range of 10,000 miles (16,093km), carrying a 10,000lb (4,535kg) bomb load for half that distance was altogether realistic. In appearance, the aircraft was very clean, with no stabilising fins or external features of note. The pressurised cockpit protruded some way

Consolidated Aircraft Large Flying Wing Bomber (1941-1942)

Crew	12
Wingspan	288ft (87.7m)
Length	78ft (23.7m)
Sweep	12° leading edge
Gross weight	237,800lb (107,864kg)
Powerplant	6 x Pratt & Whitney, 3,000hp (2,237kW) X-Wasp radial piston engines, each driving a 19ft (5.79m) diameter Curtiss three-blade pusher propeller
Maximum speed	394mph (634kph)
Ceiling	42,000ft (12,800m)
Range	10,000 miles (16,093km)
Armament	72,000lb (32,658kg) bomb load.
Defensive	Forward and rear (remote controlled) turrets with 37mm cannons. 2 x aft turrets using .50 cal (12.7mm) machine guns

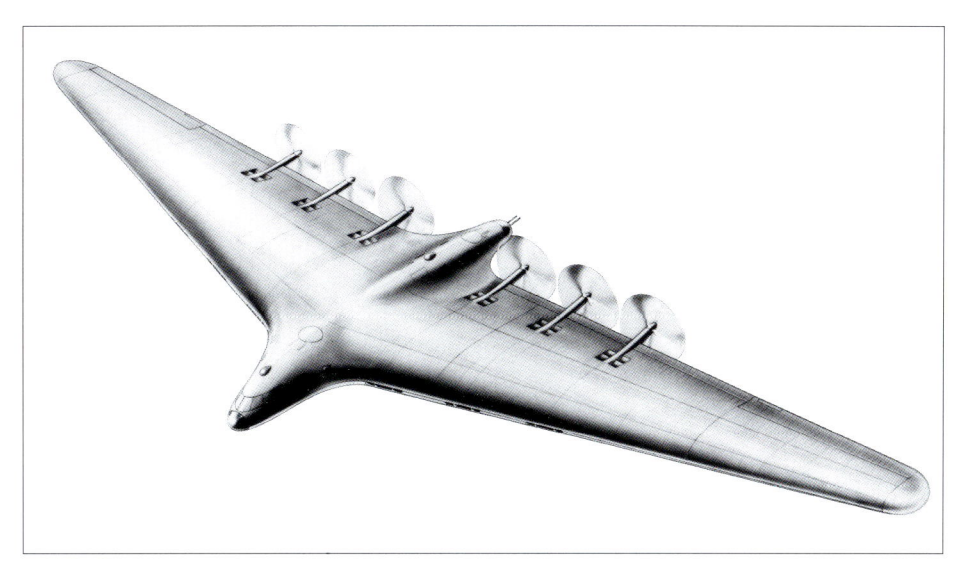

Top: **Consolidated Aircraft's flying wing alternative to the B-36 heavy bomber designed in the early 1940s.** Courtesy Robert Bradley

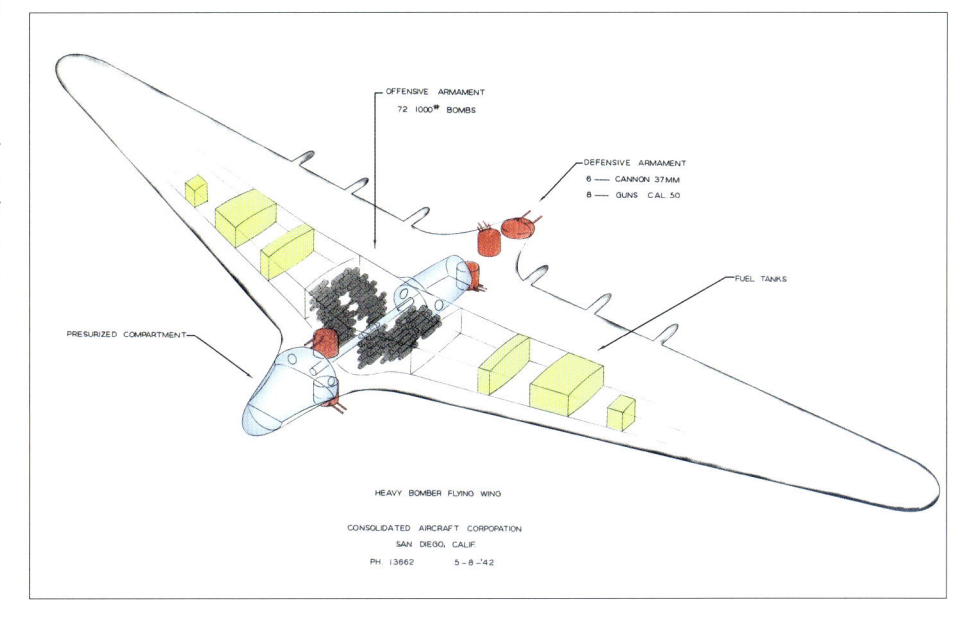

Right: **Some very basic company artwork, showing internal features of the Consolidated Aircraft six-engine flying wing proposal.**
Courtesy Robert Bradley

US Flying Wings (1935-1950)

The Burnelli UB-14B lifting fuselage, light transport aircraft (X-15320) constructed in 1935-36. It was almost identical to the earlier UB-14 (X-14740) that crashed during its test flight on 13 January 1935 at Newark, New Jersey, following detachment of both ailerons. Aspects of pre-war designs like this UB-14B would be used in the design of a wartime lifting body bomber proposed to the USAAF. Burnelli Aircraft Ltd

Burnelli B-2000B

Crew	12
Wingspan	220ft (67m)
Wing area	6,580ft² (611m²)
Length	126ft (38.4m)
Empty weight	110,000 lb (49,895kg)
Gross weight	220,000 lb (99,790kg)
Powerplant	Several proposals, utilising six or eight unspecified piston engines driving forward-mounted contra-rotating propeller units
Armament	Bomb load 72,000 lb (32,658kg). 7 defensive machine gun positions
Maximum speed	300mph (482kph)
Range (max bomb load)	2,000 miles (3,218km)

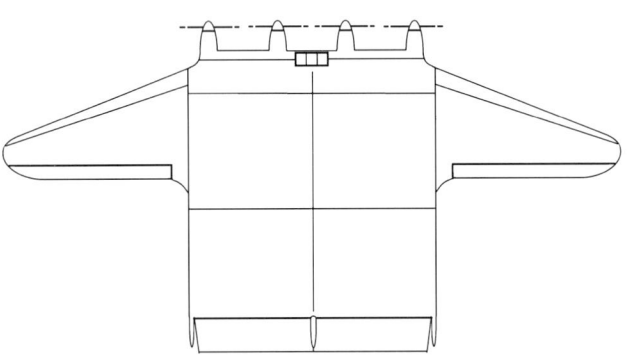

This drawing is based on US Patent Design 136249 filed on 7 October 1942. No details of this Burnelli four-engine lifting body aircraft have been located, but it appears to be part of the wartime bomber study. US Patent Office

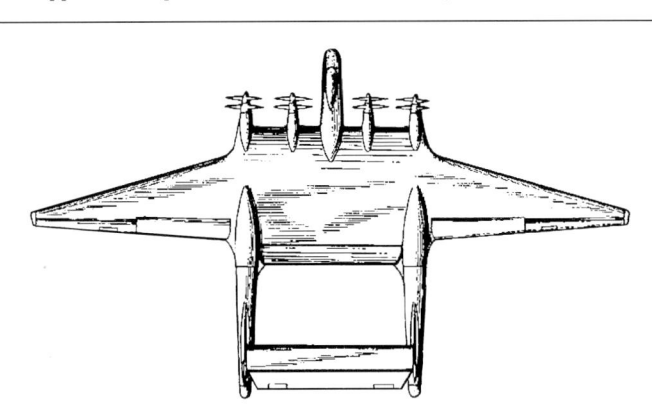

An aircraft based on the wartime Burnelli B-2000 proposal for a bomber. It is taken from US Patent Design 160842 which was filed in 1949. US Patent Office

This artwork shows the Burnelli B-1000B which was one of several submissions by Canadian Car & Foundry for the USAAF's long-range bomber proposal of 1941. Although not true flying wings, the Burnelli bomber designs offered a number of technical advantages over more conventional designs, but failed to win official support, possibly for political reasons. Bill Rose Collection

Secret Projects: Flying Wings and Tailless Aircraft

ahead of the wing, affording good visibility and it was connected to a crew compartment at the rear via an access tunnel. The aircraft was equipped with a fully retractable tricycle undercarriage comprising of a single 65in (1.64m) diameter nose wheel and 80in (2m) diameter twin-wheel sets at the rear.

The company reference for this design remains unclear and the small amount of documentation available will typically just refer to the project as the Six-Engine, Long-Range, Flying Wing Bombardment Airplane. It remains uncertain exactly when this alternative study was initiated, but available company documents suggest that work involving scale models and wind tunnel testing continued into 1942 before the project was shelved.

The CC&F submission for a long-range bomber was conceived by Vincent Justus Burnelli and although unsuccessful it remains an interesting design. Burnelli had been responsible for a number of unorthodox aircraft, often utilising lifting body features, with the emphasis on safety and load carrying efficiency. In the late 1920s, he worked on a large tailless flying wing design which was filed as a US Patent on 23 February 1933 and published two years later (Patent 1987050). This multi-engine concept was quite advanced for its time, making good use of internal space and utilising a fully retractable four-wheel undercarriage. Wingtip stabilisers and rudders were planned, although Burnelli seems to have overlooked the issue of cockpit visibility in his quest to produce a clean design. Nevertheless, the design was impressive for its time.

As a submission for the 1941 US long-range bomber proposal, CC&F produced plans and specifications for a large lifting body aircraft called the B-2000B. Based on various earlier designs, the B-2000B was essentially a development of Burnelli's 1933 flying wing fitted with two fairly substantial booms and a tailplane. The other major revision was a cockpit section that protruded forward from the straight central leading edge. Propulsion took the form of four forward-mounted contra-rotating propeller units, driven by eight unspecified piston engines. Some documentation indicates an alternative layout using six contra-rotating propeller units, each driven by a liquid-cooled Allison V-3420 engine (built from two Allison V-1710 engines using the same prop shaft) providing a total of 12,600hp (9,395kW) continuous output and a maximum speed of about 300mph (482kph). The B-2000B had a proposed wingspan of 220ft (67m), a length of 126ft (38.4m) and an estimated gross weight of 220,000lb (99,790kg). The range was dependant on the bomb load with a maximum capacity of 72,000lb. Flown by a crew of 12, the B-2000B would be fitted with seven gun turrets, mainly located in the tail booms. Burnelli also worked on a commercial airliner based on this design which would be capable of carrying 100 passengers from London to New York.

An alternative concept for the new USAAF bomber was Burnelli's B-1000. Often described as a flying wing, the B-1000 didn't really meet the terms associated with this type of aircraft and is more correctly described as a lifting body. This design would have used a substantial, but shorter tailplane unit mounted above an extension of the central trailing edge and supported by three upright fins. Other details appear similar to the B-2000B such as the propulsion layout and cockpit location. Wingspan is understood to have been 220ft (67m) with an overall length of 80ft (24.3m). By the start of 1942, the Burnelli bomber had been rejected for technical reasons, although it has since been claimed that this aircraft was the victim of a political conspiracy, possibly involving President Roosevelt.

Northrop Receives Approval

Northrop was now gearing up to develop its flying wing strategic bomber and a formal USAAF contract (W535 AC 21341) had been issued on 22 November 1941 to begin work. This covered construction of the first N-9M scale demonstrator, a mock-up of the XB-35, a prototype XB-35 and the option of building a second aircraft. Somewhat optimistically, the delivery date for the first XB-35 was November 1943.

Soon after work began on the construction of a one-third-scale size N-9M prototype, Northrop received a second contract (W535-ac-33920), which amongst other things requested two further N-9M aircraft. All three of these prototypes now received designations: N-9M-1, N-9M-2 and N-9M-3. The Northrop N-9M flying wing was intended to be a one-man aircraft, although it could be reconfigured to accommodate an observer if the 41.5gal (189 litre) fuel tank located behind the pilot was removed. The N-9M had a wingspan of 60ft (18.3m), a length of 17ft 9in (5.4m) and the first aircraft weighed 6,326lb (3,175kg) fully loaded. Two Menasco C6S-4 piston engines powered the N-9M, each rated at 275hp (205kW) and driving two-bladed pusher propellers. Like the earlier N-1M, the N-9M was built using similar methods and materials that were primarily wood, with some aluminium components and a certain amount of steel tubing. It was also equipped with a similar fully retracting tricycle undercarriage and a retractable fourth wheel to help protect the propellers during take-offs and landings. Cockpit space was tight, due to the carriage of special test equipment. Like the N-1M, the normal control stick was replaced with a column and wheel to mimic the proposed larger bomber. However, visibility from the cockpit was very good, due to its forward position and the use of a bubble canopy.

Unusually, no civil or military registrations were assigned to any of the Northrop N-9M aircraft. N-9M-1 first flew on 27 December 1941 and subsequent flights were plagued with mechanical problems, usually attributed to the Menasco engines. The prototype performed quite well delivering a maximum speed of about 250mph (400kph), a ceiling slightly better than 21,000ft (6,400m) and a range of about 500 miles (800km).

Unfortunately for Northrop, trials began to fall behind schedule due to ongoing technical problems and limited information was gathered on the aircraft's stability and drag characteristics. Then on 19 May 1943, after just 22.5 hours of accumulated flying, N-9M-1 piloted by Max Constant crashed about 12 miles (20km) west of Muroc Field. The N-9M-1 had entered a violent 60° nose-down spin and Constant tried every means to recover the aircraft. The small left hand anti-spin parachute had been released and the flaps were partially lowered, but to no avail. Having realised he was in serious trouble, Constant released the cockpit canopy and prepared to bail out, but failed to leave the aircraft and was killed. There were now serious concerns about the aircraft's stability and it was clear that the elevons on the first N-9M had undergone a control reversal during the spin. NACA Langley was asked to study a scale model in its spin tunnel to determine if changes should be made to the control surfaces and spin chutes.

The following month, N-9M-2 was completed and it took to the air on 24 June 1943. There were a series of minor problems resulting from the cockpit canopy detaching during this test-flight, but the trial was judged a success. Flights continued throughout the remainder of the year and stability and directional control were judged satisfactory rather than outstanding. Good data was being returned, although it had become apparent that drag produced by the full-sized XB-35 would be greater than indicated during tests with wind tunnel models. While development work on the full-sized XB-35 continued, Northrop completed a third N-9M, now desig-

Left: **The Northrop N-9M1 during a test flight in early 1943.** Northrop Grumman

Bottom: **Wreckage of the Northrop N-9M-1 which crashed on 19 May 1943 about 12nm (20km) west of Muroc Field.** USAF

Northrop N-1M

Crew	1
Wingspan	38ft (11.58m)
Length	17ft (5.18m)
Height	5ft (1.52m)
Empty weight	4,000lb (1,814kg)
Powerplant	2 x 65hp (48.7kW) Lycoming 0-145 four-cylinder piston engines, later replaced by 117hp (87.24kW) Franklin six-cylinder, air-cooled engines

Northrop N-9M

Crew	1 (The N-9M-1 N-9M-B were also capable of carrying an observer, achieved by removal of a fuel tank located behind the pilot)
Length	17ft 9in (5.4m)
Wingspan	60ft (18.3m)
Height	6ft 7in (2m)
Wing area	490ft² (45.5m²)
Empty weight	5,893lb (2,673kg)
Gross weight	6,326lb (3,175kg)
Powerplant N-9M	2 x Menasco C6S-4 piston engines, each rated at 275hp (205kW)
Powerplant N-9M-B	2 x Franklin O-540-7 piston engines, each rated at 300hp (223kW)
Maximum speed	258mph (415kph)
Range	500 miles (805km)
Service ceiling	21,500ft (6,555m)
Endurance	3.2 hours

nated N-9M-A and it was decided to built a fourth N-9M aircraft to replace N-9M-1 which would be known as N-9M-B.

N-9M-A was passed to the USAAF and made its acceptance flight on 28 June 1944. This aircraft incorporated numerous design changes making its handling much closer to that of the full-sized XB-35. It was equipped with split trailing edge and pitch control flaps, plus leading edge slots to reduce the possibility of stall at high angles of attack. Trials continued with the aircraft throughout the remainder of 1944 producing consistent results while the N-9M-B had soon been completed. This fourth and final prototype was equipped with more powerful 300hp (223kW) Franklin 0-540-7 supercharged 8-cylinder piston engines, driving two-blade Hamilton Standard propellers in a pusher configuration via shafts and fluid couplers. Further minor modifications had been made to this fourth prototype and like the original N-9M-1 this aircraft could be adapted to carry an observer by removal of a fuel tank. Once completed, the fourth N-9M was also passed to the USAAF for testing.

Development of the XB-35 was taking far longer than expected, largely due to a shortage of qualified engineers and skilled staff, but flights of the three smaller prototypes continued until the end of World War 2. These Northrop flying wings were never intended to be anything more than research aircraft that would demonstrate the viability of a larger military design. But it is clear from examination of patents and documentation that Northrop considered several slightly larger aircraft based on the N-9M such as a twin-engine light-bomber.

The original N-1M ended up with the National Air & Space Museum in 1949 and after several decades in storage was returned to its original condition. The N-9M-B found its way to the Chino Planes of Fame Museum in California where it was restored to flying condition. The other two N-9Ms were broken up for scrap.

The XB-35

With work underway on the XB-35 programme, Northrop received a contract to build an additional 13 pre-production aircraft. These would be designated YB-35 and the details were formalised on 17 December 1942. Furthermore, a decision had been taken to request the construction of 200 B-35 bombers to follow these test examples and this became the subject of a contract issued in June 1943. But it was already apparent that development of the B-35 would take longer than anticipated and completion of the first production aircraft was rescheduled to mid-1945. Having secured a substantial order for the new bomber, Jack Northrop began to look for additional manufacturing capacity and approached the Glenn L. Martin Company. This led to a general agreement that Northrop would produce the prototypes and pre-production aircraft, while Martin would take responsibility for building the production models at its Baltimore, Maryland, facility.

The XB-35's wingspan was 172ft (52.2m) with a tapering chord and a leading edge sweep of 27°. The wing area was 4,000ft² (370 m²), the height was 20ft 3in (6.2m) and the overall length was 53ft 1in (16.2m). It is interesting to note that the modern Northrop B-2A stealth bomber has the same wingspan, marginally less height and is approximately 13ft (3.96m) longer due to the B-2A's unusual wing profile with its 35° leading edge sweep. However, whereas the modern Northrop bomber would normally be flown by two crew members with the option of a third, the B-35 was designed from the outset to accommodate at least nine personnel (and possibly more). These would consist of the pilot and

Secret Projects: Flying Wings and Tailless Aircraft

co-pilot, a navigator, engineer and radio operator, plus a bomb aimer and three gunners. To make long missions more acceptable, there would be six folding bunk beds and a small galley. The pilot was located in a forward cockpit that was slightly offset from centre and covered by a bubble canopy. The co-pilot was located in a lower glazed section next to the bomb aimer with the navigator and engineer behind them. Like the earlier small Northrop prototype flying wings, the full-sized aircraft was supported on the ground by a retractable tricycle undercarriage.

Propulsion for the new Northrop bomber was to be provided by four substantial Pratt & Whitney Wasp Major supercharged air-cooled radial engines. Two of the engines were R-4360-17s and two were R-4360-21s. In actual fact, all the engines for this aircraft were identical and the only difference was the length of their extension shafts. Development of the R-4360 started just before the XB-35 programme and it was a very complex piece of engineering: a 28-cylinder, four-row radial engine with each row slightly offset. Although generally reliable, the engine has been described as a maintenance nightmare. This large unit utilised a complex carburettor and turbo-supercharger system. Each aluminium-alloy cylinder head was equipped with two manually adjusted valves per cylinder operated by push rods and there were a total of 56 spark plugs linked to four Bendix-Scintilla S14RN-15 low-tension dual magnetos. Early trials indicated that each engine would provide 3,000hp (2,237kW) with the possibility of higher performance as development progressed. It was decided to place cooling slots for the engines in the leading edge of the wing and each engine would be coupled to a rear-mounted contra-rotating four-blade propeller beyond the trailing edge. The engines were capable of operating at an altitude of 40,000ft (12,192m) and providing a maximum speed of about 390mph (627kph). With a take-off weight of 209,000 lb (94,800kg), the aircraft was expected to have a range of just over 8,000 miles (12,874km).

While the range of the B-35 was less than originally contemplated by the USAF, the general performance was significantly better than early versions of the Boeing B-29, which had set the benchmark for bombers of this period. The Northrop flying wing would be built almost entirely from metal using substantial amounts of a new aluminium alloy developed by Alcola. Fuel was carried in a series of self-sealing wing tanks with provision for extra tank installation within the wing and bomb bays allowing extended range missions. Double split flaps on the outer trailing edge provided lateral control or braking with substantial elevons for control of pitch and roll.

A number of defensive remote-controlled gun turrets were planned for the B-35. These would all be fitted with 0.50in (12.7mm) machine guns. The remote turrets would be mounted above and below the rear tailcone and in four units above and below the wing, outboard of the engines. The gunners would control and operate their weapons from within several stations covered with transparent domes. The aircraft was equipped with no less than eight separate bomb bays and the proposed bomb load was 16,000 lb (7,257kg). The design was structured around the central crew cabin and this rather unsatisfactory layout would eventually become a major issue for the USAAF as the type of weapons carried by heavy bombers underwent a dramatic change.

Development of the B-35 progressed at a slow pace with tests of the N-9M research aircraft continuing to indicate that performance of the full-sized flying wing bomber would be

This photograph taken in 1946 shows an X-35 wing section during assembly at Northrop's Hawthorne facility in California. USAF

The first XB-35 prototype (42-13603) is rolled out at Northrop's California plant in early 1946. Northrop Grumman

US Flying Wings (1935-1950)

less than predicted. In addition, Martin was experiencing staff shortages due to the war effort which meant that initial deliveries of the production aircraft could not be guaranteed before 1947. By spring 1944, these issues were starting to generate concerns within the Pentagon and a decision was taken on 24 May 1944 to cancel Martin's contract to build the B-35.

However, Air Technical Services Command still wanted the prototype and pre-production aircraft for test purposes and it was agreed in December 1944 that the project should continue. By mid-1945, the war in Europe was over and the USAAF was looking ahead to a time when propeller-driven warplanes would become outdated. Although work was continuing on the XB-35, the USAAF requested Northrop to adapt two of the YB-35 airframes to accept Allison J35-A-5 engines. These modified aircraft received the initial designations YB-35B (later YB-49).

Northrop YB-35

Crew	9 – pilot, co-pilot, bombardier, navigator, engineer, radio operator and three gunners
Length	53ft 1in (16.2m)
Wingspan	172ft (52.2m)
Sweep	27° (leading edge)
Wing area	4,000ft^2 (370m^2)
Wing loading	45 lb/ft^2 (220kg/m^2)
Height	20ft 3in (6.2m)
Fuselage diameter	9ft 6in (2.9m)
Empty weight	120,000 lb (54,432kg)
Loaded weight	180,000 lb (82,000kg)
Max take-off weight	209,000 lb (95,000kg)
Powerplant	4 x Pratt & Whitney R-4360 supercharged air-cooled radial engines, each rated at 3,000hp (2,200kW). Initially driving contra-props, later single rotation propellers
Maximum speed	391mph (629km/h)
Estimated range	8,150 miles (13,100km)
Service ceiling	39,700ft (12,100m)
Rate of climb	625ft/min (190m/min)
Armament	20 x .50 (12.7mm) M2 machine guns.
Bomb load	16,000 lb (7,257kg)

An air-to-air study of XB-35 (213603). Northrop Grumman

Northrop XB-35 (213603) photographed during a test flight. Northrop Grumman

An underside view of the Northrop XB-35 equipped with the troublesome contra-rotating propeller units. Northrop Grumman

Secret Projects: Flying Wings and Tailless Aircraft

Northrop XB-35 above an unspecified dry lake. The propellers have been changed to single rotation units following problems with the contra-rotating units. USAF

Further revisions to the project followed with two additional YB-35 aircraft being added as replacements for the jet versions. Various different modifications were made to the other flying wings leading to them being redesignated YB-35A.

The first XB-35 (42-13603) was ready to undertake its first test-flight from Northrop's airfield at Hawthorne, California, to Muroc AAF on 25 June 1946. The company's chief test pilot Max R. Stanley flew the aircraft and flight engineer Dale Shroeder accompanied him. Soon after take-off there were engine-related problems which would reoccur during subsequent trials. This finally brought testing to a halt on 11 September 1946 after 19 flights. Work continued on the second XB-35 prototype (42-38323) and it took to the air on 26 June 1947, but similar difficulties were encountered and the aircraft was grounded after eight flights.

Problems with the complex gearboxes operating the contra-rotating propeller units could not be resolved and it was decided to replace the entire assemblies with single-rotation propellers. Flight testing finally resumed on 12 February 1948 and continued for two months, but the substitution of these components had created unacceptable vibration issues and the aircraft's performance had worsened. Flight stability remained unsatisfactory and there were major concerns about the complexity and reliability of the powerful Pratt & Whitney engines and their elaborate exhaust systems.

By now, the first YB-35A (42-102366) had been completed and was fitted with single-rotation propellers, while efforts continued to deal with the vibration problem. This aircraft was equipped with defensive weapons and made its first test flight on 15 May 1948. Various proposals followed to use the flying wings as in-flight refuelling aircraft and to test the final YB-35 with Turbodyne XT-37 turboprop engines. This adaptation was provisionally known as EB-35B and Northrop installed the engines, but the variant was never completed. Other options for use as a reconnaissance aircraft were considered, but the propeller-driven flying wing was too unstable to function reliably as a camera platform. The first YB-35 became the only pre-production propeller driven aircraft from this series to fly and it was already clear that the days of using this method of propulsion for warplanes was drawing to a close.

The Northrop B-49

In 1944, Northrop undertook a study to determine if the B-35 flying wing bomber could be developed into a jet-powered aircraft. This led to a change in the USAAF's contract with Northrop during the following year that allowed the future conversion of two YB-35s to a new configuration using six or eight turbojets. But it was clear that a jet-powered version required additional fins to replace the yaw dampening effect provided by the prop shaft covers and the conversion would involve a fair amount of work.

Adaptation of the two YB-35s was soon underway and it had been decided to fit eight rather than six Allison J35-A15 turbojets, each rated at 4,000 lb (17.8kN) static thrust. The leading edge was modified to allow the positioning of low-drag air intakes for each engine, four sets of fins were attached to the trailing edge and wing fences were positioned on each side of the engine installations. In addition, most of the aircraft's defensive armament was removed, leaving just one remote-controlled tail barbette in the tail.

Although initially designated as YB-35B, these two prototypes were now renamed YB-49. The first YB-49 (42-102367) was completed at Hawthorne in the summer of 1947 and flown to Muroc by Max Stanley on 21 October 1947. Unlike the maiden flight of the XB-35, this mission took place without any difficulties. The second YB-49 (42-102368) was completed by the end of the year and made its first relatively trouble-free flight on 13 January 1948.

Northrop and USAF test pilots jointly undertook an extensive test programme with the first aircraft completing about 270 hours of flying and the second aircraft about 60 hours. The YB-49 was a decided improvement over the propeller-driven aircraft, although it still displayed stability problems. During tests, the maximum speed was established at 520mph (836kph) and the ceiling set at 42,000ft (12,801m), although slightly higher altitudes were achieved. On 26 April 1948, the first YB-49 set a new unofficial record by making a nine-hour flight, of which six hours were spent above 40,000ft (12,192m). But the range was considerably less than the piston-engine aircraft, allowing a distance of approximately 4,000 miles (6,437km) with a 10,000 lb (4,536kg) bomb load. The crew requirement for the new aircraft had fallen to seven, but there was the option of accommodating a replacement crew in the tail section of the aircraft for a long duration mission.

While the aircraft were performing quite well during these trials, stability remained a major issue and Lt Gen Benjamin W. Chidlaw, who was Deputy Commander of the Air Materiel Command, decided that this problem should receive top priority. Compared to the Boeing B-29, the YB-49 (when flown without autopilot) performed very badly as a bomber with the flying wing producing twice the B-29's circular average error during simulated missions. The B-29 would usually attain stability during a bomb run in 45 seconds whereas the YB-49 never managed a better time than four minutes. Despite having an autopilot, it was generally thought that the

US Flying Wings (1935-1950)

Preparation taking place for a test flight of the Northrop YB-49. USAF

lack of stability with the jet-powered flying wing was due to the inadequate stabilising fins. Northrop hoped to resolve this problem, but there were further difficulties for the company when the USAF reviewed the capabilities of the YB-49 and decided to redesignate it as a medium bomber in the same class as the Boeing XB-47 which was undergoing development.

Yet another consideration was the aircraft's ability to carry atomic weapons and the Air Materiel Command had been considering this issue for some time. Clearly there would be problems with the B-49 because of its eight separate bomb bays and the size of existing free-fall nuclear bombs.

Northrop had been examining adaptation of the B-35 to carry very large bombs since early in 1945 when the USAF began developing plans to use the T-10, which was a US-built version of the British 12,000 lb (5,443kg) Tallboy bomb and the T-14, which was a copy of the larger 22,000 lb (9,979kg) Grand Slam bomb. Both of these weapons were designed by Sir Barnes Wallis and used operationally by the RAF during World War 2 against high-value German targets. Until the arrival of nuclear weapons, they remained the only bombs capable of destroying a hardened underground facility and (excluding some trials with a modified B-29) the only post-war US bomber expected to carry them was the massive Consolidated Vultee (later Convair) B-36, which was developed in parallel to the Northrop flying wing. The B-36 could easily carry four T-10s, three T-14s or two even bigger bombs called the T-12. This was a scaled-up T-14 weighing a staggering 43,600 lb (19,776kg), which was tested but, like its predecessors, never used by the USAF.

Unfortunately, the B-35's largest bays (inboard) measured 4ft 4in (1.36m) wide, 12ft 4in (3.75m) long and 6ft 6in (1.98m) deep. But due to the need for adequate clearance, the maximum dimensions of a single bomb had to be somewhat less than this. These bays remained unchanged for the jet powered B-49, although the outer bomb bays were removed due to changes in propulsion. The largest conventional bomb that could be carried by the B-35 weighed 4,000 lb (1,814kg) and there was little scope for adaptation to carry anything bigger as the wing spars formed the front and rear walls of both inboard bomb bays. Even carrying the bomb semi-externally was impossible with the T-10 having an overall length of 21ft (6.4m) and the bigger T-14 measuring 26ft 6in (8m) including its tail.

Northrop realised from the outset that it would be impossible to make any changes to the aircraft that allowed the internal carriage of longer bombs, so it undertook a study to determine the possibility of suspending two T-10 or T-14 bombs beneath bays two and seven. This showed that carriage of these bombs would seriously degrade the aircraft's speed and the added weight of the T-14 would reduce the range considerably. In addition, the clearance between the tail of a 25ft (7.62m) long T-14 and the propeller blades would have been a mere 12in

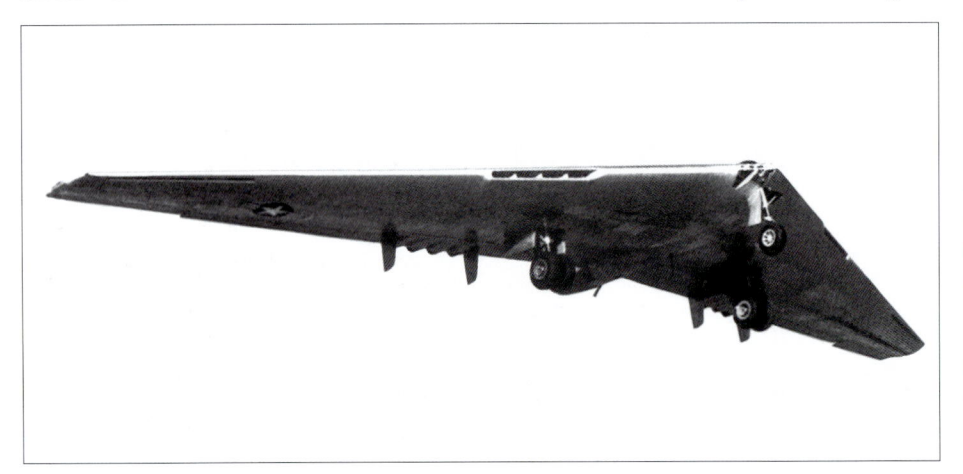

The jet-powered version of Northrop's flying wing bomber, designated YB-49. USAF

This simulated image shows an underside view of the Northrop XB-35 carrying two large ground-penetrating bombs. Although this capability was studied in detail, there were serious problems positioning these weapons and the small amount of clearance between the tail of each weapon and propeller blades created serious concerns.
Bill Rose Collection

Secret Projects: Flying Wings and Tailless Aircraft

(305mm), which was unacceptable. Whether or not a modified bomb with a shorter length was considered is unknown, but there was no possibility of moving the bomb further forward. These weapons had to be suspended from within the bays, which meant they were partly enclosed and there were issues of weight distribution.

Nevertheless, the prevailing post-war interest was the carriage of newly developed atomic weapons. The only operational aircraft capable of doing this was the B-29, but there was the Convair B-36 strategic bomber in development that could carry large weapons with ease and the future B-47 medium bomber would also be nuclear capable.

The Northrop B-35/B-49 was unable to carry the newly developed Mk3 'Fat Man' plutonium bomb which would just about fit lengthwise in a bay, but was too wide with its 5ft (1.52m) diameter and rather awkward box tail. With nuclear weapons having to be physically armed by a specialist before release, the bomb had to be accessible to the crew. So Northrop engineers carefully examined ways of modifying a bomb bay to accept the Mk3 atomic bomb and finally decided that the only practical answer was to carry the weapon semi-externally, covered by a jettisonable bathtub-shaped fairing. The problem was that the cover would have extended back over the wing flaps and was expected to significantly degrade performance. The situation improved slightly when the Mk4 atomic bomb became available in 1949. The weapon could have been carried within the B-35 or B-49's bomb bay, providing that various modifications were made to the surrounding structure. But alterations would have been very expensive and quite complicated, requiring amongst other things, new specially shaped bomb bay doors.

Despite growing concerns about the future of Northrop's flying wing bomber, the second YB-49 (42-102368) was passed to the USAF on 28 May 1948. A few days later on 5 June 1948, this aircraft crashed just north of Muroc AFB, killing the pilot Daniel Hugh Forbes Jr., his co-pilot Captain Glenn Edwards and three crew members. The aircraft was almost completely destroyed by the impact, although a section of wing was recovered several miles away. The exact cause of the accident has never been fully identified, but it was clear that a major structural failure occurred. The YB-49 had entered a dive from 40,000ft (12,192m) and one eyewitness described the aircraft as tumbling about its lateral axis prior to impact. As a result of this accident, Topeka Army Airfield, Kansas, was renamed Forbes AFB (now operated by the Kansas Air National Guard) in honour of the Kansas-born pilot on 13 July 1949. This was followed by Muroc AFB being renamed as Edwards AFB on 5 December 1949 in memory of Captain Edwards, who grew up in California.

Despite this tragic loss, the USAF intended to press on with the flying wing programme and the conversion of the YB-35 airframes continued at Northrop. With only one YB-49 available for evaluation, it was decided to extend the test period for this aircraft. The USAF also planned to place a fresh order for 30 RB-49B aircraft designed for reconnaissance missions. But the technical problems with the flying wing continued throughout the remainder of the year. Most pilots found the aircraft difficult to fly and there was constant trouble with the engines.

At the start of 1949, the USAF requested that the YB-49 was flown across the US to Andrews AFB so it could participate in a military display attended by senior officials and politicians. The YB-49 departed Muroc AFB on 9 February 1949 with USAF pilot Major Robert Cardenas at the controls. He was accompanied by co-pilot Capt W.W. Seller and Max Stanley acting as an observer and a representative of Northrop. When the aircraft arrived at Andrews AFB, it had completed the 2,258-mile (3,634km) non-stop flight in 4 hours and 20 minutes, averaging an impressive speed of 511mph (822kph).

The air show went well with no hitches and President Harry S. Truman inspected the YB-49, describing it as looking like 'one hell of an airplane'. On the return to Muroc AFB, Cardenas landed at Wright-Patterson AFB, Ohio, allowing a detailed inspection of the aircraft by USAF specialists. Having left for Muroc AFB on 23 February 1949, there were serious problems with four of the YB-49's jet engines, forcing Cardenas to make an emergency landing

Above: **Capt Glenn Edwards, who was killed when the second YB-49 (42-102368) crashed during a test flight on 5 June 1948. As a mark of respect, Muroc AFB was renamed as Edwards AFB on 5 December 1949.** USAF

Below: **Underside view of the YB-49 in flight.** Northrop Grumman

US Flying Wings (1935-1950)

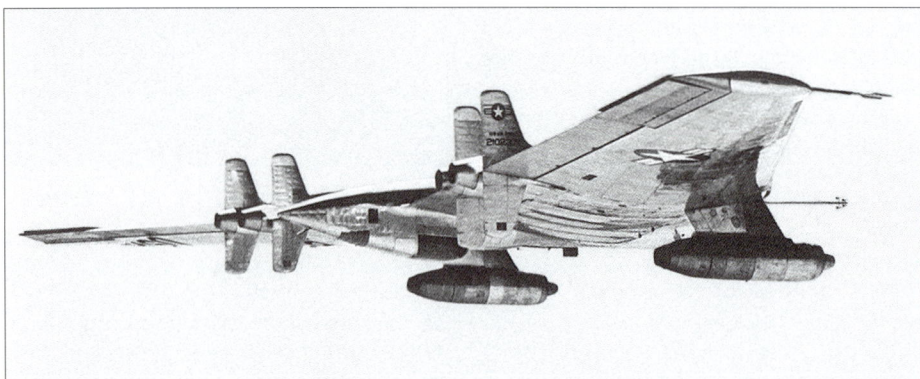

The Northrop YB-49 undertaking a test flight from Muroc AFB. USAF

The YRB-49A was the final version of the Northrop flying wing bomber. The propulsion system was extensively modified and the aircraft was reconfigured for long-range reconnaissance operations. The YRB-49A first flew on 4 May 1950, but it was not a success and was finally scrapped bringing this flying wing programme to an end. Northrop Grumman

The YRB-49 during a test flight. The reduction in engines from eight to six is clearly visible in this photograph. USAF

at Winslow Airport, Arizona. It was soon determined that the oil tanks for the J35 turbojets had not been filled before departure at Wright-Patterson and the FBI was requested to investigate, although its findings were never released and the matter was quietly forgotten.

Things continued to go wrong and on 26 April 1949, a serious engine fire caused substantial damage requiring repairs amounting to $19,000, which was a sizable amount in those days. Trials resumed and continued throughout the remainder of that year with emphasis on the ability to deliver bombs accurately with and without the E-7 autopilot. But the results were still judged unsatisfactory by most pilots. Official interest in the Northrop flying wing continued to diminish and during November 1949, the USAF decided to abandon the conversion of the remaining YB-35s to YB-49s with the exception of one aircraft that would be adapted for testing in the reconnaissance role.

Northrop YB-49

Crew	7
Wingspan	172ft (52.42m)
Wing area	4,000ft² (370m²)
Sweep	27° (leading edge)
Length	53ft (16.1m)
Height	15ft (4.57m)
Empty weight	88,442 lb (40,116kg)
Gross weight	193,938 lb (87,968kg)
Propulsion	8 x Allison J35-A-15 turbojets, each producing 3,750 lb (16.68kN) static thrust
Cruise speed	419mph (674kph)
Maximum speed	520mph (863kph)
Ceiling	42,000ft (12,801m)
Range	4,000 miles (6,537km) with a 10,000 lb (4,535kg) bomb load. 1,150 miles (1,850km) with a 36,760 lb (16,674kg) bomb load
Armament	4 x .50 (12.7mm) remotely controlled M2 machine guns in tailcone turret

Secret Projects: Flying Wings and Tailless Aircraft

The YRB-49 with its undercarriage lowered.
Northrop Grumman

Scrap metal from one (or more) of the Northrop flying wing bombers, dumped at Northrop's Hawthorne Plant. This photograph is believed to have been taken in 1953. USAF

The remaining YB-49 was destroyed in an accident while making a fast taxiing run at Edwards AFB on 15 March 1950. It began with the aircraft's nose wheel strut collapsing and although the three-man crew escaped, the aircraft caught fire. But there was no replacement for the YB-49 as the conversion programme had ended some months earlier. The remaining flying wing took to the air on 4 May 1950. Designated as the YRB-49A, this heavily-modified variant with a reconnaissance capability was a significant step away from Jack Northrop's original idea for a clean, aesthetically-pleasing and efficient aircraft. Changes to the propulsion system had resulted in the engines being reduced to six Allison J35-A-19 turbojets, each rated at 5,000 lb (22.24kN) static thrust. However, two of these engines were housed in pods below the wing to allow increased fuel within the aircraft. A crew of six would fly the aircraft with photographic equipment carried in the tail cone.

After a series of test-flights at Edwards AFB, it was clear that the aircraft could not compete with Boeing's B-47 and the flying wing project was cancelled. The YRB-49A was then placed in storage at Northrop's facility located at Ontario International Airport, California, and finally scrapped in November 1953.

The Flying Wing H-Bomber

Aside from stability problems, the major shortcoming of the B-35 and B-49 was inadequate bomb bay space. The preliminary design had been completed at a time when the idea of a huge ground-penetrating bomb had yet to be considered and atomic weapons remained ideas occasionally discussed in SF literature. As a consequence, Northrop's flying wing bomber had been built with a central cabin area and separate bomb bays positioned around it. Furthermore, by the end of the 1940s, physicists were indicating that a significantly more powerful fusion bomb was theoretically possible and assuming it could be built, such a weapon was going to be very large and the B-36 might be the only aircraft capable of carrying it.

Jack Northrop now set about designing a new flying wing aircraft with a large centrally-located bomb bay that would be able to accommodate a single 'superbomb'. Northrop was in an excellent position to know exactly where things were going with nuclear weapon design as it was undertaking highly-classified research to improve the casing for existing free-fall nuclear bombs. By 1950, he was able to present several ideas to the USAF for a long-range strategic nuclear bomber. The first proposal was for a flying wing aircraft with a forward fuselage section somewhat resembling the British Avro Vulcan.

Generally referred to as the Turbodyne V, this design had a wingspan of 128ft 4in (39.11m), a length of 74ft 8in (22.75m) and it was devoid of any upright stabilising fins. The crew of five would be housed in forward pressurised sections, with the pilot and co-pilot in tandem and two other crew members facing forward near glazed sections of each inner wing. The aircraft would be equipped with two Northrop-developed Turbodyne turboprop engines each producing 10,000hp

Northrop 1950 Flying Wing Bomber Version A: Turbodyne V

Crew	5 – pilot and co-pilot in a tandem cockpit. Two other seats were located in the leading edges of the wing roots, and had large windows for forward visibility. An additional position at the rear of the cabin
Wingspan	128ft 4in (39.11m)
Length	74ft 8in (22.75m)
Max ground weight	161,540 lb (73,227kg)
Max flight weight	222,710 lb (101,019kg) (after in-flight refuelling)
Powerplant	2 x Turbodyne V turboprop engines, each rated at 10,000hp (7,457kW) and driving a six-bladed contra-rotating propeller
Cruising speed	517mph (832kph)
Bombing altitude	43,000ft (13,106m)
Combat radius	
(un-refuelled)	2,760 miles (4,441km)
(in-flight refuelling)	5,580 miles (8,980km)
Armament	Two or four machine guns (probably .50cal) in remotely controlled tail turret
Bomb load	Unspecified

US Flying Wings (1935-1950)

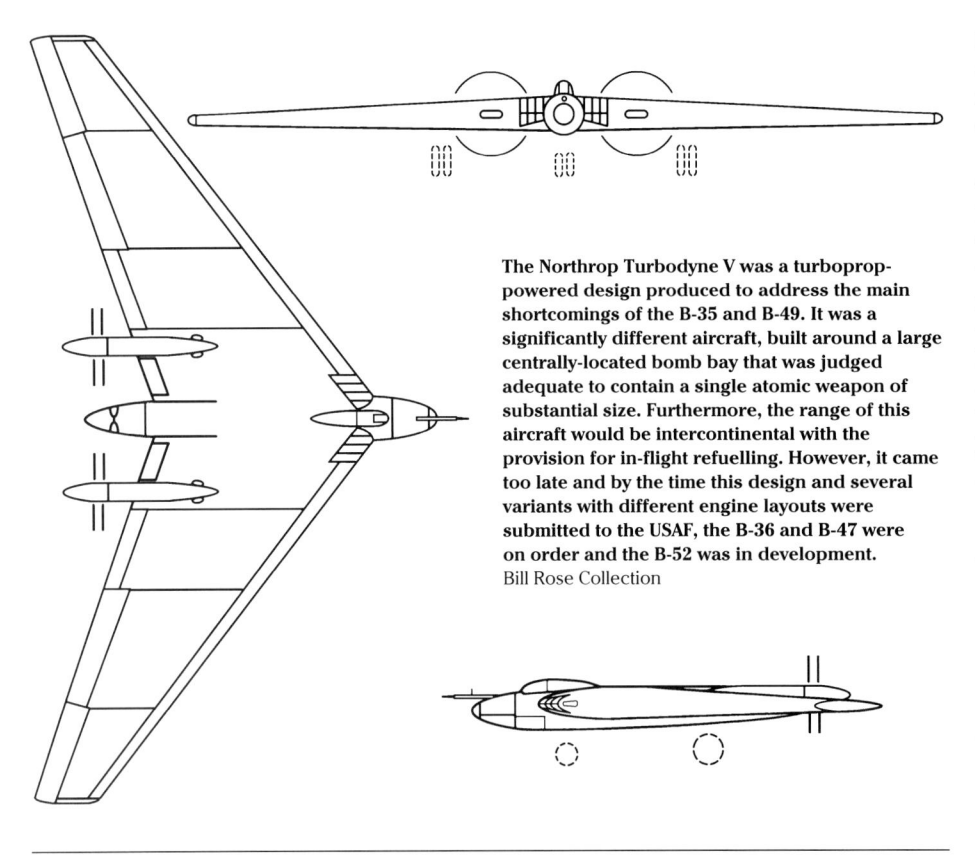

The Northrop Turbodyne V was a turboprop-powered design produced to address the main shortcomings of the B-35 and B-49. It was a significantly different aircraft, built around a large centrally-located bomb bay that was judged adequate to contain a single atomic weapon of substantial size. Furthermore, the range of this aircraft would be intercontinental with the provision for in-flight refuelling. However, it came too late and by the time this design and several variants with different engine layouts were submitted to the USAF, the B-36 and B-47 were on order and the B-52 was in development.
Bill Rose Collection

(7,457kW) and driving six-bladed contra-rotating propeller assemblies at the wing's trailing edge. The aircraft would also be equipped with the capability to refuel in-flight, allowing long-range missions. Drawings show this aircraft carrying a single bomb and it remains unclear if the aircraft was expected to have a conventional weapons capability.

Northrop 1950 Flying Wing Bomber Version B: 4 x Turboprop Engines

Crew	5
Wingspan	128ft 4in (39.11m)
Length	74ft 8in (22.75m)
Max ground weight	175,400 lb (79,560kg)
Max flight weight	212,100 lb (96,206kg) (after in-flight refuelling)
Powerplant	4 x Allison XT40 turboprops, each rated at 7,500hp (5,593kW) and each driving one six-bladed contra-rotating propeller unit
Cruising speed	506mph (814kph)
Bombing altitude	37,000ft (11,277m)
Combat radius (un-refuelled)	2,761 miles (4,443km)
(refuelled at cruising altitude)	4,027 miles (6,480km)
Armament	Two or four machine guns (probably .50cal) in remotely controlled tail turret
Bomb load	Unspecified

A remote-control tail turret equipped with .50cal machine guns was located in the tail for defence purposes. Cruising speed was an impressive 517mph (832mph) with a bombing ceiling of 43,000ft (13,106m) and an un-refuelled combat radius estimated to be 2,760 miles (4,441km). With in-flight refuelling, this could be increased to at least 5,500 miles (8,850km) and possibly further. The Turbodyne V was somewhat smaller and lighter than the B-49 with a maximum ground weight of 161,540 lb (73,227kg) and the efficient turboprop engines and in-flight refuelling capability made it an attractive proposition compared to the larger jet bomber.

An alternative version of the aircraft, having the same overall dimensions and basic layout, was to be powered by four Allison XT40 turboprop engines. Each engine was connected to contra-rotating pusher propellers producing an estimated total of 30,000hp (22,371kW). Somewhat heavier, this variant had a maximum ground weight of 175,400 lb (79,560kg) and marginally less performance. It would be capable of cruising at just over 500mph (800kph) and releasing its bomb from a maximum altitude of 37,000ft (11,277m). The un-refuelled combat radius was similar to the twin-engine version although the estimates for longer refuelled flights were not as good. But the designs failed to make an impression with the USAF,

perhaps now wary of becoming involved in another very costly flying wing project which might have technical issues that were very difficult to resolve.

Conspiracy Theories?

Before the loss of the first YB-49, Northrop was facing stiff competition from Boeing, which was well ahead of the game with its relatively sophisticated but more conventional designs. The Boeing B-47 jet bomber had originated with a USAAF requirement dating back to 1943 and this medium bomber became the B-49's main rival. The initial XB-47 had made its first flight in late 1947 and a pre-production batch of 10 B-47As was delivered to the USAF for evaluation in December 1950. At the same time, Boeing was developing the larger B-52 that would become the most successful jet bomber in history and will remain in service with the USAF well into the 21st century.

The Northrop flying wing bomber started out as an elegant, rather futuristic design, but was plagued with technical problems. As a company, Northrop was stretched to the limit during World War 2 with serious staff shortages and insufficient factory space at Hawthorne for XB-35 production. The conversion to turbojet power improved performance, but the aircraft still failed to deliver in several respects. It was unable to carry existing atomic weapons and serious stability problems made accurate bomb delivery far from satisfactory according to most of the test pilots.

By the late 1940s, Northrop was under pressure from USAF Secretary Stuart Symington to merge with rival company Convair. The Air Force felt it would be in the best interests of both organisations and was a necessary requirement for continuation of the flying wing programme as Northrop lacked adequate production capacity. Jack Northrop remained strongly opposed to the idea and some years later would claim that as a consequence of his objection to this plan Symington brought the flying wing project to an end, awarding Convair a contract for the B-36 bomber in its place.

In actuality, the USAF had been far from happy with the alternative B-36 strategic bomber and it was never given preferential treatment over the Northrop flying wing. The B-36 experienced reliability problems, lacked performance and would not have stood much chance against the rapidly improving Soviet air defences. However, significant improvements were made to the design that increased performance considerably and the bomb delivery capacity of this aircraft was in an entirely different league to the XB-49. In 1949, a Congressional investigation found that there was no favouritism behind this decision and Jack Northrop accepted the findings. But in 1979, an elderly and rather frail Jack Northrop participated in an interview conducted by KCET-TV reporter Clete Roberts and told him that undue pressure had been applied by Symington to merge his company with Convair. When he resisted the proposal, Symington scrapped the flying wing programme. Northrop added that as a direct consequence, the B-36 went ahead. While there may be an element of truth to some of this, it is clear that the decision to drop the Northrop flying wing was made by USAF specialists who rightly concluded that the aircraft was unsuitable for their needs.

Certainly the B-36 was far from perfect, but this aircraft offered superior performance to the Northrop flying wing and it seemed that the less fussy B-47 and proposed B-52 would satisfy USAF requirements for the next generation of jet bombers. Aside from bomb carriage shortcomings and stability problems, the YB-49 lacked speed and range and despite some claims, it was never designed to have a low radar cross-section or be regarded as a stealth aircraft.

A version of the B-49 was briefly considered as a passenger-carrying airliner with the tail cone replaced by a window for a small number of (presumably first class) rear-facing passengers. Northrop built a mock-up of this cabin section, but there was no serious interest in this proposal from the commercial sector. Several variants of the YB-49 also resurfaced during the mid-1950s when Northrop answered an official request to submit designs for a bomber that utilised nuclear propulsion. To protect the crew from radiation, the cockpit area was either located in a wingtip pod or at the front of a lengthy forward fuselage extension. These particular studies progressed little further than elementary concepts, although Northrop continued to work on nuclear-powered bomber designs for some time.

As a footnote to this section, some stock footage of a YB-49 in flight was used in the 1953 George Pal SF movie *War of the Worlds*. The aircraft is seen flying to drop an atomic bomb on invading Martian forces.

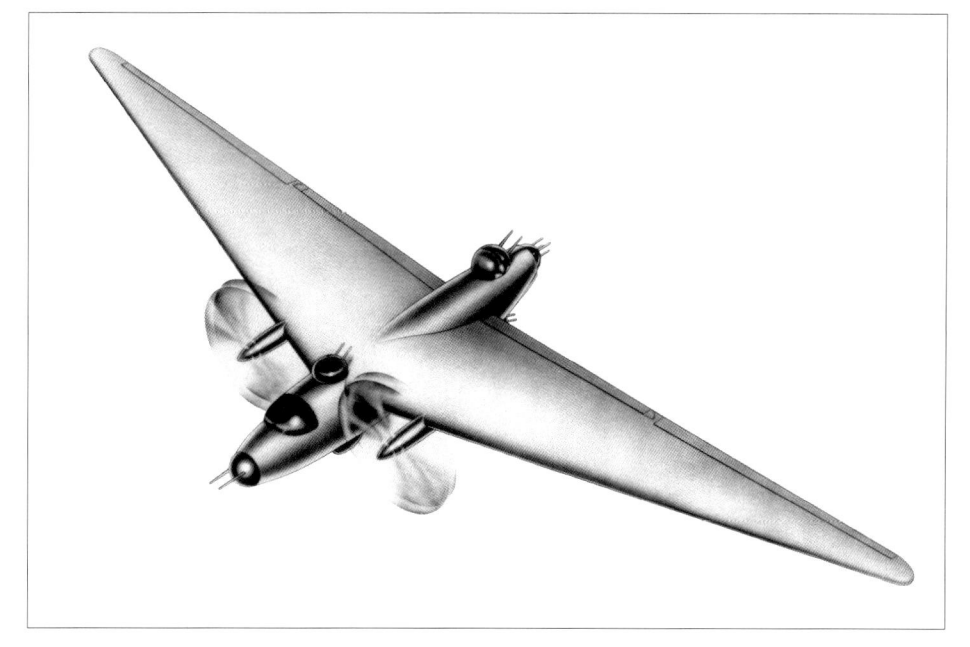

Consolidated-Vultee's initial wartime proposal for a twin-engine tailless patrol bomber. Robert Bradley

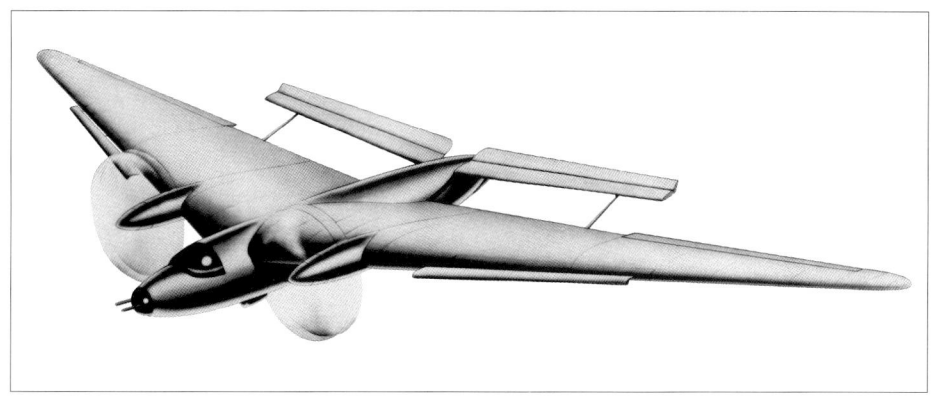

This artwork for an early Consolidated-Vultee twin-engine tailless patrol bomber design shows the auxiliary control surfaces in fully-extended position. These would normally be retracted during cruise or high-speed flight. Robert Bradley

Convair's Twin-Engine Tailless Bomber

When Consolidated and Vultee Aircraft (later known as Convair) merged in 1943, the company's engineers at Lindbergh Field, San Diego, were already working on several new tailless military aircraft. It was hoped that these designs would provide better performance and perhaps lower manufacturing costs than existing aircraft in the same class. Although design work on a flying wing alternative to the B-36 bomber had ended in 1942, wind tunnel tests of the company's two- and four-engine (tractor configuration) flying wing models continued at the California Institute of Technology (CalTech).

No details of the four-engine proposal remain and this design appears to have been abandoned at an early stage. Development of the twin-engine flying wing continued throughout 1943 with what appears to be a final set of model tests taking place in CalTech's 10ft (3m) wind tunnel from 18-30 November 1943. This led very swiftly to a company report on the project that was completed on 3 December 1943. The primary objective was to produce a new type of land-based maritime patrol bomber to replace the Consolidated PB4Y-2 Privateer, which was developed from the B-24 and had entered service with the US Navy in 1943. The Privateer undertook many different duties during World War 2 and the Korean War including reconnaissance, electronic countermeasures, communication relay, search and rescue, anti-shipping and bombing missions.

The initial flying wing design was occasionally referred to as Model P5Y-1 and sometimes a 'Two-Engine Patrol Landplane'. It comprised a wing with a span of 134ft (40.8m) and a fuselage section with an overall length of 52ft (15.8m). Two Pratt & Whitney R-4360 piston engines in wing-mounted nacelles would provide propulsion, driving forward-positioned contra-rotating propellers with eight blades and a 14ft (4.26m) diameter. The aircraft had a projected gross weight of 85,000 lb (38,555kg) and was expected to have a maximum speed of 300mph (483kph), a ceiling of 22,750ft

US Flying Wings (1935-1950)

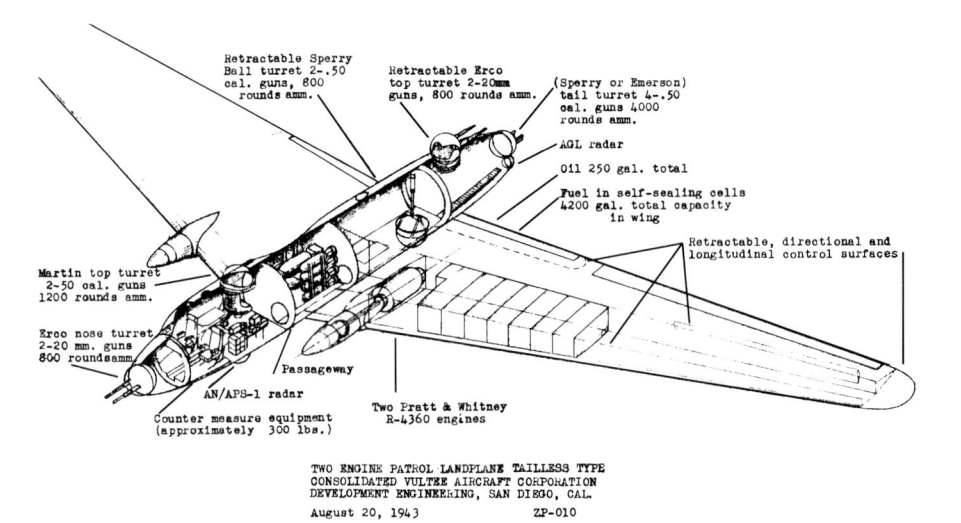

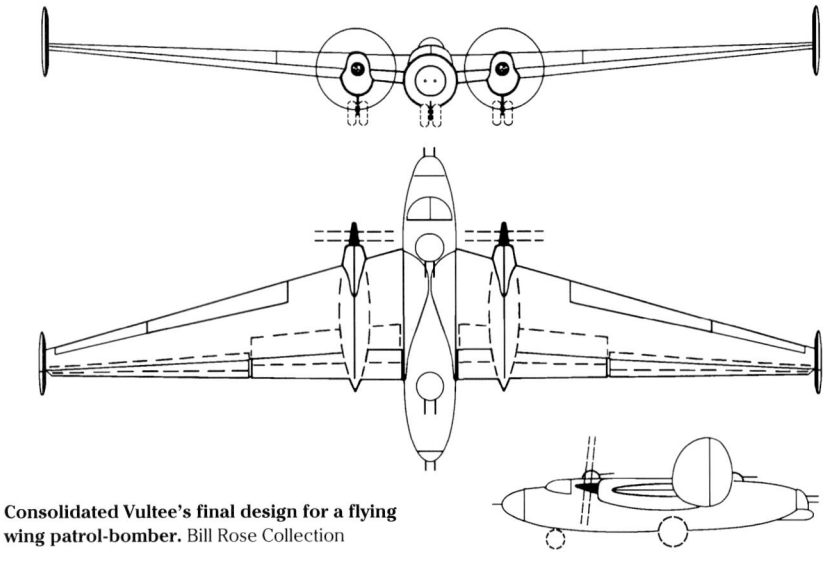

Internal layout of the initial Consolidated-Vultee twin-engine tailless patrol bomber design.
Robert Bradley

This artwork based on an original drawing shows the final design for a twin-engine flying wing patrol bomber produced by Consolidated Vultee at San Diego, California, during World War 2.
Bill Rose Collection, based on original artwork

Consolidated Vultee's final design for a flying wing patrol-bomber. Bill Rose Collection

(6,934m) and a range of 4,770 miles (7,676km) with a 10,000lb (4,536kg) payload. Flown by a crew of 10, the aircraft was expected to carry a substantial amount of defensive armament. This included two 20mm cannons in a nose turret and four .50cal in the tail. Another .50cal gun turret was located above and behind the cockpit, with two further retractable gun turrets on the upper and lower rear fuselage. Presumably, withdrawing these units into the fuselage improved the aircraft's aerodynamics. 4,200(US) gal (15,898 litres) of fuel was carried in wing tanks and a second crew compartment was located behind the centrally-positioned bomb bay. Perhaps one of the most interesting features of this design was the auxiliary directional and longitudinal control surfaces which would be fully retracted into the wing during cruise and high-speed flight.

By the time a company report on this project was produced in December 1943, the design had undergone considerable revision. Gross weight was now increased to 90,000lb (40,823kg) and the patrol range had become 5,500 miles (8,851km). The wing area was reduced from 1,900ft² (176.5m²) to 1,800ft² (167.2m²), accompanied by a small reduction in leading edge sweep from 15° to 14° and the

Consolidated Vultee Twin-Engine Tailless Patrol-Bomber (Initial Version)

Crew	10
Wingspan	134ft (40.8m)
Wing area	1,900ft² (176.5m²)
Sweep	15° (leading edge)
Length	52ft (15.8m)
Gross weight	85,000lb (38,555kg)
Powerplant	2 x Pratt & Whitney R-4360 piston engines, driving forward positioned contra-rotating propellers with eight blades and a diameter of 14ft (4.26m)
Maximum speed	300mph (483kph)
Stall speed	85mph (136kph)
Ceiling	22,750ft (6,934m)
Range	4,770 miles (7,676km) with a 10,000lb (4,536kg) payload
Armament	10,000lb (4,536kg) bomb load
Defence	2 x 20mm cannons in a nose turret, 4 x .50cal (12.7mm) in the tail, three further .50cal gun turrets

stalling speed was slightly increased from 85mph (136kph) to 89mph (143kph). Noticeable changes were a greater wingspan of 147ft (44.8m) and a nominally reduced overall length of 49ft 7in (16m). One other significant change to the design was the addition of vertical wingtip fins with rudders.

This improved stability and was found to produce a relatively little extra drag during wing tunnel testing. The aircraft was equipped with a substantial tricycle undercarriage and this underwent considerable modification to simplify its operation. Also, the hydraulic system controlling the undercarriage, brakes and bomb bay doors was replaced with an electrical AC system. Yet another change was the replacement of the eight-blade contra-rotating propellers with slightly larger six-blade versions measuring 15ft (4.5m) in diameter. It seems likely that the idea of developing this flying wing into a bomber for the USAAF was considered, but the project was finally abandoned in 1944 and then largely forgotten.

Lockheed's Atomic Bomber

The Lockheed Corporation, based at Burbank Airport, Los Angeles, California, produced artwork depicting a large passenger-carrying flying wing in 1938. Utilising six forward-positioned propellers, the aircraft was equipped with substantial wingtip fins and fitted with a fixed tricycle undercarriage. Perhaps influenced by Burnelli and Northrop designs, it remains hard to say if this pre-war concept was a realistic proposal or simply created for publicity purposes.

Lockheed does not appear to have taken any interest in flying wing aircraft during World War 2, but this changed in 1946 when US scientists decided that nuclear energy might be suitable for aircraft propulsion and the Pentagon established a programme called Nuclear Energy for the Propulsion of Aircraft (NEPA). Primarily controlled by the USAAF, the main aim was to develop a new strategic bomber, perhaps with global range. As an early submission for a nuclear-powered strategic bomber to meet NEPA requirements, Lockheed produced a massive tailless aircraft powered by a hybrid nuclear system.

This Skunk Works design was given the reference L-248-3 and it would be powered by eight highly-modified Allison turboprop engines, each driving a set of forward-mounted contra-rotating propellers. With energy provided by a nuclear reactor, the bomber was expected to have a global range. However, this meant that a sizeable crew was

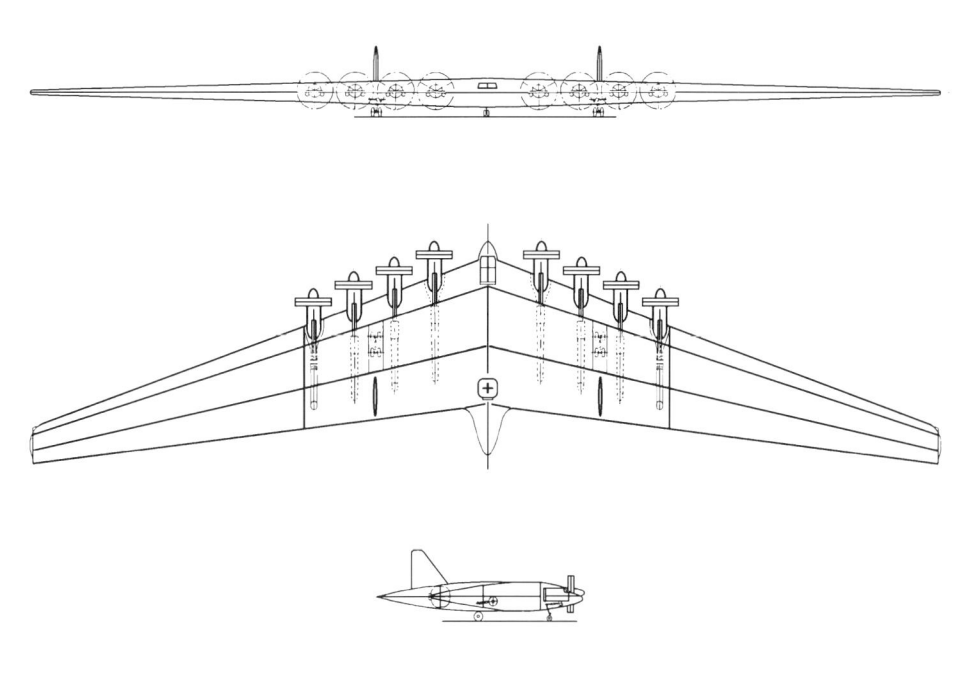

As a result of the Nuclear Energy for the Propulsion of Aircraft programme, which began in the late 1940s, Lockheed's Skunk Works investigated the possibility of building a long-range nuclear-powered bomber. Using Allison turboprops powered by a nuclear reactor, this substantial aircraft was given the design reference L-248-3. Pete Clukey/Lockheed Martin

necessary and they had to be kept as far as possible from the nuclear propulsion system. Consequently, the heavily shielded crew compartment was located at the central leading edge with the reactor positioned towards the tail.

Specifications are sketchy at best, but this huge flying wing was to have a wingspan of approximately 380ft (116m) with an estimated leading edge sweep of 20°. The aircraft's overall length was expected to be about 89ft (27m), although height is unknown. Two upright stabilising fins were located towards the trailing edge and this massive bomber was supported on the ground by a fully retractable tricycle undercarriage. Each main strut was fitted with four wheels and there were two wheels on the forward strut, although this appears somewhat inadequate. Proposed weights and estimates for performance are unknown. The L-248-3 would have been specifically designed to deliver free-fall nuclear weapons and perhaps an early hydrogen bomb. NEPA continued until 1951 when it became the USAF's Aircraft Nuclear Propulsion (ANP) programme, having determined that the technology was viable. Nevertheless, the Lockheed L-248-3 never progressed much further than engineering studies.

Northrop's Black Bullet

At the end of 1939, Jack Northrop responded to Army Air Corps request R-40C for a new fighter with superior performance to existing aircraft and significantly lower maintenance requirements. R-40C also made it clear that unorthodox designs would receive consideration. Northrop submitted a tailless proposal for RC-40C which initially carried the company designation N-2B and would compete with rival designs from Bell, Curtiss and Vultee.

The Northrop aircraft was a flying wing with a slightly bulbous fuselage and a contra-rotating propeller assembly at the rear, driven by the experimental Pratt & Whitney X-1800-A3G (H-2600) engine located in the centre of the aircraft behind the pilot. The wing profile was similar to that used on the N-1M prototype and there would be upper and lower vertical stabilisers at the rear of the fuselage. An initial US patent application for this design was filed on 10 May 1940 with a slightly modified version being applied for on 3 December 1941, which remained classified until 1946.

An Army Air Corps development contract for the Northrop N-2B was issued on 22 June 1940 and it was decided to fund the construction of a prototype on 26 September 1940. The project had now received the fighter reference P-56 (P for Pursuit was used prior to F for Fighter) and the prototype was given the registration number 41-786 and called the XP-56. But in October 1940, there was a serious setback when the Pratt & Whitney X-1800 engine chosen for the XP-56 failed to meet performance expectations and was

Often referred to by the unofficial name 'Black Bullet', Northrop's XP-56 fighter was not a great success, with the first prototype crashing in September 1943 at Muroc Dry Lake. This photograph shows the second prototype which currently resides at the National Air and Space Museum. Bill Rose Collection

abandoned by the manufacturers. The X-1800 had been a liquid-cooled 24-cylinder piston engine with an anticipated performance of 1,800-2,200hp (1,342-1,640kW) using a turbocharger at higher altitude and there was no similarly specified replacement.

In fact, the X-1800's cancellation created difficulties for all contractors entering the R-40C fighter competition as this engine had been selected for every design. It might have brought the XP-56 project (and the fighter competition) to a close, but Jack Northrop's team decided to replace the X-1800 with a Pratt & Whitney R-2800 air-cooled radial engine. Although this was a very capable design, it came with a weight penalty and extensive alterations to the fuselage were necessary. As envisaged from the outset, the engine was located just behind the un-pressurised cockpit, driving two sets of three-bladed propellers at the rear via a shaft and gearbox. However, the pusher propeller arrangement raised serious issues for the pilot should it become necessary to bail out and Northrop's solution was an explosive cord positioned around the gearbox which would be detonated to sever the rear section of the fuselage and propeller assembly.

In addition to having an unconventional shape, the XP-56's airframe was built entirely from lightweight magnesium which was joined by a newly perfected process called tungsten inert gas (TIG) welding. The XP-56 was equipped with a fully-retractable tricycle undercarriage and a lower ventral fin that offered little clearance while the XP-56 was on the ground, but provided some protection to the rear-mounted propeller blades. The wing had similarities to N-1M aircraft with elevons at the centre of the trailing edge, flaps on the angled wingtips and air intakes for engine cooling ducts at the leading edge wing roots. The wingspan was 42ft 6in (12.95m) with a wing area of 306ft^2 (28.44m^2) and a wing loading of 37lb/ft^2 (180.6kg/m^2). The overall length of the XP-56 was 23ft 6in (7.16m), the height was 9ft 8in (2.94m) and take-off weight was estimated to be 12,145 lb (5,508kg). The maximum speed would be 417mph (671kph) at sea level and 465mph (748kph) at 25,000ft (749km/h) with a ceiling of 33,000ft (10,058m) and a range of 660 miles (1,062km). No armament was fitted to the prototype but allowances were made to equip future versions with two 20mm cannons and four .50cal (12.7mm) machine guns in the nose.

With assembly of the XP-56 prototype progressing well, the USAAF decided to fund the construction of another XP-56 and a contract was issued on 13 February 1942. The second aircraft was issued with the serial number 42-38353. Work on the first prototype was relatively slow and the XP-56 does not appear to have been given high priority, although it had now received the unofficial name 'Black Bullet'. The aircraft was finally completed by Northrop in April 1943 and transported by road to Muroc Army Air Base for flight-testing. After a series of taxiing tests at Muroc Dry Lake, it was found that the aircraft tended to yaw quite badly at high speed. As a consequence, modifications were made to the vertical stabiliser and the wheel braking system.

The first attempt to fly the XP-56 was made at Muroc Dry Lake on 30 September 1943 with Northrop's, senior test pilot John Wescott Myers at the controls. He managed to briefly lift off the ground at a speed of about 140mph (225kph) but failed to become properly airborne. The flights continued with Myers managing to increase his height from the ground, although the XP-56's performance was disappointing with the aircraft handling badly. Then disaster struck while taxiing at high-speed when the rear tyre on the port side

Anticipated appearance of the Northrop P-56 flying wing fighter. Bill Rose

Northrop XP-56 Black Bullet Prototype (Original Estimates)

Crew	1
Wingspan	42ft 6in (12.95m)
Wing area	306ft² (28.44m²)
Wing loading	37 lb/ft² (180.6kg/m²)
Length	1st Prototype: 23ft 6in (7.16m).
	2nd Prototype: 27ft 6in (8.38m)
Height	1st Prototype: 9ft 8in (2.94m).
	2nd Prototype: 11ft (3.35m)
Empty weight	8,700 lb (3,946kg)
Loaded weight	11,350 lb (5,148kg)
Max take-off weight	12,145 lb (5,508kg)
Powerplant	1 x Pratt & Whitney R-2800-29 18-cylinder air-cooled radial, 2,000hp (1,491kW)
Maximum speed	465mph (748kph) at 25,000ft (749km/h)
	417mph (671kph) at sea level
Service ceiling	33,000ft (10,058m)
Range	660 miles (1,062km)
Rate of climb	3,125ft/min (952m/min) at 15,000ft (4,572m)
Armament (production model)	2 x 20mm cannons and 4 x .50cal (12.7mm) machine guns

blew out and the aircraft somersaulted before breaking up. The XP-56 was virtually a complete write-off and photographs indicate that little could have been salvaged from the wreckage. During the crash, supports holding the pilot's seat in place sheared and Myers was thrown clear of the aircraft, miraculously only suffering minor injuries.

Construction of the second prototype was now at a fairly advanced stage and it had already undergone a number of modifications. The most noticeable difference was the larger dorsal fin, accompanied by a change in weight distribution to shift the centre of gravity forward. These changes led to an increased height of 11ft (3.35m) and a greater overall length of 27ft 6in (8.38m). Improvements were also made to the wingtip rudder control system using an air-bellows fed by wingtip ducts.

The second XP-56, piloted by Harry Crosby, undertook its maiden flight on 23 March 1944 at Roach Lake. The aircraft refused to leave the ground at speeds below 160mph (257kph), but Crosby finally lifted-off and climbed to an altitude of 2,500ft (762m) with the flight lasting eight minutes. On following flights, it became clear that handling improved significantly once the undercarriage was fully retracted, although overall performance proved to be disappointing and was far less than original estimates suggested. During May 1944, it was decided that NACA would undertake wind tunnel tests at Moffett Field to investigate the aircraft's poor performance while flight-testing continued.

But having completed 10 flights, the stability and control problems appeared insoluble and further trials were cancelled. It was now clear that the days of the piston-engine fighters were coming to an end and the second XP-56 was stored in a hangar for a year before the project was scrapped. From the outset this aircraft was doomed to failure and probably should have been abandoned when Pratt & Whitney cancelled its X-1800 engine. Some other contenders for R-40C were built and test flown, such as the twin-boom Vultee XP-54 and the canard Curtiss XP-55, but in overall terms this programme was a dismal failure with none of the aircraft living up to expectations.

On 20 December 1946, the XP-56 was transported to the USAAF Storage Depot at Park Ridge, Illinois, and from there it was passed to the National Air and Space Museum.

Northrop's Wartime Rocket and Jet Fighters

By early 1942, British and American Intelligence were aware of German efforts to develop a high-performance rocket-powered tailless fighter. The US was interested in duplicating this technology and according to many sources Jack Northrop was approached to build an interceptor based on preliminary studies undertaken at Wright Field. Alternatively, it has been suggested that classified information was intentionally leaked to Northrop and this led him to approach the USAAF with plans for a rocketplane.

Whatever the truth, discussions were soon underway to develop a prototype rocket-powered fighter. As the country's leading designer of flying wings, Jack Northrop was the obvious choice for this project and by September 1942, he had submitted a series of proposals to the USAAF. This resulted in an immediate contract for three small research aircraft that would be used in the first stage of the programme. The designation MX-365 was initially assigned to the project, which then received the experimental fighter reference XP-79. The first two aircraft in this series would be gliders, referred to as MX-334. The third aircraft, designated MX-324, would differ by having an Aerojet liquid fuel rocket engine installed. Security for this undertaking was tight from the outset and it would now be regarded as a top-secret 'black' project, which for all intents and purposes didn't exist. Northrop staff simply referred to the gliders as N-12 and the rocket fighter as N-14.

Having already provided the USAAF with fairly detailed proposals for a rocket fighter, Jack Northrop submitted a complete design in early 1943. His small single-seat flying wing interceptor would be close to a delta shape with an overall wingspan of 36ft (10.97m) and a length of approximately 13ft (3.96m). The wing's root chord would be 11ft 4in (3.45m) with a wingtip chord of 3ft (0.91m) and wing area of 255ft² (23.69m²). Skin thickness at the leading edge of the wing was set at ¾in (19mm), decreasing to ⅛in (3mm) at the trailing edge. Much of the aircraft would be built from welded magnesium alloy, chosen for its

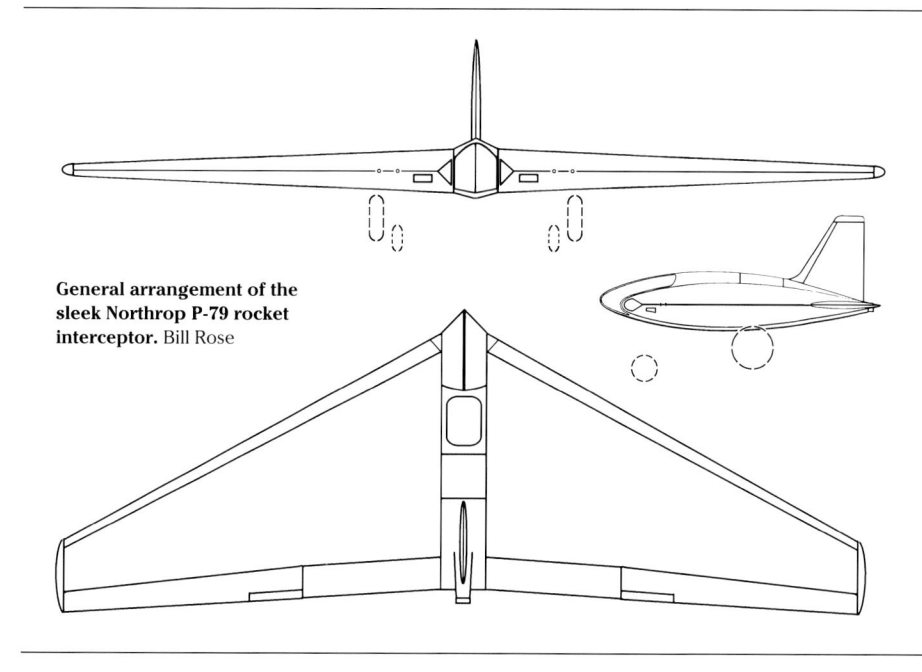

General arrangement of the sleek Northrop P-79 rocket interceptor. Bill Rose

US Flying Wings (1935-1950)

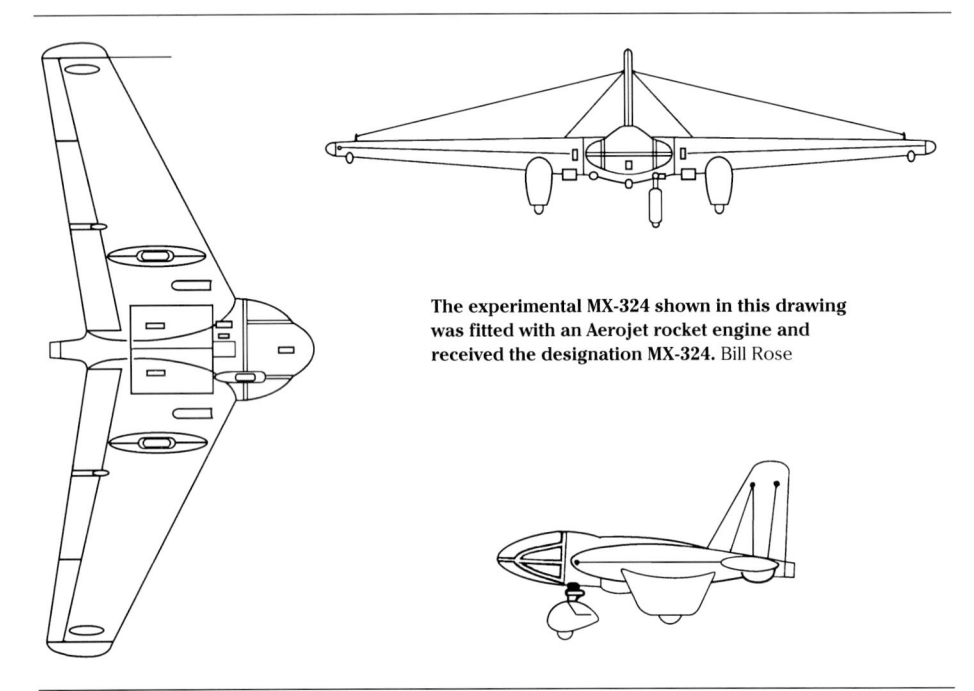

Testing at NACA Langley in the Full Scale Wind Tunnel during July 1943. This is described as a Northrop MX-324 model, but it appears to be the prototype aircraft without undercarriage. NASA

low weight and strength. The pilot was contained in a sealed but unpressurised cockpit and would lie in a prone position. This allowed Northrop to design a very sleek aircraft and it was believed that this configuration made it easier for the pilot to withstand brief periods of acceleration, perhaps as high as 12G.

Like the XP-56, this aircraft was also designed around an experimental propulsion system that was in the early stages of development and was technically risky. The proposed Aerojet rocket engine for the XP-79 would be fuelled with red fuming nitric acid and monoethylaniline (aniline) to provide a maximum thrust of about 2,000 lb (8.89kN). In addition, six solid fuel rocket-assisted take-off (RATO) units would be used for a horizontal runway take-off. They would be attached beneath the central rear area of the wing with each delivering 1,000 lb (4.44kN) of thrust and jettisoned once the fighter left the runway. The XP-79 was expected to have a gross weight of 11,400 lb (5,170kg) allowing a maximum speed of approximately 530mph (850kph) and a ceiling in excess of 45,000ft (13,716m). Estimates for range or endurance are unknown although both would have been short, restricting this aircraft's role to that of a target defence interceptor.

It is believed that Jack Northrop and his senior aerodynamicist Dr William Sears initially favoured a pure flying wing without a vertical stabiliser for the XP-79 (plus the MX-334 and MX-324), but reluctantly accepted that a fin would be necessary for high-speed flight. Directional control of the aircraft was achieved using large elevons and split manoeuvring brakes. The pilot would control the elevons with a forward-mounted crossbar fitted with handgrips and use foot pedals to adjust the manoeuvring brakes. Production fighters would be fitted with four 0.50in (12.7mm) calibre M2 machine guns with provision for 250 rounds per gun. There would also be hardened steel panels behind the inner leading edge and a bullet resistant glass screen at the front of the cockpit. The pilot's prone position made location of a fully retractable nose wheel difficult, so it was decided to use four separate wheels for the undercarriage.

Part of the contract for this project stipulated that Northrop would sub-contract the engineering and assembly work as there was a serious shortage of capacity at Northrop's factory. This resulted in construction being passed to a Los Angeles company called Avion Inc that had earlier connections to Jack Northrop. Soon after work began on the three MX prototypes, preparations started for the assembly of three XP-79 prototypes. Two would be used for flight-testing and the third for stress analysis.

The first three MX aircraft were built from inexpensive welded steel tubing, aluminium and plywood, but all were similar in appearance to the later XP-79 and accommodated the pilot in a prone position. The overall weight of the MX-334 glider was 3,000 lb (1,360kg), making it not much heavier than a medium-sized saloon car. The dimensions for the MX-324 and MX-334 were virtually the same with an overall length of 12ft (3.7m), a wingspan of 32ft (9.8m) and a wing area of 244ft^2 (22.7m^2). The controls functioned in a similar manner to the proposed XP-79 with the pilot accommodated in a prone position.

The first MX-334 was fitted with landing skids, supplemented with a four-wheel take-off trolley that was jettisoned as the aircraft became airborne. This proved unsatisfactory and it was decided to fit a fixed tricycle undercarriage to the second MX-334 and the MX-324. Fairings were fitted around each strut to improve the aerodynamics and it was necessary to offset the nose wheel because the pilot's prone position within the cockpit prevented adequate central bracing.

John Myers flew the first MX-334 on 2 October 1943 with further trials taking place at Muroc AAF. Other Northrop pilots routinely involved with this programme were Harry Crosby and Alex Papana with a number of USAAF pilots also flying the aircraft. All pilots felt that the aircraft handed reasonably well,

The experimental MX-324 shown in this drawing was fitted with an Aerojet rocket engine and received the designation MX-324. Bill Rose

Secret Projects: Flying Wings and Tailless Aircraft

although there were complaints about the rudder's responsiveness.

Two notable incidents occurred during these trials. The first took place when Alex Papana accidentally jettisoned the upper and lower escape hatches of his MX-334 after release from the Lockheed P-38 tow plane. This abrupt change to the aircraft's aerodynamic qualities generated substantial drag and forced him to make an emergency landing. Some days later while flying the second MX-334, Harry Crosby became caught in the propwash of the P-38 tow plane and the glider pitched upwards, stalled and entered a spin. It finally recovered but was now upside down with Crosby on his back and unable to reach the controls. Finding himself in a shallow glide, Crosby's only option was to bail out. During his descent, the glider continued to circle and finally landed on the lakebed, but was damaged beyond repair.

Glide flights continued at Muroc and by spring 1944, the Aerojet XCAL-200 rocket engine was ready for installation in the MX-324, increasing the gross weight of the aircraft to 3,656 lb (1,658kg) when the fuel tanks were full. The engine with its troublesome development history had been built at Aerojet Engineering's Azusa facility and was simply known as Project X. Although mainly fabricated from aluminium, the XCAL-200 was relatively heavy at 427 lb (193kg) and would provide a maximum thrust of 200 lb (0.88kN) for several minutes. The engine's exhaust protruded slightly from the rear of the aircraft, but in other respects the MX-324 was externally identical to the gliders. Internally the aircraft was somewhat different with a revised layout allowing for the engine system and fuel tanks. To offer the pilot some protection against accidental release of analine or nitric acid (which would be life threatening), thick neoprene screens were installed around the cockpit.

Now fully equipped, the aircraft was transported to Harper's Dry Lake, Lockhart, California, which was a secret test site in the Mojave Desert used by Hughes and Northrop. (Nothing remains of this facility today.) Ground tests began on 29 June 1944 and by early July, the aircraft was considered ready to undertake its maiden flight. Early on the morning of 5 June 1944, Harry Crosby eased himself into the cramped cockpit of the fully-fuelled MX-324 and was towed out across the surface of Harper's Dry Lake by the P-38 used for these trials. Having left the ground, the P-38 piloted by Martin Smith climbed to an altitude of approximately 8,000ft (2,438m) and Crosby released the towline.

Moments later, he ignited the Aerojet XCAL-200 engine and flew under rocket power for just over four minutes, reaching a speed of 270mph (435kph) before gliding to land on the lake bed. Crosby had become the first American to fly under rocket power, although this event would remain classified for some time to come. Further powered flights followed, although there were constant difficulties with the rocket engine and the USAAF was becoming concerned about this troublesome programme. Development of the full-sized Aerojet XCALR-2000A-1 liquid-fuelled rocket engine (generally referred to as the Rotajet because of its thrust chamber rotation during operation) was progressing badly and Aerojet Engineering could not guarantee reliability. As a consequence, the USAAF finally decided to terminate the rocket fighter project. Early concerns about the rocket engine had led the USAAF to hedge its bets in March 1943 with a request that the second XP-79 prototype was modified to accept two Westinghouse turbojets. This revised model was designated XP-79B and carried the registration 43-52437.

Work eventually started on the XP-79B at Avion, but due to ongoing personnel problems, the aircraft was transported to Northrop's facility at Hawthorne on 1 December 1944 for completion.

The redesigned XP-79B was now fitted with two engine bays located in the wing roots; each housed a Westinghouse axial flow 19-B turbojet (an early version of the J30) rated at 1,150 lb (51.kN) static thrust. The gross weight of the XP-79B was 8,668 lb (3,931kg), making it somewhat lighter than the rocket-powered design, but the maximum speed and ceiling were expected to be marginally less due to the different method of propulsion and aerodynamic changes. The single vertical fin mounted on the rocket-powered XP-79 was no longer in evidence, having been replaced

MX-334 and MX-324 'Rocket Wing'

Crew	1
Wingspan	32ft (9.8m)
Wing area	244ft² (22.7m²)
Sweep	30° (leading edge)
Length	12ft (3.7m)
Gross weight (MX-334)	3,000 lb (1,360kg)
(MX-324)	3,656 lb (1,658kg)
Powerplant (MX-324)	1 x Aerojet XCAL-200 rocket engine producing 200 lb thrust (0.88kN)
Aspect ratio	4.20:1
Max speed (MX-324)	300mph (482kph)
Range (MX-324)	20 miles (32km) approx
Armament	None

One of the few colour images of the Northrop MX-324 at Harper's Dry Lake. Northrop Grumman

Test pilot Harry Crosby flies the MX-324 under rocket power at Harper's Dry Lake in June 1944. Northrop Grumman

US Flying Wings (1935-1950)

by two separate stabilisers positioned above the rear of each turbojet housing producing an overall height of 7ft (2.13m).

By autumn 1945, the XP-79B had been completed and the small experimental jet plane was transported to Muroc to begin testing. After a series of taxiing trials at Muroc Dry Lake, the aircraft was finally ready to make its first flight on 12 September 1945. The aircraft lifted off with Harry Crosby at the controls and the small flying wing flew for the next 15 minutes, performing various aerial manoeuvres. Then at an altitude of about 7,000ft (2,133m), Crosby started a slow roll, but failed to recover and the aircraft began to spin. Crosby attempted to bail out but was struck by the tumbling aircraft and was killed. When the XP-79B hit the ground, it was totally destroyed. The exact cause of the accident was never fully determined, but it was thought to be a control failure. As an immediate consequence of this accident, the project was cancelled.

It is often said that the sole purpose of this small fighter was to ram enemy bombers, hence the widely used name 'Flying Ram'. Jack Northrop allegedly told colleagues that

The rocket-powered XP-79 ran into major difficulties due to its unsatisfactory propulsion system and was replaced by this alternative 'Model B' version, equipped with two turbojet engines. Bill Rose Collection

Northrop P-79 Rocket Interceptor (Initial Proposal)

Crew	1 (in prone position)
Wingspan	36ft (10.97m)
Wing area	255ft² (23.69m²)
Sweep	30° (leading edge)
Chord at root	11ft 4in (3.45m)
Chord at tip	3ft (0.91m)
Length	13ft (3.96m) approx
Gross weight	11,400 lb (5,170kg)
Powerplant	1 x Aerojet XCALR-2000A-1 'Rotajet' liquid-fuelled rocket engine providing 2,000 lb (8.89kN) thrust), plus six jettisonable RATO units, each rated at 1,000 lb (4.44kN) to assist take-off
Maximum speed	530mph (850kph) estimate
Ceiling	45,000ft (13,716m) estimate
Endurance	Uncertain
Armament	4 x .50in (12.7mm) M2 machine guns, each with 250rpg

Northrop XP-79B: Fighter Prototype

Crew	1 (in prone position)
Wingspan	38ft (11.58m)
Wing area	278ft² (25.82m²)
Length	14ft (4.26m)
Chord at root	11ft 8in (3.55m)
Chord at tip	2ft 10in (0.86m)
Height	7ft (2.13m)
Empty weight	5,840 lb (2,649kg)
Gross weight	8,668 lb (3,931kg)
Powerplant	2 x Westinghouse 19-B (J30) turbojets, each producing 1,150 lb (5.1kN) static thrust
Maximum speed	510mph (820kph)
Ceiling	40,000ft (12,192m)
Range	994 miles (1,600km)
Armament	Armament 4 x .50in (12.7mm) M2 machine guns, each with 250rpg

The completed Northrop XP-79B prototype jet fighter prior to testing at Muroc Dry Lake. USAF

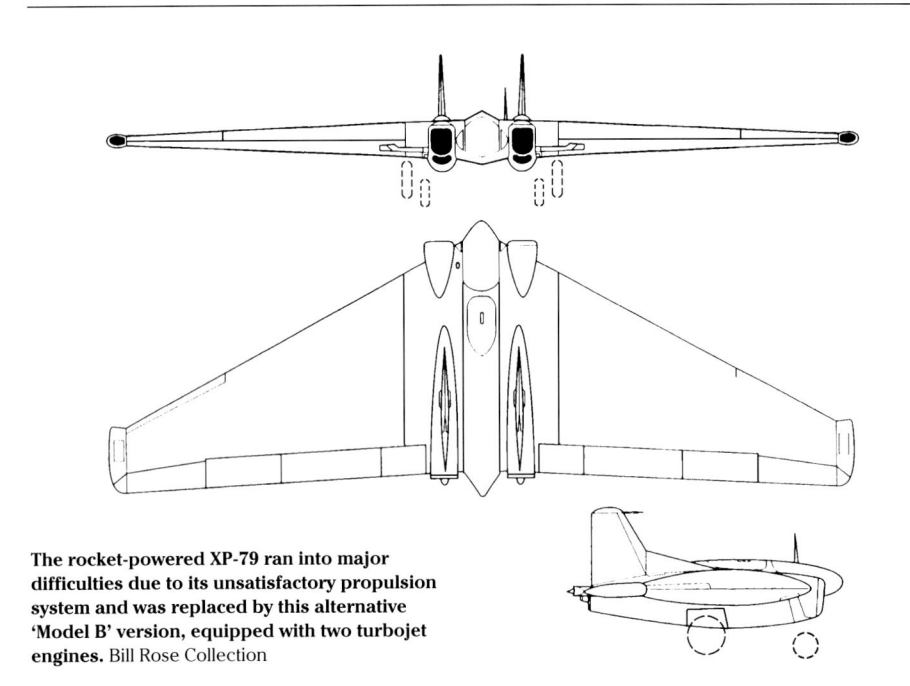

The ultimately ill-fated Northrop XP-79B twin-jet prototype. Differences between this aircraft and the original XP-79 are readily apparent due to the change in propulsion and switch to twin stabilising fins. Note the wingtip inlets for bellows type rudders, similar to those used on the XP-56. USAF

one option was to use the flying wing to 'knock wings and tails off other airplanes'. Later he would indicate the role of the XP-79 was just to intercept and shoot down enemy aircraft and ramming attacks had never been a serious consideration. But the weight of opinion suggests that there was a degree of interest in this possibility, even if the XP-79 appears to have been unsuitable for such a task.

Northrop X-4

In late 1945, the USAAF and NACA required a small aircraft to explore control and stability issues at transonic speeds of around Mach 0.85. The starting point for this project was captured research documentation for the German Me 163B rocket fighter and details of the British jet powered DH.108, which was in the process of receiving Air Ministry approval.

NACA favoured a broadly similar single-seat tailless design, although its aircraft would be powered by two turbojet engines. Northrop was considered the obvious contractor to build this type of aircraft and towards the end of 1945 it was approached to develop two prototypes. The company then submitted plans to meet this requirement and received provisional acceptance in spring 1946 for a design known as XS-4 (and also MX-810). The order was formalised as a contract (WW33-038-ac-14542) during June 1946 and the aircraft was officially called the X-4, while unofficially being given the name Bantam or Skylancer.

Northrop's senior engineer, Arthur I. Lusk, had been largely responsible for the X-4's design and was placed in charge of construction which was undertaken at the Experimental Shop at Hawthorne. But before assembly work started, a one-fifth-scale size wood and aluminium model was built for wind tunnel tests. By November 1946, a full-sized mock-up had been completed and a review panel recommended minor changes to the design which allowed the carriage of extra instrumentation.

The X-4 was an extremely compact aircraft with virtually no wasted internal space. The forward-positioned cockpit was equipped with an ejector seat and covered with a bubble canopy providing excellent visibility, although pilots found the cockpit extremely cramped. The aircraft's overall length was 22ft 3in (7.1m), its wingspan was 26ft 10in (8.2m) and a long tailfin gave the X-4 a height of 14ft 10in (4.5m). Nevertheless, most important parts of the aircraft were accessible from ground level during maintenance. Lusk drew heavily on experience gained during the XP-79 programme and many of the same constructional methods were employed for the X-4. The body was mainly built from aluminium and wings were fabricated from magnesium alloy with split flaps and elevons for control of pitch and roll.

Propulsion was provided by two Westinghouse XJ30 WE-7 turbojets (later replaced with newer versions) that were housed within the wing roots. Each engine was rated at 1,600lb (7.11kN) static thrust. With a gross weight of 7,820lb (3,550kg), the X-4's maximum speed was 630mph (1,013kph) and the maximum endurance was about 45 minutes providing a range of approximately 420 miles (675km).

The X-4 prototypes had now been assigned the serial numbers 46-676 and 46-677, with 46-676 reaching completion in late 1948 and being transported by road to Muroc AFB on 15 November 1948. During the following month, the aircraft underwent static testing, followed by taxiing trials undertaken by Northrop test pilot Charles Tucker. The aircraft made its maiden flight on 16 December 1948 and Tucker flew the X-4 for 18 minutes, reaching a maximum speed of 290mph (466kph) and climbing to an altitude of 11,000ft (3,352m). While Tucker found the handling was good, he also reported a degree of longitudinal instability. Modifications were made to the aircraft, including the installation of wingtip spin recovery parachutes and changes to the undercarriage. However, winter rains arrived which flooded Rogers Dry Lake and held up further trials until April 1949. Flight-testing then resumed, although there were ongoing reliability problems and Walt Williams who headed the NACA Muroc Flight Test Unit (now the Dryden Flight Research Center) described the X-4 as a 'lemon'.

The second X-4 (46-677) had now been delivered to Muroc and this aircraft had undergone a number of aerodynamic modifications as a result of tests with the first prototype. The second X-4 proved significantly more reliable and as a consequence it was decided to drop the first prototype from the

Northrop's second X-4 in flight. These small experimental aircraft were developed using Lippisch's research documentation for the Messerschmitt Me 163 and details of the post-war British de Havilland DH.108 Swallow. Designed to investigate transonic flight, the X-4 proved to be a valuable and successful experimental design. NASA

The first Northrop X-4 Bantam (46-676) undergoing checks at Rogers Dry Lake, California, during initial trials in late 1948. USAF

US Flying Wings (1935-1950)

The first prototype Northrop X-4 (46-676). NASA

The second Northrop X-4 research aircraft is shown split into two sections to facilitate relatively easy engine maintenance. NASA

Northrop X-4 (46-677) undertaking a test flight in 1948. NASA

programme after just 10 test flights and use it as a source of spare parts for the second X-4.

The second X-4 made its first flight on 7 June 1949 piloted by Tucker. The aircraft completed 20 flights before being passed over to the USAF and NACA in 1950. A number of USAF and NACA pilots flew the X-4 during trials that lasted until September 1953, with the best known of these being Major Charles 'Chuck' Yeager who had undertaken the world's first supersonic flight in the Bell X-1.

Lengthy delays for various reasons held up the test programme, although much was learnt during this period about the behaviour of tailless aircraft at relatively high subsonic Mach numbers. The X-4 demonstrated that it became increasingly unstable at higher speeds, although the nature of this would change from yawing and rolling at around Mach 0.75 to porpoising above Mach 0.9. Various attempts were made to counteract these problems with changes to the flaps and the elevons. There was some success and stability improved although the oscillations above Mach 0.9 remained.

The research data provided by the X-4 had a considerable impact on the future of tailless designs, indicating that this type of aircraft was unsuitable for supersonic flight. Both X-4s still exist with the first aircraft currently in storage at Edwards AFB and the second on display at the USAF National Museum at Wright-Patterson Air Force Base, Dayton, Ohio.

Northrop X-4 Bantam

Crew	1
Wingspan	26ft 10in (8.2m)
Wing area	300ft² (27.87m²)
Sweep	40° (leading edge)
Length	22ft 3in (7.1m)
Height	14ft 10in (4.5m)
Empty weight	5,507 lb (2,498kg)
Gross weight	7,820 lb (3,550kg)
Powerplant	2 x Westinghouse XJ30 WE-7 turbojets, later replaced by two slightly improved Westinghouse J30 WE-9 turbojets, each rated at 1,600 lb (7.11kN) static thrust
Cruise speed	480mph (772kph)
Maximum speed	630mph (1,013kph)
Service ceiling	42,300ft (12,839m)
Range	420 miles (675km)

Secret Projects: Flying Wings and Tailless Aircraft

Chapter Four

US Flying Wings (1950-1990)

Lockheed High-Altitude Spyplane Studies

As the Cold War intensified during the immediate post-war years, the US sought reliable ways of gathering intelligence on a wide range of activities taking place within the Soviet Union and other communist countries. Few methods were available to the US military or the CIA and there were no aircraft capable of undertaking deep reconnaissance missions while avoiding detection or interception.

At the start of the Korean War in 1950, USAF Major John D. Seaberg found himself recalled to active service from his job as an aeronautical engineer with Chance Vought. He was then assigned to the New Developments Office at Wright-Patterson AFB, working under civilian scientist William E. Lamar. Before long, Seaberg was starting to produce ideas for a specialised reconnaissance aircraft that would utilise the latest developments in turbojet technology and aerodynamics, allowing flight at extremely high altitudes. With Lamar's full support he began to develop firm proposals, which were largely completed by the end of 1952. They called for a long-range, unarmed one-man reconnaissance aircraft, carrying photographic equipment for daylight use at a minimum altitude of 70,000ft (21,336m). It was believed that the aircraft would be very difficult to detect at this height and would remain impossible to intercept for some years to come.

The proposals generated immediate high-level interest when presented in early 1953 and Lamar received full backing to place this promising programme on a formal footing. Within a matter of weeks, the proposal was officially named as Project Bald Eagle, with the reference MX-2147. Three different defence contractors were carefully selected to become involved with Bald Eagle and the first meeting with company engineers took place at Wright-Patterson AFB on 1 July 1953. From the outset, large contractors such as Boeing, Convair and Northrop were excluded as it was felt that a smaller company would handle the project more efficiently.

However, Martin Aircraft of Baltimore, Maryland, was chosen by Seaberg and Lamar because it was already building a modified version of the British twin-engine Canberra light bomber which had exceptional high altitude performance. The USAF version of this aircraft was known as the B-57 and a small number of these aircraft had been adapted for reconnaissance duties and were flying 'Sneaky Pete' missions in the Far East.

Because the B-57 already possessed some of the abilities required for Bald Eagle, it was decided to explore the idea of making modest changes to the engines and wing to improve high-altitude performance further. Seaberg and Lamar considered this aircraft to be a fairly safe bet, so Martin was issued with a contract (AF33(600)25825) to study a modified version of the B-57 which was designated Model 294. The second contractor to be approached was Bell Aircraft at Buffalo, New York, which was regarded as the leading constructor of experimental aircraft at that time. They were requested to design a completely new lightweight twin-engine jet aircraft capable of meeting the requirement. A contract (AF33(616)-2160) was issued to begin work on this project and Bell assigned the company designation Model 67 to this aircraft. The third contractor chosen for Bald Eagle was Fairchild of Hagerstown, Maryland. It was asked to undertake a design study for a single-engine, high-altitude aircraft. Fairchild received a contract (AF33(616)2182) and assigned the company reference M-195 to its project. The completion date for these studies was 31 December 1953 and all proposals had been submitted by this date.

Although the USAF initially favoured a development of the General Electric J73 turbojet for each design, every contractor recommended a modified version of the Pratt & Whitney J57. The three designs were now considered in considerable detail, with Seaberg and Lamar presenting an outline of Project Bald Eagle to several groups of USAF generals and receiving full approval to proceed during May 1954. Bell's Model 67 was considered to be the best design and a contract was issued to build a mock-up of the aircraft, with the expectation of following this with a limited production run. The Bell aircraft was assigned the designation X-16 which was intentionally misleading as this reference was normally applied to rather unusual aircraft of an experimental nature.

Fairchild's M-195 was completely eliminated from the programme, but it was decided to proceed with the construction of a modified Martin B-57 as this appeared to be a worthwhile fallback option.

As work began on both of these aircraft, there were two new developments. First, some details of Project Bald Eagle reached Clarence L. 'Kelly' Johnson who headed Lockheed's Skunk Works in California and secondly, the CIA started to take a serious interest in the programme. Kelly Johnson's approach to business was aggressive and he had no intention of allowing this project to slip from his grasp if his company was in a position to compete. Subsequently, he initiated a series of studies at the Skunk Works which appear to have evolved in three slightly different directions. The most conventional design was a long winged one-man glider-like aircraft with the design reference CL-278-1-1. This had a wingspan of 98ft 8in (30m), a wing area of 650ft^2 (60.3m^2) and utilised a tricycle undercarriage. Propulsion would be provided by the forthcoming General Electric J79 turbojet (derived from the J73).

A second Skunk Works design for Project Bald Eagle was the CL-282, based on Lockheed's prototype XF-104 Starfighter that had received a USAF contract for further development in January 1953. The fuselage of this aircraft was similar in appearance to the Starfighter, although shorter with an overall length of 44ft (13.4m). This was due to the use of a modified J79 turbojet that did not require an afterburner. A cockpit (in this case unpressurised) and tail assembly of similar design to the Starfighter would be used, but the CL-282 was not equipped with an undercarriage as such, taking off with a trolley and landing on the fuselage or perhaps small skids. Possibly the most distinctive feature of this aircraft was the proportionately wide 70ft 8in (21.5m) wingspan.

The third concept intended to meet the Bald Eagle requirement was the CL-278-1-2. This was very different from either of the other high altitude reconnaissance proposals and was based on a flying wing. It had a fuselage

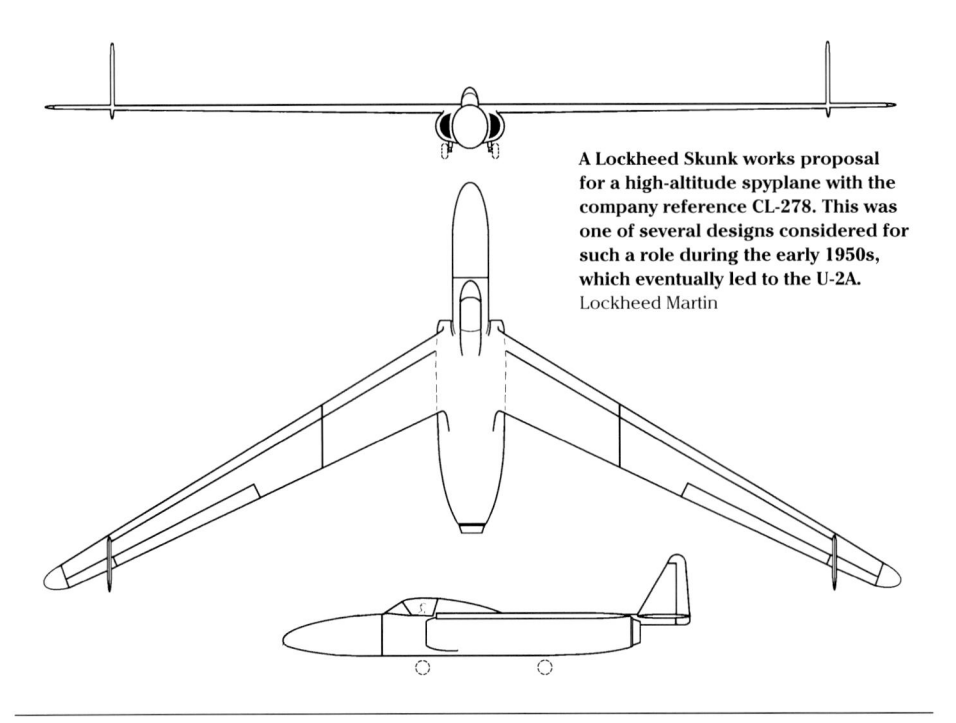

A Lockheed Skunk works proposal for a high-altitude spyplane with the company reference CL-278. This was one of several designs considered for such a role during the early 1950s, which eventually led to the U-2A. Lockheed Martin

length of 42ft (12.8m) and a single General Electric J79 turbojet when available would provide propulsion. This was the same engine chosen for the other aircraft in this study and it would be a slightly modified design with no afterburner and a static thrust in excess of 11,000 lb (49kN). The aircraft's wingspan was 100ft (30.48m) and the long slender profile provided a wing area of 650ft^2 (60.38m^2) with a leading edge sweep of 30°. Two triangular-shaped stabilising fins with rudders were located towards the wingtips with control surfaces located along the trailing edge. The overall length of the aircraft would be 48ft (14.63m) when allowing for the vertical fins.

The cockpit would be positioned with the pilot sitting upright just ahead of the wing's leading edge, allowing good visibility, and intakes for the engine would be located on either side of the cockpit area. It is not clear if an ejection seat was contemplated for this aircraft. The nose of the aircraft was rounded, rather like the earlier Lockheed P-80A fighter and two film cameras would have been carried in this section of the aircraft. Unlike CL-282, this high-altitude flying wing would have been fitted with a tricycle undercarriage. No weights are quoted in what little documentation exists. However, it is reasonable to conclude that the maximum speed would have been in the region of 500mph (804kph) with an expected operational ceiling of 70,000ft (21,336m). The estimated range is unknown, but Lockheed will have intended to meet the Bald Eagle requirements.

But it appears that CL-278-1-1 and CL-278-1-2 were discarded within the Skunk Works at an early stage, with CL-282 considered the most promising design. During May 1954, Johnson made a proposal to the New Developments Office at Wright-Patterson AFB for CL-282, but Seaberg and Lamar rejected it. Johnson then undertook a significant revision of the design and the CIA had now begun to take a serious interest in the Lockheed concept. It would lead to eventual acceptance of a new Lockheed aircraft called the U-2A and cancellation of the X-16 which proved very damaging to Bell Aircraft.

Lockheed Gusto 2

At the end of the 1950s, a new, highly-classified proposal for a high-altitude flying wing reconnaissance aircraft was produced by the Skunk Works. This was regarded as a possible replacement for the Lockheed U-2 and the cancelled Suntan supersonic spyplane. Gusto 2 was a single-seat subsonic flying wing with an estimated span of about 100ft (30.48m). It would be powered by two turbojets buried within the central section in a similar position to the Horten Ho IX. An air inlet for both engines was located in the nose and two vertical stabilisers were positioned towards the wingtips. The aim of this design was to produce an aircraft with a very low radar cross section and it is known that a number of scale models were built and tested. During trials, the design was found to be incapable of avoiding Soviet radar systems and this particular project was abandoned.

Lockheed's Flying Aircraft Carrier

Among the more bizarre military studies undertaken by any defence contractor was a Lockheed Skunk Works project to determine the feasibility of building a gigantic flying aircraft carrier or troop transporter for the US Military. With its origins in the late 1960s, this project evolved into a tailless aircraft designated CL-1201 that still looks as if it belongs in a science-fiction comic book. Four gigantic turbofan engines would have powered the CL-1201, providing a cruise thrust of 500,000 lb (2,224kn).

At altitudes below 16,000ft (4,876m), the engines would run on normal JP-5 fuel, but while operating at a greater height they would be powered by nuclear energy from a single onboard reactor. A liquid metal system would transfer energy via a heat exchanger to a secondary non-radioactive system that was coupled to heat exchangers inside each turbofan.

Conceived in the late 1950s and built as a scale-sized model, the Gusto 2 was an attempt by Lockheed's Skunk Works to produce a high-altitude low-observable subsonic aircraft. Lockheed Martin

Secret Projects: Flying Wings and Tailless Aircraft

Perhaps the most astonishing proposal ever made for a military aircraft was this massive nuclear-powered Lockheed aircraft carrier with the study reference CL-1201. Designed in the late 1960s, the CL-1201 would have taken off and landed using banks of lift jets. Once in the air, the CL-1201 would have flown for one month on nuclear power. Combat aircraft would have been carried under each wing and there was also a *Star Trek* style hangar deck for transport aircraft. It remains hard to take this concept seriously and it seems unlikely that anyone really expected such an aircraft to be built. Lockheed Martin

With a diameter of 30ft (9.1m), the reactor would provide a constant output of 1,830 megawatts. Substantial shielding would be needed to protect the crew and the reactor would be designed to have failsafe crash performance even in a high-speed head-on impact. CL-1201 would cruise at an altitude of 30,000ft (9,144m) and have an average speed of Mach 0.8. The estimated gross weight of the CL-2101 aircraft was about 5,265 tons (5,350 metric tons). The wingspan was to be approximately 1,120ft (341m) with a length of 560ft (170m) and a height of 153ft (46m). To put this in perspective, the length of the aircraft's fuselage would be almost the same as a Russian Typhoon-class nuclear powered ballistic missile submarine, which is the largest submersible vessel ever built.

The aircraft could remain in flight for one month and this might be stretched further with the reactor capable of operating for 1,000 hours (41 days) before it required refuelling. Overall life expectancy of the reactor was approximately five years. Because of the CL-1201's size and weight, it may have been initially designed as a flying boat, but company drawings show a VTOL capability, achieved by using 182 turbofan lift engines. These would provide 15 million pounds (66,723kN) of thrust and would be located along each wing behind the rear spar and in extendable units at the front of the fuselage, each containing 24 units. The lift engines would also be available for certain in-flight thrust manoeuvres.

The aircraft would be equipped with a substantial fully-retractable undercarriage comprising of four separate landing gear struts, each with six wheels positioned towards the rear of the fuselage. Two further six-wheel units would be located outboard of the wing roots, plus four-wheel stabilising gear positioned about half way along each wing. In addition, there would be a substantial four-wheel nose gear unit. The VTOL capability suggests that this undercarriage would only be used for ground handling purposes, but it is possible that operations were considered from specially built massive airfields.

Two versions of the CL-1201 were proposed. The first was the CL-1201-1-1 Attack Aircraft Carrier (AAC) and the second was the CL-1201-1-3 Logistics Support Aircraft (LSA). Both aircraft would have facilities to accommodate as many as 845 crew members for one month. A version designated CL-1201-1-2 would appear to have been considered, but nothing is held in the Lockheed-Martin archives to indicate what this concept was. The CL-1201-1-1 AAC version would carry 22 multi-role tactical aircraft below the wing on pylons and these would be recovered in-flight after completing a mission. There would be direct access to the aircraft via pylons for flight crews and maintenance staff with the aircraft being rearmed and refuelled while attached. Two additional aircraft would be carried in a hangar bay and these may have been general-purpose designs able to ferry small numbers of personnel to and from the AAC. It was also suggested that the AAC could act as an operational airborne command centre. The CL-1201-1-3 LSA was very similar to the CL-1201-1-1 AAC, but would be used to transport several hundred combat troops and their equipment to a war zone. One suggestion was to dock Boeing 707-sized transport aircraft using nose receptors positioned at the CL-1201-1-3's trailing edge and tail. However, the engineering challenge presented by this idea would have been immense. Defensive

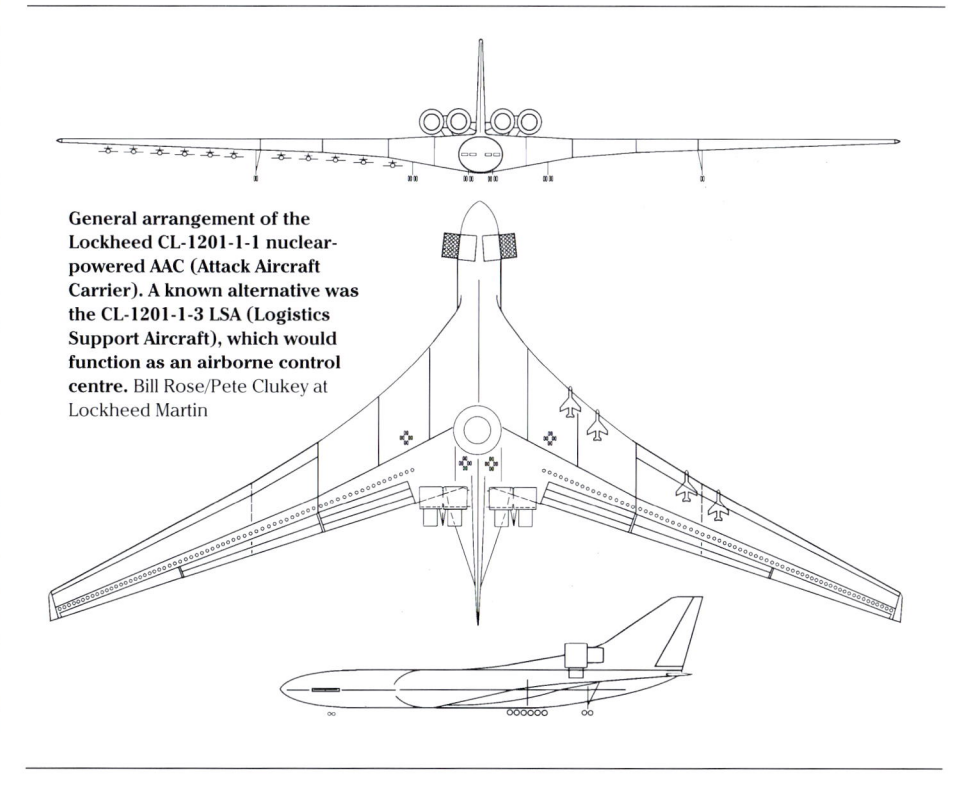

General arrangement of the Lockheed CL-1201-1-1 nuclear-powered AAC (Attack Aircraft Carrier). A known alternative was the CL-1201-1-3 LSA (Logistics Support Aircraft), which would function as an airborne control centre. Bill Rose/Pete Clukey at Lockheed Martin

US Flying Wings (1950-1990)

CL-1201-1-1 (AAC)

Wingspan	1,120ft (341m)
Wing area	125,000ft² (11612.8m²)
Length	560ft (170m)
Height	153ft (47m)
Gross weight	5,265 tons (5,350 metric tons) approx.
Powerplant	4 x turbofan engines, providing 500,000 lb (2,224kn) cruise thrust, combined with one nuclear reactor producing 1,830 megawatts
Cruise speed	Mach 0.8
Cruise altitude	30,000ft (9,144m)
Armament	Fighter aircraft carried by the CL-1201, supplemented by long-range air-to-air missiles for defence

armament for the CL-1201 aircraft is unclear, although it is likely that long-range air-to-air missiles such as the AIM-54 Phoenix were considered. In addition, some of the combat aircraft carried by the CL-1201-1-1 would have provided protection. It is also understood that the CL-1201-1-3 may have been able to launch battlefield range ballistic missiles with nuclear warheads.

Few details of the CL-1201 study remain, but most elements of this concept are hard to take seriously. Lockheed worked on this idea for an unknown period, lasting into the early 1970s and the fact that it would never be built must have been obvious to many people from the outset. Nuclear propulsion for aircraft was conceived at the end of World War 2 leading to the Convair NB-36H prototype based on the B-36. This was followed by plans to build a long-range nuclear powered bomber known as WS-125.

Tests indicated that the concept was viable, but there was strong political opposition due to the potential dangers of nuclear technology and widespread public unease about its use. In 1961, the Aircraft Nuclear Propulsion (ANP) programme was shut down by the Kennedy administration and that may have been the end of any ideas to power aircraft with atomic energy. While proposals to use nuclear propulsion for spacecraft persisted into the early 1970s, these also met with increasing resistance and were finally abandoned. But it is known that development of nuclear rocket engines was secretly revived during the US Strategic Defence Initiative of the 1980s as a means of lifting massive payloads into orbit and to power long-range high-performance missiles. This work continued throughout the remainder of the 20th century and there are suspicions that limited development of nuclear-powered aircraft or airborne platforms may have continued in the black domain. Nevertheless, even if it proved possible to build a massive aircraft like the CL-1201-1-1 and develop an advanced nuclear propulsion system for it, the operational problems would be enormous. Such an aircraft would be extremely demanding to operate, impossible to conceal and vulnerable to attack with the loss of a single multi-billion dollar asset proving catastrophic.

The Cutlass

In June 1945, Chance Vought Aircraft at Stratford, Connecticut, responded to a US Navy requirement for a future carrier-based combat aircraft. The Navy now sought a jet fighter that was capable of reaching 600mph (965km/h) and attaining an altitude of at least 40,000ft (12,192m). Vought submitted several proposals and in June 1946, the Navy selected an advanced tailless twin-engine design which would be designated XF7U-1. This aircraft promised the required level of performance, combined with the minimal amount of stowage space dictated by US carrier hangar decks. The aircraft was designed from the outset around engines equipped with afterburners and featured a pressurised cockpit, an ejection seat and a tricycle undercarriage. But the XF7U-1, which eventually received the name Cutlass, had much in common with the Arado Ar 1 jet fighter proposal (described earlier), leading to speculation that the XF7U-1 was directly based on this design.

Vought claimed to have been working on the Cutlass before any of Arado's wartime research became available, but there is a consensus of opinion that the company received help from US Intelligence during early 1945. Alternatively, the XF7U-1 proposal may have been extensively refined when documentation on the wartime Arado project became available. Whatever the truth, the XF7U-1 was developed by a team of engineers headed by Rex Beisel (1893-1972) who designed the highly successful Vought F4U Corsair fighter. Wind tunnel tests of XF7U-1 models were undertaken by NACA at Langley.

The XF7U-1 was the last aircraft developed by Chance Vought at Stratford before the Navy orchestrated a company relocation to Grand Prairie, Texas, which began in 1948. Three prototypes (122472-122474) were ordered by the Navy and subsequently

The first prototype Chance Vought XF7U-1 Cutlass (122472), which undertook its maiden flight during September 1948. NASA Langley Research Center

The first prototype Vought XF7U-1 (122472), seen in this photograph without nose probe. US Navy

assembled in Bernie Whitman's experimental shop. The first prototype XF7U-1 flew on 29 September 1948 at Patuxent River Naval Air Station with Vought's Chief Test Pilot, J. Robert Baker at the controls. Once the flight-testing was underway, the Navy placed an order for the first batch of 14 F7U-1 aircraft (124415-124428). But there were serious problems with the afterburning Westinghouse J34-WE32 turbojets that powered the prototypes and because of very real concerns about safety and reliability. A major propulsion change was made with the next batch of 16 (slightly improved) production aircraft designated F7U-3.

These were to have been powered by Westinghouse J46 turbojets, but the aircraft were fitted with less powerful (non-afterburning) Allison J35-29 engines. The Allison engines were less than ideal, but this substitution was regarded as a stopgap measure until Westinghouse resolved its technical difficulties and provided J46 engines that were reliable. While the first F7U-3 flew in December 1951, ongoing problems with the Westinghouse engines persisted and prevented the F7U-3 from entering service until autumn 1954. When the J46 finally became available, it failed to attain the anticipated level of performance. Key components would regularly fail or wear out quickly and the engines proved very difficult to maintain.

The Westinghouse J46-WE-8B was expected to deliver 7,000 lb (31kN) of static thrust and about 10,000 lb (44.5kN) with the afterburner, but in practice this engine never provided much more than about 60% of the promised figure. This led to the aircraft being named 'Gutless Cutlass' by Navy and Marine Corps pilots. The Cutlass served with the Navy until 1957, but never saw combat. It was used primarily as an interceptor that could just nudge past Mach 1 in a dive and many pilots reported that the aircraft performed favourably in mock dogfights. The fighter was armed with four 20mm cannons and unguided rockets while later versions carried Sparrow air-to-air missiles (AAMs). As a strike aircraft, the Cutlass was capable of carrying 6,000 lb (2,721.5kg) of ordnance which could include a free fall nuclear weapon.

The Vought Cutlass earned a reputation for being a difficult and dangerous aircraft to fly. The design was plagued with problems from cannon fire interfering with the engines, to landing gear failure and stall recovery issues. Worst of all were the Westinghouse engines which never delivered adequate performance and were very unreliable. These problems extended from continual failures of minor components to deadly in-flight explosions! Of the 290 F7U-3s built, no less than 49 were written off in accidents and in 25 cases the pilots were killed.

Chance Vought F7U-3 Cutlass. Bill Rose Collection

Two US Navy F7U-3 Cutlass fighters on patrol. US Navy

The first production Chance Vought Cutlass is launched from the deck of USS *Midway* (CVB-41) on 23 July 1951 during carrier trials. US Navy

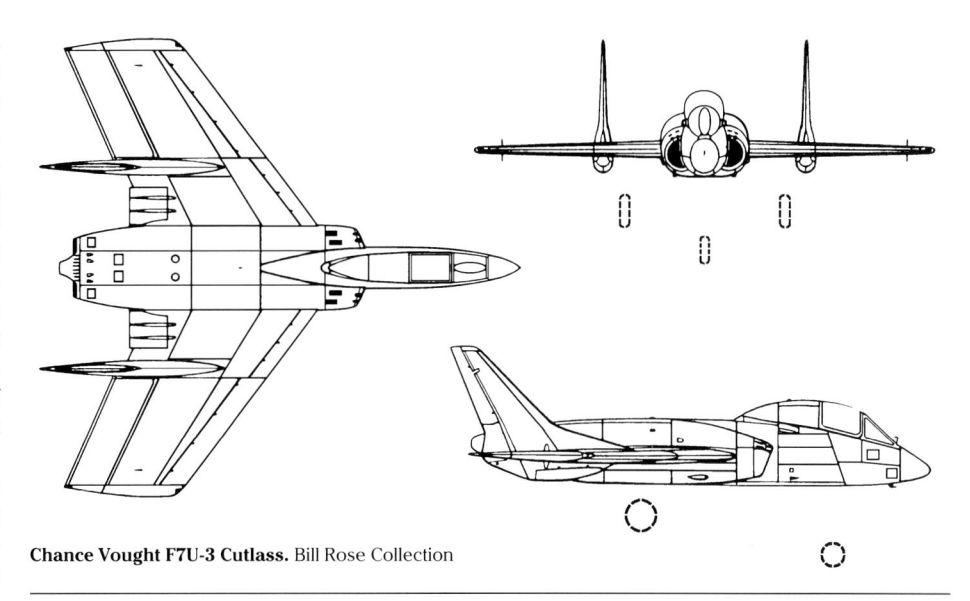

US Flying Wings (1950-1990)

A Chance Vought F7U-3 Cutlass on the ramp at Jacksonville Naval Air Station in June 1954.
US Navy

Vought F7U-1 Cutlass

Crew	1
Wingspan	38ft 8in (11.78m)
Sweep	38° (leading edge)
Length	39ft 7in (12.06m)
Height	11ft 10in (3.61m)
Empty weight	12,840 lb (5,824kg)
Loaded weight	24,000 lb (10,886kg)
Powerplant	2 x Westinghouse J34-WE-32A afterburning turbojets, each rated at 4,200 lb (18.68kN) static thrust
Maximum speed	672mph (1,081kph) at 20,000ft (6,096m) 665mph (1,070kph) at low level
Ceiling	44,000ft (13,411m)
Range	600 miles (965km)
Armament	Four 20mm cannon and three three-packs of Mighty Mouse (FFAR 2.75in) rockets (two on the wings, one under the fuselage)

Vought F-7U-3 Cutlass

Crew	1
Wingspan	39ft 8in (12.1m)
Length	44ft 3in (13.5m)
Height	14ft 7in (4.45m)
Wing area	496ft² (46.08m²)
Max take-off weight	31,642 lb (14,353kg)
Empty weight	18,210 lb (8,259kg)
Powerplant	2 x Westinghouse J46-WE-8A afterburning turbojets, each providing about 4,600 lb (20.46kN) static thrust
Maximum speed	Clean: 680mph (1,095km/h) at 20,000ft (6,096m)
Carrying missiles	648mph (1,042kph)
Ceiling	44,000ft (13,411m)
Range	1,400 miles (2,253km) with two drop tanks
Armament	Four 20mm cannons above inlet ducts, 180rpg. Four AIM-7 Sparrow air-to-air missiles, or up 6,000 lb (2,721.5kg) of external stores

Douglas Skyray

The manta-shaped Skyray jet fighter was a product of Douglas Aircraft at El Segundo, having been designed by Edward 'Ed' Henry Heinemann (1908-1991) who drew heavily on wartime research undertaken by Dr Alexander Lippisch. The history of this aircraft began the week after Germany's surrender when Douglas Aircraft's leading aerodynamicists, L. Eugene 'Gene' Root and Apollo Milton Olin 'Amo' Smith, were sent to Paris. The purpose of their trip was to meet with Dr Lippisch (who was in Allied custody) and to secure his research data on tailless high-performance aircraft.

Root and Smith were very impressed with Lippisch's work and following considerable evaluation of the data at Douglas, a programme of wind tunnel model tests began in 1946 which produced very encouraging results. Perhaps already aware of the Navy's future needs, Heinemann concentrated on the design of a tailless jet fighter and when the Navy's single-engine fighter competition was announced in 1947, Heinemann's project received the company reference Design-571. The Navy was seeking a carrier-based jet fighter capable of intercepting an enemy bomber which was travelling at 575mph (926kph) at an altitude of 50,000ft (15,240m) within a 100-mile 160km radius. Five minutes was allowed from the start of the alert to interception and engagement, which was a tough requirement to meet with prevailing technology, but Heinemann was convinced that the D-571 could meet this demand.

Initially, the fighter was very reminiscent of a Lippisch study taking the form of a delta-shaped flying wing with no significant fuselage and a single tailfin. But as the design evolved, the aircraft began to stretch and the fuselage took a more distinctive shape. With the concept formalised, a proposal was made to the Navy that decided to issue a contract to Douglas on 16 December 1948 for the construction of two prototypes receiving the official designation XF4D-1 and the BuAer serial numbers 124586 and 124587. It remains unclear when the name Skyray was applied to the design by Douglas or when it was officially adopted, but it appears to have come into use soon after construction started. Military pilots would later know the Skyray as 'The Ford' because of its F-4-D designation.

The XF4D-1 was a low-aspect ratio swept-wing tailless aircraft, falling somewhere between a flying wing and a delta design with a single tailfin. The aircraft was to be powered by one of the new afterburning Westinghouse turbojets, fed from air intakes located at the leading edge wing roots. The XF4D-1 would be equipped with a tricycle undercarriage, folding wings for hangar deck storage and a forward-positioned pressurised cockpit fitted with an ejector seat developed by Douglas. Production aircraft would be fitted with four 20mm M-12 cannons in the wing's inner leading edges and use a forward located Westinghouse radar system. Provision was also made for the future carriage of underwing stores, including drop tanks and air-to-air missiles when they became a practical proposition.

The production aircraft would have an overall length of 45ft 3in (14.5m) and a wingspan of 33ft 6in (10.21m), making it similar in size to the Vought Cutlass and, with the wings folded, would occupy much the same storage space within an aircraft carrier's hangar deck. The Navy had specified the Westinghouse XJ-40-WE-6 afterburning turbojet for the Skyray. It was rated at 7,000 lb (31.13kN) static thrust and Douglas was confident that its new fighter had the potential to reach Mach 1 in level flight with this engine. The Westinghouse turbojet had been chosen to power several other Navy aircraft, but it was experiencing serious development problems that led Heinemann to make modest alterations to the XF-4D-1's airframe, allowing the installation of alternative engines with diameters up to 42in (1.06m).

This proved to be a shrewd decision because when the airframe was completed in early 1950, the Westinghouse turbojet was still unavailable due to ongoing technical difficulties. As a consequence, it was decided during June 1950 to install the less powerful Allison J35-A-17 providing 5,000 lb (22.24kN) static thrust in each prototype for trial purposes. Subsequently, the first XF4D-1 (124586) took to the air on 21 January 1951 at Edwards AFB, piloted by Douglas' test pilot Larry Peyton. The flight proved to be quite

A Douglas F4D-1 equipped with drop tanks and Sidewinder AAMs above San Diego, California. US Navy

A Douglas F4D landing on the aircraft carrier USS Bon Homme Richard during 1957. US Navy

demanding with Peyton reporting various control and handling problems and he never flew another Skyray. The aircraft was then test flown by Douglas test pilots Russ Thaw and Robert O. Rahn who both reported problems with yaw immediately after the undercarriage was retracted and unusual difficulties controlling pitch. Some years later, Rahn wrote his memoirs in a book called *Tempting Fate* and he had the following to say about the aircraft. 'I flew on manual flight control and quickly learned why Larry wanted no part of the Skyray. The stick forces were exorbitant for the small control-surface deflection achieved. The plane was tough to handle unless below 200kts and in smooth air – not a good sign for a fighter.' That aside, Rahn went on to praise the Skyray's agility, describing it as the best machine he had flown since the Spitfire.

The second prototype featured minor experimental differences such as a sliding cockpit canopy that was not adopted. The Skyray continued to exhibit various control problems that needed to be addressed and was the first Douglas aircraft to show signs of inertia coupling at high roll rates. Nevertheless, the Navy was sufficiently impressed to order a small batch of production F4D-1s in February 1951. With work underway on these aircraft, the Navy then placed an order for a second batch of 230 Skyrays in early 1952 which would be manufactured at the company's plant at Torrance, California.

Problems persisted with the generally unsatisfactory Westinghouse XJ40-WE-6 turbojet, although units were provided for installation in both prototype aircraft. The improved performance allowed XF4D-1 (124587) flown by Navy Lt-Cdr James B. Verdin to set a new world air speed record of 752.944mph (1211.746kph) over a 1.86 mile 9 (3km) course above the Salton Sea, California, on 3 October 1953.

But the Westinghouse engines remained unreliable and liable to failure in flight, some-

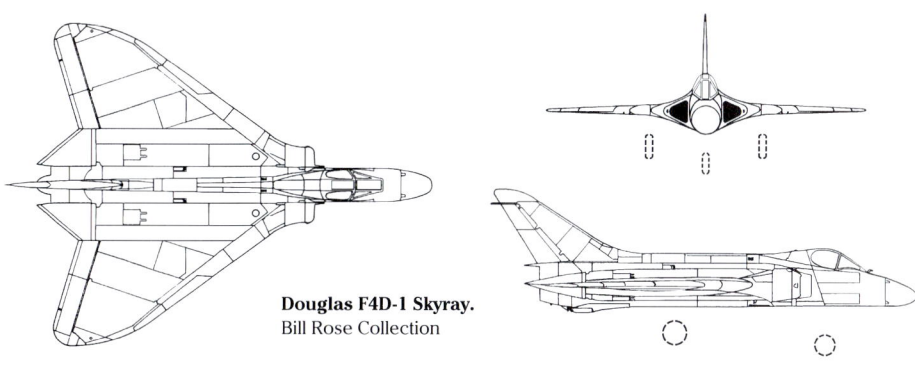

Douglas F4D-1 Skyray

Crew	1
Wingspan	33ft 6in (10.2m)
Wing area	557ft² (51.8m²)
Length	45ft 3in (14.5m)
Height	13ft (4m)
Wing loading	41 lb/ft² (198kg/m²)
Empty weight	16,024 lb (7,268kg)
Combat weight	22,648 lb (10,272kg)
Gross weight	25,000 lb (11,339kg)
Max permissible weight	27,116 lb (12,299kg)
Maximum speed	722mph (1,162kph)
Cruising speed	520mph (837kph)
Landing speed	134mph (215kph)
Initial rate of climb	18,300ft/min (5,578m/min)
Ceiling	55,000ft (16,764m)
Range (external tanks)	700 miles (1,126km)
Ferry range	1,200 miles (1,931km)
Powerplant (production aircraft)	1 x Pratt & Whitney J57-P-8, 8A, or 8B turbofan providing 10,200 lb (4,627kg) static thrust and 16,000 lb (7,258kg) with afterburner
Internal fuel capacity	640 US gal (2,422 litres)
External fuel capacity	Two 150 US gal (568 litre) or two 300 US gal (1,135 litre) drop tanks
Armament	Four 20mm cannons in wings and seven fuselage/underwing hardpoints able to carry up to 4,000 lb (1,815kg) in stores.

Douglas F4D-1 Skyray. Bill Rose Collection

US Flying Wings (1950-1990)

Douglas F4D-1 Skyray (134806) belonging to VMF-542 of the US Marine Corps. US Dept of Defense

US Navy Douglas F-6A Skyray (139083) photographed at MCAS El Toro, California, during July 1964. The aircraft shown was being used for training purposes. US Dept of Defense

Lockheed Naval Jet Bomber

During 1947, the US Navy's Bureau of Aeronautics (BuAer) produced a preliminary specification for a carrier-based jet bomber. This document known as OS-111 was issued to 14 major aircraft contractors in December 1947. BuAer sought a fast jet aircraft capable of carrying a single atomic weapon (Mk3 Fat Man plutonium bomb) with a weight of 10,200 lb (4,630kg), a length of 10ft 8in (3.25m) and a diameter of 5ft (1.52m) to a target 2,000nm (2,300 miles or 3,700km) distant and returning to the carrier.

The military think-tank Project RAND (Research ANd Development) had suggested that 150,000 lb (68,000kg) should be the minimum gross weight considered for an aircraft undertaking such a mission. However, BuAer decided this was an unrealistic demand, even allowing for the 1,088ft (331m) flight decks of the five proposed 'Supercarriers', so they set the gross weight at 100,000 lb (45,359kg). More than half the contractors approached had soon dropped out stating they felt it was impossible to balance the requirement for a bomber with this gross weight against a compact design that used prevailing or near-term engine technology. The remaining contractors indicated that performance compromises were necessary and progressively abandoned the contest, leaving a design produced by Curtiss and a lightweight proposal from Douglas that was capable of operating from a 45,000-ton (40,823-metric ton) Midway class carrier.

Then on 23 April 1949, the five supercarriers were cancelled and two months later Douglas received a development contract to build two XA3D-1 prototypes and a static test airframe. Among the numerous earlier proposals for OS-111 were two Lockheed designs which had different types of engines but broadly similar features. Both featured swept wings and tails with twin underwing engines, either for turbojets or turboprops. Designated with the company reference CL-187 (also referred to as L-187 in some documents), these designs resembled something of a cross between the larger B-47 and the smaller Douglas A-3.

A third completely different proposal was the CL-187-3 flying wing. This design comprised a short fuselage section with no tail and

times with catastrophic results. The upshot of this was a decision taken in March 1953 to adapt the Skyray to accept the more powerful and more reliable Pratt & Whitney J57-P-2 axial-flow afterburning engine that had an anticipated rating of 10,000 lb (44.48kN) static thrust. Trials of a Westinghouse-powered XF4D-1 onboard the USS *Coral Sea* continued, but the fate of this engine was now sealed and Westinghouse soon found itself out of the jet engine manufacturing business.

The first Skyray powered by a J57 flew on 5 June 1954 and the re-engined fighter soon showed itself to be a more capable aircraft than initially envisaged. It had a maximum speed of almost Mach 1, an outstanding rate of climb and a ceiling in excess of 50,000ft (15,240m). The maximum take-off loaded weight was 27,116 lb (12,299kg) that was partly due to the use of two 300 US gal (1,136 litre) fuel tanks, which extended the operational range to about 700 miles (1,126km), depending on the mission profile. Ferry range was somewhat greater at 1,200 miles (1,931km). Although designed from the outset as a high-performance interceptor, changing requirements resulted in adaptation to a limited strike capability, but the Skyray was seldom configured for this role.

The first production fighters reached the Navy in early 1957 and the US Marine Corps began receiving Skyrays soon after this. With many of the initial bugs ironed out, the Skyray proved to be reliable and reasonably popular with pilots. It never saw combat but was deployed operationally during two separate periods of international tension. The first was Taiwan in 1958 and then throughout the 1962 Cuban Missile Crisis when fully-armed Skyrays patrolled from the Naval Air Station at Key West, Florida, and Guantanamo, Cuba. In total, 421 Skyrays were built with the aircraft designation being changed to F6A. The Skyray was finally retired in 1962 when it was replaced by the outstanding McDonnell F-4B Phantom II.

Heinemann followed the Douglas Skyray with a naval attack aircraft called the A-4 Skyhawk which used the same basic design philosophy of compactness and functionality. The Skyhawk entered production in 1954 and continued to be built until 1979. Some 2,980 examples were sold to the US Navy, Marine Corps and a number of overseas customers making it one of the company's most successful products.

Secret Projects: Flying Wings and Tailless Aircraft

a forward-positioned tandem cockpit. The substantial swept wing would be fitted with split flaps and elevons, plus wingtip stabilising fins and rudders. CL-187-3 used three turbojets for propulsion with two mounted above the wings in nacelles that extended beyond the trailing edge. The third engine was located in a dorsal fairing at the centre of the wing. For hangar storage, the wings would fold and the crew access to the bomb bay was required to arm a nuclear weapon. Presumably, this aircraft was also capable of accommodating conventional bombs and perhaps carrying photo-reconnaissance equipment. Two 20mm cannons would have been fitted in a rear remote-control tail unit which was a requirement of OS-111. No details of dimensions, weights or performance for this rather obscure proposal appear to have survived, but the wingspan was probably in the region of 85ft (25m) to 90ft (27.4m). Maximum speed would have been about 500mph (804kph) with a ceiling of 40,000ft (12,192m). Nothing came of this interesting design and the scant details of CL-187-3 remained in Lockheed's archives until relatively recently.

This drawing of Lockheed's proposed tailless L-187 carrier-based bomber clearly shows the multi-engine layout for a design that stretched the limits of what was technically possible in the late 1940s. Pete Clukey/Lockheed Martin

Northrop N-381

During the 1970s, the Navy began to replace its propeller-driven anti-submarine warfare (ASW) Grumman S-2 Tracker aircraft with the more advanced turbofan-powered Lockheed S-3 Viking. The Viking was developed by a consortium of companies headed by Lockheed that built the airframe, supported by Ling-Temco-Vought (LTV) and Univac Federal Systems. Although the four-man Viking was designed primarily for ASW operations, it was capable of undertaking many other duties and a 'Weapon Systems Improvement Program' (WSIP) was initiated in 1981, leading to the S-3B Viking. This versatile subsonic carrier-based aircraft could easily be adapted to anti-shipping operations or used to attack land targets. Vikings have also been used for refuelling purposes, sea surveillance and even trialled as airborne early warning (AEW) platforms.

The Viking has been used in many different military campaigns which include the first Gulf War, the Balkans War and operations in Afghanistan. At the time of writing, the Navy is expected to keep the Viking in service until about 2015. But since the early 1980s, the Navy has been considering an eventual successor to the Viking that would be similar in size, but capable of being easily configured to many different tasks. Northrop was one defence contractor to conduct studies for a possible multi-role successor to the Viking S-3 with a definitive design known as N-381 which has its origins in the early 1980s.

Some details of N-381 remain sensitive and are not available, although the design was based on a compact fuselage not totally dissimilar to the S-3 with a substantial wing section that almost blends into the body with the leading edge beginning next to the centre of the forward-positioned cockpit. The aircraft would be powered by two unspecified non-afterburning turbofan engines, largely buried within the wings and fed by leading edge air intakes on either side of the wing roots. This suggests that some consideration was given to reducing the radar signature of the aircraft. There is no tail, but there are two slightly inward leaning tail fins with rudders which

The Northrop N-381 multi-role carrier-based flying wing aircraft designed as a possible replacement for the Grumman S-2 Tracker and Lockheed S-3 Viking. George Cox/Bill Rose Collection

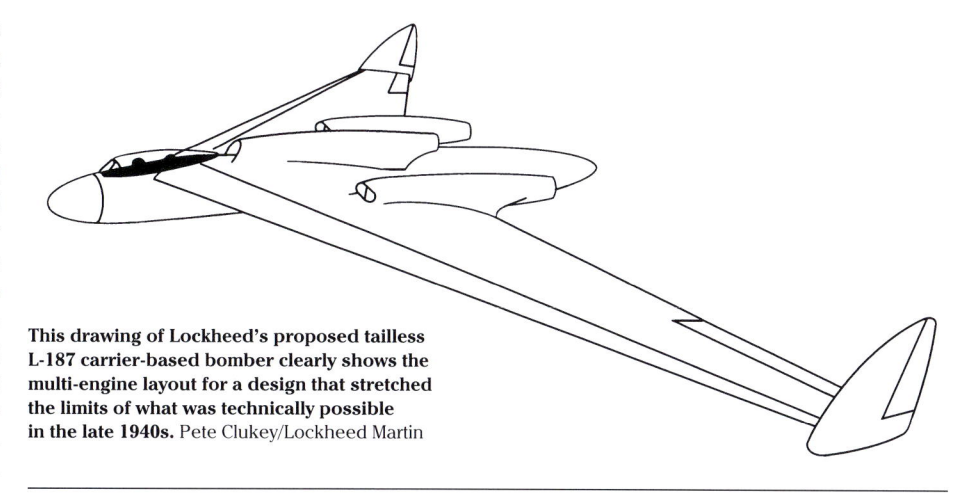

US Flying Wings (1950-1990)

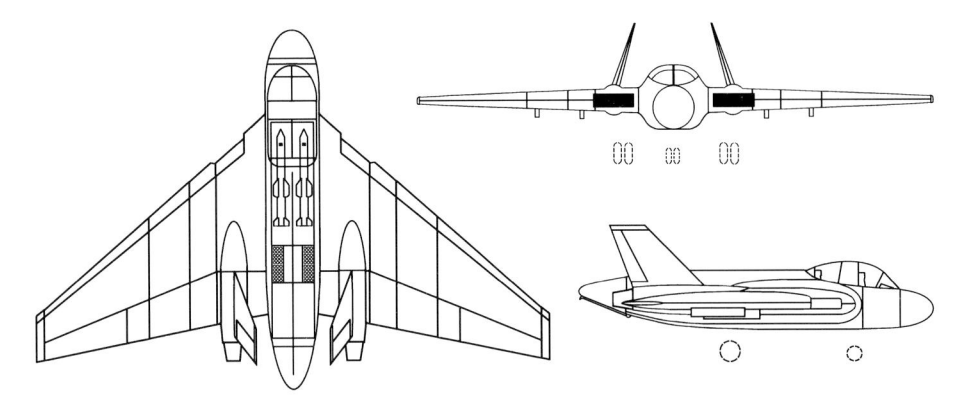

Three-view drawing of the Northrop N-381 multi-role aircraft showing internal carriage of two AGM-84A Harpoon missiles. Bill Rose Collection

are mounted above each engine unit towards the trailing edge. The wing is fitted with elevons and split flaps, while also having the ability to fold for hangar deck storage.

The forward-positioned four-man pressurised cockpit appears fairly similar to the EA-6B Prowler design, although the windshield is slightly different. All crew members faced forward in ejector seats with a pilot and co-pilot in the front seats and system specialists behind. The total number of roles envisaged for the N-381 remains undisclosed, but it was primarily designed as an ASW successor to the Lockheed S-3 with the probable ability to replace several other Navy aircraft. Typically, the N-381 would carry two banks of sonobuoy launchers, chaff and flare dispensers and two AGM-84A Harpoon missiles internally.

Alternatively, the aircraft could carry Mk46 or Mk50 torpedoes, mines, depth charges, free fall conventional bombs and B57 or B61 nuclear weapons. Four underwing pylons would allow additional stores. These could be AIM-9 Sidewinder AAMs for self-defence, AGM-88 high-speed Anti-Radiation Missiles (HARM), AGM-65F Maverick air-to-surface missiles, free fall bombs, unguided rockets, fuel tanks or various specialised pods.

The N-381 would be equipped with radar modules at the front and rear of the fuselage. In addition to ocean surveillance, Northrop almost certainly proposed a variant that was specifically designed to replace the EA-6B Prowler electronic warfare aircraft. The N-381 would be capable of in-flight refuelling and could be configured as a refuelling aircraft. Generally speaking, it seems reasonable to suppose that this design was expected to provide significant improvements over the S-3 Viking. N-381 would utilise a fully-retractable tricycle undercarriage and arresting gear. The wingspan was 70ft (21.3m) with an estimated leading edge sweep of 42° and it is probable that part of the reason for angling the tail fins inwards would be to assist with wing folding during storage. The overall length of the aircraft was 47ft 6in (14.4m) and the height was 18ft (5.5m). N-381 would have a maximum speed in the region of 520-550mph (836-885kph) and a ceiling of about 40,000ft (12,192m).

This design was finally rejected for unknown reasons, but the Common Support Aircraft (CSA) project began in 1993 with the intention of finding a single design capable of replacing the S-3B Viking, ES-3A Shadow surveillance aircraft, E-2C Hawkeye airborne AEW platform, EA-6B Prowler EW aircraft and C-2A Greyhound transporter. Although there would be differences between each variant, the basic airframe and propulsion system would be standardised, leading to obvious advantages with maintenance and training, while theoretically reducing the cost of manufacturing.

However, financial restraints and the focus of attention switching to programmes like the F/A-18E/F Super Hornet and the Joint Strike Fighter (now F-35 Lightning II) caused the CSA programme to slow. CSA Phase II began in 1997 with Lockheed-Martin as an active participant. They suggested improvements to the S-3 Viking, followed by an advanced canard variant equipped with a triangular shaped radome that was mounted on the tailfin. This was followed by various unusually-shaped proposals with stealthy characteristics. The CSA project remains on the shelf and it would be too costly to implement at present. As things stand, the F/A-18 Super Hornet has largely replaced the S-3 Viking in the anti-shipping and tanker roles. The EA-6B Prowler is also being superseded by the EA-18G Growler derived from the Super Hornet and there has been a reappraisal of ASW missions.

It is impossible to predict development of carrier-based aircraft during the next 20-30 years, but the introduction of a new multi-role manned aircraft seems unlikely in the near-term.

Lockheed Long Endurance Patrol Aircraft

During 1968 the US Navy's Naval Air Systems Command (NAVAIR) at Patuxent River, Maryland, began to consider future requirements for an aircraft that could replace and improve on the very reliable and extremely versatile land-based Lockheed P-3 Orion maritime patrol aircraft that had been in service since 1962. This resulted in Lockheed being approached to develop new designs that might be introduced in the late 1970s. The company accepted the commission and began a six-month programme which received the umbrella reference CL-1170. Its emphasis was on long-duration missions.

Initially, the designers looked at fairly conventional two- and four-engine designs that were configured to meet two different gross weight requirements of 150,000 lb (68,038kg) and 500,000 lb (226,796kg). The smaller aircraft would have a fuselage that was similar to the P-3 Orion, giving it an overall size that was close to a Boeing 737. The larger aircraft would be somewhat similar to a Boeing 747.

A parallel series of studies considered two different sizes of all-wing aircraft which were designed to the same overall gross weight requirements. These concepts incorporated laminar flow control and anticipated advances in high-bypass ratio turbofan engines allowing lengthy, fuel-efficient loitering. Mass would be carefully controlled through the use of composite materials and aluminium alloy wherever possible. At the end of this study, Lockheed engineers determined that the larger CL-1170-6-2 all-wing design using a mixture of turbofan and turboprop propulsion would perform better than its conventional equivalent on long-range missions. This was due in part to the proposed laminar flow control.

The CL-1170-6-2 would have a projected endurance of 90 hours and a mission radius of 3,000nm (3,452 miles, or 5,556km) and it appears that four turbofans became the preferred choice for this tailless aircraft, offering slightly better all-round performance. In the case of the smaller all-wing aircraft, it seems there were no significant gains over the conventional design. Under CL-1170, Lockheed considered six different basic configurations (conventional and all-wing), with outlines for several variants. Each aircraft utilised multiple wheel, tricycle landing gear, although the smaller all-wing design was expected to require outriggers to ensure stability. Other common design features for the all-wing aircraft were elevons and flaps, plus a single large tail fin with a rudder. All versions

Secret Projects: Flying Wings and Tailless Aircraft

Lockheed CL-1170-4-1

Crew	10
Wingspan	131ft (40m)
Wing area	1,890ft² (175m²)
Sweep	25° (leading edge).
Length	97ft (29.5m)
Height	27ft (8m)
Gross weight	150,000 lb (68,038kg)
Powerplant	2 x advanced high-bypass ratio turbofans each rated at 22,500 lb (100kN) static thrust. Alternatively, 2 x advanced turboprop engines
Maximum speed	Unspecified
Ceiling	Unspecified
Armament	Mk46 or Mk50 torpedoes, mines, depth charges, free fall bombs, AGM-84A Harpoon missiles, AGM-65F Maverick air-to-surface missiles

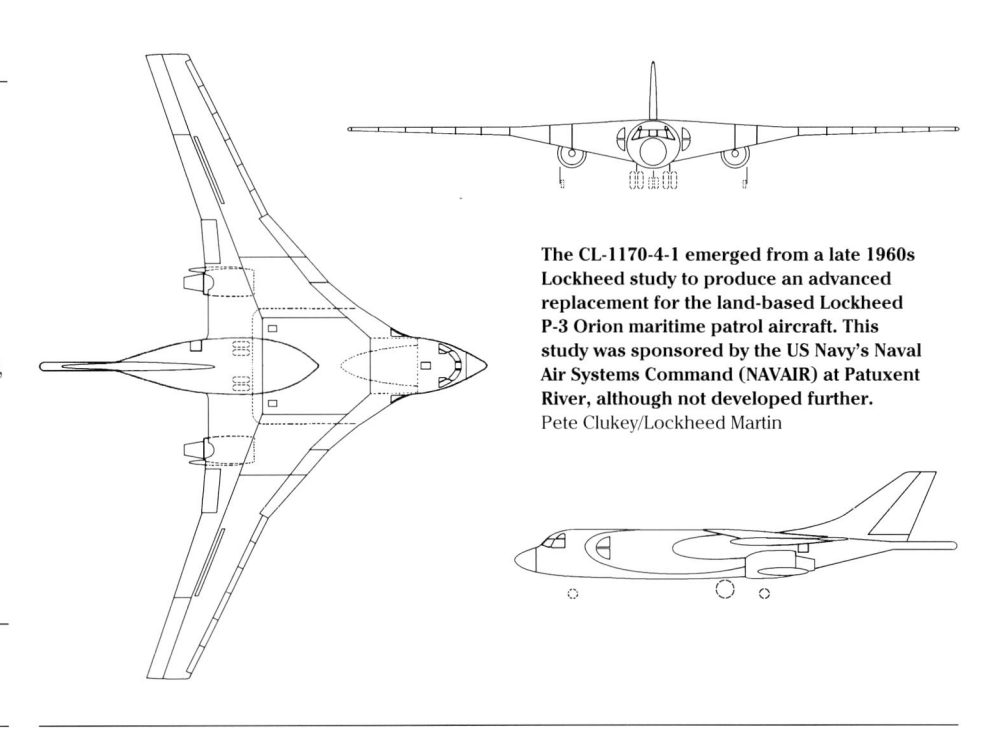

The CL-1170-4-1 emerged from a late 1960s Lockheed study to produce an advanced replacement for the land-based Lockheed P-3 Orion maritime patrol aircraft. This study was sponsored by the US Navy's Naval Air Systems Command (NAVAIR) at Patuxent River, although not developed further.
Pete Clukey/Lockheed Martin

Lockheed CL-1170-6-2

Crew	Unknown
Wingspan	224ft (68m)
Wing area	5,000ft² (464.5m²)
Length	95ft 6in (29m)
Height	36ft 9in (11m)
Gross weight	500,000 lb (226,796kg)
Powerplant	4 x advanced high-bypass ratio turbofans or 2 x turbofans and 2 x turboprops
Maximum speed	Unspecified
Ceiling	Unspecified
Endurance	90 hours at a mission radius of 3,000nm (3,452 miles, or 5,556km) using mixed turbofan/turboprop propulsion system
Armament	Unspecified, but probably similar to CL-1170-4-1

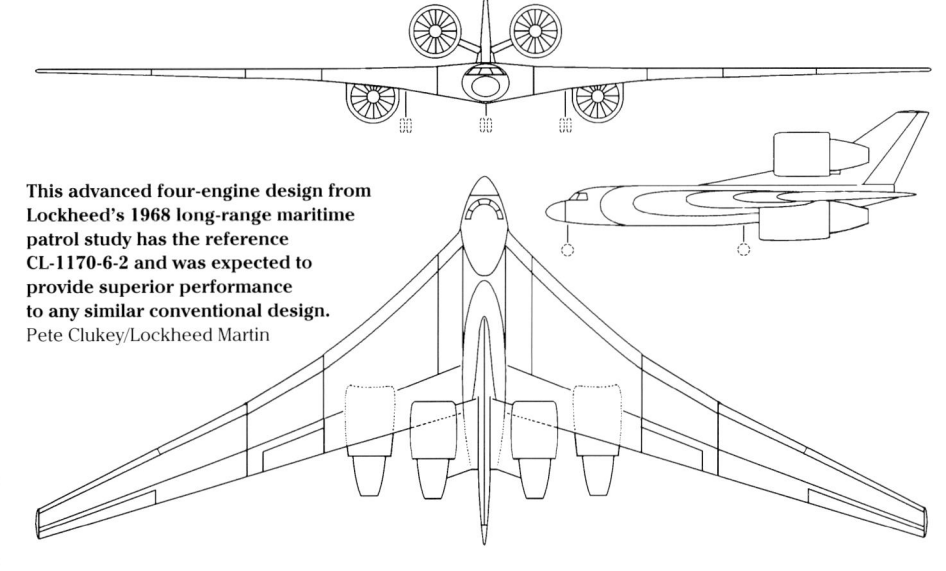

This advanced four-engine design from Lockheed's 1968 long-range maritime patrol study has the reference CL-1170-6-2 and was expected to provide superior performance to any similar conventional design.
Pete Clukey/Lockheed Martin

would be capable of in-flight refuelling.

Engines for the all-wing designs were suspended in pods beneath the wing with their thrustline positioned at the chordline. The four-engine versions of the all-wing aircraft would be fitted with two additional engines in nacelles supported by struts on each side of the lower forward tailfin section. With mixed propulsion designs it was determined that the turboprops needed to be installed in the outboard locations. The smaller tailless aircraft was intended to carry similar armament to the P-3 Orion, ranging from free fall bombs, various missiles, torpedoes, mines and depth charges. There would also be provision for sonobuoys. There are no details of external hardpoints and the capability of the larger all-wing aircraft is unknown, but it would be similar or slightly better. No action was taken on development of this advanced study and apparently no preference was stated for a specific design by NAVAIR.

The CL-1170 project was the subject of a Freedom of Information Request to NAVAIR during the writing of this book. However, despite considerable assistance from this office, it was not a cost effective proposition to undertake a full search for details of CL-1170 and most of the information used in this section is based on documents provided by Lockheed-Martin. Currently, the Navy's P-3 Orions will start to be replaced in 2010 by the Boeing P-8 Poseidon which is a development of the Boeing 737-800.

The Advanced Tactical Aircraft – A-12A Avenger II

During the mid-1970s, the US Navy began to take a serious interest in the possibilities offered by an aircraft using 'low observable technology'. Lockheed and Northrop were already working on a top-secret 'radar invisible' interdictor project for the USAF which appeared to be progressing well. However, the Navy wanted a 'stealth' warplane and it was decided to embark on a more ambitious programme with seemingly little concern about the massive cost that would be incurred.

US Flying Wings (1950-1990)

Several modest research projects were already underway, but in 1983, the Navy officially began its Advanced Tactical Aircraft (ATA) project that aimed to replace the carrier-based Grumman A-6 Intruder with a versatile and highly sophisticated stealth strike aircraft. General Dynamics had been undertaking studies into stealth technology for the Navy and now teamed up with McDonnell Douglas to work on a flying wing design for the ATA project. In direct competition were Northrop in association with Grumman and Ling Temco Vought. At the present time, large gaps exist in the early history of the ATA project, but it seems probable that General Dynamics and Northrop both received black budget funding to produce wind tunnel, radar and flying models, followed by scale-sized, manned demonstrators.

An early General Dynamics concept for a manned stealth aircraft received the codename Cold Pigeon. This 1970s design was a flying wing, with rounded wingtips. Power would be provided by two deeply buried turbofan engines, fed by leading edge intakes, with trough-shaped exhaust ducts in the central area of the trailing edge.

Cold Pigeon was built as a scale model and it may have also been known as Sneaky Pete. An alternative stealthy proposal from General Dynamics and McDonnell Douglas was a swing-wing strike aircraft resembling a cross between the F-14 and F-111 with a Mach 1.5 capability. Known as Configuration 403, it progressed no further than the initial design stage. Lockheed also submitted plans for a navalised version of the F-117 during this period, but the Navy rejected this aircraft due to its limited range and payload capability.

The appearance of Northrop's ATA proposal remains unclear, although the initial design is thought to have resembled a smaller twin-engine version of the B-2A bomber. It is also possible that Northrop produced a twin-engine arrowhead shaped design and US Patent Des: 342,717 filed on 29 October 1992 may provide some indication of how this looked. Whether or not small manned demonstrators were built and tested for the ATA programme remains a matter of speculation, but it has been suggested that Northrop built at least one proof-of-concept aircraft. It is also rumoured that General Dynamics produced a scale-sized prototype called the Model 100, which bore some resemblance to the later A-12A.

Assuming there were tests of manned ATA demonstrators during the 1980s, these would have been flown from China Lake, California, or Groom Lake, Nevada, perhaps being occasionally glimpsed by the public and reported as triangular-shaped UFOs. While there is no documentation to prove these aircraft existed, the sheer scale and importance of the multi-billion dollar ATA programme would suggest that this project did not proceed from testing models to full-scale production without any form of prototyping.

On 13 January 1988, the Navy finally selected the General Dynamics design for further development; a contract ultimately worth around $4.5 billion was issued which requested an initial four test and eight pre-production aircraft. The designation of this new aircraft would be the A-12A, although an official name had yet to be chosen. Congress was exerting pressure on the USAF to accept a version of this aircraft as a replacement for the aging F-111 and despite some resistance within the Air Force, General Dynamics was awarded a $7.9 million contract to study a version more suited to USAF needs. Although the project had become public knowledge, the design of the Navy's new aircraft remained a mystery. In 1989, a number of names were considered for the A-12A which included the Avenger, Enforcer, Ghost, Penetrator, Seabat, Shadow and Stingray. These names were released to the public domain and some hinted at what the aircraft was like. The final choice was Avenger II which must have been met with a degree of anger by Grumman who built the original wartime Avenger aircraft and had lost out on the ATA programme.

It is known that different forward engine inlet positions and contoured wingtip stabilising fins were considered for the General Dynamics A-12A design. There were also various engine exhaust systems tested with one configuration ducting air into the exhaust stream via upper and lower slots in the rear fuselage. The final appearance of the aircraft was a very clean triangle with few protuberances. The wingspan of the A-12A was 70ft 3in (21.4m) and this reduced to 36ft 3in (11m) when the wings were folded for hangar deck storage. With a length of 37ft 3in (11.35m), this produced a wing area of 1,308ft^2 (122m^2). The overall height of the aircraft was 11ft 3in (3.4m). The A-12A was fitted with a fully retractable tricycle undercarriage and composite materials were used extensively in the aircraft's construction.

General Dynamics and McDonnell Douglas both asserted that maintenance would be half that of the A-6 and reliability was expected to be better than any other aircraft in Navy service. Although undoubtedly true, it has been suggested that the special surface coatings required for this aircraft to reduce its radar signature were susceptible to damage in the harsher marine environment and this would have become a significant issue.

The gross weight of the A-12A was set at about 80,000lb (36,300kg) which included 15,000lb (6,803kg) of ordnance. Designed as a subsonic aircraft with a maximum speed of 580mph (930kph), propulsion was provided by two deeply buried General Electric F412-GE-D5F2 non-afterburning turbofans, each rated at 13,000lb (58kN). Each engine would be fed from two trapezoidal intakes at the lower leading edge linked by stealthy inlet ducts. The F412 engine was based on the design used for the F-117A and it provided slightly better thrust, although supersonic speed was never a consideration with the A-12A as it degrades the ability to hide from radar. While the A-12A was not intended to undertake air combat, it was expected to be very agile due to its low wing loading and highly sophisticated flight control system. The A-12A's service ceiling remains unclear, but it would have been in excess of 40,000ft (12,200m) and the un-refuelled combat radius was about 800nm (920 miles, or 1,480km).

Flown by a crew of two in a tandem-configured cockpit, the primary role of the A-12A was to attack heavily defended land targets or shipping in all weather conditions and at night. A mission well suited to this aircraft would have been the surprise attack mounted against targets within the Libyan capital Tripoli during April 1986. Known as Operation 'Eldorado Canyon', it was undertaken by F-111s flown from England and Navy carrier-based F-18s. The still secret F-117 was considered but it lacked sufficient range. Nevertheless, there can be little doubt that this operation encouraged the Navy to proceed with development of the A-12A. In addition to delivering bombs (conventional and nuclear) or air-to-surface missiles, the A-12A could carry two High Speed Anti-Radiation Missiles (HARM). For self-defence, four (later two) air-to-air missiles (AAMs) would be carried internally. The options were AIM-9 Sidewinders or AIM-120 Advanced Medium Range Air-to-Air Missiles (AMRAAM). These weapons would be supported by an advanced Westinghouse AN/APQ-183 multimode radar system that would also provide high-resolution groundmapping and surface search capabilities. In addition, the A-12A would have used a sophisticated threat management system known as Radar Warning Receiver/Electronic Support Measures (RWR/ESM).

The Navy planned to buy no less than 620 copies of the A-12A and the US Marine Corps was considering a further 238 aircraft. In addition, the USAF was being encouraged to purchase 400 of the land-based variant

This aircraft would have lacked the arrester gear and folding wings necessary for carrier-based operations and there will have been system and weapons carriage differences. It is also believed that the USAF favoured the side-by-side cockpit arrangement that was originally proposed for the ATA Model-21. Finally, the RAF had expressed an interest in eventually buying land-based A-12s to replace the Panavia Tornado GR4.

But when the cost of each A-12A reached $96.2 million in January 1990, it was clear that all was not well with the programme and these spiralling costs were accompanied by some serious ongoing technical difficulties. Of primary concern was the aircraft's weight which had steadily increased beyond the original specification. The extensive use of composites had not produced the anticipated weight savings and as a consequence some components were now being fabricated from lightweight alloys. There were also unresolved difficulties with the advanced avionics and the state-of-the-art synthetic aperture radar system.

The A-12A programme may have seemed unstoppable, but alarm bells were now sounding in Washington and during April 1990 the Secretary of Defense Dick Cheney ordered a major review. It emerged that apart from serious technical issues, the project faced a $2 billion over-run and the first flight would be delayed until late 1991. The first eight aircraft were already under construction at Tulsa and enough parts had been manufactured to complete a total of 14 aircraft.

Intense negotiations took place and the Navy

Below left: **Simulated image of an A-12A stealth attack aircraft in flight.** McDonnell Douglas/Bill Rose Collection

Below right: **An early proposal for the Advanced Tactical Aircraft (ATA) programme built as a test model. Many of the features seen here, such as the upturned wingtip fins and engine inlets, were dispensed with.** General Dynamics

Bottom left: **This twin-engine, low-observable strike aircraft was a 1990s British Aerospace concept for the UK's Future Offensive Strike Aircraft Project. It may have been directly based on a US design such as the unsuccessful Northrop ATA proposal.** BAE Systems

Bottom right: **This artwork shows the possible appearance of a scale-size, one-man proof-of-concept demonstrator that preceded the A-12 Avenger II. This aircraft may have been known as the Model 100.** Bill Rose Collection

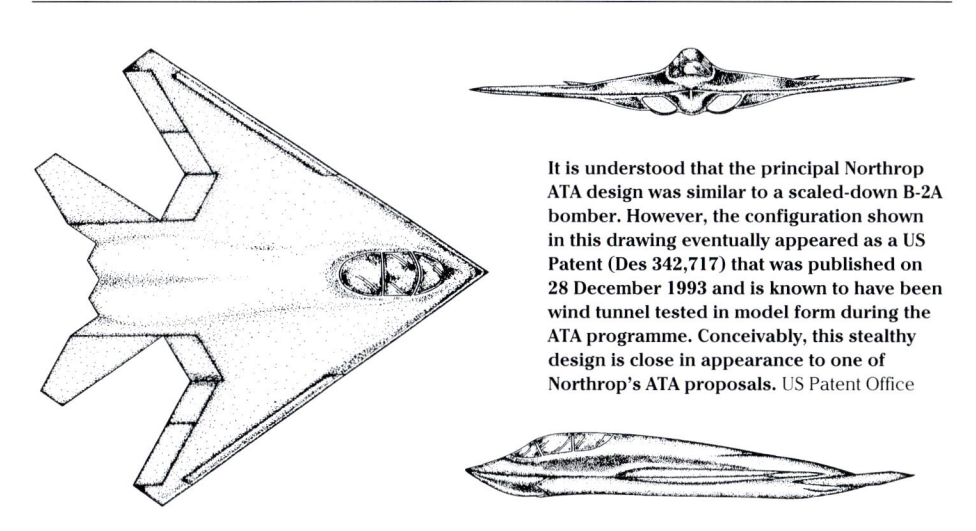

It is understood that the principal Northrop ATA design was similar to a scaled-down B-2A bomber. However, the configuration shown in this drawing eventually appeared as a US Patent (Des 342,717) that was published on 28 December 1993 and is known to have been wind tunnel tested in model form during the ATA programme. Conceivably, this stealthy design is close in appearance to one of Northrop's ATA proposals. US Patent Office

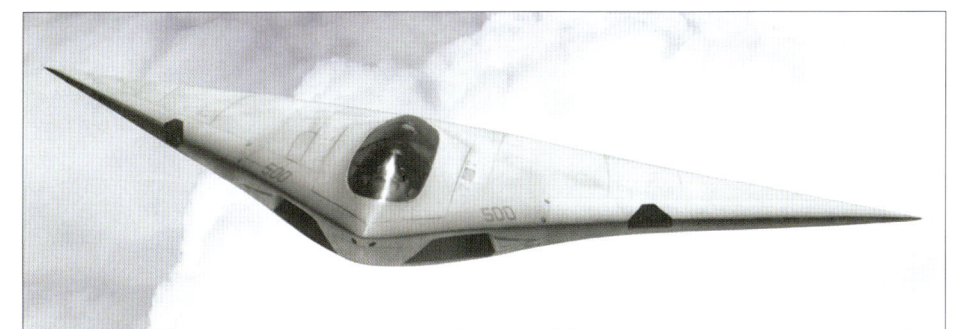

US Flying Wings (1950-1990)

This three-view drawing shows the A-12 in its final form for the US Navy. Bill Rose Collection

The General Dynamics/McDonnell Douglas A-12 Avenger II configured with a side-by-side cockpit arrangement. Initially, this was the favoured arrangement and it is believed that the USAF opted for this version. Bill Rose Collection

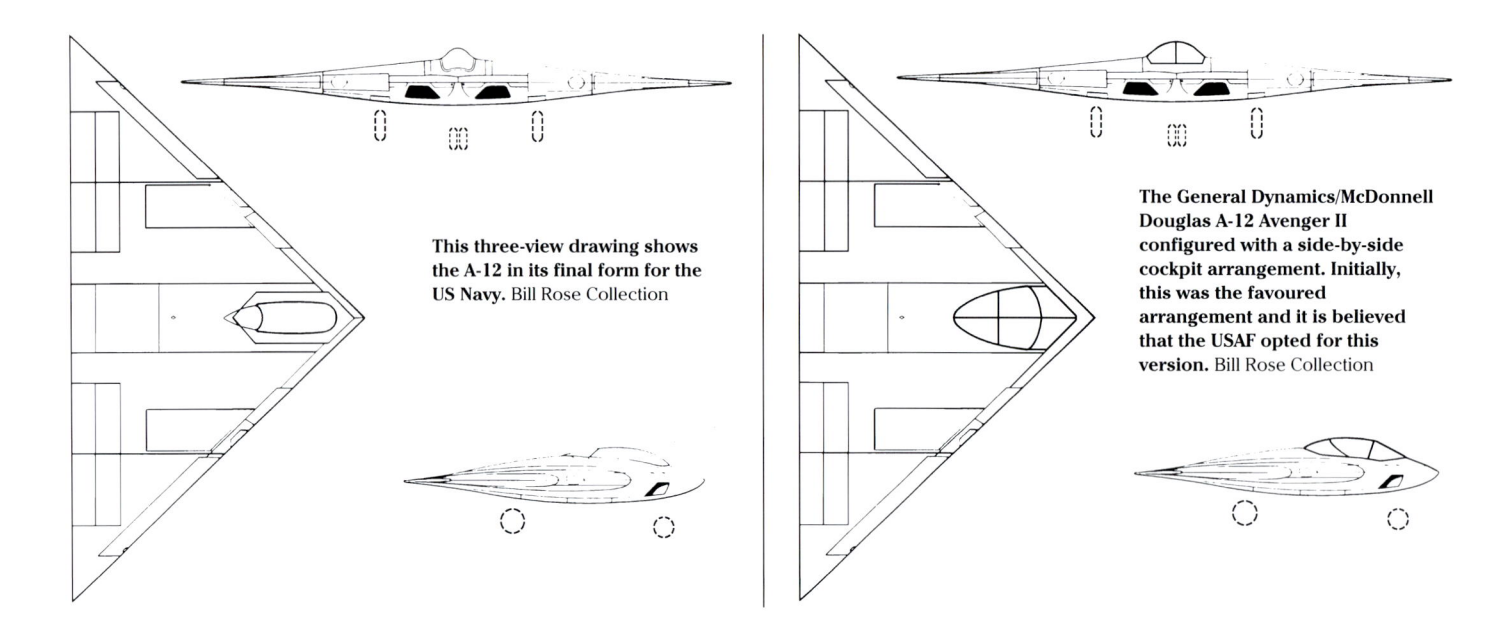

Intense negotiations took place and the Navy modified its contract to allow delivery of the first aircraft by the last day of 1991. But the contractors now insisted that it would be impossible to build the A-12A for the agreed price and some estimates put the total cost of completing the programme at about $10 billion. On 7 January 1991, Cheney announced that the A-12 programme had been cancelled and cited rising costs and unacceptable delays. Just under $3 billion had been spent on the A-12A and the government wanted some of its money back. This led to a major legal dispute between General Dynamics, McDonnell Douglas (later Boeing) and the Department of Defense that would roll-on into the 21st century.

With the shock cancellation of the A-12A programme, the Navy was left without its planned next-generation strike aircraft and the contractors made efforts to rescue the deal by providing a lower cost, stripped down version of the A-12A. Northrop and Lockheed also submitted plans for suitable aircraft, but the Navy was reluctant to embark on any new projects with an element of risk. Subsequently, it was decided to buy a larger, improved version of the F/A-18 known as the F/A-18E/F Super Hornet and wait to see how the Joint Strike Fighter (JSF) project progressed (later the Lockheed F-35 Lightning II). Clearly, the Super Hornet was never going to be a direct substitute for the stealthy A-12A, but it remains a rugged and reliable combat aircraft which is capable of undertaking a wide range of missions.

During the A-12A programme at least one full-sized A-12A mock-up was built and there have been persistent rumours that a small batch of production aircraft were completed by late 1995 and secretly supplied to the USAF. If the USAF did take these A-12s, they may have been considered for special deniable missions or optimised for use as low observable spyplanes. Another rumour concerns the secret development of an Unmanned Combat Aerial Vehicle (UCAV) for the USAF which was directly based on the A-12A. This may or may not be true, but it could be many years before all the details of this programme become public knowledge.

McDonnell Douglas/General Dynamics A-12 Avenger II

Crew	2
Wingspan (unfolded)	70ft 3in (21.4m)
Wingspan (folded)	36ft 3in (11m)
Wing area	1,308ft² (122m²)
Length	37ft 3in (11.35m)
Height	11ft 3in (3.4m)
Empty weight	39,000 lb (17,700kg)
Gross weight	80,000 lb (36,300kg)
Powerplant	2 x General Electric F412-GE-D5F2 non-afterburning turbofans, each rated at 13,000 lb (58kN)
Maximum speed	580mph (930kph)
Ceiling	40,000ft (12,200m)
Range	800nm (920 miles or 1,480km)
Armament	A maximum of 15,000 lb (6,803kg) bombs or ASMs. 2 x (originally 4) AIM-9 AAMs or AIM-120 Advanced Medium Range Air-to-Air Missiles (AMRAAM) and 2 x High Speed Anti-Radiation Missiles (HARM)

Early artwork showing the very clean triangular-shaped A-12 in US Navy service. US Navy

Secret Projects: Flying Wings and Tailless Aircraft

Chapter Five

US Manned Tailless Aircraft (1980-2030)

The Defense Advanced Research Projects Agency (DARPA) funded a series of highly classified studies in 1974 to examine new technologies that might give aircraft the ability to avoid detection by Soviet radar networks. The initial contractors who undertook this work were Northrop and McDonnell Douglas with the programme being extended to include Lockheed in 1975. Following radar trials at White Sands, Lockheed and Northrop received further USAF and DARPA funding to continue research.

In 1978, Rockwell International at Los Angeles, California, completed a major study (partly sponsored by the US Air Force) to examine bomber needs for the 1990 to 2000 period, taking note of stealth developments. Several new designs emerged from this project that included a forward-swept, twin-engine, canard penetrator with supersonic performance, a four-engine flying wing equipped with a rear-mounted (possibly retractable) turret containing a defensive laser weapon and a stealthy twin-engine delta bomber, simply referred to as the Spanloader.

To fully exploit the latest developments in stealth technology, the USAF partnered Rockwell with Lockheed while Northrop was teamed up with Boeing and Vought. Both groups would design new low-observable aircraft and at the same time DARPA awarded Northrop a contract to construct a 'one-off' manned stealth test-bed which was given the codename Tacit Blue.

It was now clear to senior Pentagon officials that within a few years it would only be possible to penetrate Soviet air space with stealthy aircraft. Consequently, it was decided to develop a light bomber as quickly as possible which utilised technologies developed by Lockheed during the Have Blue programme. It was also accepted that a more ambitious stealth bomber was needed in the longer term. As a result, Lockheed

This four-engine flying wing concept was produced by Rockwell International, possibly within the late 1970s D-645 stealth bomber study. Note the turret containing a laser weapon mounted at the rear of the fuselage for self-defence. Bill Rose Collection (based on Rockwell artwork)

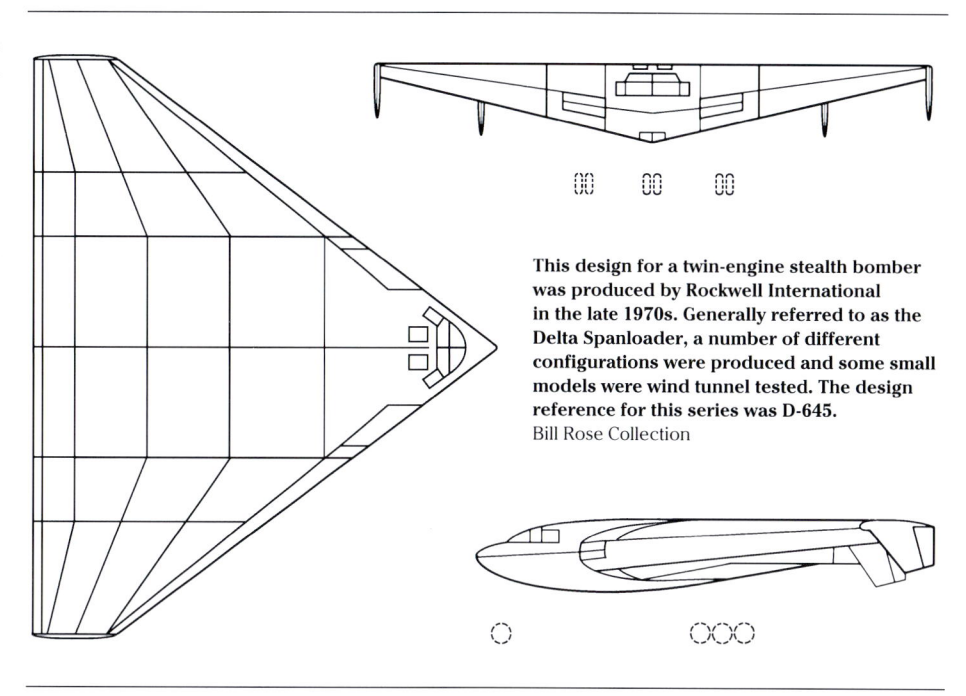

This design for a twin-engine stealth bomber was produced by Rockwell International in the late 1970s. Generally referred to as the Delta Spanloader, a number of different configurations were produced and some small models were wind tunnel tested. The design reference for this series was D-645. Bill Rose Collection

was contracted to study a light-bomber under a highly-classified programme called Senior Peg and Northrop was asked to produce proposals for a more advanced strategic nuclear bomber under the codename Senior Ice.

Senior Peg

The Senior Peg programme began with Lockheed basing the design of a new light-bomber on work undertaken during the Hopeless Diamond programme that had produced the

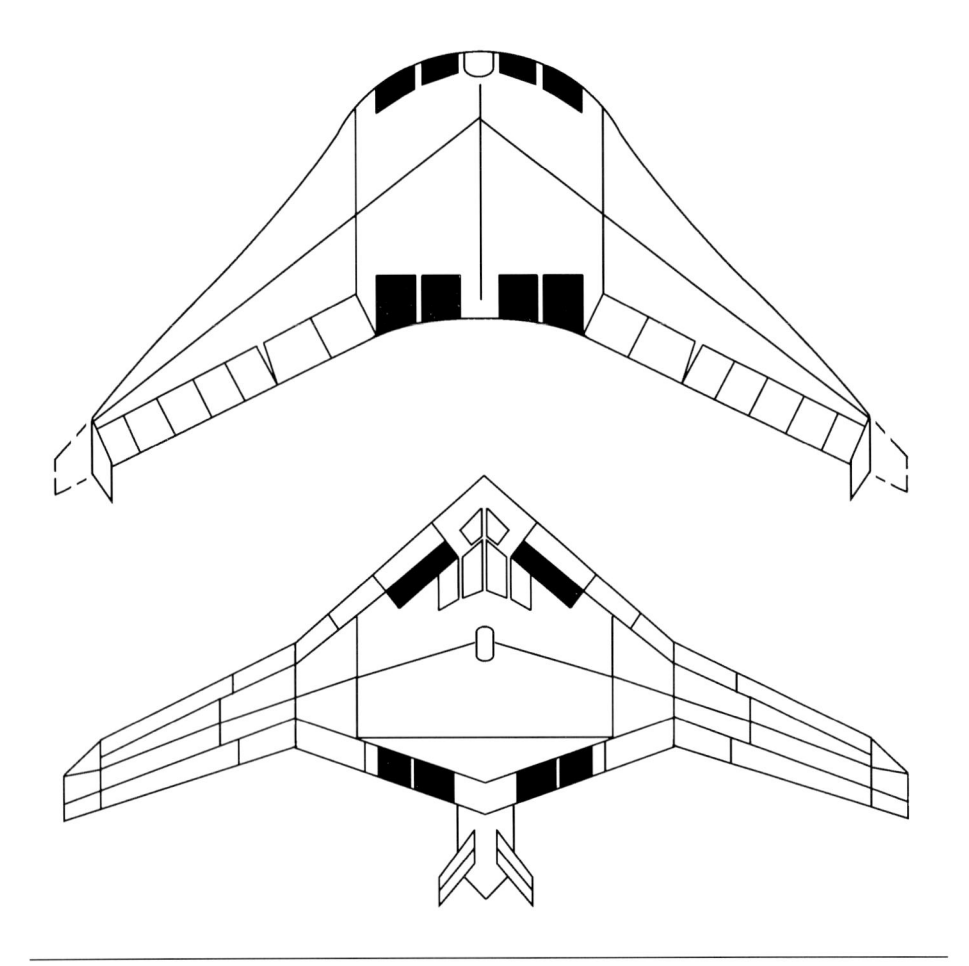

Two designs from the Lockheed Skunk Works that are believed to have fallen within the Senior Peg programme for a new advanced bomber utilising stealth technology. The top drawing has the company reference CL-2120-2 and was optimised for very low-level operations. The bottom drawing is based on information from several sources, which is thought to show Lockheed's proposal for a high-altitude stealth bomber. It remains unclear if this development work was utilised for any further projects that remain within the black domain. Bill Rose Collection

Rockwell D645-4A Stealth Delta Spanloader

Wingspan	100ft (30m) estimated*
Sweep	55° (leading edge)
Length	76ft (23m) estimated*
Height	Unknown
Powerplant	2 x afterburning turbofan engines providing a total of 60,000 lb thrust. The engines would utilise noise reduction measures and two-dimensional Asymmetric Load-Balanced Exhaust Nozzles (ALBEN)
Gross weight	412,000 lb (186,880kg)
Maximum speed	Unknown but subsonic
Ceiling	Unknown
Range	Unknown
Armament	50,000 lb (22,679kg) bombs and missiles. The possibility of carrying a defensive laser weapon may have been considered, if the technology became available

* Figure from a reliable source, but not definitive.

Lockheed CL-2102-2 Low Level Penetrator

Crew	4
Wingspan	183ft 4in (56m)
Wingspan (tips down)	205ft (62.4m)
Wing area	7,278ft² (676m²)
Wing area (tips down)	7,528ft² (699m²)
Sweep	45° (leading edge)
Load factor	3.0G
Aspect ratio	4.62
(tips down)	5.58
Length	99.7ft (30.38m)
Height	25.75ft (7.84m)
Empty weight	145,240 lb (65,879kg)
Gross weight	526,140 lb (238,653kg)
Powerplant	4 x turbofan engines. Possibly afterburning.
Maximum speed	Mach 0.80
Ceiling	50,000ft (15,240m)
Optimised for operations at 200ft (61m)	
Range (un-refuelled)	5,753 miles (9,260km), with 2,300 miles (3,700km) flow at low-level
Armament	40,000 lb (18,143kg) payload

F-117A stealth interdictor. Most of the details remain secret, but it is believed that the early Senior Peg studies resulted in several four-engine aircraft concepts roughly in the class of the F-111. In appearance, these designs were almost flying wings with flat undersides and faceted upper surfaces. It is also reported that Lockheed favoured a narrow tail section fitted with two V-shaped stabilising fins. Although USAF interest shifted towards the Northrop proposal, it has been suggested that Lockheed may have studied a strategic bomber with a wingspan in the region of 170-180ft (50-55m), perhaps loosely based on the Rockwell Spanloader. Built mainly from composite materials, this aircraft would have been manned by a crew of three.

Little is presently known about the Senior Peg proposals, but the Skunk Works later produced designs for a strategic stealth bomber specifically optimised for low-level penetration. This came about in late 1980 when concerns were expressed within the USAF that Soviet defences would eventually be capable of detecting and tracking high-altitude stealth bombers and a low-level option was needed as a fallback.

Whether or not this design work was part of the Senior Peg project remains unknown, but Lockheed assigned a company reference CL-2120 to the study and it has been possible to find some details of CL-2120-2. This was a flying wing with a leading edge sweep of about 45° that was optimised to fly at altitudes in the region of 200ft (60m). Several possibilities were considered for central stabilisers and the aircraft would have been equipped with movable wingtip fins with rudders. Propulsion took the form of four deeply buried turbofan engines with stealthy leading edge intakes located on each side of the cockpit and carefully configured rectangular exhaust outlets at the centre of the trailing edge. The wingspan was 183ft 4in (56m), which could be increased to 205ft (62.4m) by lowering the wingtips during a fully laden take-off. Length of the CL-2102-2 was 99ft 8in (30.38m) and height 25ft 8½in (7.84m). Empty, the aircraft was expected to weigh 145,240 lb (65,879kg) and gross weight was estimated at 526,140 lb (238,653kg), including a 40,000 lb (18,143kg) payload. Maximum speed at very low altitude was Mach 0.6-0.7 with a service ceiling of about 50,000ft (15,240m). Maximum un-refuelled range was expected to be 5,753 miles (9,260km) with 2,300 miles (3,700km) flown at low-level during an attack mission.

Secret Projects: Flying Wings and Tailless Aircraft

Senior Ice

The Northrop high-altitude proposal code-named Senior Ice was a flying wing that is clearly recognisable as an early incarnation of the B-2A bomber. Project Director Hal Markarian was directly responsible for the Senior Ice programme and he reported directly to Welko E. Gasich who was the Senior Vice-President for Advanced Projects. Contrary to some opinion, this design was not a development of the earlier Northrop YB-49 or heavily-influenced by the wartime Horten Ho IX and its appearance was initially dictated by complex calculations to achieve the lowest possible radar-cross-section within an operational environment. Secondary considerations were the use of new materials and a sophisticated flight management system. However, the study was enlarged in early 1981 to include concepts for low-level missions. This branch of the project remains largely classified, although Northrop may have worked on a tailless triangular design for this role which was the subject of a DARPA study.

Although this design was very different to the Skunk Works low-altitude penetrator, it was conceived (like the Lockheed CL-2120-2) to fly the last part of a strike mission at altitude of about 200ft (61m) and speeds in the region of Mach 0.7. But either the cost of operating two different types of aircraft was prohibitive or there were too many unforeseen technical challenges. Stability control was considered a major issue for a stealth aircraft operating at treetop height and afterburners were regarded as essential to meet take-off requirements. So it was finally determined that the most cost effective solution was to proceed with the high-altitude design and introduce a modified low-level version of this aircraft if the need should arise.

Nevertheless, as something of a compromise, President Reagan authorised the construction of 100 B-1B bombers on 2 October 1981 which were modified variants of the original supersonic variable-geometry B-1. This version was quite stealthy, but the lower radar cross-section came with a performance penalty. Nevertheless, the B-1B was capable of being flown at almost the speed of sound just 500ft (152m) above the ground. Lockheed was regarded as the leading exponents of stealth technology and its partner Rockwell had developed the B-1 bomber, so the industry expected them to win this competition and envisaged the Northrop design being placed on the back burner. But surprisingly, the USAF rejected Senior Peg and Northrop was selected on 17 October 1981 to build the new strategic bomber, receiving a development contract on 4 December 1981. By the time this contract was signed, the existence of an advanced bomber programme had been public knowledge for about a year and Northrop now began a major engineering development review that would last until June 1983.

The aircraft was assigned the name Advanced Technology Bomber (ATB), although the programme was officially known as Senior Cejay. The Reagan Administration planned to eventually have 127 ATBs in USAF service, plus the five initial evaluation aircraft, which would be upgraded to full specification with the first examples entering service during 1987.

LOW ALTITUDE CONCEPT

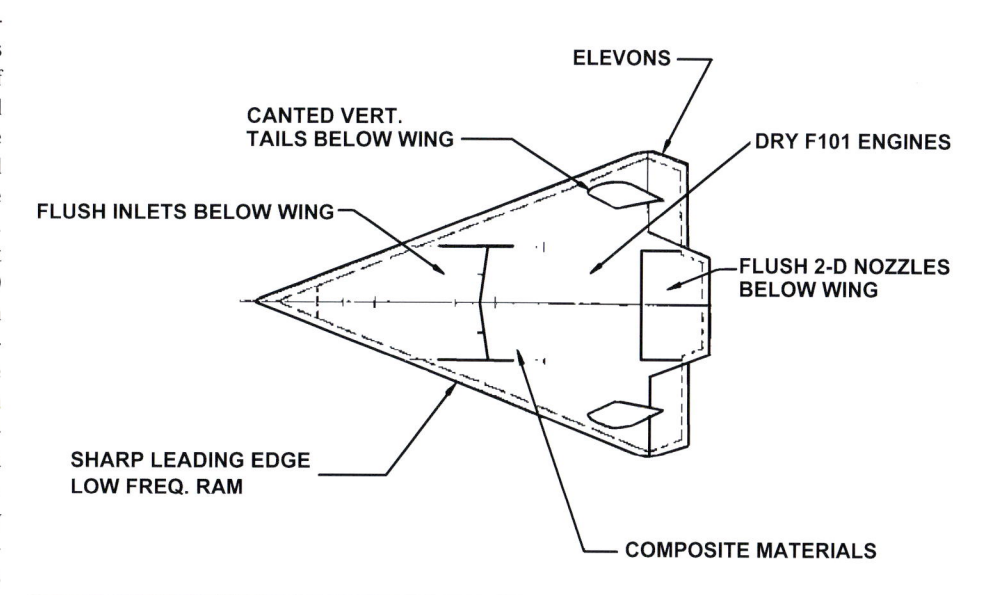

- ELEVONS
- CANTED VERT. TAILS BELOW WING
- DRY F101 ENGINES
- FLUSH INLETS BELOW WING
- FLUSH 2-D NOZZLES BELOW WING
- SHARP LEADING EDGE LOW FREQ. RAM
- COMPOSITE MATERIALS

A DARPA illustration for a low-altitude stealth bomber that was considered during an early stage of what became the Advanced Technology Bomber (ATB) programme in the early 1980s. DARPA

USAF artwork released into the public domain during the 1980s which depicted the forthcoming B-2 bomber. Although some of the details such as engine exhausts were not revealed, this image was reasonably accurate and reflects acceptance that this high-profile aircraft would eventually become impossible to hide. USAF

US Manned Tailless Aircraft (1980-2030)

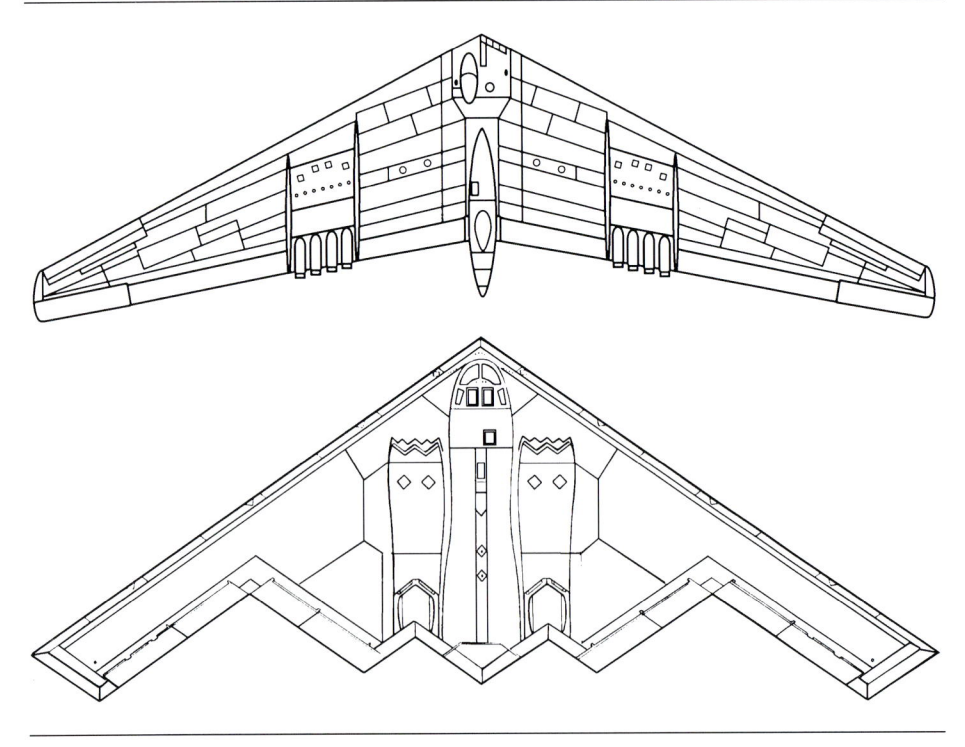

This image is directly based on USAF artwork released in the early 1980s that allegedly showed an early proposal for the Advanced Technology Bomber (ATB). Many experts dismissed this concept as unlikely to bear any resemblance to the new bomber. However, it may have been partly derived from one of the Rockwell Delta Spanloader designs or a proposed low-level penetrator, finished with an experimental camouflage finish intended for this role. Bill Rose Collection

Northrop B-2A

The ATB was officially renamed as the B-2A in September 1984 and security at Northrop and the sub-contractors remained oppressive. In addition to intrusive surveillance methods, large numbers of Northrop workers at the Pico Rivera B-2 plant and Palmdale were made to undergo polygraph tests. False companies were established to receive B-2 components which were delivered by sub-contractors, computers were isolated within screened enclosures to prevent electronic eavesdropping and USAF top brass who visited the plant always arrived in civilian clothing.

While the new bomber was still in the development phase, the strange-looking Tacit Blue low-speed technology demonstrator was undergoing secret tests at Groom Dry Lake and it would remain classified until 1996. Described initially as an experimental reconnaissance platform, this compact 55ft 10in (17m) long aircraft, which looked like an inverted bathtub with stubby wings, was used to develop various technologies that would find their way into the B-2A. However, Tacit Blue bore almost no resemblance to the B-2A apart from perhaps the cockpit canopy and it is believed that Tacit Blue was also used to develop the AGM-137 TSSAM (Tri-Service Standoff Attack Missile). While there is no proof or admission that prototypes were built during the B-2A programme, there were reliable reports of small flying wings being sighted in areas associated with secret aircraft trials that hint at the possibility.

On 22 November 1988, the first B-2A (AV-1) was unveiled at Northrop's Palmdale facility in California. Many aspects of the programme remained secret, but it was felt that keeping the B-2A under wraps any longer would raise too many unnecessary problems and serve no useful purpose. Attending this ceremony were USAF officials and members of the media, with access to the aircraft carefully restricted to avoid anyone seeing sensitive areas such as the engine exhausts. But a reporter called Michael A. Dornheim was one step ahead of these measures and flew a light plane over the facility with a photographer onboard. Nobody had considered this possibility and it led to a major scoop which showed many of the aircraft's features that Northrop and the Air Force would have preferred to remain under wraps.

AV-1 undertook its first test flight on 17 July 1989 at Palmdale, flown by Northrop's Test Pilot Bruce Hinds and USAF Col Richard Couch. The second aircraft (AV-2) would fly just over a year later. At this time, the USAF confidently anticipated paying $550 million for each new B-2A that rolled off the production line. Amazingly, this had risen to $865 million by 1991 and when the development costs were added, the price of each aircraft was closer to that of a space shuttle at more than $2 billion. This spiralling price tag would soon lead to widespread political criticism and allegations of wrongdoing.

A side-by-side comparison between the Northrop B-49 bomber (top) and the modern Northrop Grumman B-2A Spirit stealth bomber. These aircraft are approximately to scale and the purpose of this drawing is to show that the B-2A has almost nothing in common with the original Northrop flying wing bomber. Bill Rose Collection

A B-2A Spirit bomber crossing rugged desert terrain. USAF

B-2A *Spirit of Mississippi* which was delivered to the USAF in 1993 and has since been upgraded to Block 30 specification. USAF

A B-2A of the 509th Bomb Wing at Whiteman AFB in Missouri. USAF

On 1 March 1990, the *Washington Post* reported that Northrop admitted in court to 34 counts of overcharging the Government during development of the B-2A. While a further 141 charges were dropped, Northrop ended up with a record fine of $17 million. Evidently, there was – and may still be – plenty of scope for misappropriation of funds within a highly classified big budget project. There were also reports that the B-2A's range and payload capability was somewhat less than anticipated and the aircraft remained visible to radar systems in certain conditions. In 1991, the USAF admitted that tests had revealed various weaknesses in the B-2A's ability to avoid detection and steps had been taken to correct the problem with the application of more RAM in some areas. This sounded worse that it probably was because stealth technology is hardly perfect and does have limitations.

The first production B-2A Spirit (AV-8) was accepted into USAF service on 17 December 1993 at Whiteman AFB, Missouri, and there can be little doubt that the B-2A is an extremely sophisticated and potent aircraft. It is ideal for special operations using conventional or nuclear weapons and has a far superior delivery performance to the B-1B. Just six aircraft could have undertaken the entire 1986 attack on Libya, operating from the US mainland. Many new cutting-edge processes were employed for the construction of this aircraft with components manufactured from aluminium and titanium alloys, steel and composites. A special elastomeric coating was developed for the aircraft's exterior, to maintain uniform conductivity and avoid radar hot spots at seams.

Northrop was responsible for producing the forward body, cockpit, leading and trailing edges and control surfaces. Boeing manufactured most of the remainder of the B-2A with Ling-Temco-Vought providing components for the wing and engine intakes/ exhausts. Each aircraft was to be completed at Palmdale, California, before delivery to the USAF. Because the aircraft is inherently unstable, the Digital Flight Control System (DFCS) is the B-2A's most important piece of equipment. Using a quadruplex fly-by-wire system, the DFCS manages a series of control

US Manned Tailless Aircraft (1980-2030)

surfaces located along the trailing edge. This includes two sets of combined brake-rudders towards the wingtips that control yaw, two three-part sets of elevons and the Gust Load Alleviation System (GLAS) located at the rear of the centre line which is mainly used to control pitch. It is also thought that yaw can be controlled in certain situations by varying port or starboard engine thrust.

The B-2A has a wingspan of 172ft (52.42m) making it similar in size to the original Northrop flying wing bombers. The overall length is 69ft (21m) and the aircraft's height is 17ft (5.18m). Empty, the B-2A weighs about 153,700 lb (69,717kg) and the maximum take-off weight is 376,000 lb (170,550kg). Propulsion is provided by four non-afterburning General Electric F-118-GE-100 turbofan engines each rated at 17,300 lb (77kN) static thrust which allows a maximum speed of Mach 0.95, a ceiling of 50,000ft (15,240m) and an un-refuelled range in excess of 6,000 miles (9,600km) carrying a 37,300 lb (15,920kg) payload. A wide range of conventional and nuclear free fall or guided weapons can be carried by the B-2A. The maximum weapons payload is quoted as 49,317 lb (22,369kg). A later Block 30 upgrade known as the Generic Weapons Interface System (GWIS) would allow the B-2A to carry different mixes of weapons making it possible to attack as many as four different targets during a single mission.

The B-2A was originally equipped with the Raytheon AN/APQ-181 covert strike radar operating at the J band. This is a very sophisticated multi-function radar system that could be used for terrain following and hazard avoidance at low altitude. Significant and costly upgrades to the B-2A's radar system have been undertaken in recent years with the installation of several classified modules and a new Active Electronically Scanned

A full load of conventional free-fall bombs is released by a B-2A during trials. USAF

A Mk84 2,000 lb bomb about to be loaded into a B-2 Spirit bomber at Andersen AFB, Guam. USAF

The Joint Direct Attack Munition (JDAM) is a family of cost-effective and highly accurate weapons that can be carried by a number of US and European military warplanes. This photograph shows a GBU-31 JDAM bomb during transport to a warplane. JDAMs have been used by a number of US aircraft during several recent conflicts. The B-2A made its combat debut during Operation Allied Force in 1999, delivering more than 650 JDAMs to Serbian targets. The most controversial B-2A mission involving JDAMs was the 'accidental' bombing of the Chinese embassy in Belgrade on 7 May 1999 when three JDAMs hit sensitive parts of the building. USAF

An inert practice B-61 nuclear weapon is released from a B-2A at the Tonopah Test Range in Nevada on 20 November 1996. USAF

A B-2A refuels from a KC-135 tanker above the Pacific Ocean while flying to Andersen AFB, Guam. The unusual shape of the aircraft in this photograph is caused by the use of a fisheye lens. USAF

A Northrop Grumman B-2A in flight. USAF

Array (AESA) antenna. No defensive armament is carried by the B-2A which relies on its ability to hide from radar. But having said that, each B-2A is equipped with a Defensive Management Subsystem (DMS). This includes the Lockheed Martin AN/APR-50 (also known as the ZSR-63) radar warning system that detects and identifies threats. It is thought that this equipment may have the ability to cancel out radar returns. Honeywell and Raytheon have provided other classified components of the DMS, but their functions are unknown. Normally, a crew of two fly this aircraft, but there is provision for a third member who may be required for certain specialised missions.

By the mid-1990s, there was growing opposition within Congress to the very expensive B-2A programme and an amendment to the 1997 Defense Authorisation Bill was tabled to cap production of the B-2A at 21 aircraft. Although this proposal was narrowly defeated, it was not just Congress which was concerned about costs, but the USAF who feared that procurement of further stealth bombers would mean severe funding restrictions in other areas. As a result, Congress never approved the construction of further B-2As and three optional aircraft (AV-22-76, AV-77-133, AV-134-165) belonging to the initial batch were cancelled.

Military Operations
The B-2A was used in combat for the first time on 24 March 1999 when two aircraft delivered precision-guided munitions to targets in Yugoslavia. The objective of this NATO campaign was to secure the withdrawal of Serbian military, paramilitary and police forces from Kosovo by means of a substantial air attack on the Serbian military and civilian infrastructure. Known as Operation 'Allied Force', the raids lasted until 11 June 1999 and during this time six different B-2A aircraft flew 45 long-range missions from the USA. Typically, each flight would last for 30 hours and in total the B-2As delivered 656 Joint Defence Air Munition (JDAM) bombs to Serbian targets.

Unquestionably, the most controversial mission involving a B-2A during this cam-

US Manned Tailless Aircraft (1980-2030)

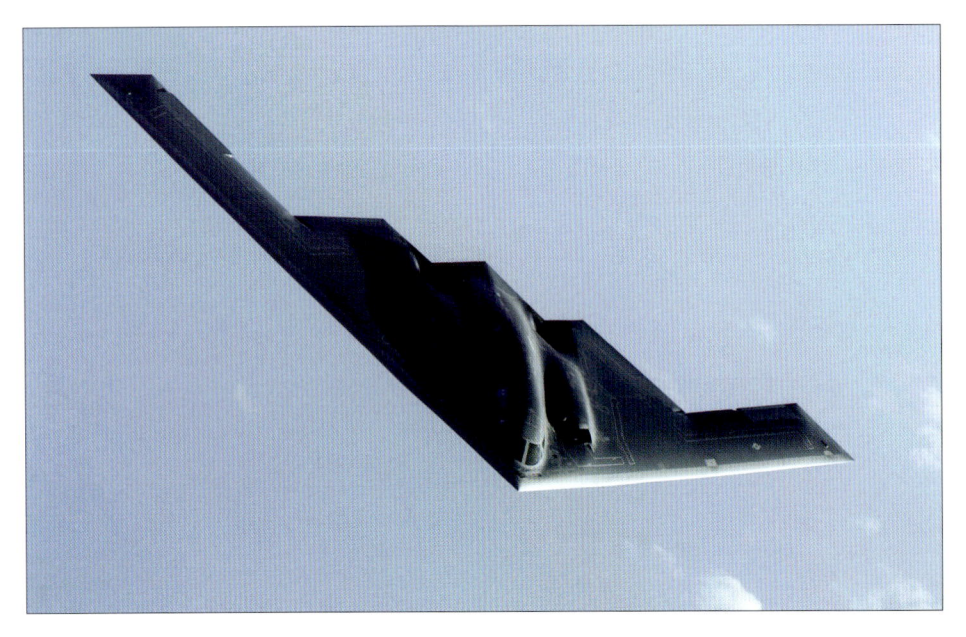

paign took place on 7 May 1999 when a single B-2A escorted by EA-6B Prowlers and F-15C fighters dropped three JDAM bombs on the Chinese embassy in the Novi Beograd district of Belgrade. President Bill Clinton and CIA director George J. Tenet both insisted that the bombing had been a terrible accident due to the use of an outdated map. However, the Chinese embassy was one of many

Northrop-Grumman B-2A Spirit Stealth Bomber

Crew	2 with provision for 3rd member
Wingspan	172ft (52.42m)
Wing area	5,140ft² (478m²)
Length	69ft (21m)
Height	17ft (5.18m)
Empty weight	153,700 lb (69,717kg)
Take-off weight	336,500 lb (152,635kg)
Max take-off weight	376,000 lb (170,550kg)
Powerplant	4 x non-afterburning General Electric F-118-GE-100 turbofan engines, each rated at 17,300 lb (77kN) static thrust
Maximum speed	Mach 0.95, approx 570mph (915km/h) at sea level
Ceiling	50,000ft (15,240m)
Range	Nuclear strike mission with mix of 16 AGM-129/B61 weapons (weighing 37,300 lb – 15,920kg) 6,330 miles (10,186km). Similar Mission with 1x refuelling: 11,508 miles (18,529km)
Normal payload	40,000 lb (18,144kg)
Max weapons load	49,317 lb (22,369kg)
Armament	

(Carried by 2 Boeing Rotary Launcher Assemblies in each bomb bay): AGM-129 ACM W80 Nuclear Warhead; AGM-131 SRAM 2 W89 Nuclear Warhead; AGM-137 TSSAM HE or submunitions; AGM-154 JSOW submunitions; B61 Nuclear Penetrator; B83 Nuclear Variable Yield; BLU-118/B Thermobaric Weapon; Mk64 2,000 lb (907kg) Sea Mine; Mk82 500 lb (226kg) HE Bomb; Mk83 1,000 lb (453kg) HE Bomb; Mk84 2,000 lb (907kg) HE Bomb; CBU-87 Cluster; CBU-89 Cluster; CBU-97 Cluster; GBU-27 Paveway III 2,000 lb (900kg) HE Laser Guided EGBU-27 Enhanced version of GBU-27, with additional GPS guidance; GBU-31/2 JDAM Mk83/84 HE or BLU-109 Penetrator Warhead; GBU-37 4,700 lb (2,131kg) Penetrator

Demonstrating its true global capability, *Spirit of Missouri* prepares to touch down at Whiteman AFB after flying a long-range mission to Iraq. USAF

These portable B-2 shelters were assembled at Diego Garcia by the USAF's 49th Material Squadron. USAF

A Northrop Grumman B-2A returning from a mission during Operation Iraqi Freedom on 27 March 2003. USAF

Secret Projects: Flying Wings and Tailless Aircraft

buildings that were marked for avoidance by NATO warplanes and it seems very unlikely that the strike was an accident. It was later claimed that the intended target had been the headquarters of the Yugoslav Federal Directorate for Supply and Procurement (FDSP), but few observers believed this to be true. There are several possible reasons for the attack and it has been suggested that the Chinese embassy was being used to relay radio messages to irregular forces under the direction of the late Zeljko Raznatovic (usually known as Arkan). This is a possibility, but it's more likely that Chinese intelligence were monitoring NATO operations and testing advanced passive detection equipment capable of tracking stealth aircraft. Perhaps they were passing immediate details to the Serbs?

On 27 March 1999, a F-117A stealth aircraft was shot down near the village of Budjanovci in Serbia and in a separate incident a F-117A is understood to have returned to base badly damaged. Conceivably both events resulted from newly-developed methods of detection. There may also be a link to the destruction of Belgrade's RTS television station on 23 April 1999 by two Tomahawk cruise missiles. This reportedly killed 16 people and injured 20. NATO refused to apologise for the attack, claiming the station was broadcasting unacceptable propaganda. But the TV transmitter's powerful output may have been assisting passive stealth detection technology controlled from the embassy.

When the embassy raid took place the building was largely empty, but three personnel were killed, 20 were injured and there was substantial damage. Chinese President Jiang Zemin expressed outrage at the attack and relations with America were strained for some time. The US administration apologised to China, eventually paying $28 million in compensation, but it could be decades before the truth emerges about this incident.

Following the events of 11 September 2001, it was determined that Osama bin Laden was responsible for organising the attacks on American targets. The CIA was confident that he was hiding in Afghanistan and Washington insisted that the Taliban government hand over bin Laden and the al-Qaeda leadership. They refused and a major military operation began initially involving air power.

B-2As were used on three consecutive days to strike al-Qaeda and Taliban positions in Afghanistan with stopovers at the British base at Diego Garcia in the Indian Ocean. The next operational use of the B-2A would take place during the second Gulf War (or Iraq War) that began in March 2003. This US-led campaign was based on the suggestion that Iraq was continuing to develop weapons of mass destruction which threatened regional stability. As a prequel to operations, 20 members of the USAF's 49th Material Squadron arrived at Diego Garcia during December 2002 and organised the assembly of two huge portable shelters for B-2A bombers.

USAF Capt Jennifer Wilson, who became the first woman to fly the B-2A operationally on 1 April 2003 during the Iraq conflict. USAF

The task took 70 days to complete and it was the first time these sophisticated units with their high-tech environmental systems had been used operationally. Each fully air-conditioned shelter measured 55ft (16.76m) in height and 250ft (76m) wide. Each shelter was shipped by air to the operational site in sections requiring 29 C-130 Hercules flights. With the ability to undertake some B-2A missions from Diego Garcia, the strike distance to Baghdad could be reduced to less than half that from Whiteman AFB, Missouri.

From early in the campaign, B-2As attacked key Iraqi targets with JDAM munitions and these aircraft were often used to take out Iraqi radar and communications facilities. Although combat missions with the most advanced US warplanes are generally regarded as a male preserve, Capt Jennifer Wilson, who was stationed with the 393rd Expeditionary Bomb Squadron at Diego Garcia, became the first woman to fly a B-2A operationally on 1 April 2003. But this was not the first combat mission for 30-year-old Captain Wilson, who had already flown B-1Bs during Operation Allied Force.

No B-2As were lost or reported damaged during the 2003 Iraq campaign. Enemy air defences proved largely ineffective and the Iraqi Air Force are not thought to have operated any fighter aircraft during this period. In addition to the B-2A being flown by women on combat missions, RAF Squadron Leader David Arthurton became the first foreign pilot to fly the B-2A in 2006 while participating in the Personnel Exchange Program.

Evolution

Recent improvements to the B-2A fleet include the Link 16 aircraft-to-aircraft data transmission system, the introduction of a virtually unjammable EHF (Extremely High Frequency) satellite connection, a digital engine control system to replace the troublesome analogue controllers and the capability to attack moving targets with precision-guided weapons.

Since the aircraft's introduction, there have been proposals for new or modified versions. One possibility considered was the installation of a multi-role sensor package that would result in the aircraft being redesignated as the RB-2A. Another suggestion was a Signals Intelligence (SIGINT) variant called the EB-2A. A further proposal was to turn the B-2 fleet into remotely piloted vehicles capable of refuelling automatically and carrying much larger payloads. It is likely there was considerable resistance to the idea of converting such an expensive warplane into an unmanned vehicle and equally probable that dependable technology to allow such a thing was lacking when the idea first surfaced. At the start of the 21st century, there was considerable interest in the idea of producing a second batch of 40 B-2 bombers to meet USAF needs. This would have resulted in a modified design known as the B-2C. The 'C' reference would stand for conventional, indicating it was not specifically designed to deliver nuclear weapons. The exact differences from the B-2A remain unclear, but the B-2C was described as 'improved'.

In 2001, Northrop-Grumman suggested that production could be restarted for about $3 billion, with each aircraft costing $735 million, but Northrop's Pico Rivera facility where the production of B-2A aircraft began had been closed down, so this meant that Boeing would undertake most of the work. Both the Vice President Dick Cheney and Defense Secretary Donald Rumsfeld were in favour of proceeding with this option, but there was considerable political opposition and eventually the plan was abandoned.

Russian Designs

Soviet designers studied US stealth development in great detail and it has been a topic of occasional discussion that a Russian equivalent was never built. In fact, there was a Myasishchev project conducted during the 1980s to develop a high-altitude spyplane bearing the codename M-67, which produced at least one manned proposal that vaguely resembled the B-2A (see Chapter Six). Whether or not this design came about as the result of information gathered by Soviet Intelligence is unknown. In early 1996, the MiG Design Bureau released artwork of a canard-shaped stealth bomber that loosely resembled the B-2A. The drawing is certainly interesting, but Russia was no longer in a position to fund such an expensive programme and the MiG stealth bomber was clearly little more than wishful thinking.

Chinese Stealth Bomber

According to some recent reports circulating in the Far East, China has been working on an advanced stealth strike aircraft known as the Xian H-8. Apparently, the H-8 project was initiated in 1994 with the aim of equalling America's B-2A bomber. Said to possess marginal supersonic performance, an intercontinental range and the ability to carry advanced weapons, it has been claimed that the H-8 is about to enter production. Illustrations of unknown origin suggest that the H-8 is a compact, highly swept flying wing, possibly powered by two deeply recessed engines. Nobody would deny that the Chinese have made huge technological strides in recent years, but there seems little likelihood that a warplane with this capability is about to enter service or even exists.

B-2A Loss

The B-2A has a good record of safety with the loss of only one aircraft since its introduction into service. This accident took place at Andersen AFB, Guam, on 23 February 2008 when B-2A (AV-12 *Spirit of Kansas*) was taking off. The crew believed that the aircraft had reached take-off speed, when it was actually travelling 10kts (11.5mph or 18.5kph) slower. The problem was caused by moisture in three of the 24 air pressure sensors providing incorrect information to the flight computer. This reported that the aircraft was in a nose down position and required a 30° pitch change, leading to a stall. Consequently, the aircraft swerved off the runway and as the left wingtip hit the ground Major Ryan Link and Captain Justin Grieve ejected. Both were injured with Grieve suffering some compression fractures to his spine. The aircraft was a complete write-off.

Left: **It is now clear that Russian scientists and engineers studied US stealth developments in great detail. Many western observers expected Russia to match the Northrop Grumman B-2A with a similarly specified bomber, but this never happened, perhaps due in part to the high cost and deteriorating Soviet economy. The only hint of such a possibility was in early 1996 when the MiG Design Bureau released artwork of canard stealth bomber vaguely resembling the B-2A. However, Russia was not in a position to develop such an expensive aircraft and it remains unlikely. This illustration has been developed from the original artwork as a representation of the MiG design.** Bill Rose Collection

Below left: **This poor quality image, lifted from video footage, shows the moment when *Spirit of Kansas* ran into serious trouble during take-off at Andersen AFB, Guam, in February 2008. The crew were forced to eject and the aircraft was destroyed.** USAF

Below: **Wreckage of the B-2A that crashed during take-off at Andersen AFB, Guam. Smoke continues to issue from the aircraft, which was a total write-off. The cause of the accident was moisture in three of the 24 air pressure sensors that supply data to the flight computer.** USAF

Secret Projects: Flying Wings and Tailless Aircraft

Senior Citizen

On 24 April 1980, the United States undertook a daring multi-services covert mission to rescue 52 hostages being held at the US Embassy in Tehran, Iran. Known as 'Eagle Claw', the operation degenerated into a total disaster. Retired Chief of Naval Operations Adm James L. Holloway III was given the task of heading an official investigation which found major deficiencies in planning and co-ordination. While the failure of 'Eagle Claw' cannot be blamed on the aircraft used, it highlighted the fact that some Special Forces operations would benefit from transporters possessing a helicopter's VTOL ability and the speed, range and payload capability of a fixed wing aircraft.

An aircraft of this type was the dream of aeronautical designers for decades with German engineers at Focke Achgelis making a serious effort to develop just such a 'convertiplane' during World War 2. This design, which combined aspects of the helicopter and fixed wing aircraft, was never completed, but Bell saw the tilt-rotor's potential during the early post-war years and it led to the experimental XV-3 which first flew in 1955. This research project would eventually result in the Bell Helicopter Textron and Boeing Helicopters V-22 Osprey which took a tremendous effort to develop and was almost cancelled on several occasions due to serious accidents and rising costs.

Today, this unique aircraft is in service with the US Marine Corps and the USAF, so should a similar situation to the Iranian hostage crisis arise, there is every possibility that the Osprey would be used. It can carry at least 24 soldiers and their equipment with a combat radius of 428 miles (690km) that can be extended with in-flight refuelling. The Osprey can cruise at about 316mph (508kph), well above the reach of small-arms fire or shoulder-launched missiles. As such, it appears well suited to Special Forces operations, medevac and the recovery of downed pilots in hostile territory. Unfortunately, the Osprey remains an imperfect design. Aside from the sheer engineering complexity of this aircraft, there are some doubts about the Osprey's ability to survive in a harsh combat environment and the huge 38ft (11.6m) diameter rotors make the aircraft far from stealthy.

'Eagle Claw' spurred the Department of Defense (DoD) to initiate full development of the V-22 Osprey in 1981 which was then known as the Joint-service Vertical take-off/landing Experimental (JVX) aircraft. However, there was already major interest in low-observable aircraft and the idea of a larger, faster stealthy transport aircraft with STOL or ideally a VTOL capability seems to have caught the attention of senior officials at the Pentagon.

A series of highly-classified studies was undertaken by the major aerospace contractors to design an aircraft to meet specifications for a stealthy tactical transporter. Nothing reached the public domain about these proposals, but a Department of Defense document DoD7045.7-H, 'FYDP Program Structure', October 1993, would eventually come to light and it mentioned a project called Senior Citizen, Program Element 0401316F. The codename was initially believed to refer to a hypersonic spyplane project, but was then identified as a stealthy tactical transport aircraft.

Some design work undertaken at Wright-Patterson AFB (probably in the 1980s) had suggested two favourable approaches to lift propulsion for a VTOL special operations aircraft. The first way of generating lift was the use of additional upright turbojets, while the second was to use large shaft-driven fans in ducts. Although these ideas were hardly new, this work provided a useful framework for the Senior Citizen programme which is rumoured to have considered many different concepts including lighter-than-air designs.

One participant in the Senior Citizen project is understood to have been Northrop which is thought to have proposed a design loosely based on the B-2A Spirit bomber. The central section of the aircraft is presumed to have similarities with the B-2, while the overall appearance is manta-shaped with clipped wingtips. Lift and hover would be achieved by the use of four vertical ducts containing large constant RPM fans covered by shutters and louvers during normal flight. Propulsion details of this study are unclear, but horizontal flight would be achieved using two or four deeply-buried turbofans and the aircraft would be capable of making conventional take-offs and landings.

A US Marine Corps crew prepares a V-22 Osprey for night operations in Central Iraq during early 2008. This aircraft is well suited to special missions, although it lacks the ability to hide from enemy forces. US Navy photo by Chief Petty Officer Joe Kane.

Details of what appear to be alternative designs from Boeing and/or Lockheed suggest an aircraft with semi-arrowhead shape using engines for horizontal flight in a rear dorsal duct and two vertical stabilising fins on either side towards the rear wing area. Two banks of four upright turbojets are positioned on each side of the fuselage. These provide lift and would be covered by shutters during horizontal flight. A clearer idea of what may have been under consideration for the Senior Citizen programme can be found by studying a Lockheed propulsion system patent (5,320305) filed on 22 July 1992 and published two years later.

A small team at the Skunk Works, headed by the Chief Engineer of Advanced Development Projects, Dr Leland Malcolm Nicolai, produced this interesting concept that appears to be specifically developed as a stealthy flying wing aircraft. The propulsion system comprises two ducted cruise fans for horizontal flight which are buried within the fuselage. Intakes for the engines are positioned towards the centre of the leading edge and there are two-dimensional exhaust outlets at the centre of wing's trailing edge. The VTOL capability is provided by two substantial, constant RPM ducted fans which are driven by two (or possibly four) engines located between both units with cross shafting to allow power redistribution in an emergency. To balance and control pitch during take-off, landing, hover and flight transition, air from the cruise engine's bypass ducts would be diverted to forward and aft nozzles. To control downward thrust, each fan would have variable pitch propellers. Each fan duct would be fitted with covers on the upper side and louvered shutters on the wing's underside which would be adjustable for directional control.

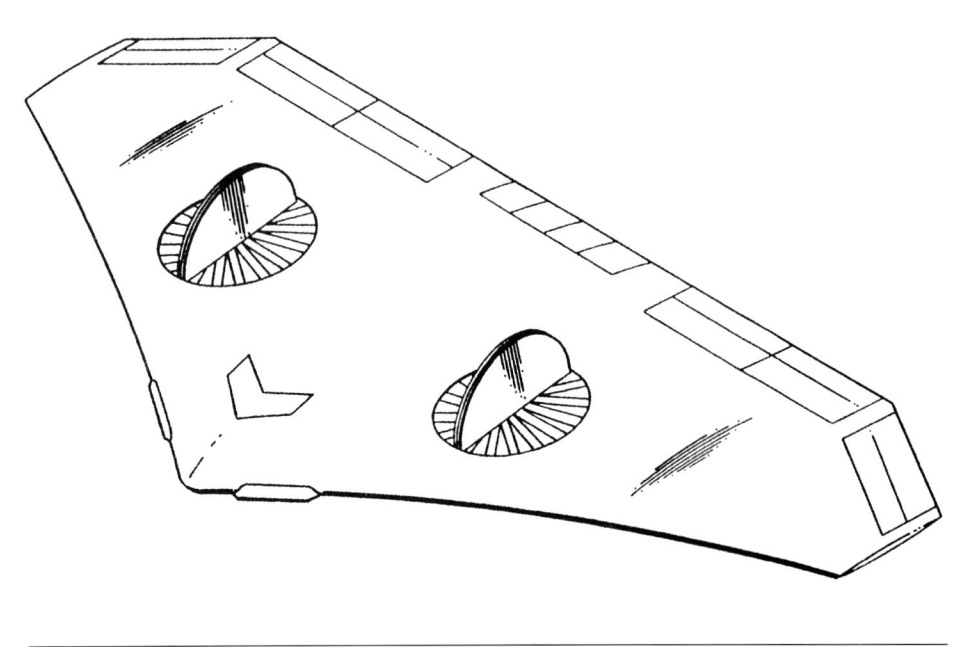

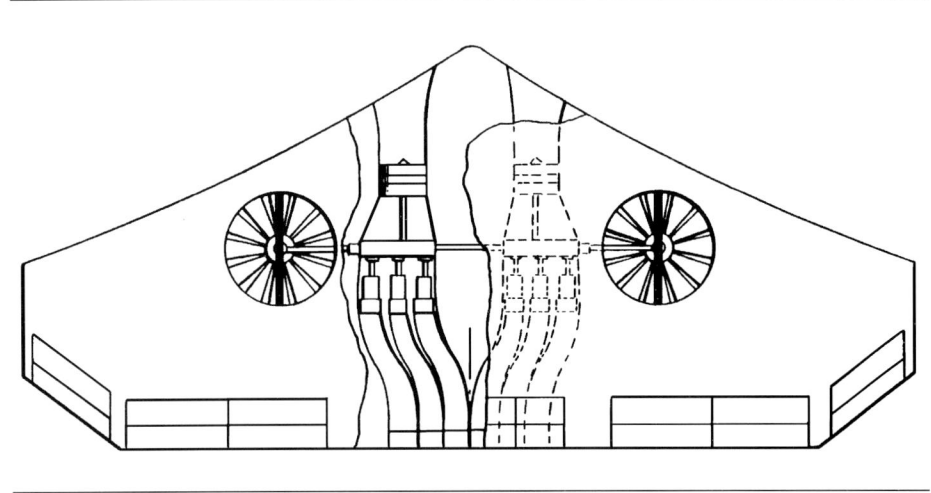

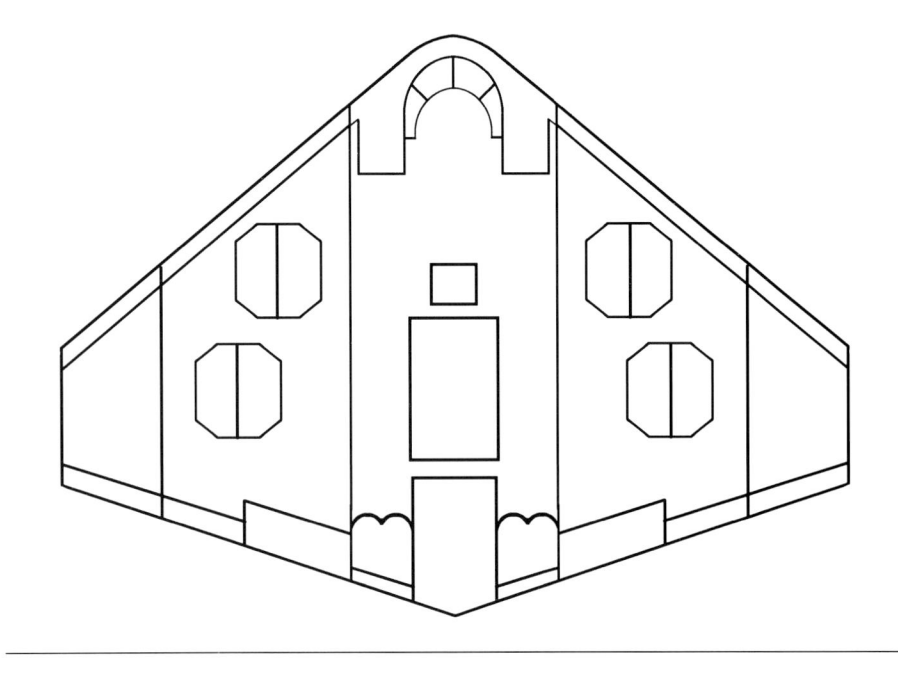

At take-off, all engines would be operating and the wing fan ducts would be fully open. Having left the ground, the lower louvers would slowly move rearwards and once the aircraft had reached sufficient speed to provide lift, there would be a full transition to horizontal flight with the cruise fans taking over and the fans shutting down and the covers closing. Landing would be a reverse of this procedure. This propulsion system seems to be completely tied into the flying wing design which would probably differ considerably from the patent drawings. However, this very stealthy design has no vertical surfaces and uses ailerons, elevators and drag rudders for flight control. It is also shown with a multi wheel tricycle undercarriage.

Whether or not a Senior Citizen design has been prototyped by one of the major contractors or even built as a small batch of special ops aircraft is impossible to say. But occasional sightings of unidentified triangular-shaped aircraft by the public may (in a few reliable cases) indicate that small numbers of stealthy transporters exist and might be available for a high-priority clandestine mission. Such an aircraft would probably be able to carry 30-35 soldiers with their equipment. It would be capable of in-flight refuelling and have an operational range of about 2,500 miles (4,000km). Depending on the propulsion system, the maximum speed might be somewhat better than the V-22 with a ceiling of perhaps 35,000ft (10,668m) which assumes a fully pressurised cabin. Another possibility is a stealthy gunship variant. This might lack the VTOL capability but could be heavily armed and perhaps equipped with a chemical laser weapon for use against ground targets.

This drawing taken from a US Patent shows a Lockheed VTOL aircraft proposal that may be related to black budget 'Senior Citizen' project to develop a stealthy theatre transport aircraft for high-risk covert Special Forces operations.
Bill Rose Collection/US Patent Office

The unusual ducted and lift-fan propulsion system for a Lockheed VTOL stealth aircraft design.
Bill Rose Collection/US Patent Office

Based on a number of different sources, this may be the general appearance of a Boeing design for a stealthy special operations transport aircraft with a full VTOL capability. Derived in part from the B-2A bomber, it is not know if this project progressed beyond initial studies. Bill Rose Collection

Secret Projects: Flying Wings and Tailless Aircraft

Next Generation Bomber B-3

The Pentagon currently plans to keep the B-52, the B-1B and the B-2A in service until 2037 with the already ancient B-52 perhaps remaining operational until 2045. These 'Legacy Bombers' will be subject to an ongoing programme of improvements until their retirement. There are plans to supplement the Legacy Bombers with an unmanned strike aircraft, but a new manned strategic strike aircraft is needed and the USAF would like to see this reaching operational status by 2018. The new bomber must be capable of handling any air defence system currently envisaged. It will be subsonic, possess intercontinental range and have the ability to deliver a significant conventional or nuclear payload.

While it has been suggested that the next manned US bomber should be a cutting-edge design capable of high supersonic speed, the Pentagon is not prepared to initiate another financially challenging A-12A or B-2A programme. So this aircraft must be available in the short term, affordable and effective as a warplane. Two teams of contractors have now been chosen to develop detailed proposals for this project which is currently known as the Next-Generation Bomber (NGB). Significant funding for NGB development is expected to become available shortly and the contractors hoping to win this contest are Northrop-Grumman and Lockheed-Martin which have teamed up with Boeing.

Both groups are thought to be drawing heavily on experience gained with unmanned aircraft programmes for this project. Northrop-Grumman have been responsible for the X-47B Pegasus Uninhabited Combat Air Vehicle (UCAV) programme

Northrop Grumman's initial Next Generation Bomber proposal. The chosen design is expected to reach operational service by 2018. To some extent, this aircraft is a next-generation version of the existing B-2A stealth bomber, drawing on advances made during the development of unmanned aircraft such as the X-47B Pegasus. It is expected to receive the designation B-3. Northrop Grumman/Bill Rose Collection

An early Lockheed Martin proposal for the USAF's Next Generation Bomber. Like the Northrop Grumman design, this also makes extensive use of new materials and advances in stealth technology made during the development of unmanned military aircraft. Northrop Grumman/ Bill Rose Collection

The experimental Northrop Grumman X-47B Pegasus Unmanned Combat Aircraft (UCAV) which has been used to develop new technologies that will be employed in the crewed Next Generation Bomber. Northrop Grumman

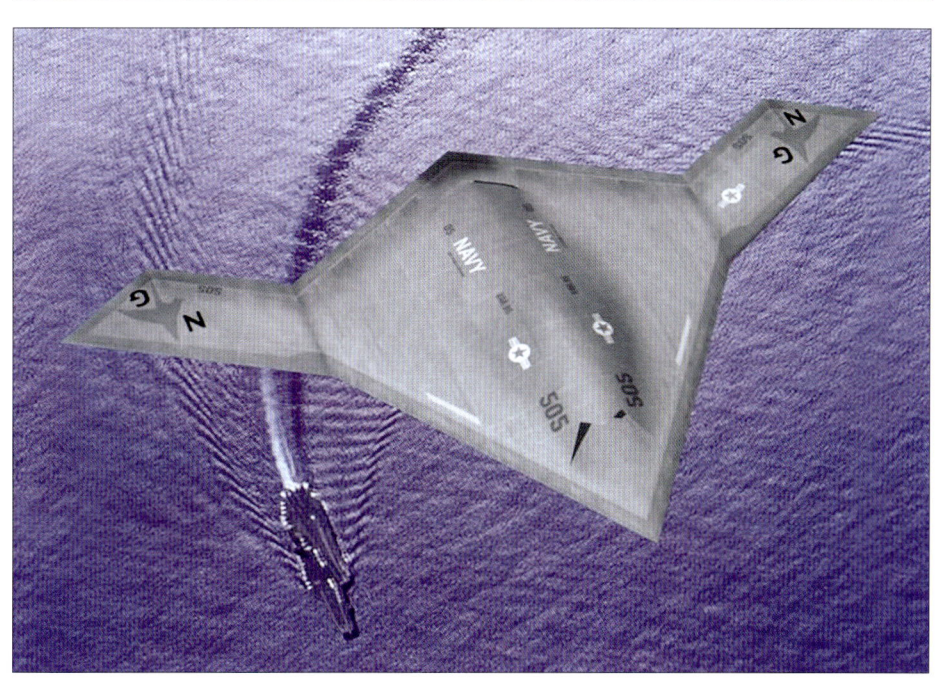

US Manned Tailless Aircraft (1980-2030)

which is now part of the US Navy's UCAS-D carrier-based aircraft project. Boeing produced the X-45 series of unmanned demonstrators leading to the advanced Phantom Ray which is due to fly in 2010. In the case of Lockheed's Skunk Works, it already had considerable expertise with low-observable technology and recently flew the P-175 Polecat unmanned stealth aircraft as a company funded technology development venture.

Preliminary artwork for the NGB shows that the principle designs hold no big surprises with concepts from both groups resembling a cross between the B-2A and a scaled up high-tech UCAV. It is interesting to note that Northrop-Grumman has already proposed an unmanned X-47C with a 172ft (52,4m) wingspan and a 10,000lb (4,536kg) payload capability.

A straightforward approach to development of the NGB is favoured by the US Air Force which requires an aircraft with a realistic delivery date. Noticeable improvements will be in low-observable, avionics, fuel efficiency and maintenance requirements. It is anticipated that the 2018 NGB will receive the designation B-3, although this new bomber is seen as something of a stopgap until a more advanced stealthy long-range supersonic aircraft becomes available in 2037.

NGB Specifications

Powerplant	Readily available turbofan engines
Maximum speed	Subsonic
Combat radius	+2,000 miles (+3,200km)
Ability to carry nuclear weapons	
Weapons load	14,000-28,000lb (6,350-12,700kg)
First flight	By 2018

Lockheed-Martin FB-22

When it became clear that the USAF would need to supplement or start to replace its existing bomber fleet by 2018, several designs were proposed that built on existing technology and could be delivered within an acceptable timeframe. One suggestion was to replace the existing B-1B Lancer with a new version of the aircraft called the B-1R (Regional). Re-engined with new avionics, a new radar system, external hardpoints and air-to-air missiles, the B-1R would regain the B-1A's Mach 2+ performance. It is also possible that the B-1R might be configured to launch cruise missiles, although this capability is currently restricted by the Strategic Arms Limitation Treaty 1 (SALT 1). While this proposal has obvious merits, the existing B-1B has a reputation for being unreliable, it is demanding to maintain and the B-1R will not be any stealthier than the current aircraft. These observations may help to explain why the B-1R was rejected as an interim solution to USAF requirements.

Another possibility that is rumoured to have received serious consideration was a stealthy strike aircraft based on the unsuccessful Northrop YF-23 fighter. This does not appear to have been regarded as a realistic option, either for technical reasons or on the grounds of cost. But a third idea that generated considerable interest was a strike aircraft based on the advanced, stealthy Lockheed-Martin F-22 Raptor fighter. This suggestion originated within the Skunk Works during 2002 and a detailed study was funded by the company. The design may have been linked to a proposed experimental tailless version of the F-22 called the X-44A.

Although described as an F-22 modified to become a stealthy light bomber, the FB-22 would effectively be a brand-new aircraft with a completely new wing and probably no tail or vertical stabilisers. This cleaner design would improve the aircraft's stealthiness, aerodynamic properties and help to reduce manufacturing costs. The fuselage would be stretched by about 10ft (3m) and approximately 80 per cent more fuel would be carried. There would be enough internal storage for up to 30 small diameter 250lb (113kg) bombs utilising GPS for precise targeting. The FB-22 would also be capable of delivering anti-radiation missiles and nuclear weapons.

For self-defence, the FB-22 would carry at least two and perhaps four AMRAAMs internally or possibly a laser weapon, but this is not an aircraft that is intended for use as a fighter. Engines would be upgraded to two powerful Pratt & Whitney F135s developed from the afterburning turbofans used for the F-22. Air for the engines would be drawn through two reconfigured stealthy intakes and the ability to cruise at supersonic speed has been suggested but this remains unclear. However, the FB-22 would be the fastest bomber in USAF service. Possessing a maximum speed of Mach 1.8, the two-man FB-22 would have an unrefuelled range of 1,600 miles (2,575km) and deliver its bomb load from an altitude of 60,000ft (18,288m). The FB-22 would be equipped with sophisticated threat determination systems and have the ability to capture high quality radar images of ground targets which could be relayed to a command centre in real time.

A completely tailless technology demonstrator based on an F-22A airframe was proposed and it received the designation X-44A. This experimental aircraft was intended to use thrust vectoring for all flight control functions and the project would have provided useful research data for the FB-22, but at the time of writing the X-44 remains officially unbuilt. The FB-22 would fill the place once occupied by the variable-geometry F-111. It would effectively replace the F-15E, taking over some missions currently better suited to the B-1B and B-2A. It is probable that various FB-22 models have undergone wind tunnel and radar tests. This aircraft remains an interesting and viable

This artwork shows the possible appearance of a strike aircraft based on the F-22A Raptor stealth fighter which would receive the designation FB-22. This would be almost an entirely new aircraft with a stretched fuselage, new wing and more advanced engines. Although this proposal has much in its favour, the cost of development is likely to remain prohibitive and there are no plans at present to initiate such a programme. Bill Rose Collection

concept that may simply be too expensive to develop as a parallel programme to the NGB with recent estimates for the FB-22 programme varying from $7-10 billion.

FB-22

Crew	2
Wingspan	Unknown
Wing area	Unknown
Length	72ft (22m) approx
Height	Unknown
Gross weight	84,000-100,000 lb (38,100-45,000kg)
Propulsion	2 x Pratt & Whitney F135 afterburning turbofan engines, based on the F119 developed for the F-22. The F135 engine can produce 34,000 lb (151kN) dry thrust and 50,000 lb (222kN) afterburning thrust. The General Electric/Rolls-Royce F136 afterburning turbofan, which was proposed at one stage, would offer similar performance
Maximum speed	Mach 1.8
Ceiling	65,000ft (19,812m)
Combat range	1,600 miles (2,575km) un-refuelled
Armament	30 x 250 lb (113kg) Small Diameter Bombs (SDB). Larger conventional or nuclear bombs, guided weapons. Anti-radiation missiles and 2-4 AMRAAM air-to-air missiles for self-defence. Perhaps later, stealthy underwing pods carrying ordnance, fuel or EW equipment

Boeing F/A-XX

Many aviation observers have suggested that the F-35 Lightning II will be the last manned fighter aircraft of any significance, but artwork released in July 2009 by Boeing's Phantom Works shows a manned 'sixth generation' combat aircraft intended to replace the current F/A-18E/F Super Hornet after 2025. This tailless design has been proposed to meet the US Navy's future F/A-XX requirements and it will have been conceived from the outset to be as stealthy as possible. That said, it goes without saying that current illustrations do not reveal any important or innovative design features.

The exact definition of 'sixth generation' remains unclear, although we should expect an aircraft with supercruise, increased range, thrust vectoring, internal weapons carriage, advanced sensors, lower maintenance requirements and improved stealth. Primarily intended for carrier-based operations, the aircraft would be designed for compact storage. Flown by a crew of two, the aircraft may be configurable for unmanned operations or built as a UCAV version.

Whether or not such an aircraft will become a reality when faced with the next generation of completely unmanned designs is hard to determine at present. But it is possible to say with some degree of certainty that a manned F/A-18E/F replacement will be costly to develop, especially if undertaken separately from any future manned multi-role combat aircraft requested by the USAF.

Blended Wing Body Designs

The Blended Wing Body (BWB) aircraft can be traced back to Junkers and Burnelli, although the modern BWB design is generally attributed to a research programme initiated by McDonnell Douglas at Long Beach, California.

Work on this project began in late 1988 with the aim of developing a more efficient transport aircraft. The McDonnell Douglas team, which included Bob Liebeck, Mark A. Page and Blaine K. Rawdon, steadily refined the concept into a proposal resembling a hybrid-flying wing. The aim was to utilise an effective aerofoil-shaped body fitted with high-lift wings, but it was also important to allow the internal installation of easily fabricated pressurised tubular compartments. As the project evolved, it became increasingly clear that the BWB design would offer significantly improved aerodynamic efficiency over existing aircraft designed for the same purpose. A 10-15 per cent reduction in weight would also be possible if composite materials were used extensively in the aircraft's construction. These factors would mean lower engine thrust for the same payload and therefore a considerable reduction in operating costs. Comparisons with similarly specified conventional jet airliners suggested a 20-25 per cent improvement in fuel efficiency.

Boeing's Phantom Works has revealed a new concept for a US Navy F/A-XX fighter to replace the F/A-18E/F Super Hornet in the mid-2020s. The two-seat, blended-wing, twin-engine, tailless design is dubbed a 'sixth-generation fighter' and will embrace technologies such as visual stealth, advanced electronic attack capabilities and optional manning. Although not yet a formal requirement, the Navy is thought to be considering both manned and unmanned options for F/A-XX. Boeing

NASA has supported the BWB design from the outset. It determined that this type of aircraft showed great potential as a large capacity subsonic airliner. This led to BWB models being wind tunnel tested at NASA Langley and the commission of a scale-size remote-control prototype that was built at Stanford University by a team directed by Dr Ben Tigner and Associate Professor Ilan Kroo. This small aircraft was designated BWB-17 (because of the 17ft (5.18m) wingspan) and it flew for the first time on 29 July 1997 at El Mirage Dry Lake, California.

It seemed that there were relatively few negative features to the BWB design. Longitudinal stability, which is often a major problem with tailless designs, could be maintained by the latest active flight management systems, although there were concerns about the suitability of BWB aircraft for many existing airports and the fact that there would be few, if any windows available for passengers. Early proposals for a 368-passenger BWB airliner were based on a proposed range of 9,500 miles (15,000km) and Mach 0.85 cruise. By 1994, NASA was suggesting that the McDonnell Douglas engineers should consider a much larger aircraft capable of carrying 800 passengers for 8,000 miles

(12,800km). This scaled-up design would require two layers of cylindrical pressurised compartments, at least four engines, an increased wingspan approaching 350ft (106m) and an empty weight of approximately 200 tons (180 metric tons).

In 1997, McDonnell Douglas became part of the restructured Boeing Company and it was decided to continue with the promising BWB programme. But there were concerns that the project was distancing itself from any near-term commercial applications. The European Airbus Corporation was pushing ahead with development of a super Jumbo jet and as a consequence Boeing decided that there was no immediate room in the market for another aircraft in this class. It meant that further development of an 800-seat passenger BWB airliner was suspended with a 450-seat aircraft using unconventional aerofoils becoming the new primary objective. A series of in-house classifications were introduced for the BWB designs with the 450-seat aircraft becoming the BWB-450. This model would have a wingspan of 249ft (75.8m) and use three large turbofans for propulsion.

The outcome to this change in direction was the construction of several wind tunnel models that were tested at NASA Langley and a small-scale unmanned proof-of-concept demonstrator that was initially designated as the BWB-LSV (Low Speed Vehicle). Work began on the 35ft (10.6m) wingspan BWB-LSV at Langley in 2000 with the name changed to X-48A in 2001 to reflect its experimental nature. The X-48A was essentially a 14 per cent scale sized version of the BWB-450, making extensive use of composites in its construction. Unfortunately, unforeseen problems with the flight control system and budgetary restraints brought the project to a halt in 2002.

Soon after this, the X-48A was scrapped. Small wind tunnel models replaced the demonstrator and it was planned to build two compact unmanned prototypes with 21ft (6.4m) wingspans. Development and construction of these aircraft was undertaken by Cranfield University in Britain with the designations X-48B being assigned to both models in June 2005. The first X-48B was wind tunnel tested by NASA in May 2006 and then shipped to Dryden Flight Research Center at Edwards AFB where it would act as a backup for the second aircraft that was scheduled to begin flight-testing.

Powered by three small jet engines, each rated at 50lb (.22kN) thrust and having a take-off weight of 520lb (235kg), the X-48B was still expected to attain a maximum speed of 138mph (222kph) and achieve an altitude of 10,000ft (3,048m). Ground testing began in late 2006 with the first flight taking place on 20 July 2007. This lasted for 31min and the aircraft climbed to an altitude of 7,500ft (2,286m). Trials have continued with increased participation from the Air Force Research Laboratory (AFRL) which recognised the military potential of the BWB design some time ago.

Boeing has developed a series of commercial configurations for the BWB configuration known as the BWB-250, BWB-350 and

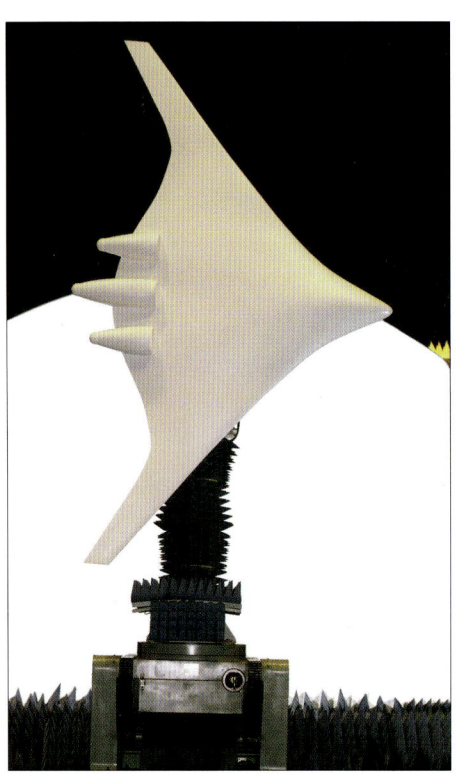

Above: **A three-engine blended wing body test model undergoing antenna pattern measurements during 1998.** NASA

Above right: **Rear view of a Boeing Blended Wing Body (BWB) 450-passenger subsonic transport test model in the wind tunnel at the NASA Langley Research Center during 2000.** NASA

Right: **The sleek looking sub-scale X-48B BWB prototype is prepared for testing in the full-scale wind tunnel at NASA Langley in May 2006.** Boeing

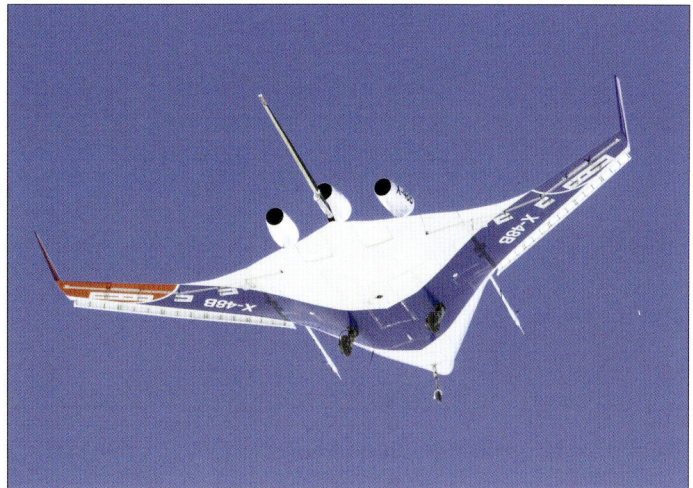

BWB-450. These designs had wingspans from 199ft (60m) to 222ft (67.6m), although a very large version known as the BWB-1000 was studied. This would have a wingspan of 262ft 6in (80m), a length of 193ft 10in (59m) and a gross weight of 650 tons (589 metric tons). While a fuel-efficient airliner was the original aim of this long-term programme, it now seems likely that BWB technology will be applied to military designs first. Boeing is known to have conducted extensive studies into military adaptations of the BWB design with proposals for a BWB tanker to meet future USAF requirements. The BWB tanker would be equipped with two hose/drogue refuelling stations and up to three smart booms capable of fully automated refuelling of multiple numbers of piloted or unmanned aircraft.

An obvious military application for the larger BWB aircraft would be a transporter, while a long range and the ability to loiter for lengthy periods would make this aircraft suitable for command control, surveillance, reconnaissance or maritime operations. It is also likely that a BWB aircraft would make a suitable platform for one or more laser weapons, either to intercept ballistic missiles during their boost

Top left: **The Blended Wing Body X-48B demonstrator undertakes its first test flight at Edwards AFB on 20 July 2007.** NASA

Top right: **Tail view of the unmanned X-48B BWB demonstrator during its first test flight at Edwards AFB.** NASA

Above right: **The general layout for a three-engine, intercontinental 529-seat airliner. One factor often discussed with this design would be the lack of windows, although video displays would provide external views for passengers.** NASA

Right: **One of several Boeing proposals for a BWB tanker aircraft. This would be capable of fully automated refuelling operations involving manned and unmanned aircraft.** Bill Rose Collection

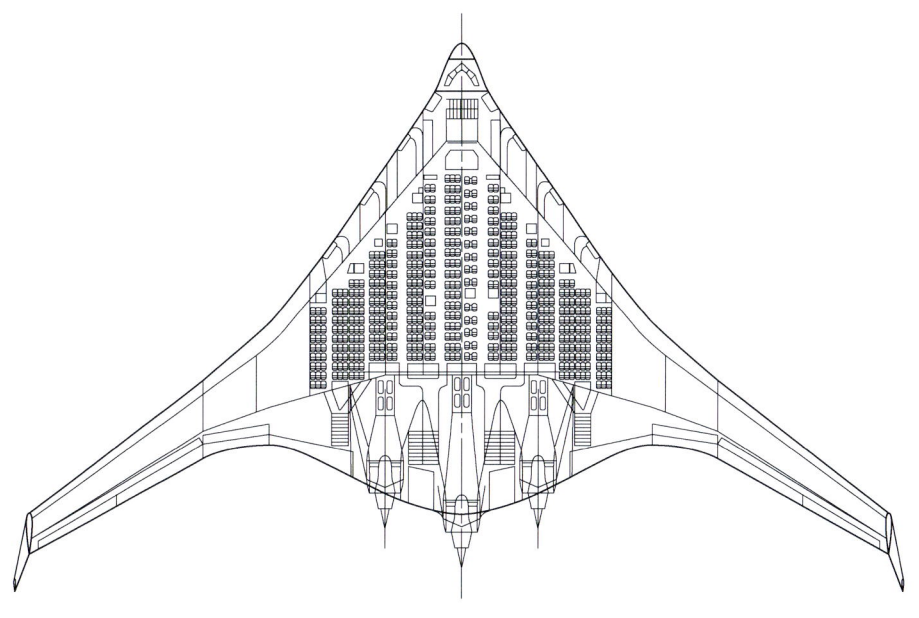

US Manned Tailless Aircraft (1980-2030)

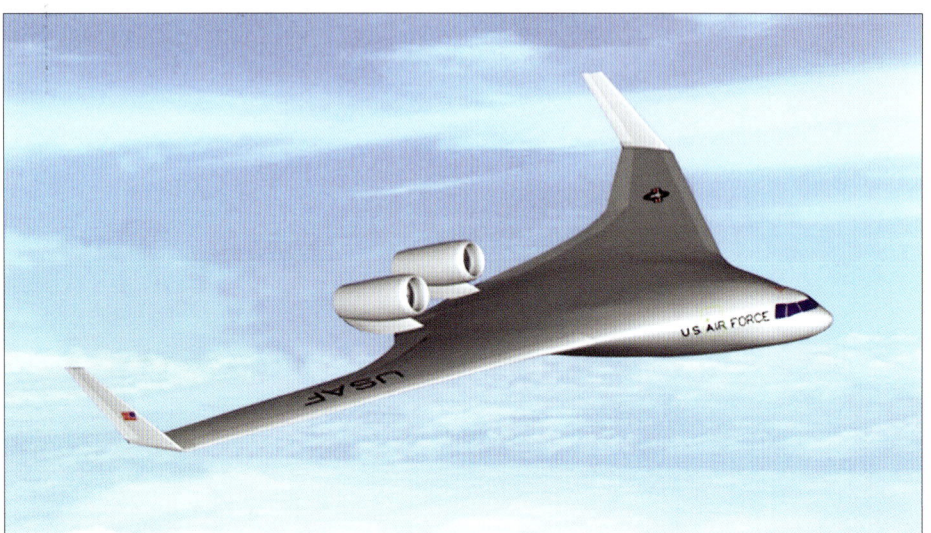

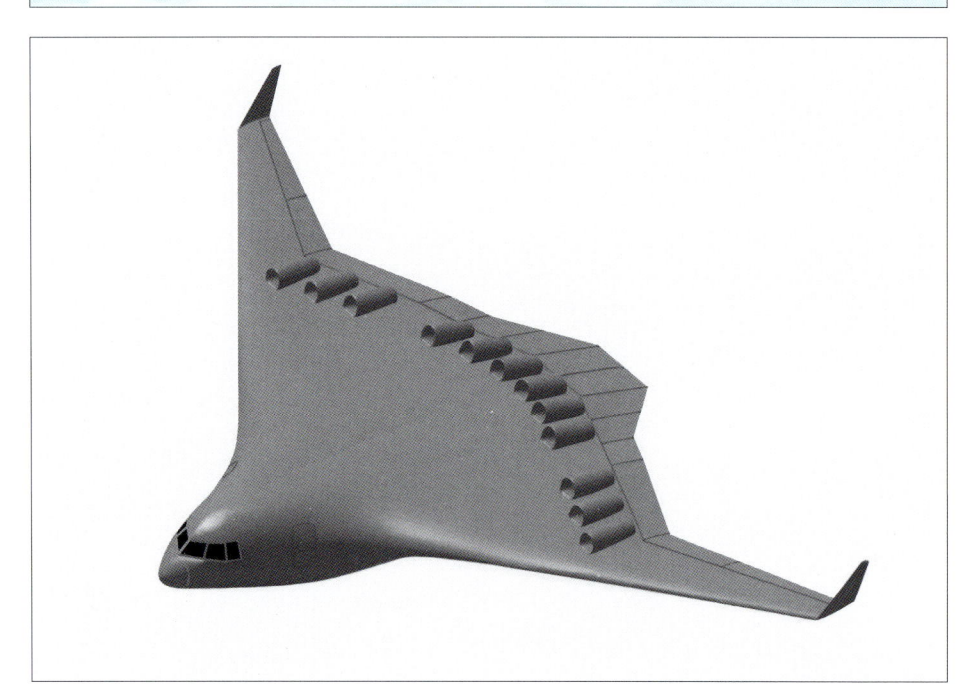

Artwork depicting a twin-engine Boeing BWB tanker design. Boeing

A twin-engine Boeing BWB proposal, suitable for use as a military transport aircraft. Boeing

A BWB design produced in 2005 by the Boeing Phantom Works for a CESTOL (Cruise Efficient Short Take-off & Landing) aircraft. This design with the reference AB32 would use 12 embedded ATSE (Advanced Technology Short Engines), each providing 5,000 lb (22.2kN) thrust. An initial application could be a military transport aircraft. Boeing Phantom Works

phase or for use against ground targets. Other possibilities are a launch platform for the next generation of high-performance cruise missiles or the delivery of free fall bombs or JDAMS. In this respect, such an aircraft could eventually replace the B-52 bomber, perhaps as the B-4. Sufficient clearance beneath the aircraft might also permit the carriage of a small orbital manned or unmanned spacecraft for release at altitude.

The stealthiness of a BWB design remains largely unknown or classified and while technical opinion appears divided on this issue, it has been suggested that engines and their locations may present problems. The BWB design has been the subject of a long-term study at Lockheed-Martin, while Aerospatiale considered the BWB for the Very Efficient Large Aircraft (VELA) programme. In Russia, there has been a number of state-sponsored research programmes producing concepts broadly similar to those created in the West. It is impossible to accurately predict the state of aviation by the middle of this century, but it seems highly probable that by then, the BWB design will have become a familiar sight in our skies.

Oblique Flying Wings

A flying wing aircraft that could swivel about its vertical axis during flight would theoretically provide good performance at low speeds while also allowing high-speed or supersonic flight when moved to an oblique angle. Unfortunately, the engineering complexity of such a design remains considerable, and to date there have been no practical applications of this idea.

It's probable that Dr Richard Vogt of Blohm & Voss made the earliest serious proposal for utilisation of an oblique wing during World War 2. He conceived a variable-geometry jet fighter known as the P.202 with a wing that swivelled around a central pivot to provide variable sweep. Models are believed to have been wind tunnel tested, but the concept progressed no further. The oblique wing was also studied by

Messerschmitt at Oberammergau as part of the P.1101 experimental fighter project, but it was considered too radical for further development. In the post-war years, the idea was studied over a lengthy period by the American NACA/NASA aerodynamicist Dr Robert Thomas Jones (1910-1999) who recognised the advantages of an oblique (or asymmetrically-swept) wing aircraft. He also realised from the outset that major design challenges existed which might take years to resolve.

In 1958, Jones outlined his ideas for an oblique flying wing (OFW) concept at the first International Congress of the Aeronautical Sciences held in Madrid. Attending the conference were Handley Page aerodynamicists Lachmann and Lee who took serious notice of Jones' ideas. As a consequence, Godfrey Lee began work on his own OFW design study for a 150-seat, Mach 2 airliner that he completed in early 1961 calling it Sycamore. The aircraft was very unusual in appearance, taking the form of large semi-elliptical wing with an overall length of about 300ft (91m). This was fitted with a swivelling crew nacelle at the starboard wingtip and a stabilising fin at the other. Beneath the centre of the wing were four swivelling jet engines in pods that controlled the yaw angle from 25° at low speeds to 72° during supersonic flight. The RAE undertook wind tunnel tests, but Lee's Sycamore airliner was generally considered too far ahead of its time to be a practical proposition.

Interest in oblique wings faded until the early 1970s, when R.T. Jones re-generated awareness with a number of supersonic transport aircraft proposals, including a very unusual twin fuselage concept. This led to several short-term studies undertaken by Boeing, General Dynamics and Lockheed which tried to determine civil applications for the OFW. At the same time NASA Ames undertook studies into military applications of the OFW, initially producing designs for a land-based anti-submarine warfare (ASW) aircraft

Similar in many ways to the earlier British Sycamore concept, this long-range supersonic oblique wing airliner was one of several concepts to be produced by NASA during the early 1990s. NASA

This multiple exposure photograph of NASA's Oblique Wing Research Aircraft made in 1976 shows the wing rotation limits to 45 degrees. This small, unmanned research vehicle provided invaluable data, which allowed construction of a much larger experimental manned aircraft. NASA

NASA's Oblique AD-1 (Ames-Dryden-1) research aircraft in flight. This small single-seat jet-powered research vehicle was built after extensive testing of wind tunnel models and first flew on 21 December 1979 at Edwards AFB. A very successful series of trials followed, lasting until autumn 1982. NASA

with modest supersonic performance and good endurance. Another proposal was an unmanned air-combat aircraft which looked rather like a large surfboard with a swivelling fuselage section below the wing that carried two external missiles. Air launched and powered by two afterburning turbojets, this UCAV would have a maximum speed of Mach 1.6 and high manoeuvrability with an 11G limit. The folded length was about 35ft (10.6m), so it is conceivable that a couple of these aircraft might have been carried beneath a B-52 bomber for defensive purposes. After firing its missiles, the UCAV could have been flown into the path of an enemy aircraft as the UCAV was considered expendable once launched. However, making such an advanced system work with 1970s technology might have proved rather demanding.

Further applications of the oblique wing were an advanced tactical fighter with a fairly conventional fuselage, an unusual strategic missile launch aircraft and several missile designs. Although these studies were undertaken just to establish the limits of what might be possible with the oblique wing, R.T. Jones was already involved with the building and successful testing of small radio-controlled OFW models. It is also worth mentioning that Teledyne-Ryan was asked to investigate the possibility of adapting a supersonic BQM-34F Firebee II remotely-piloted research vehicle as an oblique wing test-bed and a model was wind tunnel tested during the early 1970s. That seems to have been the full extent of this project which ended in the mid-1970s.

NASA Ames Research Center and NASA Dryden Flight Research Center were now collaborating on plans for a manned aircraft and a decision was made to proceed with a small, low-speed jet powered prototype called the AD-1 (Ames-Dryden-1). Initially, NASA Ames and NASA Langley conducted wind tunnel tests with scale-sized models, and then Ames Industrial (no connection to NASA) was contracted to build a single prototype. The one-man AD-1 made its first flight on 21 December 1979 at Edwards AFB, piloted by Thomas C. McMurtry. In total, the AD-1 undertook 79 flights and the last of these took place on 7 August 1982 with McMurtry at the controls. During testing, the wing was swept to a maximum of 60° with several landings made with the wing positioned at 45°. The AD-1 is now on display at the Hiller Aviation Museum in San Carlos, California.

There were plans to follow the AD-1 with a supersonic Oblique Wing Research Aircraft based on NASA's Digital Fly-By-Wire (DFBW) Vought F-8 demonstrator. But it became clear that problems would arise using the F-8 because the undercarriage would have prevented landings at high angles of attack. Furthermore, flight simulations indicated unacceptable issues would arise with lateral acceleration during pitch manoeuvres that needed to be addressed, so it was decided not to proceed with the construction of this aircraft which would have been partly funded by the US Navy. Rockwell also studied a carrier-based fighter equipped with an oblique wing during the 1980s. A fighter with the ability to loiter for long periods and then intercept enemy aircraft at supersonic speed would be an attractive proposition and as a bonus, the oblique wing would allow very efficient storage onboard a carrier. But the US Navy was unwilling to divert substantial funding from its costly A-12A programme and the project was abandoned. Jones officially retired from NASA in 1981 and accepted a senior position at Stanford University, although he continued to act as a consultant for NASA Ames until 1997.

Despite cancellation of the oblique wing F-8, NASA Ames continued to work on oblique all-wing designs. In 1991, several designs that were not totally dissimilar to Lee's Sycamore were completed. The aim was to produce a 480-seat supersonic airliner with a range of 6,329 miles (10,000km) for possible introduction by 2020. The estimated maximum speed was about Mach 1.8 and the wing would have an oblique sweep of 37.5° during take-off and landing, moving to 68° during supersonic cruise. One of the biggest problems to emerge during this study was undercarriage design and airport handling, although it now seemed that the oblique wing would be capable of providing supersonic performance for about the same operating costs as a conventional long-range jet airliner.

In August 1992, the study was expanded to include engineers from Boeing and McDonnell Douglas, plus a small research group from Stanford University. This led to many design refinements and two definitive proposals known as OAW-1 and DAC-1. Wind tunnel models were tested and NASA Ames funded the construction of two small remote control OFW aircraft at Stanford University. These were built by Steve Morris and flown in 1993 and 1994. However, at the end of this programme, the representatives of Boeing and McDonnell Douglas were both in agreement that the design had no near-term commercial potential and their involvement with OFW development came to an end.

DARPA was the next US Government agency to take an interest in the OFW and it envisaged an unmanned vehicle, configured for specialised reconnaissance or strike missions. Its initial specification was for a reconnaissance aircraft with an operational radius of 2,858 miles (4,600km) and the ability to loiter for 15 hours at 60,000ft (18,288m) while carrying a 4,000lb (1,800kg) payload. The strike aircraft would have the same operational radius with a larger 15,000lb (6,800kg) payload, a cruise speed of Mach 1.6, subsonic loiter and a maximum speed of Mach 2.0. It was hoped that one design could be adapted for either role with the provisional service entry date set at 2020.

In March 2006, DARPA awarded Northrop-Grumman a $10.3 million contract for a two-year design and development programme that would result in proposals for an experimental OFW demonstrator. DARPA hoped that this project would lead to the construction of a supersonic test vehicle within five years. By autumn 2007, Northrop-Grumman had started supersonic wind-tunnel trials of models at

A Northrop Grumman concept for an unmanned oblique flying wing aircraft. This artwork shows the wing configured for low subsonic speeds. The propulsion system is contained in a single pod below the wing. Northrop Grumman

Right: **This illustration shows a proposed Northrop Grumman oblique flying wing aircraft with the wing swept for supersonic speed.** Northrop Grumman

Middle: **Equipped with swivelling engine pods, this Northrop Grumman proposal for a supersonic oblique wing demonstrator shows the wing configured for a speed of Mach 0.73 (upper illustration) and fully swept (below) at Mach 1.2. The design was part of a multi-million dollar study funded by DARPA leading to the construction of an unmanned flying prototype. However, the programme came to an end in 2008 and at the present time, there seems little likelihood of further development.** DARPA

Bottom: **An advanced Northrop concept for an unmanned oblique flying wing releasing a JDAM. Details of the integral engine system have been intentionally left unclear, but it seems likely that the central section of the wing containing the propulsion system would rotate within the wing.** Northrop Grumman

Calspan, Buffalo, New York. As the project progressed, the name Switchblade was being loosely used for the proposed Mach 1.2 demonstrator. The wing would have a span of 56ft (17m) and the oblique sweep could be varied from 0° to 65°. Two General Electric J85-21 afterburning turbojets would be housed in a centrally-positioned swivelling unit, but tests indicated that individual pods were more satisfactory and the design was modified.

The undercarriage is understood to have represented something of an engineering challenge and finally consisted of fully retractable main gear located between the engines with a castoring tailwheel. A further design for a proposed production aircraft carried the engines in a central swivelling section that was integral with the wing, but no details of this have been released.

A review of the OFW project was scheduled for March 2008 and Northrop-Grumman hoped it would lead to the construction of a demonstrator, but within a matter of months, DARPA had decided to conclude the programme. The exact reasons are unclear, but it is believed that financial restraints were responsible.

At the present time, it is hard to say if there is a future for the manned or unmanned oblique flying wing, but it seems probable that the concept will reappear at some point.

Northrop Switchblade: Production Version

Crew	Unmanned
Wingspan	200ft (61m)
Sweep	0° to 60°
Powerplant	2 x unspecified afterburning turbofan engines
Maximum speed	Mach 1.8 - 2
Ceiling	60,000ft (18,288m)
Range (approximately)	5,600 miles (9,000km)

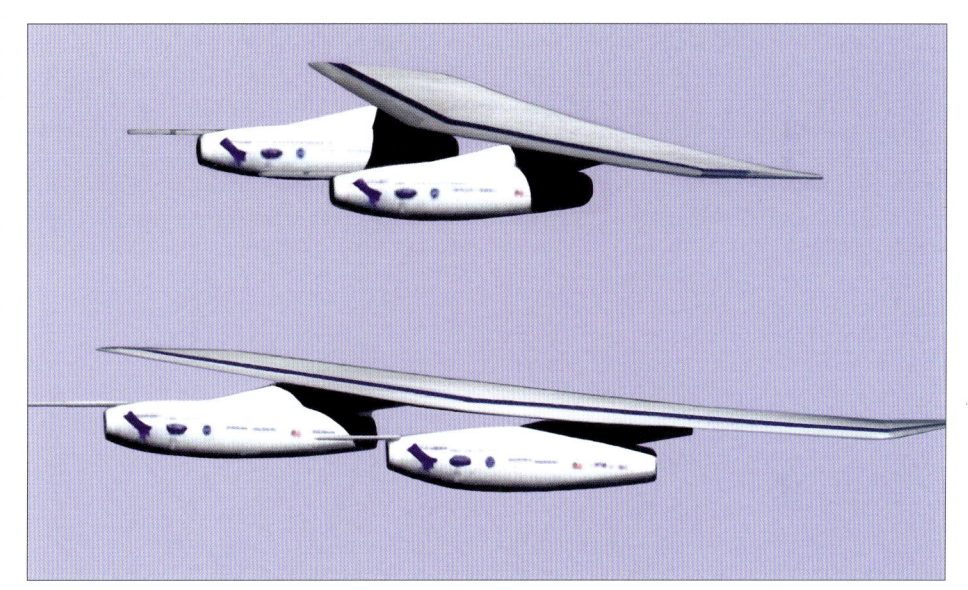

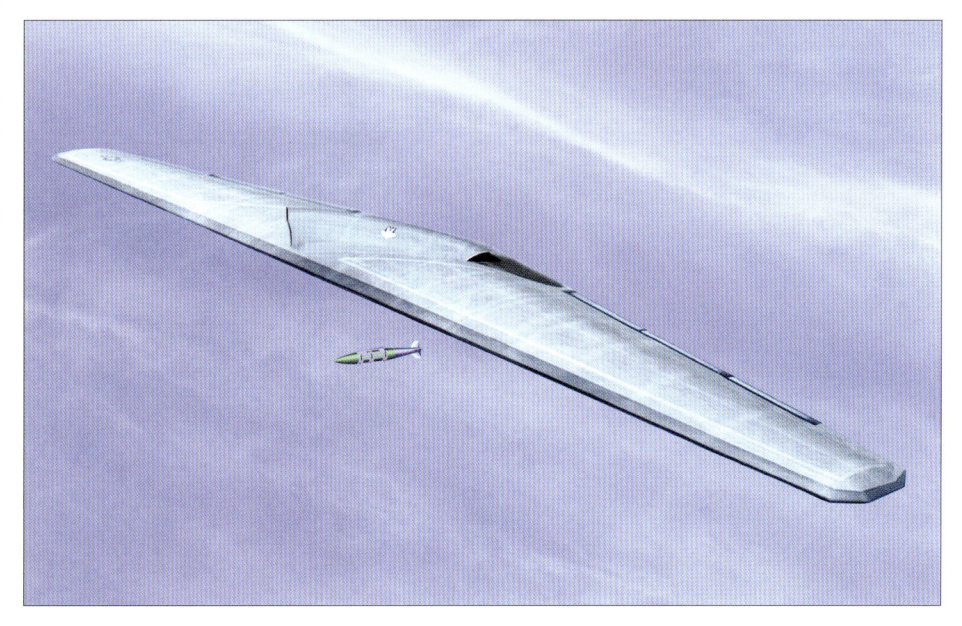

US Manned Tailless Aircraft (1980-2030)

Chapter Six

Soviet Tailless Designs

Many innovative and advanced aircraft were designed and built within the Soviet Union. Engineers were encouraged to experiment with unorthodox concepts and the history of Russian tailless aircraft design and construction stretches back to the pre-war years. During this time, designers such as Cheranovsky, Kalinin and Belyaev all saw their tailless concepts progress from the drawing board to functional hardware, although none of these aircraft reached production.

At the end of World War 2, vast amounts of advanced German military technology were captured by the Russians and shipped east for evaluation and exploitation. This equipment was accompanied by thousands of German engineers and scientists who were interned by the Russians and one of these prisoners was Professor Günter Boch (1898-1970) who headed Germany's wartime flying wing projects. As the war progressed Germany had given increasing priority to the development of tailless combat aircraft, seeing various aerodynamic and production advantages over more conventional designs. Subsequently, the Russians decided to study and capitalise on this approach, keeping Boch and his associates in custody for many years. Aware of this situation, the Pentagon believed that advanced flying wing jet bombers were being developed which had the ability to reach North America.

During the immediate post-war period, information gathered by Western intelligence agencies on military developments within the Soviet Union was extremely limited and unreliable. So when the CIA circulated the idea that Russia was building a massive fleet of 1,800 flying wing bombers based on Horten designs, it was taken very seriously.

One declassified US Intelligence document from 1949 (USAF Directorate of Intelligence 100-203-79 CY) had the following to say: 'It is believed that Dr Boch has made available all German plans for flying wing type aircraft to the Soviets.' The document goes on to say: 'Among the designs considered by the Germans and possibly exploited by the USSR, are jet-propelled, flying wing type aircraft whose configuration would be similar to descriptions of certain objects reported flying over the US. The estimated speeds of such aircraft are within range of the lower limits of speed attributed to flying objects over the US. It is not impossible that emphasis on surpassing foreign developments has led to unusual progress in fuels and propulsion by the USSR.'

These concerns were totally groundless and while wartime German know-how was fully utilised for the first generation of Soviet combat jets, these aircraft were relatively conventional, with tailless designs progressing little further than the prototype stage. During the decades that followed, Soviet designers would occasionally propose tailless configurations, but nothing significant was produced.

However, the Americans were making rapid advances in stealth technology and this encouraged the Soviets to consider new long-range manned and unmanned high-altitude spyplanes and bombers, often utilising flying wing layouts. Most details of this work remain classified, but the main programme appears to have been abandoned when the Soviet economy collapsed in the early 1990s. Nevertheless, it is possible that this research resumed, perhaps being utilised for an unmanned high-altitude spyplane.

Cheranovsky's Tailless Designs

The first notable tailless Russian aircraft was designed by Boris Ivanovich Cheranovsky (1896-1960). He had grown up with a fascination for manned flight and joined the Zhukovsky Academy in 1922, making initial proposals for a flying wing aircraft during the same year.

In 1924, he completed work on two small single-seat parabolic-shaped gliders which received the names BICh-1 and BICh-2. These experimental aircraft were considered quite avant-garde for their time, especially as the entire trailing edge was taken up with control surfaces. It appears that there were handling problems with BICh-1, but BICh-2 is said to have performed somewhat better in flight showing improved stability. The next design, BICh-3, was based on BICh-2. The main difference was a small 18hp (13.4kW) Blackburn-Tomtit 698cc inverted V-twin engine, driving a 4ft 7in (140cm) propeller at the front of the aircraft. Completed by Cheranovsky by the end of 1925, BICh-3 had a

A demonstration flight of Boris Cheranovsky's small one-man parabola-shaped BICh-2 glider, probably during the 1924 glider contest.
Bill Rose Collection

A scaled-up version of the BICh-3, the two-man BICh-7 powered by a 100hp (74.5kW) Bristol Lucifer radial engine, undertook its first flight in 1929. Bill Rose Collection

wingspan of 31ft 2in (9.5m), a wing area of 215ft² (20m²), an overall length of 11ft 6in (3.5m) and a gross weight of approximately 507 lb (230kg).

BICh-3 was mainly constructed from wood and covered in fabric. The pilot sat in a centrally-located cockpit which was faired into the tailfin. A fixed undercarriage was used, comprising of two forward wheels with fairings and a simple tailskid. The aircraft made its first flight in February 1926, piloted by B.N. Kudrin and there are mixed reports about BICh-3's capabilities. BICh-3 could reach a maximum speed of about 85mph (136kph) and the landing speed was an impressive 24mph (40kph), allowing touchdowns in a remarkably short distance. It is also said that the aircraft handled quite well, but still exhibited stability problems. During the remainder of the 1920s, Cheranovsky continued to design unusual parabolic-shaped tailless aircraft, including the BICh-5 twin-engine bomber, but none progressed beyond plans or small models.

His next full-sized experimental design to reach construction and testing was the more substantial two-man BICh-7 which undertook its first flight in 1929. BICh-7 had a wingspan of 40ft (12.2m), a length of 15ft 5in (4.74m) and a wing area of 323ft² (30m²). Power was provided by a 100hp (74.5kW) Bristol Lucifer three-cylinder air-cooled radial engine driving a forward mounted two-blade propeller. BICh-7 was fitted with two tandem open cockpits and a rather unsatisfactory undercarriage that consisted of a central wheel and wingtip skids. With a gross weight of about 1,907 lb (865kg), this allowed a maximum speed in the region of 100mph (160kph) and a landing speed of 43mph (70kph). There was no tailfin, but rudders were fitted to the wingtips. Exactly how many test flights were undertaken is uncertain, but it quickly became apparent that BICh-7 was very difficult to fly and dangerous to land, leading Cheranovsky to extensively modify the design.

This resulted in the BICh-7A being fitted with a conventional fixed-position undercarriage and a re-designed fully-enclosed cockpit that trailed into the tailfin. Cheranovsky was now heavily involved with other projects, so the work progressed slowly. These other projects included two small gliders (BICh-8 and BICh-11) with the BICh-11 being intended for trials with a small rocket engine.

It appears these experiments were cancelled on the grounds of safety and BICh-11 may have flown with a small piston engine driving a rear mounted pusher propeller.

Work on BICh-7A was finally completed in early 1932 and the reconfigured aircraft made its first flight soon afterwards with N.A. Blagin undertaking all the initial tests. Despite some problems with engine vibration, the BICh-7A was a considerable improvement over its predecessor, but the aircraft remained something of an experimental curiosity and Cheranovsky returned to the drawing board to continue with development of his parabolic designs. This led to the twin engine BICh-14 which was designed as a light utility aircraft.

As another State-sponsored project, the BICh-14 was produced at the Menzhinsky Factory. Most of the airframe was built from wood or aluminium alloy and the aircraft was covered with fabric. Powered by two M-11 100hp (74.5kW) piston engines, the BICh-14 had a wingspan of 53ft 2in (16.2m), a wing area of 646ft² (60m²) and an overall length of 19ft 8in (6m). With the provision for five seats, BICh-14 had a maximum take-off weight of 4,188 lb (1,900kg), allowing a maximum speed of 136mph (220kph) and a useful landing speed of 43mph (70kph). BICh-14 flew for the first time in 1934, but it was not a success and like the earlier Cheranovsky aircraft, it lacked stability and suffered with various aerodynamic shortcomings. BICh-14 continued to fly until 1937 when it was finally scrapped.

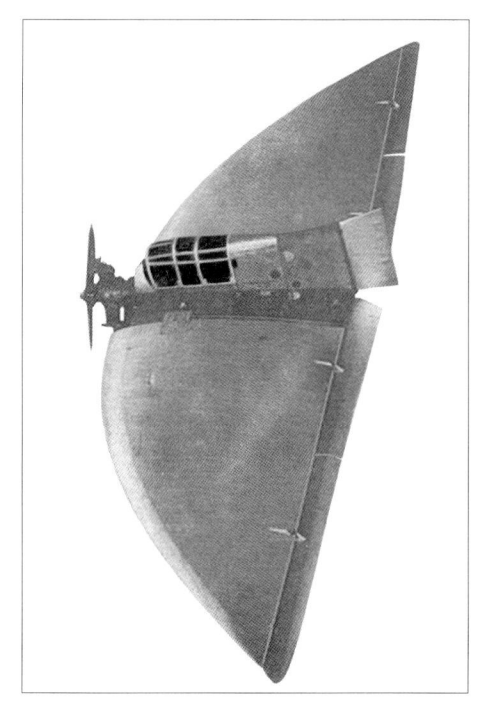

In early 1935, Cheranovsky was sent to work for Leonid. V. Kurchevsky who ran the Special Tasks Collective. Kurchevsky had designed a series of recoilless guns and it was now planned to build a new fighter aircraft that could carry two specially designed large calibre APK cannons. Cheranovsky proposed an improved version of the BICh-7A with the cannons mounted in the wings. There is some confusion about these cannons which are usually described as being of a recoilless design with an 80mm calibre. Research suggests this weapon may have been a modified version of the APK 76.2mm recoilless cannon using a reloading system operated by compressed air and fed from a magazine carrying 5 or 6 rounds. Whatever the exact specification, it seems this weapon was not a great

Various problems with the BICh-7 led Cheranovsky to extensively modify the design leading to a re-designation of this aircraft as the BICh-7A. Bill Rose Collection

Soviet Tailless Designs

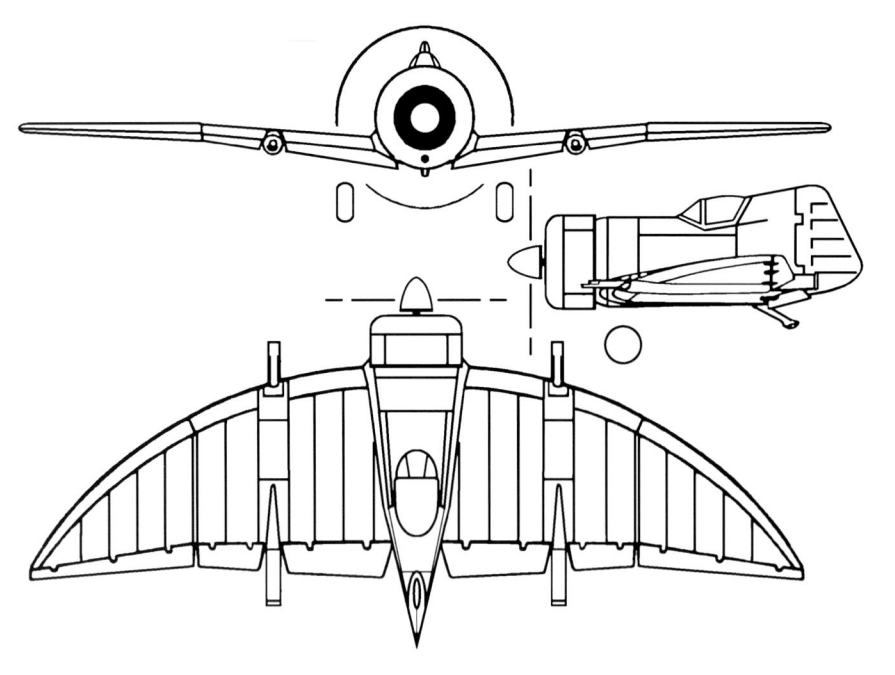

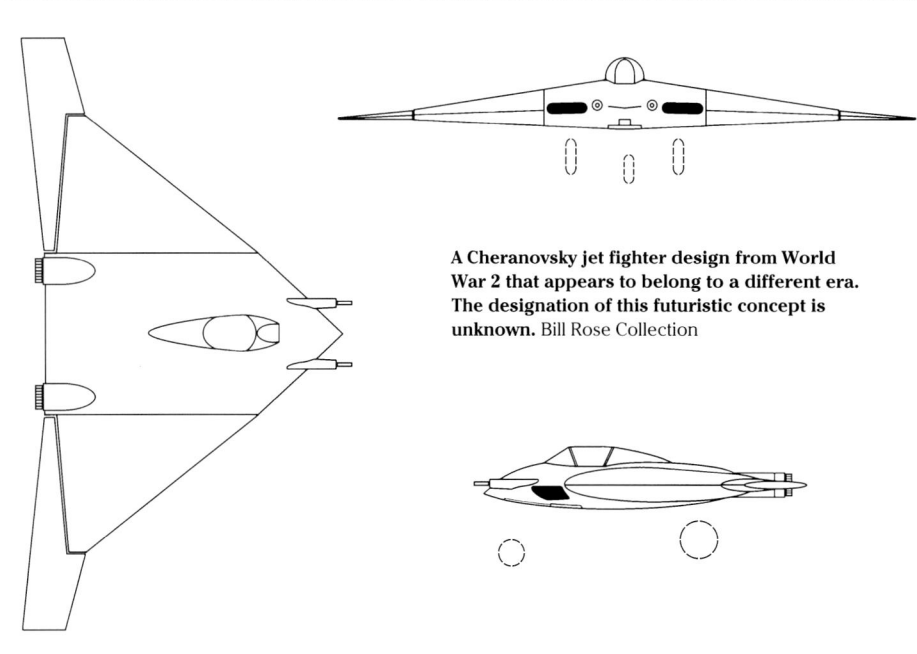

Left: **The tailless BICh-17 fighter was specifically designed to carry two large-calibre recoilless APK cannons. A prototype of this aircraft was about 60 per cent complete by February 1936 when the project was scrapped on Stalin's direct orders.** Bill Rose Collection

Middle: **A small model of the BICh-17 fighter, equipped with large calibre APK recoilless cannons. This mid-1930s project was never completed.** Bill Rose Collection

BICh-3

Crew	1
Wingspan	31ft 2in (9.5m)
Wing area	215ft² (20m²)
Length	11ft 6in (3.5m)
Empty weight	309 lb (140kg)
Loaded weight	507 lb (230kg)
Powerplant	1 x Blackburn-Tomtit 18hp (13.4kW) piston engine
Maximum speed	85mph (137kph) approx
Landing speed	24mph (40kph)

BICh-7A

Crew	2
Wingspan	40ft (12.2m)
Wing area	323ft² (30m²)
Length	15ft 5in (4.74m)
Empty weight	1,382 lb (627kg)
Loaded weight	1,940 lb (880kg)
Powerplant	1 x Bristol-Lucifer 100hp (74.5kW) piston engine
Maximum speed	102mph (165kph)
Landing speed	43mph (70kph)

BICh-17

Wingspan	40ft (12.2m)
Wing area	Unknown
Length	16ft 5in (5m)
Powerplant	1 x M-22 480hp (357kW) piston engine
Armament	2 x APK recoilless cannons (probably 76.2mm)

BICH-26

Crew	1
Wingspan	23ft (7m)
Wing area	291ft² (27m²)
Length	29ft 7in (9m)
Gross weight	9,921 lb (4,500kg)
Powerplant	1 x Mikulin AM-5 turbojet producing 4,409 lb (19.6kN) static thrust
Maximum speed	Mach 1.7 at 23,000ft (7,000m) estimated
Ceiling	72,000ft (22,000m) estimated
Armament	Unspecified, probably forward fuselage mounted cannons

A Cheranovsky jet fighter design from World War 2 that appears to belong to a different era. The designation of this futuristic concept is unknown. Bill Rose Collection

A small wind tunnel model of the BICh-24 jet fighter. Looking rather like the Douglas F-4D Skyray, it remains uncertain if this design progressed to the hardware stage, although the aircraft was expected to appear in public during 1949. Bill Rose Collection

The advanced BICh-26 (Che-26) jet fighter appears to have been based on the BICh-24 and was expected to have a supersonic and high altitude capability, which appears rather optimistic bearing in mind the engine technology of that era.
Bill Rose Collection

success and there were serious problems with the reliability of the loading system. However, the Cheranovsky fighter was approved for construction by mid-1935 and assigned the reference BICh-17. The new aircraft had a wingspan of 40ft (12.2m) and a length of 16ft 5in (5m). Power was provided by an M-22 engine rated at 480hp (358kW). The airframe was mainly constructed from wood and fitted with a fully-retractable undercarriage. By February 1936, about 60 per cent of the BICH-17 had been completed when Kurchevsky's operation was disbanded on the direct orders of Stalin and the fighter project was scrapped.

Boris Cheranovsky continued to design unconventional aircraft, leading to the BICh-21. This was an advanced, very sleek tailless design that was built by 1940 and flew for the first time in June 1941. It was planned to enter BiCH-21 for the All-Union Air Race scheduled for August 1941, but the event was cancelled due to the war. Little is known of Cheranovsky's wartime activities, although a remarkable design was unearthed by Yefim Gordon and Bill Gunston while researching the book *Soviet X-Planes* (Midland Counties, 2005).

The reference for this design is unknown, but it dates from 1944 and shows a surprisingly futuristic jet fighter, looking rather like the cancelled A-12 Avenger II stealth attack aircraft which was developed during the late 1980s. Cheranovsky's small, one-man fighter was to be powered by two turbojets buried in the wings with leading edge air intakes. It has been suggested that the intended jet engine may have been the Lyul'ka VRD-2 design which was under development at the time. Almost triangular with no upright stabiliser, the jet fighter used two large elevons for flight control and was equipped with a tricycle undercarriage. Two cannons were positioned on each side of the cockpit with the barrels protruding beyond the leading edge. No specifications for this little-known design are thought to exist.

After World War 2 ended, Cheranovsky continued to work on proposals for jet fighters with the BICh-24, also referred to as the Che-24. Looking rather like the Douglas F-4D Skyray, this design was expected to appear in public during 1949.

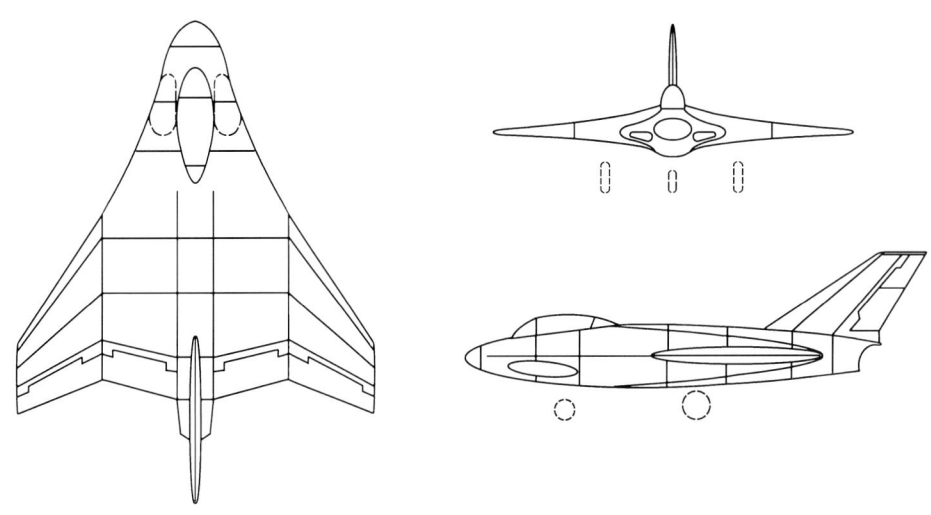

An image showing a wind tunnel model does not reveal the position of air intakes for a jet engine. Conceivably, a prototype was built, but there is no documentation to support this. The BICh-25 (Che-25) is understood to have been a variable-geometry concept and Cheranovsky followed this with a supersonic fighter design in 1948, bearing the reference BICh-26 (Che-26) and clearly a development of the BICh-24. The airframe and skin would be built almost entirely from lightweight alloy and steel with a wingspan of 23ft (7m), a wing area of 291ft² (27m²) and a length of 29ft 7in (9m). The gross weight was set at 9,921 lb (4,500kg) with control surfaces on the trailing edge of the wing and a swept tailfin with a rudder. A tricycle undercarriage would support the BICh-26 on the ground. The forward pressurised cockpit was flanked by contoured engine intakes which supplied air to the single Mikulin AM-5 turbojet rated at 4,409 lb (44kN) static thrust. It was claimed that this aircraft could attain a maximum speed of Mach 1.7 at 23,000ft (7,000m) and reach an altitude of 72,000ft (21,945m). This appears to be rather wishful thinking! No details of armaments are quoted, but cannons located towards the nose of the aircraft would seem probable.

BICh-26 was never built and it is believed to be Cheranovsky's last major design. He is understood to have retired soon after completing work on this proposal, suffering with poor health. Cheranovsky died in Moscow during 1960.

Soviet Tailless Designs

Kalinin's Flying Wing Bomber

Konstantin Alekseyevich Kalinin (1889-1940) was a Soviet engineer responsible for a number of interesting civil and military aircraft designs during the interwar period. He began his career in 1916 as a military pilot and following several years in service, he attended the Moscow Air Force Engineering Academy. An exceptional student, Kalinin was put in charge of an OKB during 1926 which was primarily responsible for developing civil aircraft.

In 1933, Kalinin produced plans for a new bomber that might also have potential as a civil aircraft. He submitted three different proposals to the NII-VSS (Scientific Test Institute) which were a conventional monoplane, a twin boom design and a tailless aircraft. The tailless design was accepted on the grounds of lower drag and reduced weight with Kalinin receiving approval to develop a prototype that was given the reference K-12. Initially, there were wind tunnel tests with models and it was then decided to build a half-sized manned glider with a wingspan of 29ft 6in (9.0m) and a length of 17ft (5.2m). The aircraft was equipped with a fixed undercarriage comprising of two main wheels and a tailskid. Slats and ailerons were fitted to the trailing edge with wingtip stabilisers and rudders. Construction was mainly from wood with a fabric covering. It appears that sufficient space existed behind the pilot to accommodate an observer, although no records confirm this. Following completion of the K-12 glider in 1934, the test pilot V.O. Borisov made more than 100 flights.

During 1935, work began on a full-sized K-12 prototype at GAZ State Aviation Factory No 18 at Voronezh, with the first test-flight taking place in July 1936 with Borisov at the controls. 46 flights were completed and the aircraft was then flown to Moscow in October 1936 for further trials that were undertaken by the NII's test pilot P. Stefanovsky. The K-12 prototype had a wingspan of 59ft (18m), a wing area of 783ft² (72.75m²) and an overall length of 26ft 3in (8m). There was provision for three crew members and positions for forward and rear manually-operated defensive machine guns, although no weapons were installed on the prototype. It was intended to

This photograph shows the Kalinin K-12 glider under construction in 1934. The glider was used in the development of the much larger K-12 tailless bomber. Bill Rose Collection

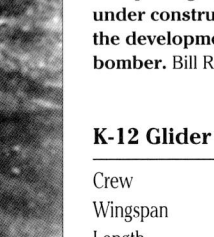

The Kalinin K-12 glider. Bill Rose Collection

K-12 Glider

Crew	1 (possible space for an observer)
Wingspan	29ft 6in (9.0m)
Length	17ft (5.2m)
Weight	Unknown

K-12

Crew	3
Wingspan	59ft (18m)
Wing area	783ft² (72.75m²)
Length	26ft 3in (8m)
Empty weight	6,768 lb (3,070kg)
Loaded weight	9,259 lb (4,200kg)
Powerplant	2 x M-22 (licence-built Bristol Jupiter) 9-cylinder radial piston engines each rated at 435hp (324kW) continuous power
Maximum speed	149mph (240kph) at 9,840ft (3,000m)
Ceiling	23,524ft (7,170m)
Range	435 miles (700km)
Take-off run	2,297ft (700m)
Landing run	984ft (300m)
Armament (production aircraft)	

2 x 7.62mm ShKAS machine guns in nose and in tail turrets. 1,102 lb (500kg) bomb load in a vertical rack

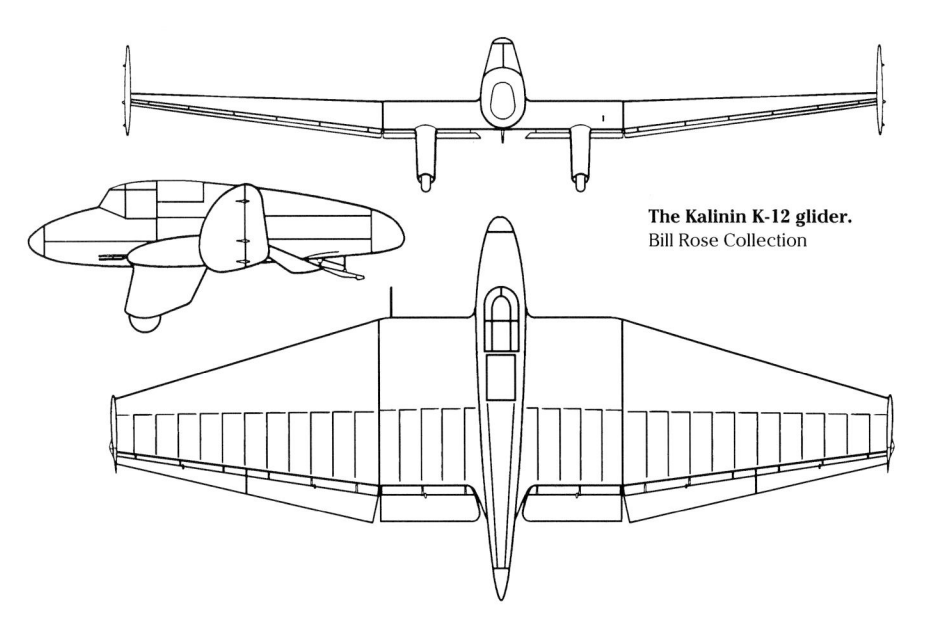

Painted in spectacular markings, the K-12 appeared at the Tushino Air Day Parade in August 1937. Bill Rose Collection

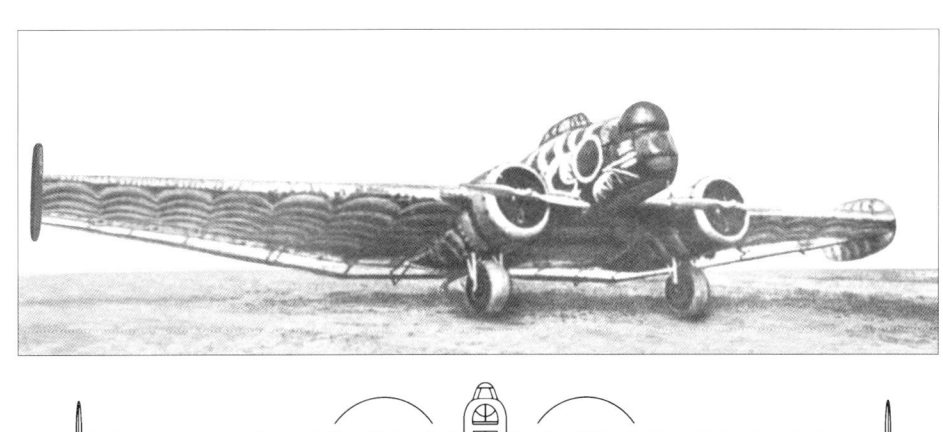

power the K-12 with M-25 engines driving variable pitch propellers, but these were not available, so M-22 (licence-built Bristol Jupiter) nine-cylinder radial piston engines were fitted rated at 435hp (324kW) continuous power, driving two-blade propellers. Because these engines were judged to be inadequate for the task, extensive weight-saving alterations were made to the undercarriage resulting in the proposed electrically powered retractable main wheels being fixed in position.

As a result, the take-off weight was lowered to 9,259 lb (4,200kg) which allowed a maximum speed of 149mph (240kph), a ceiling of 23,524ft (7,170m) and a range of 435 miles (700km). Much of the airframe was fabricated from welded Chromansil steel tubing which was covered by fabric. Kalinin hoped this aircraft would pave the way to an improved all-metal variant called the K-14 and a larger four-engine long-range tailless bomber with the reference K-17. Kalinin had made a number of enemies in high places who managed to delay the K-12 project and tried to have it scrapped. The situation finally changed when K-12 was flown at the August 1937 Tushino Air Day Parade having been repainted in bright high-profile colours. The aircraft made an immediate impression on senior officials who ordered a resumption of testing in early 1938 and requested preparation for production as a light-bomber.

Nevertheless, Kalinin was arrested by the secret police on trumped-up charges of spying. The 10 pre-production K-12s being assembled were scrapped and his design bureau was disbanded. In 1940, Kalinin was executed on orders issued by Stalin, although finally pardoned during the 1950s after Stalin's death. As an aircraft, the K-12 was far from perfect with some reports indicating that it was often difficult to fly and suffered with various problems associated with tailless designs.

Putilov's Attack Aircraft

In the early 1930s, several Moscow-based engineers and designers formed a small group to study steel airframes. Known as OOS (Russian abbreviation for Experimental Aeroplane Construction Section), the group was headed by Sergei Grigoryevich Kozlov and Alexander Ivanovich Putilov. They began working on a series of studies for bombers

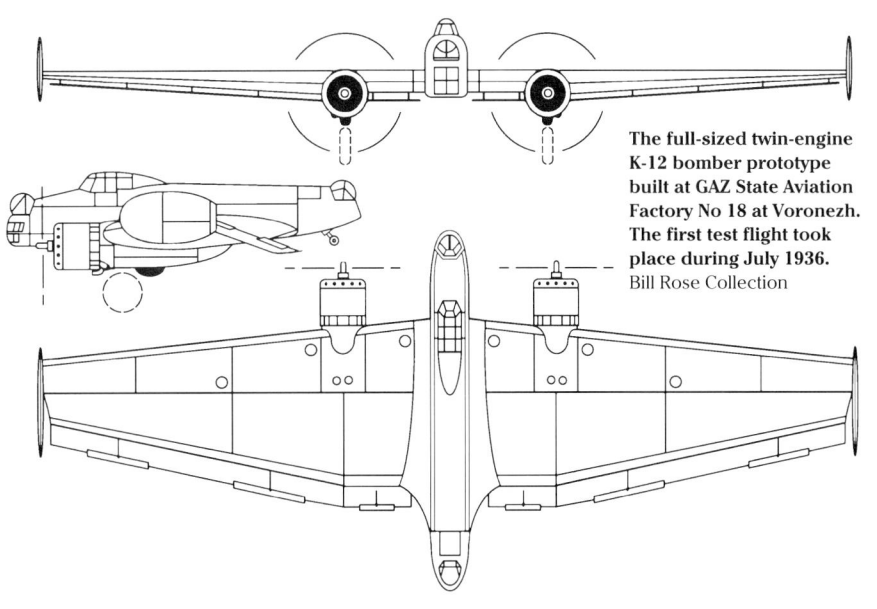

The full-sized twin-engine K-12 bomber prototype built at GAZ State Aviation Factory No 18 at Voronezh. The first test flight took place during July 1936. Bill Rose Collection

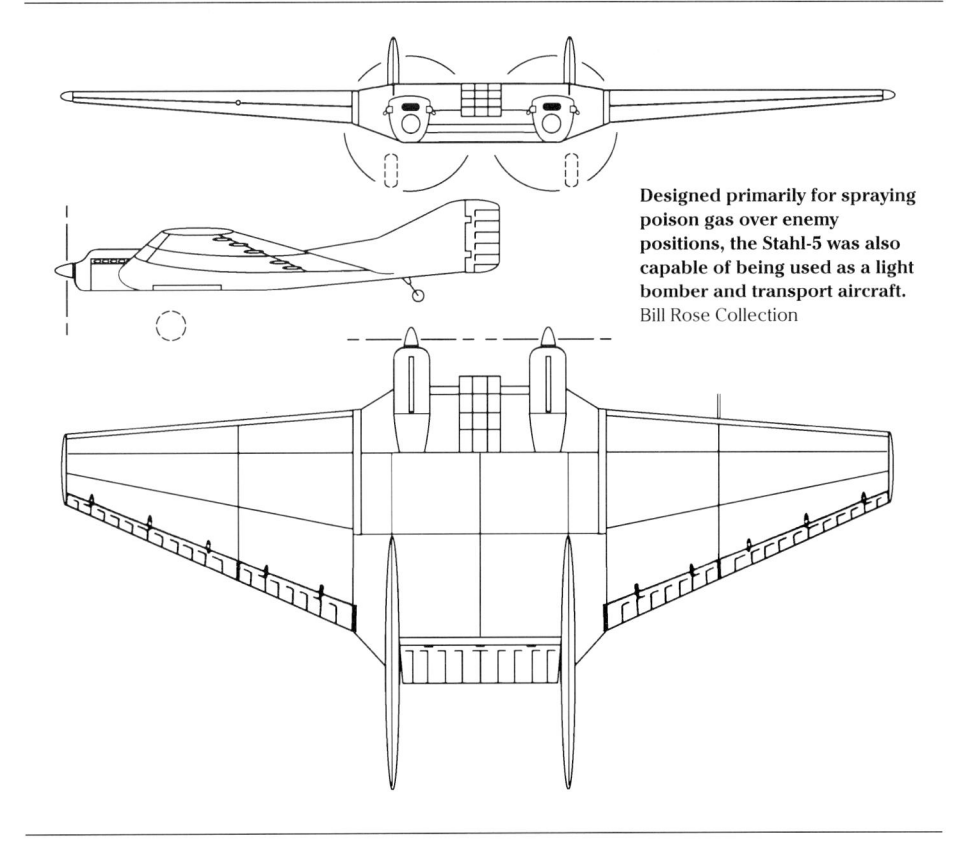

Designed primarily for spraying poison gas over enemy positions, the Stahl-5 was also capable of being used as a light bomber and transport aircraft. Bill Rose Collection

Soviet Tailless Designs

and transport aircraft which all received the reference Stahl (Steel).

The most promising design was the Stahl-5, completed in 1933. Stahl-5 was a tailless, transport aircraft or light bomber, also capable of spraying poison gas. This was a twin-engine aircraft with a thick central wing section and a flush cockpit canopy positioned at the leading edge. The wingspan was to be 75ft 5in (23m) with a wing area of 1,292ft² (120m²) and an overall length of 41ft (12.5m). A retractable undercarriage would be fitted and propulsion took the form of two M-34F V-12 water-cooled engines, each rated at 750hp (559kW) driving three-blade, forward-mounted propellers. The airframe would be built almost entirely from Enerzh-6 stainless steel, with a Bakelite bonded veneer used to cover the central section and fabric in other parts. The wing was equipped with slotted flaps and a central aileron, plus two substantial stabilising fins with rudders that extended behind the trailing edge. In 1934, an experimental wing spar was completed and used for static testing, while a small proof-of-concept Stahl-5 demonstrator was built and flown in 1935. This small tailless aircraft had a span of 19ft 7in (6m) and was powered by two nine-cylinder Salmson 9ADB radial engines, each producing 45hp (33.5kW). It is not clear if this was an unmanned vehicle or flown by a pilot, but it proved extremely difficult to control and the idea of building a full-sized prototype was finally dropped.

Belyaev's Db-LK

Victor Nikolaevich Belyaev (1896-1958) was a talented Russian aviation designer who evolved ideas for a bat-wing aircraft during the 1920s and early 1930s. He believed that a flying wing designed with a small degree of forward sweep and a slightly curved back would help to overcome longitudinal stability problems and provide a noticeable reduction of induced drag.

In 1933, some of Belyaev's theoretical work was proven with trials of his BP-2 glider which was towed from the Crimean resort of Koktebel (much favoured for early glider trials) to Moscow. The following year, he entered the Avianito Competition for a new transport aircraft submitting plans for an unusual twin-fuselage aircraft capable of carrying 10 passengers. The entry was unsuccessful, but Belyaev progressively refined his design with the emphasis shifting towards a military role. Belyaev now regarded his concept as a flying wing, although in the strictest sense it wasn't this, or even a tailless aircraft. In early 1938, Belyaev submitted plans for his bomber to TsAGI (Central Aerohydrodynamic Institute – Russia's equivalent to NACA/NASA) at Zhukovsky, Moscow. The aircraft was now called the DB-LK (meaning long-range flying wing bomber in Russian) and it won favour with senior officials who informally approved the assembly of a mock-up and construction of a prototype.

The DB-LK project was assigned the rather non-descript reference 'Order 350' and it was officially approved in Defence Committee Decree No 248. A wooden mock-up was completed in the same year at Belyaev's KB-4 Design Bureau in Moscow (Aircraft Factory 156) and the prototype was authorised, reaching completion in September 1939. The circular fuselage sections and wing were mainly constructed from aluminium alloy, with fabric covering some external areas. The pilot flew the aircraft from a cockpit in the left fuselage section, which also accommodated a rear-facing gunner. The right fuselage section carried the navigator in a forward-facing cockpit and a rear-facing radio operator who acted as another gunner.

Each fuselage section housed a forward positioned Mikulin KB (later Tumansky) M-87B supercharged 14-cylinder radial engine (based on a Gnome Rhone design) providing 950hp (708kW) and driving a VISh-23D three-blade 10ft 10in (3.3m) propeller. The DB-LK had a wingspan of 70ft 10½in (21.6m), an overall length of 32ft (9.78m) and a height of 11ft 11in (3.65m). Flaps and ailerons were fitted to the wings and there was a central tailfin with a rudder and a tailplane linked to the ailerons.

The aircraft was equipped with retractable main wheels in each fuselage section and a single tail wheel. At the rear of each fuselage section was a completely glazed tail cone with a position for a single ShKAS 7.62mm machine gun. The second crew member in each fuselage section would operate this weapon when necessary and an additional rear firing machine gun was proposed for each wing's inner trailing edge. In addition to the four rearward firing weapons, two ShKAS 7.62mm machine guns controlled by the pilot were positioned between the propellers in the central wing section. There would be 4,500 rounds available for all six guns. A bomb bay was located behind each wheel housing and the possibility of carrying additional bombs under the centre section (or perhaps extra fuel tanks) was considered. It is also

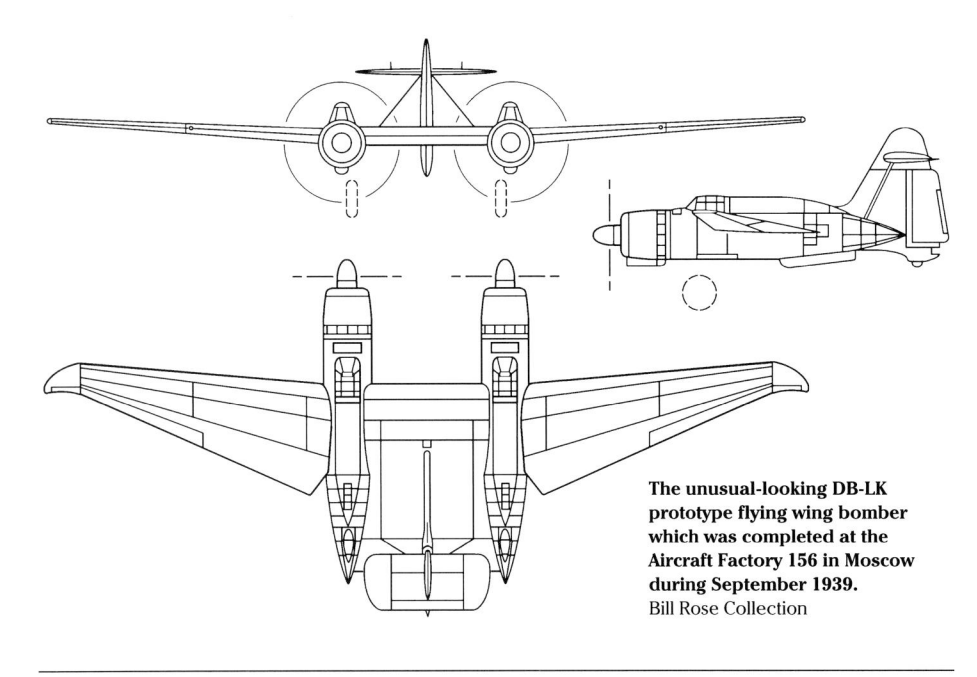

Putilov Stahl-5

Crew	3?
Wingspan	75ft 5in (23m)
Wing area	1,292ft² (120m²)
Length	41ft (12.5m)
Empty weight	12,125 lb (5,500kg)
Gross weight	17,640 lb (8,000kg)
Powerplant	2 x M-34F V-12 water-cooled engines, each rated at 750hp (559kW)
Maximum speed	Unknown
Ceiling	Unknown
Armament	Unspecified bomb load. Could carry tanks holding chemical agents for dispersal during flight.

The unusual-looking DB-LK prototype flying wing bomber which was completed at the Aircraft Factory 156 in Moscow during September 1939.
Bill Rose Collection

During fast taxiing trials of the DB-LK in early 1940, Chief Engineer A. I. Filin ran over a tree stump buried by snow on the edge of an airfield. The aircraft was quite badly damaged, but was repaired and testing resumed. Bill Rose Collection

conceivable that the DB-LK might have been adapted to the reconnaissance role.

The NII-VVS was now given the task of preliminary testing, but there were various difficulties encountered during taxiing trials and finally a bad accident when Chief Engineer A. I. Filin hit a tree stump on the edge of the airfield that was buried by snow. This removed most of the port undercarriage and damaged the propellers beyond repair, although the aircraft itself was repaired and underwent various additional modifications. Testing resumed in 1940 with the DB-LK taking to the air. It is said to have performed well and as a consequence, the aircraft was flown above Red Square during the 1940 May Day Parade.

But there was considerable resistance to the unorthodox design and a number of serious problems began to surface during the continuing trials, such as the rear gun positions being too close to each other. More worrying, were health issues caused by engine exhaust fumes entering the fuselage and apparently, there was no simple solution to this. Test pilots and engineers also complained about poor forward visibility from the cockpits. Belyaev was now working on a revised design powered by two 1,700hp (1,267kW) M-71 piston engines, but the project met with cancellation in late 1940.

BOK-5

BOK (Buro Osovikh Konstruktskii) at Smolensk was an OKB established in 1930 to develop experimental designs and modify aviation equipment for special purposes. Having produced a small research aircraft called BOK-2, the bureau was officially encouraged to begin work on a new design for a compact one-man flying wing called BOK-5.

A team was assembled under the direction of Vladimir Antonovich Chizhevsky and funding for this project was made available in 1935. Design work started almost immediately and swiftly moved to the construction phase. BOK-5 had a span of 32ft 4½in (9.86m) and a length of 14ft 4in (4.365m). A Shvetsov M-11 radial engine was installed which produced 100hp (74.7kW) during cruise, with slightly more available during take off and it was coupled to a two-blade metal propeller. The airframe was mainly built from aluminium alloy, the wing followed the CAHI (TsAGI) 890/15 profile and the fuselage section was described as semi-monocoque in design. Much of the aircraft's skin was fabric and BOK-5 was equipped with a fixed undercarriage comprising two main wheels and a tailskid. When completed, this compact aircraft had an empty weight of 1,314lb (596kg).

BOK-5 was completed at the beginning of 1937, but a number of late modifications were introduced, holding up flight-testing until the

BOK-5

Crew	1
Wingspan	32ft 4½in (9.86m)
Wing area	249ft² (23.15m²)
Length	14ft 4in (4.365m)
Height	Unspecified
Empty weight	1,314lb (596kg)
Gross weight	1,684lb (764kg)
Powerplant	1 x Shvetsov M-11 5-cylinder air-cooled radial engine producing 100hp (74.7kW)
Maximum speed	108mph (174kph)
Landing speed	53mph (85kph)
Ceiling	15,900ft (4,850m)
Range	373 miles (600km)
Endurance	4 hours

DB-LK

Crew	4
Wingspan	70ft 10½in (21.6m)
Wing area	612.14ft² (56.87m²)
Wing sweep	-5° 42' (outer wing leading edge)
Length	32ft (9.78m)
Height	11ft 11in (3.65m)
Empty weight	13,236lb (6,004kg)
Gross weight	23,258lb (10,672kg)
Powerplant	2 x Mikulin (Tumansky) M-87B supercharged 14-cylinder radial engines, each producing 950hp (708kW)
Maximum speed	245mph at sea level, 303mph (488kph) at 17,057ft (5,100m)
Take-off speed	90mph (145kph)
Landing speed	93mph (150kph)
Ceiling	27,890ft (8,500m)
Range	1,800 miles (2,900km), reduced to 789 miles (1,269km) fully laden
Armament	6 x defensive 7.62mm machine guns. 4,409lb (2,000kg) of bombs

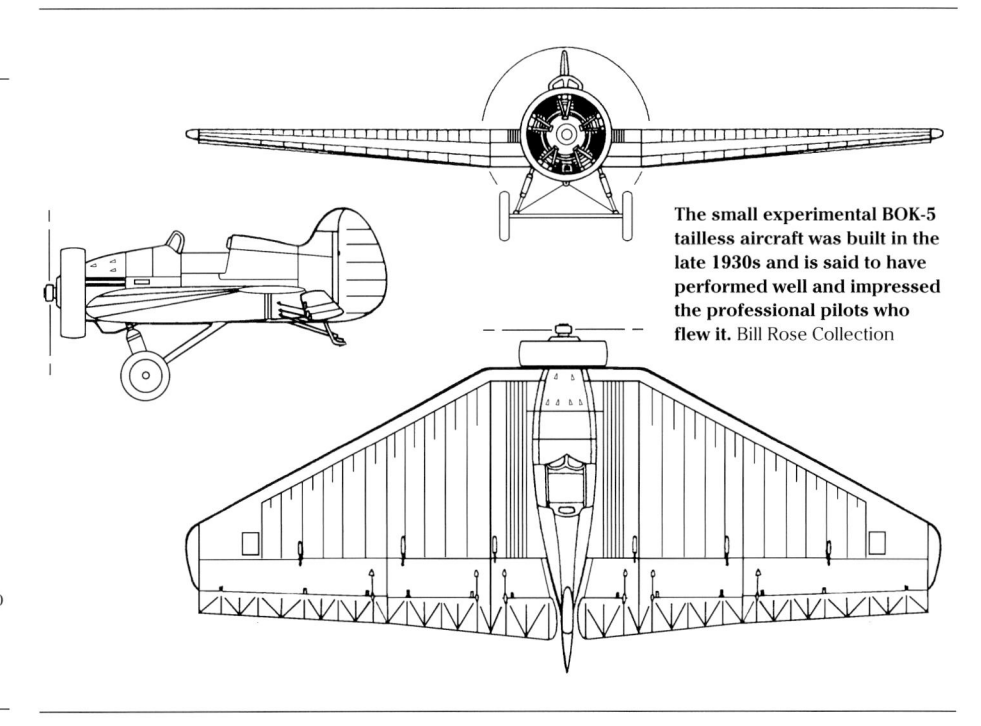

The small experimental BOK-5 tailless aircraft was built in the late 1930s and is said to have performed well and impressed the professional pilots who flew it. Bill Rose Collection

Soviet Tailless Designs

autumn. Test pilot I.F. Petrov was at the controls for the first flight, although he made a hard landing on his return and BOK-5 was damaged. Repairs and further modifications lasted for the remainder of the year and the BOK-5's handling characteristics were considerably improved. One of these changes may have been to the three control surfaces on each wing. In mid-1938, testing was undertaken by pilots from NII-VVS, one of whom, P.M. Stefanovkii, is said to have remarked that BOK-5 was very easy to fly. There were suggestions that experience gained from the BOK-5 could be used to build a new long-range tailless bomber and a prototype was provisionally pencilled in as BOK-6. But the proposal went no further and in 1940, BOK was absorbed by the Sukhoi OKB.

Russia's First Flying Wing Jet Bomber Proposal

Igor Vyacheslavovich Chetverikov (1909-1987) was officially requested to commence design work on a jet-powered, twin-engine light bomber in May 1947. His design bureau normally specialised in flying boats and it is unclear why the Chetverikov OKB was chosen to undertake this project. It has been suggested that the bureau was short of work and Chetverikov had been allocated several German engineers with knowledge of Arado jet aircraft, but this explanation may be speculative.

Work on an engineering study of the proposed bomber was soon underway with a tailless, swept wing considered the best option. The aircraft was assigned the codename RK-1 and it was agreed that a mock-up would be completed by the following year and a prototype completed before the end of 1948.

Details of this project have proved difficult to locate, but available documents show that the RK-1 would have been flown by a crew of three and carried a maximum bomb load of 4,409 lb (2,000kg) in a centrally-located bay. It was also intended to position two manually-operated 7.62mm machine guns in the aircraft's tail for defensive purposes. Propulsion would be provided by two Klimov RD-45 turbojets, each producing about 5,000 lb (22.24kN) of static thrust. These were reverse-engineered copies of the Rolls-Royce Nene centrifugal engine manufactured in Russia without UK approval.

Dimensions of the RK-1 are not available, but comparisons with the British twin-engine Canberra bomber (initially tested with the Nene engines before adoption of the Avon) and the Ilyushin Il-28 allow for some very rough estimates. Wingspan of the proposed RK1 was about 60-70ft (18-21m), suggesting an overall length of approximately 40-45ft (12-13m). It is also fair to assume that the designers were aiming at a maximum speed of at least 500mph (800kph), but these figures are little more than guesses. A fin and rudder would be mounted at each wingtip and control surfaces were positioned along the trailing edge of each wing. Lightweight alloy would be used for most of the airframe and the aircraft was equipped with a fully-retractable tricycle undercarriage. The forward-positioned, fully-pressurised cockpit would have provided good visibility and this part of the design seems to have been adopted from the wartime Arado Blitz jet bomber.

It is not clear how far the RK1 project progressed. Wind tunnel models were tested and a mock-up is believed to have been built, but the RK1 was formally cancelled in 1948. Soon after this, Chetverikov's OKB was shut down and he accepted a teaching post in Leningrad.

RK1

Crew	3
Wingspan	60-70ft (18-21m) estimate
Length	40-45ft (12-13m) estimate
Gross weight	Unknown
Powerplant	2 x Klimov RD-45 turbojets (unauthorised Rolls-Royce Nene copies), each produced about 5,000 lb (22.24kN) of static thrust
Maximum speed	+500mph (+800kph) estimate
Ceiling	40,000ft (12,192m) estimate
Range	Unknown
Armament	4,409 lb (2,000kg) bomb load. 2 x 7.62mm machine guns in tail

Antonov M (Masha) Jet Fighter

The name Oleg Constantinovich Antonov (1906-1984) is generally associated with transport aircraft and not fighters, although during World War 2, Antonov was Yakovlev's deputy and made numerous contributions to the evolution of Yak fighters.

On 6 March 1946, Antonov took control of his own OKB (153) at Novosibirsk for the development of civil aircraft, but towards the end of the year, there was insufficient work for his design team, so Antonov began to consider the possibility of building a new jet fighter. He had been impressed by the German Heinkel He 162A Salamander, praising the designer's straightforward, cost-effective approach. This led Antonov to produce the basic outline for a fighter that would be powered by a single RD-10 turbojet (Soviet copy of the Junkers Jumo 004B) mounted in a dorsal position. He regarded this as a good configuration that avoided the ingestion of debris when operating from poor sites. But Antonov is known to have expressed concerns about the quality of Russian engines which were no more reliable than the German originals and also lacked power. In early 1947, he received official approval for the project and tests were soon underway with wind tunnel models. By April, Antonov had been instructed to halt the programme and begin work on a flying wing design powered by two RD-10 turbojets.

Antonov now created the outline of an entirely new aircraft which was given the name Masha, usually abbreviated to 'M'. Chief designers for this new project were A.A. Batumov and V.A. Dominikoviskiy, with I.I. Yegorychev being assigned responsibility for tooling and construction. Work continued throughout 1947 on the fighter, which was

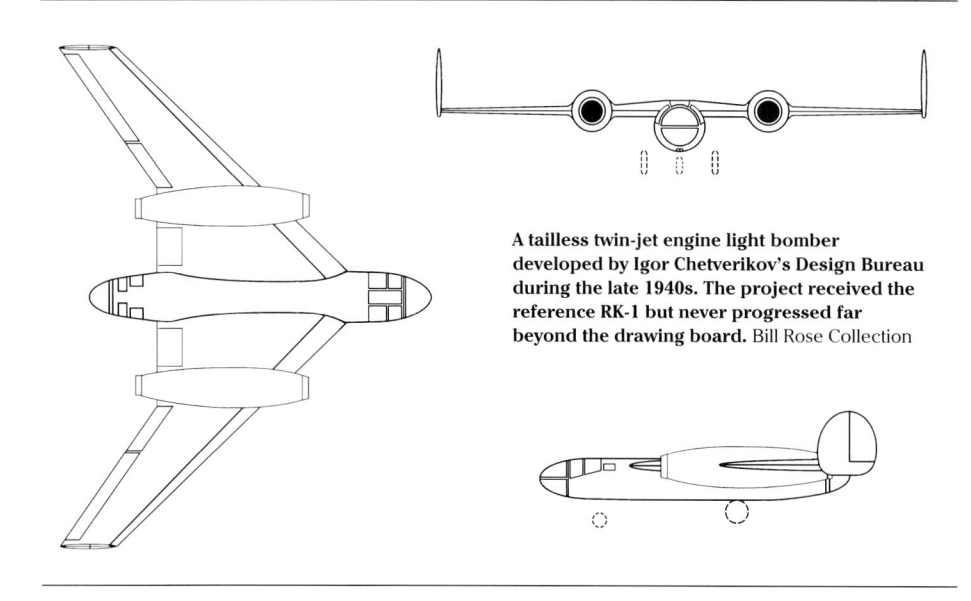

A tailless twin-jet engine light bomber developed by Igor Chetverikov's Design Bureau during the late 1940s. The project received the reference RK-1 but never progressed far beyond the drawing board. Bill Rose Collection

highly classified, like every other Soviet military programme undertaken during the Cold War era. The design was somewhat unusual in appearance, using two upright wing-mounted stabilisers with rudders and forward swept wingtip ailerons. A fully-retractable tricycle undercarriage was fitted with intakes for the engines on each side of the cockpit. Proposed armament was four cannons located in the nose and below the cockpit.

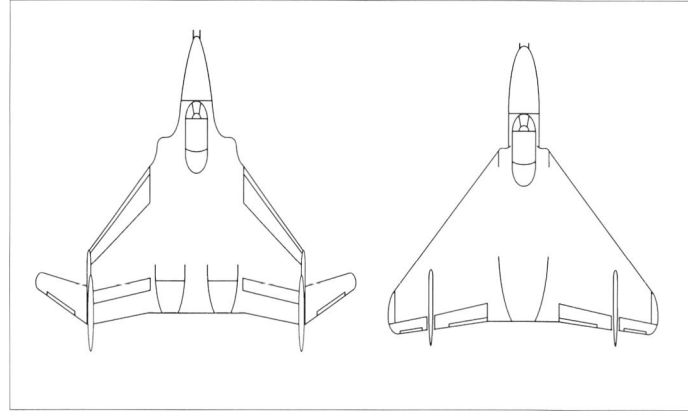

In late 1947, Project M was officially halted and Antonov received instructions to redesign the aircraft so it would accept the new RD-45 engine. The RD-45 was superior in all respects to the earlier engines, although it was a centrifugal design with a larger diameter, so the aircraft required extensive revision apart from the forward section. This resulted in a broader fuselage with engine intakes at the leading edge of the wing roots. Two upright stabilising fins with rudders were fitted, but the outer section of the wing was now rounded with control surfaces on the trailing edge of the wing. The wingspan was reduced to just over 30ft (9.1m) and the length was almost the same as the earlier design at 34ft 10⅝in (10.64m). Armament also remained the same as the 1947 version, along the undercarriage gear, although the rear wheels were positioned slightly differently. It is assumed that the cockpit was pressurised and an ejector seat was fitted although this is not mentioned in any surviving Russian documentation.

The next stage in development of the revised Masha was wind tunnel testing at TsAGI and once this was successfully concluded, the construction of a full-sized mock-up that could also be flown as a glider was approved.

Given the reference E-153, the mock-up was built mainly from wood and equipped with jettisonable wheels for take-off and a skid for landing. Having been shown to officials in spring 1948, it was then prepared for trials as a towed glider. Test pilot Mark L. Gallai was ready to undertake the first flight of E-153 in July 1948, but the fighter project was unexpectedly cancelled. It is believed that a jet-powered prototype of the 'M' had now reached an advanced stage of construction, but this remains unclear.

Apparently, it was decided at a high-level that the La-15, MiG-15 and Yak-23 were sufficient for the country's immediate needs and any new combat aircraft would have to show a significant improvement over these designs. Subsequently, the Masha and a number of other programmes were terminated. Antonov is known to have been disappointed by this decision and considered the Masha well suited to future upgrades such as improved engines and radar equipment. In 1953, he designed another flying wing fighter powered by AL-7F turbojets, but this never progressed beyond the concept stage and Antonov's fighters were soon completely forgotten about.

Antonov 'M' Masha

Crew	1
Wingspan (1947)	35ft 5in (10.8m)
Wingspan (1948)	30ft 6⅜in (9.3m)
Length (1947)	34ft 9¼in (10.6m)
Length (1948)	34ft 10⅝in (10.64m)
Empty/gross weight	Unknown
Powerplant	1 x Klimov RD-45 turbojet (unauthorised Rolls-Royce Nene copies), produced about 5,000 lb (22.24kN) of static thrust
Maximum speed	Unknown
Armament (both versions)	2 x 23mm Volkov-Yartsev VYa-23 + 2 x 20mm Berezin B-20 cannons

Top left: **This artwork shows an early configuration for the proposed twin-engine Antonov 'Masha' jet fighter.** Bill Rose Collection

Top right: **These drawings show the initial layout for the Antonov 'Masha' jet fighter (left) and the final configuration (right).** Bill Rose Collection

Bottom left: **An illustration of the Antonov E-153 glider, built and test flown during the unsuccessful Antonov 'Masha' jet fighter project of the late 1940s.** Bill Rose Collection

Bottom right: **An original Soviet drawing showing the underside of the Antonov 'Masha' jet fighter.** Bill Rose Collection

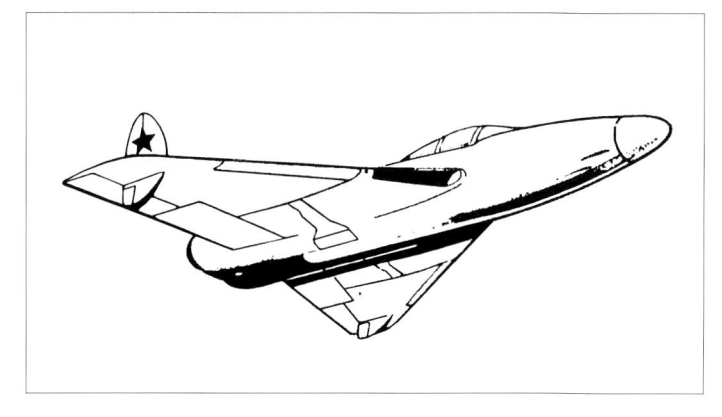

Soviet Tailless Designs

Ilyushin Il-52 Flying Wing Bomber

This interesting design dates from the early 1950s, although relatively little is known about it at present. It was a four-engine long-range jet bomber concept, probably intended to match the capability of a Western aircraft like the Boeing B-47. It would be designed to carrying conventional bombs, probably an early Soviet atomic weapon, or undertake reconnaissance operations. The bomb bay was located at the centre of the aircraft.

The Il-52 would be supported on the ground by a fully-retractable twin-wheel bicycle undercarriage with two outrigger wheels. The proposed wingspan was substantial and lengthy ailerons were proposed, although it has not been possible to find details of any dimensions. Two upright stabilising fins with rudders were located towards the wingtips and underwing pods close to these accommodate the outrigger wheels and might also contain extra fuel. One interesting feature was the remote-control cannons located in pods at the centre of each main wing section to defend the rear. Propulsion would be provided by four turbojet engines located in a cluster towards the tail, with air intakes on each side of the fuselage just behind the cockpit. The type of engine considered for this concept is unknown. Nothing came of the Il-52 and it is probable that this design progressed little further than the drawing board.

Although relatively little is known about this four-engine flying wing bomber at present, the Ilyushin Il-52 was probably designed to be comparable to the US B-47. Bill Rose Collection

DSB-LK Strategic Flying Wing Bomber

In 1957, a project was initiated at the Soviet Mozhaisky Air Force Engineering Academy to produce concepts for an advanced long-range supersonic flying wing bomber. The name of this aircraft was DSB-LK (Dalniy Strategicheskiy Bombardirovshchik – Letayushcheye Krylo – Long Range Strategic Bomber – Flying Wing) and heading the project were the designers Alexander Moskalyov and A. Smirnov. While it might be argued that the DSB-LK is neither a true flying wing or tailless aircraft, it is sufficiently interesting to warrant inclusion in this chapter.

The idea was to develop an operational aircraft as opposed to an experimental prototype and the specifications were very demanding. This was a significant project and it involved several other academies, a number of TsAGI departments and the Myasishchev OKB-23 design bureau. Numerous concepts were studied with the aim of producing a supersonic bomber with intercontinental range that would out-perform all existing Western fighters and fly above the reach of surface-to-air missiles. Initial specifications for the DSB-LK were a requirement to cruise at a speed of Mach 2 and perhaps have a maximum speed of Mach 4 while operating at an altitude of about 114,829ft (35,000m). Estimates for take-off weight were 1,102,290lb (500 metric tons). The DSB-LK would be powered by a number of advanced turbojets or turbo ramjet engines and the aircraft would carry a 33,069lb (15,000kg) nuclear or conventional payload. By mid-1958, the design had been extensively revised. It would be powered by a combination of 6-10 turbojets and ramjets and the airframe would be mainly built from titanium alloy. The maximum take-off weight would be 660,000lb (299 metric tons), allowing a maximum speed of Mach 4.4 and a ceiling of 114,829ft (35,000m). It was also planned to equip the DSB-LK with defensive weapons that included four internally carried air-to-air missiles with a range of 6.3 miles (10km) and two cannons. In addition, there would be electronic countermeasures and the Rubin-1 radar system that was in development at that time. It remains unclear why some of the defensive features were considered necessary, especially the cannons.

It was now agreed that this aircraft was feasible using prevailing or near-term technology and it would be possible to build a prototype. Revisions continued into 1959 and the DSB-LK was beginning to take shape as a viable design. The aircraft would be flown by a crew of three – the pilot, co-pilot and a navigator/electronics operative. DSB-LK now had a wingspan of 123ft 4in (37.6m) and an overall length of 170ft 7in (52m). The cranked wing would have an initial sweep of about 72° and a secondary sweep of 42°. Two large upright swept fins with rudders were located above the engine bays and ailerons were located on the wing's outer trailing edges. A multi-wheeled bicycle undercarriage was planned and the aircraft would be capable of

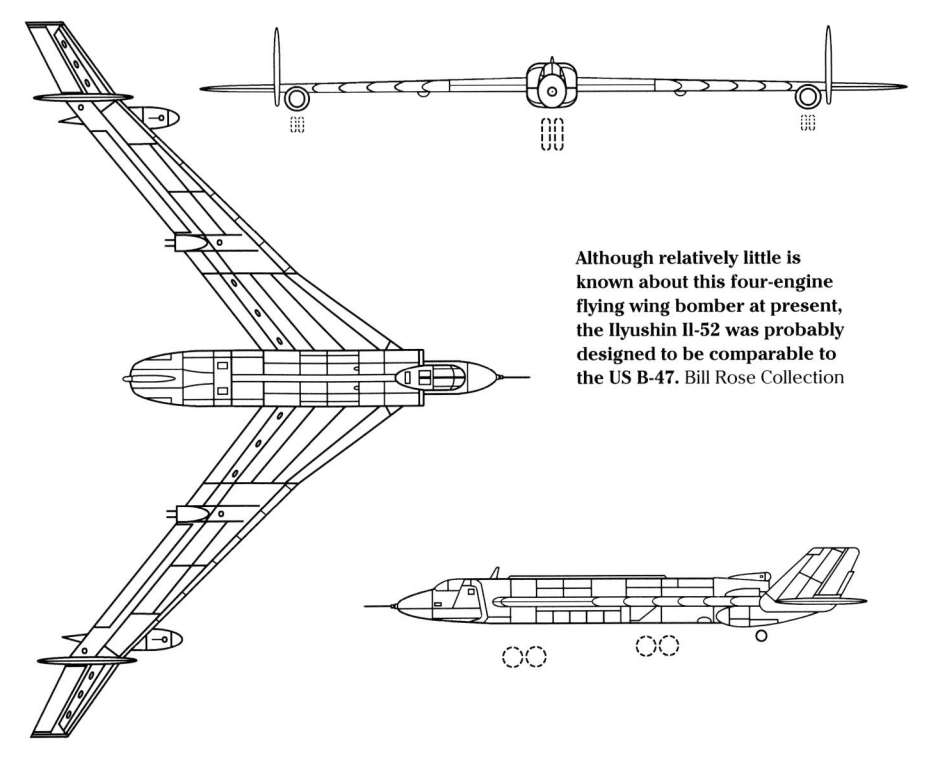

DSB-LK Strategic Flying Wing Bomber

Crew	2-3
Wingspan	123ft 4in (37.6m)
Sweep	Cranked delta wing, swept 72° (approx) inboard and 42° outboard
Length	170ft 7in (52m)
Empty weight	195,109lb (88.5 metric tons)
Max take-off weight	660,000lb (299 metric tons)
Powerplant	6 x TRDF-VK-15M turbojets, generating a total of 34,830lb (155kN) of thrust
Speed	Mach 2.8+
Altitude	114,829ft (35,000m)
Range	10,439 miles (16,800km)
Armament (defensive)	Four air-to-air missiles and two cannons.
Armament (offensive)	Up to 11,023lb (15 metric tons) of free fall conventional and nuclear weapons, or air-to-surface missiles

carrying bombs or air-to-surface missiles. Propulsion would be provided by two sets of three TRDF-VK-15M turbojet engines producing a total thrust of 34,830lb (155kN). This would allow the aircraft to cruise at Mach 2.8 while sustaining a maximum altitude of 114,829ft (35,000m) and the range would be at least 10,000 miles (16,000km). Myasishchev was interesting in fully developing this concept, but there was insufficient funding available to make it a reality due to strategic missiles and the space programme being given priority.

The DSB-LK project was formally concluded in 1960, with research documentation being provided to the Myasishchev, Sukhoi and Tupolev design bureaus. Some of this data is said to have been used in the development of future military aircraft such as the advanced Mach 3.5 variable-geometry delta-winged Sukhoi T-4MS (200) that was designed in the early 1970s but never built and the later Tupolev Tu-160 *Blackjack* supersonic bomber, which remains in Russian Air Force service.

There is little doubt that Soviet engineers could have built the DBS-LK during the early 1960s given sufficient funding, but whether this aircraft would have met the intended requirements is questionable.

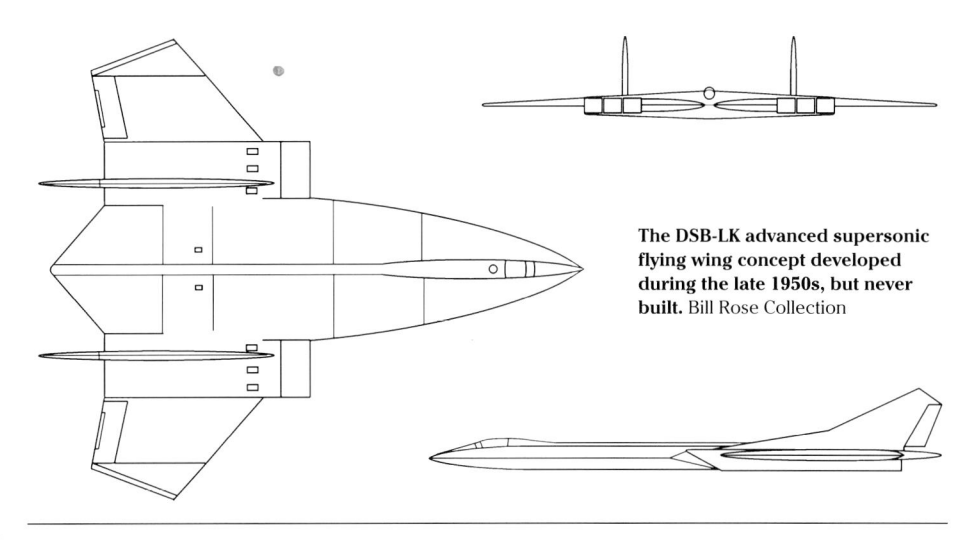

Late Cold War High-Altitude Surveillance/Reconnaissance Projects

East-West relations had reached a very low point when NATO Exercise 'Able Archer 83' began on 2 November 1983. This simulated a major clash with Soviet forces in Europe and while it took place, NATO forces maintained radio silence and only used highly-encrypted communication links. The exercise culminated with a DEFCON 1 alert and the authorisation to use battlefield nuclear weapons. In the lead-up to this exercise, concerns began to develop within the Kremlin that the US planned to use 'Able Archer 83' as cover for a pre-emptive nuclear strike against Russia. Consequently, a decision was taken at the highest level to secretly bring Soviet nuclear forces to full readiness. Tension continued to mount until the exercise concluded on 11 November 1983 and Russia's strategic forces were returned to stand-by. Little was disclosed to the public about this crisis during the remainder of the century and some details remain classified. However, many historians believe it was the closest mankind has come to nuclear war since the Cuban Missile Crisis of 1962.

'Able Archer 83' was clearly a major wake-up call for the Soviet armed forces which found themselves under considerable pressure to improve their intelligence gathering abilities and upgrade early warning systems. One result was a proposal to develop specialised high-altitude aircraft equipped with state-of-the-art passive infrared sensors capable of detecting missile launches and new stealthy high-altitude manned and unmanned spyplanes. This project is thought to have started in 1984 with Myasishchev receiving an urgent request from the Ministry of Defence to initiate a study which was given the reference M-67.

New types of aircraft considered during this programme were high-altitude manned flying wings and various highly sophisticated long-range unmanned aerial vehicles (UAVs). Many aspects of the M-67 project remain secret, but the leading manned design was a large four-engine flying wing called the M-67LK (Cruiser) that was capable of accommodating a crew of 10 to 15 for up to eight hours. Designed with a protruding nose section, presumably housing optical sensors, this aircraft had a huge, although currently undisclosed, wingspan and was fitted with two upright inward angled tailfins with rudders. Intakes for the four jet engines are carefully positioned above the centre of the wing and just like the letterbox exhaust ports they were designed with stealth in mind. A tricycle undercarriage was planned, but drawings do not indicate outrigger wheels that would appear necessary due to the substantial wingspan. Because an aircraft of this nature would be a high-priority target in any surprise attack, considerable attention was paid to reducing the radar cross-section (RCS) and the M-67LK would probably use radar-absorbing materials (RAM) in many areas of its construction.

M-67LK would loiter at altitudes of 66,000-70,000ft (20,000-21,300m) for lengthy periods without detection, providing advanced warn-

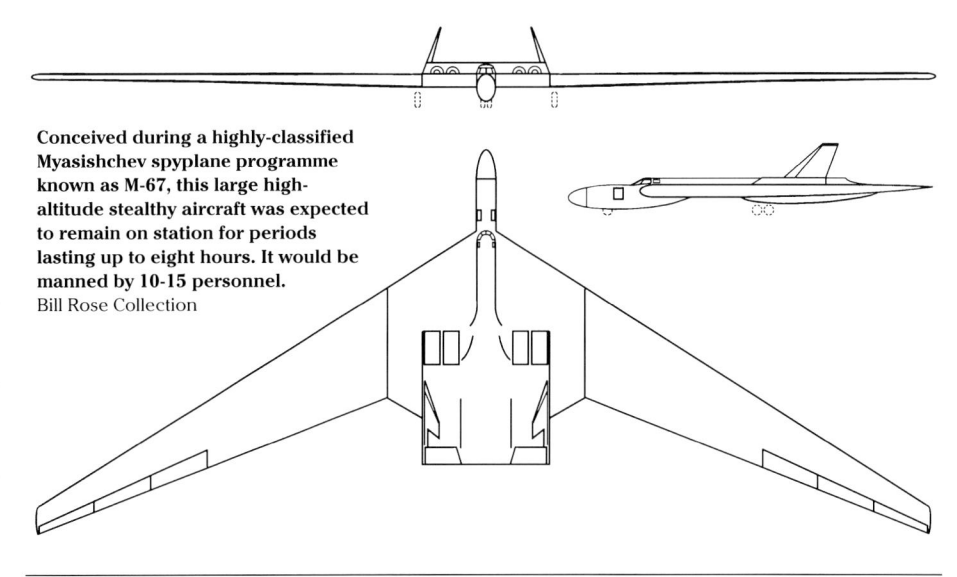

The DSB-LK advanced supersonic flying wing concept developed during the late 1950s, but never built. Bill Rose Collection

Conceived during a highly-classified Myasishchev spyplane programme known as M-67, this large high-altitude stealthy aircraft was expected to remain on station for periods lasting up to eight hours. It would be manned by 10-15 personnel. Bill Rose Collection

Soviet Tailless Designs

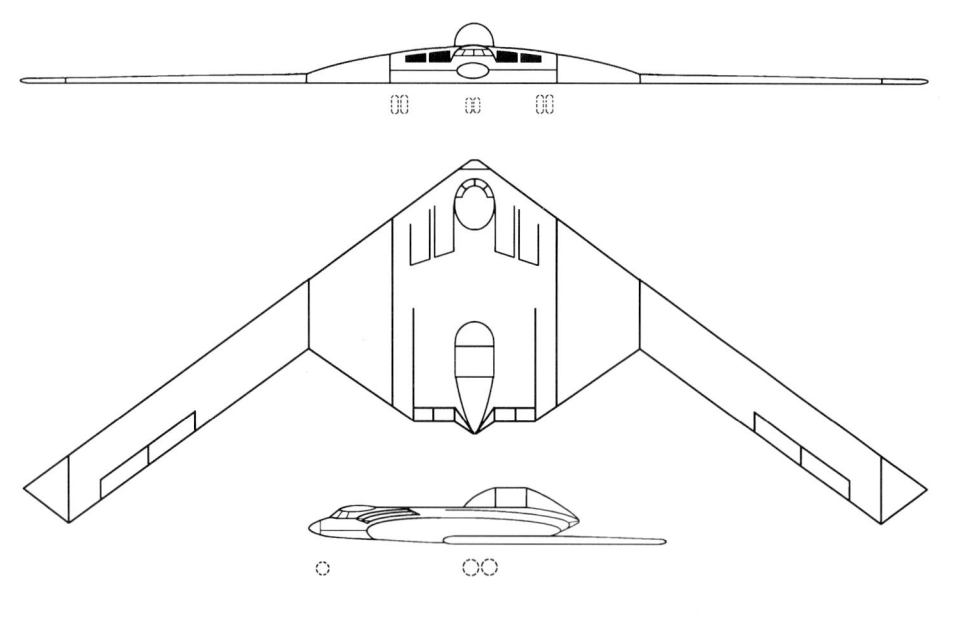

ing of missile launches at times of heightened tension. Equipment carried by the aircraft would have been designed to recognise launches of theatre ballistic missiles such as the newly-introduced super-accurate US Pershing II stationed in West Germany. An ability to detect and track long-range strategic nuclear missiles would also appear to be part of the M-67 project and this aircraft may have been considered for the role.

A second very different Myasishchev manned aircraft bears some resemblance to early proposals for America's ATB (eventually the Northrop B-2A) and also suggests a good awareness of US military developments. The designation of this concept appears to be M-67LK-M and very little is currently known about it. The design is a pure flying wing with no vertical control surfaces. The leading edge sweep is about 36° and the extended wing section had a constant chord with flaps and elevons. Four jet engines power the M-67LK-M and there are stealthy dorsal air intakes behind the cockpit area and carefully designed rectangular exhaust ports.

Dimensions, weights and performance of this aircraft are unknown, although it would employ a multi-wheeled tricycle undercarriage. On the upper rear of the fuselage is a substantial teardrop-shaped pod for unspecified purposes, perhaps containing optical sensors, although the exact role of this aircraft is unclear. It may have been intended to undertake the same missions as the previously described M-67LK Cruiser, or it may have been proposed as a stealthy high-altitude reconnaissance aircraft using passive sensors and linking to a ground station via a secure orbital relay platform. There is also the possibility that the M-67LK-M was derived from a Myasishchev study to match America's B-2A stealth bomber.

Other proposals for M-67 include a fairly conventional looking manned aircraft with a long, straight wing and what appear to be tandem cockpits. Powered by two jet engines, it would carry a large sensor pod above the centre of the wing. This design may be known as the M-67VDS. Two unmanned high-altitude proposals include a single-engine swept-wing aircraft referred to as the M-67 Boomerang carrying side-looking optical equipment in the nose. This UAV could be quite substantial in size and utilises a tricycle undercarriage. The wing has a similar profile to the manned M-67LK-M and in addition to elevons there are small wingtip fins that may be rudders.

A second long wing UAV would perform the same role as the Boomerang, but appears to have been designed from the outset to have a very low radar cross section. Designated as the M-67BVS-LK, this aircraft has a smoothly contoured rounded and flattened nose leading directly to the wings. Above this, is an upper fuselage section containing forward-positioned windows for side-looking optical equipment. A single jet engine contained in the rear of the fuselage draws air from two rectangular air intakes just behind the sensor windows and the exhaust outlet is hidden by two inward-leaning fins with rudders. Control surfaces are located on the outer trailing edges of the wing and the aircraft is supported on the ground by a fully retractable tricycle undercarriage. Nothing else is currently known about this fascinating programme, which presumably ended with the economic collapse of the Soviet Union.

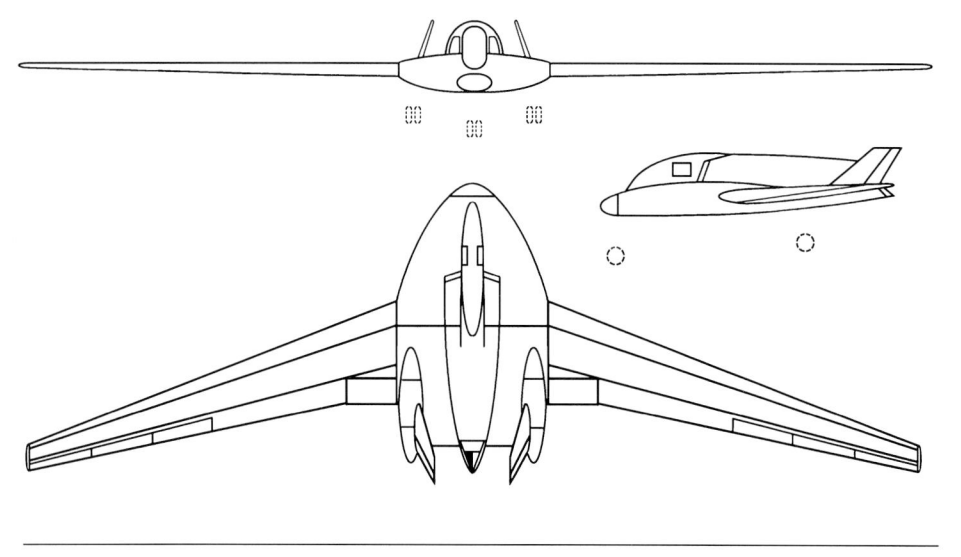

Above: **This M-67 Myasishchev design (thought to be M-67LK-M) from the 1980s bears a degree of resemblance to some proposals for America's ATB (eventually the Northrop B-2A). The design is clearly stealthy, having carefully-configured engine intakes and exhaust ports and most of the exterior would be covered in RAM (Radar Absorbing Material). The primary purpose of this aircraft would be to look for unannounced missile launches using state-of-the-art, passive infra-red sensors. However, it seems likely that Myasishchev also considered this design as a reconnaissance aircraft or bomber.** Bill Rose Collection

Left: **This unmanned proposal for the M-67 project is believed to have been assigned the reference M-67BVS-LK. It would loiter unobserved at very high altitudes for extended periods of time, using passive optical equipment to look for signs of NATO missile launches and provide advanced warning of a pre-emptive attack.** Bill Rose Collection

Glossary

AAM	Air-to-Air Missile
ALBEN	Asymmetric, Load-Balanced Exhaust Nozzles
ATB	Advanced Technology Bomber
AFB	Air Force Base
AFEE	Airborne Forces Experimental Establishment, Sherburn-in-Elmet, Yorkshire
ANP	1950s USAF Aircraft Nuclear Propulsion programme
BAC	British Aircraft Corporation
BAT	Baynes Aerial Tank
Black Projects	Highly-classified, secretly-funded programmes usually involving the development of new military systems. These can remain hidden for years, perhaps decades, sometimes progressing no further than studies.
BLC	Boundary Layer Control, a method of drag reduction
BLT	Boundary Layer Theory
BuAer	US Navy's Bureau of Aeronautics
BWB	Blended Wing Body aircraft design
BTZ	Bureau Technique Zborowski. An aircraft design organisation, operating in post-war France and headed by Dr Helmut Zborowski
CIA	Central Intelligence Agency
DARPA	US Defense Advanced Research Projects Agency
DFS	Deutsche Forschungsanstalt fur Segelflug – German Research Institute for Soaring Flight
DoD	US Department of Defense
FE	US WW2 prefix for Foreign Equipment serial number
KTS	Knots (1 knot = 1.5mph)
Laser	Light amplification by stimulated emission of radiation – monochromatic visible/invisible light
Luftwaffe	German Air Force
MoA	UK Ministry of Aviation, 1959-1967
MoD	UK Ministry of Defence, 1964-Present Day
MoS	UK Ministry of Supply, 1939-1959
Mt	Megaton
NACA	National Advisory Committee for Aeronautics
NASA	National Aeronautics & Space Administration
NEPA	US post-war Nuclear Energy for the Propulsion of Aircraft project
NGTE	National Gas Turbine Establishment (UK)
NM	Nautical Mile (1 NM = 1.15mile)
Nurflugel	German term for wing only aircraft
OKB	Opytnoe Konstruktorskoe Byuro – Soviet Experimental Design Bureau
OKL	Oberkommando der Luftwaffe (Luftwaffe High Command)
Payload	Normally cargo or equipment, but can refer to military ordnance
RAE	Royal Aircraft Establishment
RLM	Reichsluftfahrtsministerium (wartime German Air Ministry)
ROC	Royal Observer Corps
RRG	Rhön-Rossitten Gesellschaft – early German gliding society. In 1933, RRG became the DFS
SALT 1	Strategic Arms Limitation Treaty 1
SBAC	Society of British Aircraft Constructors
Senior Citizen	Codename for classified US stealth transport aircraft
SNCASE	Société Nationale de Constructions Aéronautiques du Sud-est. France
Stealth	Low-visibility technologies
STOL	Short Take-Off and Landing
Technische Luftrüstung	German wartime Technical Air Armaments Office
TFW	Tactical Fighter Wing
Tons/tonnes	Throughout this book the value for 'ton' equates to an American short ton, which equals 2,000 lb. The metric tonne is 1,000kg, and the conversion factor is 0.9072
TsAGI	*Tsentrahl'nyy Aero-i Ghidrodinameecheskiy Instituot* (Central State Aerodynamic and Hydrodynamic Institute), Zhukovsky
UCAV	Uninhabited Combat Air Vehicle
USAAF	United States Army Air Force
USAF	United States Air Force
Volksjäger	German wartime People's Jet Fighter
VTO	Vertical Take-Off
VTOL	Vertical Take-Off and Landing
Walter RII-203b rocket engine fuel	T Stoff: Concentrated hydrogen peroxide Z Stoff: Calcium permanganate liquid catalyst C Stoff: Methyl alcohol, hydrazine hydrate and water mixture catalyst (replaced Z Stoff)
WSMR	White Sands Missile Range

Index

AD-1 NASA Oblique Aircraft *127-128*
Aerojet XCAL-200 Rocket Engine *91*
Aerojet Liquid Fuel Rocket Engine *89, 90*
Airborne Forces Experimental Establishment (AFEE) *12*
Alan Muntz Company *12*
Allison J35-A15 Turbojet *79*
Allison V-3420 Engine *75*
Allison XT40 Turboprop Engines *84*
Amerika Bomber *51, 53*
Andrews AFB *81*
ANP: USAF Nuclear Propulsion Programme *87, 98*
Antonov M (Masha) Jet Fighter *138-139*
Arado Ar 1 *36-37, 98*
Arado E.555-1 to E.555-15 *35-36*
Arado E.581-4/5 *36*
Armstrong Whitworth AW.50 *16-19*
Armstrong Whitworth AW.52 *19-20, 31*
Armstrong Whitworth AW.52G *17-19*
Armstrong Whitworth AW.56 *19-21, 26*
Armstrong Whitworth AW.171 *21*
Armstrong Whitworth MkVII Light Tank Tetrarch *12, 13*
Arnoux, René *6, 7*
ATA: Advanced Tactical Aircraft (A-12A Avenger) *106-108, 121, 128*
ATB: Advanced Technology Bomber *111-112, 142*
Avro Vulcan *7, 8, 21, 26-27, 83*

B-2A Northrop-Grumman Spirit *8, 112-119*
B-3 Next Generation Bomber *121-122*
BAT: Baynes Aerial Tank *12-13*
Baynes, Leslie Everett (1902-1989) *11-13*
Belyaev, Victor Nikolaevich (1896-1958) *130, 136-137*
Bishop, Ronald *21*
Blohm und Voss Ae 607 *39*
Blohm und Voss BV P.208 *37*
Blohm und Voss P.210-01 BV *37-38*
Blohm und Voss P.212 BV *38-39, 41*
Blohm und Voss P.215 BV *39*
Blohm und Voss P.217 *39*
Blohm und Voss Shipbuilding Company *37*
BMW Strahlbomber II *40*
Boeing B-1R *122*
Boeing F/A XX *123*
Boeing Model 306 Bomber *70*
Boeing Model 306 Flying Boat *71*
Boeing Model 306A Airliner *71*
Boeing Model 306B Fighter (Single Engine) *71*
Boeing Model 306C Fighter (Twin Engine) *71*
Boeing XB-15 *70*
Boeing X-Programme *122*
BOK (Buro Osovikh Konstruktskii) *5 137-138*
Bouncing Bomb Project (UK) *13, 27*
Brandis Airfield *45, 49, 58-59*
Bristol Cherub Engine *10*
Brown, Captain Eric Melrose 'Winkle' *13, 15, 62*
Burnelli, Vincent (1895-1964) *7, 75, 87, 123*
Burnelli Flying Wings *75*
Butler, James William *6*
BWB: Blended Wing Body Aircraft *123-126*

Carden, Sir John *11*
Carden-Baynes Aircraft *11*
Cardenas, Major Robert *81*
Cayley, Sir George (1773-1857) *6*
Chadwick, Roy (1893-1947) *26-27*
Chance Vought Aircraft at Stratford, Connecticut *98*
Chance Vought XF7U-1 Cutlass *98-99*
Cheranovsky, Boris Ivanovich (1896-1960) *130-133*
Cheranovsky Advanced Jet Fighter *132, 133*
Cheranovsky BICh-2 *130*
Cheranovsky BICh-7 *131*
Cheranovsky BICh-14 *131*
Cheranovsky BICh-24 *133*
Cheranovsky BICh-26 *133*
Chetverikov RK-1 *138*
Chinese Embassy (Belgrade) Bombing Incident 1999 *114, 116-117*
Consolidated Aircraft Flying Wing Bomber *73*
Consolidated-Vultee 2 Eng Patrol-Bomber *85-86*
Coplin, John *25*

Cornwall, George (1897-1960) *29*
Crosby, Harry *89-92*
Cunningham, John (1917-2002) *23*

da Vinci, Leonardo (1452-1519) *6*
Dams, Ruhr, Germany, Möhne, Sorpe & Eder *27*
Davies, Stuart *26*
DB-LK Bomber *136-137*
de Havilland, Geoffrey Roald OBE (1910-1946) *22*
de Havilland DH.108 Swallow *21-23, 62, 69, 93*
de Havilland Gipsy Major II 4-cylinder Piston Engine *14*
Derry, John (1921-1952) *23*
DFS: Deutsche Forschungsanstalt fur Segelflug *34, 35, 53, 54*
DFS 194 *54-55*
Dittmar, Heinrich 'Heini' *55, 56, 58*
Dornheim, Michael A. *112*
DSB-LK Strategic Flying Wing Bomber *140-141*
Dunne, John William (1875-1949) *6, 10*

Edwards, Edmund *6*
Edwards, George *26*
Edwards, Glenn (1918-1948) *81*
Egypt Bay near Gravesend, Kent, Accident Scene *23*
EHK: Entwicklungs-HauptKomission *35*
Espenlaub, Gottlob *34*
Etrich, Igo (1879-1967) *6*

Falk, Roland 'Roly' (1915-1985) *27, 62*
Focke-Wulf Fw1000 x 1000 x 1000 Bomber *40*
Forbes, Daniel Hugh (1920-1948) *81*
Franklin, Eric *19*

GAL: General Aircraft Ltd *9, 13-16*
Genders, Squadron Leader George *23*
General Dynamics Cold Pigeon *106*
General Dynamics-McDonnell Douglas A-12A Avenger II *8, 105*
General Electric F-118-GE-100 Turbofan Engine *114, 116*
GLAS: Gust Load Alleviation System *114*
Glenn L. Martin Company *76*
Goblin 2 Turbojet Engine *21*
Göring, Reichsmarschall Hermann *43, 45, 51*
Gotha Waggonfabrik A.G *46, 48*
Gotha Go 229A *46, 48*
Gotha P.60A *48*
GRD-2M-3V Rocket Engine *65*
Green Lizard *28*
Günter, Siegfried (1899-1969) *41-42*

Handley Page HP.75 Manx *13-14*
Handley Page HP.117 *31-32*
Harper's Dry Lake, Lockhart, California *91*
Hartley Wintney, Hants, Accident Scene *23*
Hawker-Siddeley P.1077 Tailless Two-man Jet Fighter *25*
Heinkel He S 011 Turbojet *35*
Heinkel P.1078A/B/C Fighters *41*
Heinkel P.1080 Ramjet Fighter *42*
Henschel, Friedrich Nicolaus *43*
Henschel P.135 *42-43*
Hertel, Dr Heinrich (1902-1982) *53-54, 60*
Heston JC.9 *29*
Hill, Geoffrey Terence Roland (1895-1955) *10-11*
Hill Pterodactyl Bomber *10-11*
Horten, Reimar (1915-1994) *7, 34, 43, 46, 49-52, 72*
Horten, Walter (1903-1998) *7, 34, 43, 45, 49-52, 72*
Horten Ho VII *43*
Horten Ho IX Fighter *43, 45-49, 51, 52, 66, 96, 111*
Horten Ho X *49-50*
Horten Ho XIIIa Glider *50*
Horten Ho XIIIb Fighter *50*
Horten Ho XVIIIb *52*

Ilyushin Il-52 *140*
Instituto Aerotécnico at Córdoba *52*

Jones, Dr Robert Thomas (1910-1999) *127-128*
Junkers, Hugo (1859-1935) *6-8, 34*
Junkers EF.128 *24, 53*

Junkers EF.130 *53*
Junkers Ju 248 *60*

Kalinin, Konstantin Alekseyevich (1889-1940) *134-135*
Kalinin K-12 Bomber *135*
Kalinin K-12 Test Glider *134*
Kauba, Otto *37*
Klimov RD-45 Turbojet *138-139*
Kozlov, Sergei Grigoryevich *135*
Kronfeld, Robert (1904-1948) *12, 13, 15, 16*

Lachman, Dr Gustav Victor (1896-1966) *13*
Laute, Dr W. *35*
Lean, David *23*
Leuna Synthetic Fuel Plant *59*
Lilienthal, Otto (1848-1896) *6*
Lindley, Bob *26*
Lippisch, Alexander Martin (1894-1976) *7, 26, 34-35, 41, 50-51, 54-57, 59, 62, 65-68, 93, 100*
Lippisch Li P.04-106A *65*
Lippisch P.09 *65*
Lippisch P.10 *65-67*
Lippisch P.11 *65-67*
Lippisch P.15 *57-58*
Lippisch Delta VI *66-67*
Little Brickhill, Buckinghamshire, Accident Scene *23*
Lloyd, John 'Jimmy' (1888-1978) *16-17, 19*
Lockheed CL-187-3 *102-103*
Lockheed CL-278-1-2 *95-96*
Lockheed CL-1170 *104-105*
Lockheed CL-1201 Atomic Powered Aircraft *96-98*
Lockheed F-117A *8, 106, 110, 117*
Lockheed Gusto 2 *96*
Lockheed L-248-3 Atomic Powered Bomber *87*
Lockheed Senior Peg *109-111*
Lockheed Martin AN/APR-50 (also known as the ZSR-63) Radar Warning System *115*
Lockheed-Martin FB-22 *122-123*
Lockheed-Martin Next Generation Bomber *121*
Lockheed-Martin X-44A *122*
Lusk, Arthur *93*
Lycoming R-680-13 Radial Engine *14*

M22 Locust Light Tank (US) *13*
Martin XB-16 *70*
Matsu I-29, Japanese Diesel Electric Submarine *60*
Messerschmitt Me 163A *55-58*
Messerschmitt Me 163B *22, 49, 55-65, 93*
Messerschmitt Me 163C *57-60*
Messerschmitt Me 263 *60, 64, 65*
Messerschmitt Me 329 *67-68*
Messerschmitt P.08.01 *68*
Messerschmitt P.1108.11 *69*
Messerschmitt P.1111 *69*
Metropolitan-Vickers (Metrovick) F.2/4 Beryl Turbojet *17*
MiG I-270 (Zh) *64-65*
MiG Stealth Bomber *118*
Mikulin (Tumansky) M-87B Radial Engine *136, 137*
Mitsubishi J8M1 Shusui *61, 63*
Mk3 Atomic Bomb (US) *81, 102*
Mk4 Atomic Bomb (US) *81*
Mouillard, Louis Pierre (1834-1897) *6*
Muller-Rowland, Squadron Leader Stuart (1921-1950) *23*
Multhropp, Hans *62*
Muroc Field (now Edwards AFB) *62, 63, 75, 76, 79, 81, 82, 89, 90, 91, 92, 93*
Myasishchev M-67 *118, 141-142*

National Advisory Committee for Aeronautics (NACA – the forerunner of NASA) *10, 31, 32, 65, 75, 89, 90, 93, 94, 98, 127, 136*
National Air and Space Museum (US) *46, 63, 88, 89*
National Physical Laboratory at Teddington, Middlesex *28*
Northrop, John 'Jack' Knudsen (1895-1981) *72*
Northrop B-49 *7, 8, 79-81, 83, 84, 112*
Northrop MX-324 *89-91*
Northrop MX-334 *89-91*
Northrop N-1M *9, 16, 72, 73, 75, 76, 87, 88*

Northrop N-9M *75-77*
Northrop N-381 *103-104*
Northrop Senior Ice *109, 111*
Northrop Switchblade *129*
Northrop Turbodyne V *83-84*
Northrop X-4 *93-94*
Northrop XB-35 *75-80, 84*
Northrop XP-56 Black Bullit *87-90, 92*
Northrop XP-79 *89-93*
Northrop XP-79B *91-92*
Northrop YB-35 *76, 78, 79, 81*
Northrop YB-49 *78-85*
Northrop YRB-49A *82, 83*
Northrop-Grumman B-2A Spirit Stealth Bomber *8, 51, 68, 76, 106, 107, 111, 112-122*
Northrop-Grumman B-2C *117*
Northrop-Grumman EB-2A *117*
Northrop-Grumman RB-2A *117*
Northrop-Grumman Next Generation Bomber *8, 9, 121-122, 128-129*

Oblique Flying Wings *126-129*
OKB: Opytnoe Konstructorskoe Byuro (Experimental Design Bureau) *63-65, 134, 137, 138, 140, 143*
Operational Requirement OR.229 *19-20, 26*
Operational Requirement OR.246 *24*

Peenemünde-Karlshagen *55, 58*
Pénaud, Alphonse (1850-1880) *6*
Pratt & Whitney Wasp Major Radial Engine *77*
Predannack Aerodrome, Cornwall *28, 29*
Pterodactyl Aircraft *10-11*
Putilov, Alexander Ivanovich *135*
Putilov Stahl-5 *135-136*

Raytheon AN/APQ-181 Covert Strike Radar *114*
Reitsch, Hanna (1912-1979) *34, 58*
Rockwell B-1B bomber *29, 30, 111, 113, 117, 121, 122*
Rolls-Royce VTOL aircraft *25*

Scud 1 Light Sailplane *11*
Senior Citizen *119-120*
SG-500 Jagdfaust (Fighter Fist) *59, 60*
Short PD.7 *62*
Shvetsov M-11 Radial Engine *137*
Skoda-Kauba SK V-6 *37, 38*
Slingsby Sailplanes *12*
SNCASE SE.1800 *54*
Specification N.40/46 (UK) *24-25*
Symington, USAF Secretary Stuart *84-85*

T-10 12,000 lb (5,443kg) Bomb *80*
T-14 22,000 lb (9,979kg) Bomb *80*
Tailless Aircraft Advisory Committee (TAAC) *10, 14*
Talbot, James Richard (1909-1945) *13, 14*

UCAS-D Carrier Based UCAV Project *108, 121, 122, 123, 128*

Vickers Swallow *9, 27-31*
Vogt, Dr Richard (1894-1979) *37-39, 126*
Vought F-8 Demonstrator *128*

Wallis, Sir Barnes Kt, CBE, FRS, RDI, FRAeS (1887-1979) *13, 27-31, 80*
Walter HWK109-509C Rocket Engine *60*
Westinghouse 19-B Turbojet *91, 92*
Westinghouse J46 Turbojet *99, 100*
Westinghouse XJ30W-7 Turbojet *93, 94*
Westland PJD.144 *24-25*
Wild Goose *28-29*
Wilde, Geoffrey Light (1917-2007) *25*
Wilson, Captain Jennifer USAF *117*
Winter, Martin *62*
Wood, Donald *26*
Wright, Edgar Alexander 'Ginger' (1914-1945) *13, 14*
Wright, Orville *34*
Wright-Patterson AFB, Ohio *62, 70, 81, 82, 89, 94, 95, 96, 119*

X-47B Pegasus UCAV *121*

Yokosuka MXY8 Glider *61*
Yuganov, Victor (1922-1964) *65*

Ziller, Leutnant Erwin *45*